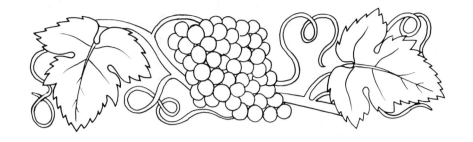

THE WINES AND WINELANDS OF FRANCE

Geological journeys

under the direction of Charles Pomerol

Robertson McCarta

LONDON

List of Authors

History, wines and soils	André Combaz, Robert Lautel, Charles Pomerol
Alsace	Claude Sittler
Champagne	Hubert Guérin and Michel Laurain
Bourgogne-Beaujolais	Noël Leneuf, Robert Lautel and Pierre Rat
Jura	
— Côtes du Jura	Nöel Leneuf, Robert Lautel and Pierre Rat
— Bugey	Gérard Demarcq
Savoie	Jean-Paul Rampnoux
Côtes du Rhône and Diois	
— Northern Côtes du Rhône	Gérard Demarcq
— Southern Côtes du Rhône	Georges Truc
— Tavel and Lirac, Costières du Gard	Claude Rousset
— Diois	Georges Truc
Provence	Claude Rousset
Corsica	Alain Gauthier
Eastern Aquitaine and Languedoc-Roussillon	Albert Cavaillé
Bordelais	Jean-Pierre Doazan, Jean-Claude Dumon, Claude Latouche, Louis Pratviel, Gérard Seguin and Michel Vigneaux
South-West	
— **Armagnac**	Michel Pujos and Michel Vigneaux
— Chalosse, Béarn, Basque Country	Robert Bourrouilh and Jean Delfaud
Vineyards of Charentes: Cognac and Pineau	Pierre Moreau
Bourbonnais, Auvergne and Loire region	
— Bourbonnais, Auvergne	Jean-Marc Peterlongo
— Loire region	Jean-Jacques Macaire
Lorraine	Claude Sittler
In search of lost vineyards	
— Paris region	Charles Pomerol
— Lyonnais	Louis David
English translation	Charles Polley and Graham Cross in association with First Edition; and Sally M. Tyner

Contents

FOREWORD

Although numerous books on wine have been published over the past few decades, we feel that not one of them examined precisely and systematically the relationships between the vine and the land. This could be done theoretically but for the purpose of this book we chose to actually go out to the wine regions and follow itineraries which highlight not only the vine but also the deep sub-soil, or more precisely the rocks whose weathering created the soils which feed it. This was made possible thanks to the assistance of twenty-five authors, geologists and oenologists, and involved exploring with them, by way of minor roads, even the smallest corners of the land where both grands crus and vins de pays are grown and tasted.

The authors provide, for each of the fifteen major wine-growing regions of France, a brief insight into the history of the vineyard and of the wine- growers. They then present the terrain (rocks, soils, climate, exposure) as well as the types of vine encountered along the proposed itineraries. At the end of these journeys, the reader is invited to celebrate the marriage of choice wines and fine dishes which best complement them.

Although this guide describes some fifty itineraries in the main wine- growing regions of France, it has not been possible to mention every single vins de pays. South of the Loire, for example, almost all the terrain of low or average elevation tends to produce wines of this category, in any of the regions of Thouarsais, Poitou, Forez, Vivarais or Aveyron. Wine lovers who wish to visit these vineyards and study their soils can obtain relevant information in the collection of Guides géologiques régionaux (published by Masson, Paris). The vineyard area demarcation shown on the geological map at the beginning of each chapter is thus only approximate and is of purely indicative value. For more precise information, it is necessary to refer to the major viticultural establishments such as the co-operatives, wine-growing syndicates, inter-professional committees and in particular the Institut National des Appellations d'Origine (INAO).

It is not possible to thank individually the numerous people in the profession who have provided documentation and information to the various authors involved. We would like to express our gratitude to them and hope that this book will make a modest contribution to the promotion of French wine. If, above all, it can both help the public to appreciate the work of the wine-grower and provide the latter with an understanding of the part played by geology, then our purpose will have been achieved.

Additional geological information is provided in the geological time-scale and glossary which appear at the end of the book before the index of vines and the geographical index.

The general concept of the book was developed in collaboration with André Combaz, Robert Lautel and Jean Ricour with the dedicated assistance of Michel Arnould and Robert Lautel in the editing of the manuscript. The majority of the drawings are the work of Odile Fernandez and the 1/1,000,000 scale demarcation maps have been produced at the Bureau de Recherches Géologiques et Minières (BRGM). Editorial responsibility has been undertaken by André Combaz (TOTAL Édition-Presse), Jean-Claude Dumort, Jacqueline Goyallon and Marie-Claude Guim-baud (BRGM).

In taking into account the observations of numerous readers, the second edition includes improvements in the text and illustrations as well as additional information, notably with regard to the wines of Lorraine, the regions of the Rhône and Provence, eastern Aquitaine, Bordeaux, Languedoc and the Loire area.

Finally, this book would not have been possible without the participation of Crédit Agricole.

Charles POMEROL

HISTORY, WINES AND SOILS . . .

The link between geology and wine is not always immediately evident since the vine can, in fact, adapt to almost any type of terrain providing the climate is temperate. This is why, in the past, it was cultivated throughout France, before the existence of practical and fast means of transport. A relationship does exist nevertheless and the aim of this chapter is to illustrate how, beneath the soils of the vineyards of France, the subsoil plays a part in the quality of the wine produced: in Bourgogne, the link will be plain to see since the only varieties of vine (pinot noir for red wines and chardonnay for white) grow on a specific geological formation; similarly in Beaujolais where another type of vine, gamay, produces different grands crus on schist and granite. In other areas where several types of vine are cultivated on varied terrain often disturbed with transport, it is more difficult to establish to what extent the wine is influenced by the nature of the subsoil, in spite of an age-old understanding of the compatibility between the variety of vine selected and the type of soil involved. The problem becomes even more complex when, as in Bordelais, wine is produced from assemblages of several varieties of vine.

Outside Europe, the major foreign vineyards depended above all, at their outset, on the *savoir-faire* of the vine-grower in selecting and creating a suitable soil. Nowadays these vineyards are exploited in order to produce the greatest possible amount of an industrial sort of wine in which physics and chemistry play a leading part. Consequently, the wine is often acceptable and of a consistent quality, but there are never created any of those miraculous bottles which, in certain French vineyards, are the product of a soil and a wine-grower putting into practice expertise passed down through age-old traditions.

Origins of vine and wine

The first question usually asked by the wine lover is: for how long has the vine been cultivated and where did it first appear? Its evolution goes back a very long way. It has flourished on French soil for many tens of millions of years. In 1880, the geologist E. Munier-Chalmas discovered, in a limestone deposit formed at the beginning of the Tertiary era, approximately sixty million years ago (Sézanne travertine located at the foot of the Côte de Champagne, 40 kms south of Épernay) leaf imprints of the vine designated *Vitis sezannensis* by G. de Saporta. It belongs, however, to a subtropical climate variety found today in southern North America. It is totally distinct from the cultivated vine, *Vitis vinifera*. This latter species belongs to the flora originating from western Asia and southern Europe. Pollen analyses have shown that it was from these South Caspian and Mediterranean domains that it spread throughout Europe, as far as Sweden, in accordance with the climatic alternations of the Quaternary.

On account of its physiological characteristics, this wild vine, *Vitis vinifera silvestris*, differs from our *Vitis vinifera sativa* whose multiple varieties of vine seem to be derived from *Vitis vinifera caucasica* which thrives from the Black Sea to the Indus. Cherished by the Greeks, perpetuated and promoted by the Romans, the vine was introduced into Provence and Languedoc towards the fifth century B.C. Through the Rhône Valley and the Garonne Basin, it gradually gained ground further and further north and west through Brittany, Normandy, Flanders, Champagne and Alsace. Another plausible route is often put forward, which would have joined the Roman route and passed through the centre of Europe from Greece and Asia.

Such propagation would tend to indicate that the vine is less dependent upon physical conditions than is often supposed nowadays.

It is now known that the vine has been dedicated to the production of wine for time immemorial. It has always been a symbol associated with beliefs, mythology, religions and civilizations. It is also something of a mystery, touching on the divine, with gods (Bacchus and others) and the Bible making some six hundred references to it, the most well known episode being Noah's ordeals. In France, the vineyard was generally much more widely spread. Means of transport were difficult if not dangerous and to be able to drink wine, everyone had to produce it on location. If we take the example of a region with a harsh and cold continental climate such as Lorraine, spring frosts mean good harvests only about every four years. Nevertheless, the vine was planted everywhere.

Admittedly, quality was not extraordinary when ripening of the grapes was poor. It was not a matter of adding sugar to the must since this was only begun in the seventeenth century. Wine would not stand transportation, except for that which had been produced since ancient times by certain exceptional vineyards, as in Auxerrois, Bourgogne and Bordelais. Two types of recipients were used at the time: firstly the Greek and Roman amphorae, difficult to cork and fragile, and secondly casks, the virtues of which were only realized by the Gauls. In fact, only the vineyards having access to a river or seaway could sell or exchange their wines. It was the navigable Yonne which opened the Parisian market to the Auxerrois region, planted continuously as far as Sens, while Bourgogne was handicapped by the necessity to use carts as far as the Yonne. As for the wines of Bordelais, they went by sea to England and Holland. Those from Alsace were transported down the Rhine to Holland or down the Danube to Vienna.

The use of cork assuring hermetic stopping of the liquid while still allowing subtle exchanges of the surrounding air, essential to a good ageing of the wine, began as recently as the eighteenth century.

Some historical facts to remember are the following: the vigour of the Gallic vineyard challenged the Roman wines to such a point that Domitian ordered the uprooting of the vine stocks in Gaule between the years 91 to 95. But he incited such resistance that Probus had to repeal these decrees from 272 to 282. The Merovingians encouraged production, as did the Carolingians, after the destruction perpetrated by the Alemans and the Franks. But the evolution of the vineyard was due above all to the clergy to which one in every five men belonged at that time and meaning that wine was required in profusion for the purpose of mass. Bishop's palaces and abbeys were very active in the fifteenth and sixteenth centuries with certain brotherhoods even making it their duty to guarantee the quality of the wine, a practice which has survived to this day. Finally, the scientific and industrial revolutions of the nineteenth century contributed significantly to the success of the wine trade, although in other respects tolled the knell of badly situated vineyards, such as those in Lorraine.

For a very long time then, up until the end of the nineteenth century, the vine grew everywhere but wine hardly ever travelled. Like the wine-growers of Ancient Egypt, the French peasants only drank a small amount of wine, selling most of it to the clergy, the nobility and the middle classes. For their own consumption they produced, out of the remains of the musts or verjuices, beverages which were refreshing and non-intoxicating through lack of alcohol.

Various factors were to concur to change the geographical distribution of the French vineyard: first the damage caused by oidium after 1830 and later by phylloxera; then the coming of the railways, allowing fast and easy transportation and opening the access of the whole of France to good table wines, notably those from the Midi, and to fine wines. It was no longer necessary for every region to produce its own

6

wine as it became possible to buy it at affordable prices for family consumption. This meant the end of vineyards producing vins ordinaires – and their replacement with other types of crops. Only those vineyards producing notable quality wines were to survive.

Wines and their soil

What were the prevailing factors, then, which decided the survival or disappearance of a vineyard? In varying degrees of importance they include: climate, exposure, nature of the terrain, planting of the vine and tradition.

The vine could survive when the climate was favourable (meaning not too much freezing during the spring), especially on the hillslopes, since freezing is more common and causes more damage in the valley bottoms. Neither should there be too much rain in the spring since freezing in wet weather is fatal for the shoots. It is in July and August when rain is needed to swell the bunches of grapes, although it should not lie on the ground for too long. The September sun ripens the bunches of grapes, but if it rains before the grape harvest, there is the risk of harmful rotting setting in and the wastage of the musts if the wine grower is not careful to sort the fruit during harvesting.

The shoots or the grapes can be damaged by storms and heavy rain which can also wash away the soil leaving only a thin layer. It was once the task of the women to place back on the top of the slopes the soil which accumulated behind the low walls erected by the wine-grower downhill from his vines.

The role of the sun is of primordial importance and the vines are planted preferably facing south and east. Microclimates also play an important part; they result from the favourable joint effects of the hygrometric index, sunshine and altitude, all producing exceptional protection determining a vineyard.

Victor Rendu writes in his *"Ampélographie française"*, of 1857, that "the vine adapts to any sort of terrain provided that it is not a place where water stands" and also asks the question which is still valid today: "Would it not be short-sighted to determine the type of soil preferred by the vine excluding all others? In France, in fact, the vine thrives on the chalks of the Marne and also tolerates heavy and marly soils perfectly well, such as those of the best Jura crus; it turns to account the oolitic limestone of the Côte d'Or just as it exploits granite debris, evidenced by the excellent Côte-Rotie and Hermitage wines; the vines of La Malgue, near Toulon, are set on schist, as are those of Banyuls; the vineyards of Cap- Breton lie on almost pure sand. . ." One could add to this list volcano-sedimentary soils (grauwackes), Permo-Triassic sandstone and alluvial deposits in Alsace, not forgetting, of course, for the same region, the granite, gneiss, schist and limestone. . . . besides all the sedimentary, metamorphic or eruptive rock types which can accommodate the vineyard.

These rocks, as seen in cross-section in quarries, were deposited and consolidated many millions of years ago. They make up the "subsoil" which also incorporates loose deposits caused by the erosion and/or transportation of rocks from the substratum and constitute surface formations. These include, for example, residual clays resulting from the break-down of limestone; clay with flint and millstone and slope deposits transported by gravity . . . Their deposition only goes back a few hundred thousand years.

Soil results from the interaction, layer upon layer, of the mineral elements of the subsoil, the biological activity (plant and animal) and the cultivation practices which sometimes go down some fifty centimetres and endow the soil with considerable diversity. Although the subsoil may retain its homogeneity for areas often in excess of

7

a square kilometre, the uniformity of the soil hardly goes beyond a few hundred square metres . . .

With regard to the personality of a wine, it is not only the rock type of the subsoil which is a determining factor, but also the composition and properties of the soil derived from it. The vine, in actual fact, is fond of stony soils where no other type of cultivation would be able to flourish and this characteristic of stony soils repelling other crops has facilitated the introduction of the vine which, paradoxically, produces better grapes in stony soils than in rich soils.

Even if the soil is barren, it must still be intensively worked. It is firstly ploughed up, deeper down (0.60 m) the drier the climate is. It is then improved through the careful addition of enriching agents. The vine, in fact, prefers heterogeneous to homogeneous soils, hence its partiality for scree-covered slopes. Man has often intervened and still intervenes with this preference in mind, for example in Champagne, where the chalky soil is blended with 'earth' extracted from Sparnacian lignite-bearing clay outcrops. These practices go back to ancient times.

Dion (1959) quotes an extract from the accounts of the Duke of Lorraine (1625) which records the transporting of grass in 3 800 cartloads to improve the great vines of the Château de Condé-sur-Moselle (nowadays Custines). The result of these ancestral practices is that, in the Mâconnais for example, the soils of the vineyards are different today to those found elsewhere, even on the same substratum.

In most of the chapters in this book, the authors demonstrate the relationship between the characteristics of the wine and those of the soil, for example in Alsace where the late sylvaner vine ripens on very varied soils and the gewurztraminer vine is found on granite, limestone-marl and alluvial deposits.

The same applies to the different varieties of Beaujolais — "fruity, plump, flavoursome, robust and distinguished" on granitic sand, or "plump, generous, robust, of a fine deep red colour, with a characteristic taste of the soil", on schist and porphyrite.

The relationship between the rock and the soil derived from it on the one hand and the wine which is the result of it on the other hand, is then clearly established, but the biochemical mechanisms brought into play are far from being well elucidated. Leneuf and Rat, for instance, have formulated hypotheses on the role of certain chemical elements present in the environment, such as potassium, manganese and magnesium, a role which is evident in the growth and productivity of the vine, but which remains unclear with regard to the type or the quality of the wine. These same authors explain that a certain number of physical characteristics (slopes, "stoniness", clay and total limestone content) have been analysed and linked to levels of quality.

It still remains a mystery how the vine searches out, through its roots, nutritional elements which the sap will concentrate in the grapes, the juice of which will develop into a fine wine. Superficial analyses cannot give an accurate picture of the whole living and changing function of this vital earth sap which circulates through the roots of the vine. While geology, that is the nature of the subsoil in which the roots grow, cannot explain everything, it is certain that the personality of a wine is strongly marked by the geo-pedological substratum.

In a soil based on compact limestone, the vine roots go down no further than 0.70 metre. If a dry summer occurs, water supply is poor, and yet satisfactory, as the limestone rock will supply, through capillary migration, up to 35% of the water consumed by the vine in between flowering and harvesting.

On the other hand, in a sandy textured subsoil, during the same summer, supply from the ground water will remain in superabundance and this will not contribute favourably to the quality of the harvest.

The regulation of water supply is, in fact, an essential element to the quality of a soil. Thus, rather than its chemical composition it is the physical characteristics of the soil which determine the quality of the wine, through optimal water retention and restitution capacity according to climatic conditions. In the Graves region of Bordelais the soils show the same gravelly appearance, but the subsoil, colonized by roots as far down as 4, 5 or 6 metres, is very varied.

The water supply regulation mechanism provided by the roots maintains a constant internal environment for the vine, a guarantee of good maturation of quality grapes. The character of wines bearing the appellation Graves is strongly influenced by the nature of the strata down below, which have no gravel content. If reduction in water supply does not fall below 45% or 35% of normal quantity, the result is an improvement in the quality of the harvest. Sugar contents vary little, while the grapes are less acid, and in particular they are richer in phenolic compounds, essential factors in determining quality. The result of an abundant water supply is increased yields which degrade the crus by diluting the aromatic and gustatory elements and colour pigments. Factors limiting yield, such as water deficiency or poor nitrogen supply, are often responsible for the creation of a great wine.

Personality and quality of a wine

With regard to the "personality" of a wine, apparently related to the intrinsic nature of the soil, one might imagine that it is dependent on chemical factors. But as our knowledge stands at present, it must be agreed that this is only a matter of hypothesis . . . Nature is probably more subtle and what essentially gives a wine its personality (aroma and bouquet) is rather the result of a complicated biological "alchemy" — the intimate secret of each bunch of grapes as it matures its sugars and acids. At the moment of pressing, the rupturing of the grape will release these to the yeasts, for the great molecular frenzy that takes place in fermentation.

It is thus essential to distinguish between the personality and the quality of a wine, the latter being related above all to the climatic environment of the particular vintage.

In fact, this qualitative relationship is one that is formed between the climate, the soil and the plant, with each variety of vine contributing its own particular thoroughbred to the wine it produces. All throughout history, French wine-growers have searched for vines suited to the soil used for cultivation.

There are, in France, several hundred well demarcated wines each with their own character, which are produced from some forty main varieties of vine.

For a long time experts have dedicated themselves to the study of vines (ampelography) and, according to Louis Orizet, three categories can be considered: the "grande noblesse" of vines which produce the great wines, then further quality vines which are blended together to make certain grands crus and finally vines which are termed "regional" producing pleasant and quite fine wines. For each wine-growing region of France, each author mentions in this book the main types of vine used. Let us mention just here that in the case of the "grande noblesse" vines, the white juice of pinot noir produces not only the great red Bourgognes after ageing, but also Champagne, by pressing and immediately drawing off the white juice. The gamay grape forms the basis of Beaujolais, grenache produces the wines of the Midi, while the Médocs, the great red Bordeaux, are made from cabernet-sauvignon with two quality additions, merlot and malbec. With regard to white wines we should mention chardonnay which produces the grands crus of the Bourgogne and Champagne regions, chenin which grows along the Loire, riesling in Alsace, sauvignon in Sancerre and the south-west, and finally sémillon in Bordeaux.

Much time is required, however, to experiment in vine cultivating. The first harvest only takes place after three years, is not significant until after fifteen years and the vine only attains its best qualities after a period of thirty or forty years.

Vine-growing and wine-producing methods owe much in France to savoir-faire passed down through the centuries from generation to generation. It is the privilege of the old wine-growing areas to enjoy traditions which have been kept alive in the vineyard as well as in the winery and the cellar. Let us hope that mechanization does not drastically reduce human intervention, for that would be the end of the magnificent French grands crus whose true creators we wish to make known through this book. These wine-growing craftsmen are the heirs of the pioneer monks of the Middle Ages who have adapted wine-growing practices in the selection and establishment of vineyards which still produce, almost every year, masterpieces beyond compare.

An encounter with the soil, the vine and its wine brings great pleasure but the most enriching experience of all is to visit the wine-grower in his vineyard and his cellar for he is fond of discussing his art. Choose a wine, savour it, and you will create a solid bond of friendship so that you may recall the experience with him several years later.

As complex as life — the secrets of wine

Wines, like old masters, are not a matter of science but of art. It is still hard, nevertheless, to resist scientific curiosity just as many a sample taken from antique paintings has been the subject of chemical analyses.

The best wines have also been subjected to analysis and the intimate secrets of this fascinating beverage are now a little better understood. Water is its principal constituent, making up roughly 80% of its weight, as in the human body. Ethyl alcohol in solution in the water, represents a little over half of the remainder, with traces of many tens of other alcohols. This is what structures the wine. It provides a medium for the various fragrant components, whilst the water dissolves the sugars, the remainders of the original glucides produced in the grape under the rays of the sun. Glycerine as well as several other polyalcohols give the wine its luscious quality. It is glycerine which is left on the surface of the glass when the wine is spun round just before tasting.

Then there are the organic acids, totalling a good thirty, which are essential partners of the alcohols. These are called lauric, malic, lactic, citric, succinic, tartaric, propionic and acetic acids. They exist in a free state and notably in the form of potassium salts. Their balanced proportions give the wine its "freshness", its "vigour". The dominance of tartaric acid is importunate but fortunately it precipitates, with time, in the form of potassium bitartrate. With an excess of acetic acid, however, all that time will do is turn the wine into vinegar.

Besides nitrogenous substances, including a collection of amino-acids, there remains a whole group of rarer and more complex substances: tannins, polyphenols produced from catechic acid, derived from the raffle, seeds and even the oak casks in which the young wine is kept; pigments: flavines, anthocyans; vitamins, particularly C and B, and still further substances, the most complex not even yet identified. And finally, for all that, some mineral salts: a dozen anions and some twenty identified cations. These are the salts from the earth, which have come up in the water of the sap: chlorides, sulphates, phosphates . . . of sodium, potassium, calcium, magnesium with, finally, various trace elements: fluorine, boron, iodine, silicon, zinc, iron, manganese . . .

Even from its very beginnings, this limpid liquid called wine is already amazingly complex. But an old wine is much more complicated again. Time ennobles great wines. Slowly, alcohols and acids come together; they merge into different esters: ethyl tartrate, amyl citrate, butyl propionate, . . . Their olfactory and gustatory properties are distinctive and with the passing of the years, they enrich the wine and endow each cru with its own personality. This process continues as further chemical processes concur in the form of very slow oxidations, turning alcohols into aldehydes and the latter into ketones.

Wine-tasting and the art of living

Produced from living matter, tended with expert care and attention for man's enjoyment, wine behaves like a living substance, with its youth, its zenith, its waning and its death. Its amazing alchemy maintains in it a perpetual pursuit of balance. Its constituents may react in two different ways for if the wine is of princely stock and solid constitution, the tranquility of a cool cellar will assure it of a long life. Inversely, however, a wine can die from an accident (of "stress"), chemical disease (oxidization, ferric or copper "casses" – a condition caused by diastatic ferments) or from bacterial disease (aerobiosis or anaerobioses). A wine can equally die of old age. Its deterioration is marked by unmistakable symptoms: colour turning brown, cloudiness, oxidization, and acidity.

But just as sad an ending is to be rejected. Just like the oyster, wine must be savoured absolutely fresh, by the eyes, nose and the palate . . . Firstly, whether pale or deep, wine has a 'robe'. This is the pleasure of the eyes. "White", "grey", "yellow", "rosé", "onion skin", "red" . . . Every range of wine has countless shades, light hues often being enhanced by bubbles sparkling in the transparity. So how could such a complicated blend of molecules in the limpidity and often brilliance of a thoroughbred wine be doubted? – while the more vigorous wines evoke rather more the thickness of velvet than the elegance of shimmering silks of many others.

Let us pass to the delightful and sensuous sampling of the wine. The bouquet is savoured by the olfactory senses of the nose. The aroma of young crus, inherited straight from the grape, evokes the perfumes of summer. Having fermented and aged a little, the wine takes on a secondary bouquet. Its floral and fruity nuances soften into a spectre of wild smells of the undergrowth; fungus, truffle and amber, and even musk and venison. The wine must be inhaled at length before the great moment when it surrenders to the mouth. In the warmth of the mucous membranes, the wine surrenders itself entirely: exhaling its volatile essences and ethers into the nasal fossae, it impregnates the taste buds, the palate, the base of the cheeks and the throat with a whole range of different tastes, to finally melt there into a myriad of harmonies.

Ten to twenty more years or so of subtle improvement in a still and cool environment. . . . All that jealous care and attention must patiently await the arrival of this great moment: the opening and savouring of a good bottle. This should not therefore be hurried . . ., the aroma will often linger in the mouth thanks to the long-lasting sensation of taste. It is quite rightly said that such a wine "has length", and this is the best moment of wine tasting.

The pleasures of wine tasting are not difficult to come by and may involve a good vin de pays as much as a great vintage. All that is needed is a little care and preparation in order to enjoy to the full a culture which is still too uncommon in France as in the rest of the world. In France and abroad, one comes across more and more wine drinkers, but still very few "connaisseurs". A true appreciation, both of its qualitites and of its imperfections, demands not only a refined and trained palate, but also a cultivated mind. These truly intellectual prerequisites are not improvised, they are the preserve of the initiated, as in all things of art. If indeed man was meant to be first and foremost a wine consumer, any industrial wine, dull and devoid of character would amply suffice. On the contrary, education in wine appreciation must, through educating public taste, increase the number of connaisseurs capable of insisting on wines that have not been blended, of expressing the genius of their soil and their extreme diversity.

The only means of understanding is through initiation and for this there is no better way than to return to the source; an excursion into the wine-growing regions, to discover the world of the wine growers on their soil, to learn how their "savoir-faire" has evolved. They belong to the spirit of France and they have a long and rich history. It should also be known that never in the past have wines been as good as they are today, never have they been as numerous and diverse, and never have they been kept so long. Our era has its own glories . . .

Finally it should be said that while science has had a part in this, it notes, rather than explains the magic of good wine which transcends its compass. Between an ordinary wine and a very good wine, chemical analysis only reveals minute differences while it is from this very margin that the "soul of the wine" is conjured up by the connaisseur.

Wine-tasting is a psychic process which is based on the stimulation of the senses. It requires an ability to recall odours as well as a capacity for concentrated attention. Wine, itself a product of "haute culture", requires a taster worthy of it, that is to say someone of suitable refinement. Since wine is the ideal companion of gastronomy, initiation should take place within the context of the family. Why not develop in our children the senses of smell and taste? We should go a step further than merely allowing them to appreciate beautiful things from afar; they should also be allowed to experience them . . . at the same time as they learn temperance. Art and ethics can go hand in hand perfectly. The more enquiring mind of the child would thus more easily recognize real values in all spheres and would become broadened as it acquired the vocabulary granting the child the means of expressing experiences of taste and smell.

The region of good cuisine is also known for its good wine. Eating and drinking involve the same palate. And then art is a vehicle of the soul. In France, nation of many artistic traditions, there is Bourgogne for example, which upholds the glory of its art in wine side by side with that of its Roman art, two traditions bound together at the height of their spiritual richness.

Refinement is the supreme expression of civilization. The art of living feeds on wordly goods sublimated by the genius and love of mankind. The substance is mastered and ennobled until it is transcended, bringing joy with it. Is this not, finally, a perfect form of moderation?

WINE REGULATION

The idea of regulating wine was first thought of by Baron Le Roy de Boiseaumarié who wanted to protect the distinctive characteristics of the Côtes-du-Rhône wines. Then, in 1919, a law was introduced stipulating that, in order to benefit from such a designation, a wine must be derived from varieties of vines and an area of production which had been sanctioned by "local, loyal and constant use". In practice, the demarcation of production areas of wines bearing the mark "appellation d'origine" is carried out under the jurisdiction of the Institut National des Appellations d'Origine des Vins et Eaux-de-Vie (INAO) and, in the statutory procedure, the role of the soil is vital with commissions of enquiry, including geologists, noting the close relationship between the quality of a wine and the nature of the terrain which produced it i.e. the geological nature of the source rock, the texture and structure of the soil, its stoniness, depth and chemical composition. Other intervening factors are topographical location, altitude, slope, exposure and natural drainage capacity, the latter feature being of particular importance. Whether it is a matter of one or several well suited varieties of vine, the distinctive characteristics of each appellation are demonstrated and noted thanks to these criteria among which the nature of the subsoil and the soil play a determining part.

The wine trade is a closely scrutinized world and French wine-growing is strictly controlled at the national level, by the INAO and by fraud detection services, as well as at the European level. Since 15th June 1970 there has been a European wine common market in which two categories of wine are distinguished; vins ordinaires and quality wines. In the case of the former, a subdivision is made between:

Table wines with alcohol percentage shown on the label. This category can include blends of wines from different countries of the European Common Market without this being indicated on the label.

Vins de pays with indication of geographical origin are table wines whose area of origin is laid down by ministerial order. They are wines produced from traditional vines and not from hybrids and which are subjected to this control by analysis and tasting. The right to the simple appellation d'origine, that is to say to the mention of the area of production, can be claimed outside any legal decision and constitutes a sort of natural right Abased on local, loyal and constant use.

In the case of *quality wines*, the EEC distinguishes quality wines produced in determined regions (VQPRD). In France these are the vins délimités de qualité supérieure (VDQS) and those bearing the mark "appellation d'origine contrôlée" (AOC), decided by decree. Geographical demarcation is very strict, and vine-planting, methods of cultivation, vine-dressing, maximum yield per hectare, natural alcohol percentage, and possible enrichment are systematically regulated and controlled.

Actually, the borderline between VDQS and AOC is vague and in practice it essentially comes down to evaluating a certain degree of reputation acquired by wines produced in accordance with local, loyal and constant use, or in other words according to a very well-established technical tradition. The geological and pedological nature of the area in question is a criterion applied to an increasing extent in the demarcation of appellations. In the case of the Bourgogne and Beaujolais grands crus, it is the geological nature of the soil which is the determining factor. For other regions, this criterion is only used for better definition, through continual factual observations, of certain fundamental characteristics of a soil. It is an invaluable criterion for determining the best variety of vine for a given soil.

An important example is shown in the case of Alsace whose wines come under the general geographical appellation of Alsace followed by the identification of the vine, riesling for example. But the need for a tighter geographic appellation is felt here today to provide better promotion of the product and plans have in fact been realized for a broken up demarcation of Alsace AOC and grands crus localities.

How should the information on the label be put to use when buying "appellation wines?"

The denotation "mise en bouteille" (bottled) is a useful piece of information providing the identity of the bottler: his name, address and profession. It is important to know whether he is a wine-grower or a wine merchant. Appellation and vintage are essential items of information: in the case of the latter, there are numerous promotional type maps in table form classifying, for every major vineyard area, the vintage in terms of quality of wine and ageing capacity. Making use of this information will help towards building up a good wine cellar. The appellation VQPRD is only found on the labels of foreign wines since in France it is the distinction between VDQS and AOC which is most important, being more precise and more restrictive than the European appellation.

BIBLIOGRAPHY

OENOLOGY

ANGLADE P. and PUISAIS J. (1987). – Vins et vignoble de France. Published by Larousse.

CLOS-JOUVE H. (1974) – Itinéraires à travers les vins de France. De la Romanée-Conti au Piccolo d'Argenteuil. Published by Denoël.

DEBUIGNE G. (1970). – Larousse des vins. Published by Larousse.

DION R. (1959). – Histoire de la vigne et du vin de France des origines au XIX siècle. Published by Flammarion.

DUMAY R. (1967). – Guide du vin. Published by Stock. (New edition 1983).

ENGALBERT H. and B. (1987). – Histoire de la vigne et du vin. Published by Bordas.

JACQUELIN L. and POULIN P. (1960). – Vignes et vins de France. Published by Flammarion.

JOHNSON H. (1984). – Le Guide mondial du vin. Published by Laffont.

LACHIVER M. (1988). – Vins, vignes et vignerons — Histoire du vignoble français. Published by Fayard.

LICHINE A. (1972). – Vins et vignobles de France, Robert Laffont, Paris.

MASTROJANNI M. (1982). – Grand livre des vins de France. Published by Solar.

PEYNAUD R. (1980). – Le got du vin ; grand livre de la dégustation. Published by Dunod.

RENDU V. (1857). – Ampélographie française.

RIBEREAU-GAYON J., PEYNAUD E., RIBEREAU-GAYON P. and SUDRAUD P. (1975) – Traité d'oenologie – Sciences et techniques du vin. Published by Dunod.

ROGER CL. (1981). – Les vignerons. Published by Berger-Levrault

ROUPNEL G. (1932). – Histoire de la campagne française.

GEOLOGY

BELLAIR P. and POMEROL CH. (1982). – Éléments de géologie, 8e ed. Published by Colin. Collect. U.

DEBELMAS J. (1974). – Géologie de la France, 2 vol., published by Doin.

DELMAS J. (1971). – Les sols des vignobles, in: Ribereau-Gayon J. and Peynaud E., Sciences et techniques de la vigne, t.I. Published by Dunod.

DERCOURT J., PAQUET J. (1978). – Géologie. Objets et méthodes. Published by Dunod.

DUCHAUFOUR PH. (1970). – Précis de pédologie. Published by Masson.

FISCHER J.-C. (1980). – Fossiles de France et des régions limitrophes. Published by Masson.

FOUCAULT A. and RAOULT J.-F. (1983). – Dictionnaire de géologie. 3rd ed. Published by Masson.

POMEROL CH. (1980). – France géologique. Grands itinéraires. Published by Masson.

POMEROL CH., BLONDEAU A. (1980). – Initiation à la géologie. Mémento du géologue. 2nd ed. Published by Boubée.

Geological map of France and of the continental margin to the scale 1/1,500,000. Published by BRGM.

N.B. A more specialized bibliography is included at the end of the chapters dedicated to the wine-growing regions.

SEDIMENTARY ROCKS

a^2	Recent Quaternary
a^1	Older Quarternary
	Glacial deposits
p	Pliocene
	Oligocene
J^2 J	Middle Jurassic (Dogger) Undifferentiated Jurassic
J^1	Lower Jurassic (Lias)
t^3	Upper Triassic (Keuper)

t^2 t	Middle Triassic (Muschelkalk) Undifferentiated Triassic
t^1	Lower Triassic
r	Permian
h^4	Stephanian
h^1	Dinantian
d^2 d	Upper and Middle Devonian Undifferentiated Devonian
s^2	Silurian
v	Precambrian (Brioverian)

METAMORPHIC AND PLUTONIC ROCKS

γ γ^b	Granite Biotite granite
γ^m γ^r	Muscovite (and biotite) granite Riebeckite granite
η	Diorite, quartz diorite Granodiorite

VOLCANIC ROCKS

Tertiary

β^3	Basalt and labradorite
φ^3	Phonolite

Palaeozoic and Precambrian

ρ^1 τ^1 α^1	Rhyolite, trachyte and Trachy-andesite, andesite
	Devonian and Carboniferous tuff

DEMARCATION

	Extent of A.O.C. vineyard area

Fig. 1 – Geological map and demarcation of the Alsatian vineyard region

Alsace

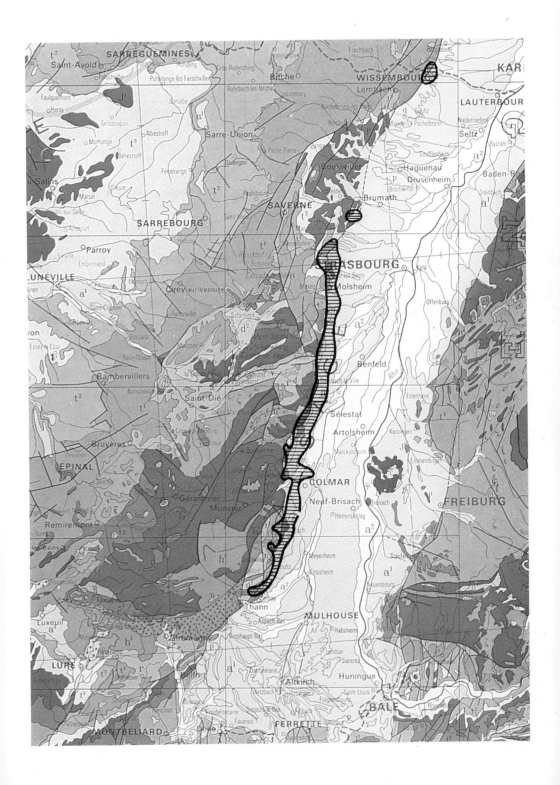

Whilst today we know of several varieties of wild vines of the species *Ampelopsis* and *Vitis*, especially in the forests of the Rhine, it cannot be certain that these "lambrusques" are the true precursors of the vines of Alsace. Admittedly, the riverside forests of the great river valleys provided domains of refuge for the wild vine which thus escaped the rigours of the climates of the Quaternary. In fact, we have found, in various postglacial deposits of the Rhine and Neckar valleys, dating back to 5 000 years B.C., fossilized seeds and wood of the *Vitis silvestris* species, and leaves and even grape seeds accumulated in the soil of neolithic lakeside settlements dating from 5 000 to 3 000 years B.C. These prehistoric populations appreciated even then the fruits of the vines of the Alsace plain. Consequently, it is not surprising that in this well sheltered region, one of the most beautiful northern vineyard regions of Europe should have evolved.

Extent and subdivision of the vineyard area

The Alsatian vineyard region extends along the Vosges, from north to south, over a hundred kilometres or so, from Marlenheim, on the same latitude as Strasbourg (Lower Rhine), to Thann, level with Mulhouse (Upper Rhine). It is laid out in terraced rows principally on the hillsides situated at the foot of the chain of mountains and around a multitude of small ancestral towns, full of charm, housing some ten thousand families who live off the vine (fig. 1). But this region has not always possessed the charming appearance for which it is known today.

Forty-five million years ago, the cornerstone of an old Vosgian-Black Forest massif subsided, gradually at first, then more violently when two series of cracks stretching north-south came to demarcate the classic Rhine Graben (Sittler, 1969, 1982-1986). It was thus that, in the course of Otime, three morpho-structural units became identified as the Vosges Mountains, the Vosges foothills and the alluvial Rhine plain, the domains of the Alsatian vineyards. Quite rarely, however, are they situated on the side of the mountains and it is only out of economic considerations that they extend as far as the plain. The preferred domain of the vine remains the area of the Vosges foothills, the hillsides which the geologist sometimes terms the vineyard area. This wine-growing area, however, is not subdivided as in other great French vineyard regions, according to areas of production or localities of origin. The dominant factor in Alsace is the vine variety, since no less than *nine different varieties* are cultivated here, introduced according to the soil and micro-climate; these are what characterize the different wines of Alsace, whether they are denominated "AOC" without precise origin or are from a grand cru locality.

The AOC vineyards in production in 1985, comprised 12 600 hectares out of the 20 200 hectares demarcated AOC. This only represents 5% of the agricultural surface area of Alsace, but 25% of its production (35% of just vegetable products).

Terrain and soils of the vineyards of Alsace

The extension of the vineyard area over the three morphological and structural regions of Alsace is conditioned by the nature of favourable terrain and exposure. On the side of the mountains, the ground consists of generally siliceous rocks where drainage and sunshine play a major part; on the hillslopes, calcareous soils predominate and an optimum climate is found here; on the plain, the water storage capacity of the ground, of a much more recent age and thus less well evolved than the other two areas, is critical.

In these three different areas, the diversity of the subsoil, combined with very different environmental conditions, generates a great variety of soils of distinct chemical fertility and structure which lie side by side but also amalgamate owing to ancient or recent landslides, erosion and declivities. For each type of geological terrain, we will indicate the soil types usually derived from them.

Mountainside

The expanse of each of the geological formations being quite considerable here, there results a certain regional uniformity. The altitude of the wine-growing terrain rarely exceeds 400 metres; it is generally in the region of 250 to 360 metres and the slope of the land which is occasionally steep (65°), requires the erection of terraces. The soils are very shallow (0.30 m), except on colluvial deposits at the slope bottoms and are as follows:

— on granitic and gneissose ground — colluvial soils, brown acid to leached soils, chemically fertile sands;
— on schistose ground — brown stony or clayey soils;
— on volcano-sedimentary ground — varied brown soils, very rich in fertilising mineral elements;
— on sandstone ground — brown leached to podzolic, sandy, light and poor soils, with no water retention capacity.

Vosges foothills

The juxtaposition of terrain of varied age and lithology over slight distances characterizes this sector from a geological point of view. Surface weathering and rearrangement, however, in addition to Quaternary solifluxion, make the distinctive pedological features which one would naturally expect from the various types of terrain, less well defined; overall, it is almost all of a more or less calcareous and marly nature although in detail, this terrain is far from uniform. The vineyards here are situated at an altitude of between 200 and 360 metres and occupy very variable slopes, generally of around 25°. Soil thickness also varies, according to the terrain and the slopes, from about 0.50 to 2.00 metres. The soils are as follows:

— on calcareous ground — brown rendzines, stony and dry soils;
— on sandstone chalk — rendziniform soils and brown soils, sandy, aerated and permeable limestone, rarely fertile;
— on marly clay ground — heavy, impermeable soils with good chemical fertility;
— on calcareous marl ground — red to brown rendzines, very favourable to the vineyard: tertiary limestone conglomerates along the edge of the hills.

Alluvial plain of the Rhine

It is only along the edge of the Vosges foothills that we encounter favourable wine-growing terrain. Here, Quaternary, rarely Pliocene deposits, are a reflection of the different lithological materials of the hinterland from which they emanate. Altitude is generally in the region of between 170 and 220 metres. The soils are quite thick and uniform here, since they benefit from being fertilized by run-off from the hills so that certain wine-growing stretches of the plain are justified by their good hydrological characteristics and their longer daily sunshine. The soils are as follows:

— on alluvial, sandy-clay, gravelly ground — poorly evolved soils or varied brown acid soils which, from time to time, are water-logged (pseudogleis);
— on loess and loam ground — brown calcareous soils and pararendzines.

Climate and sunshine of the Alsace vineyard area

Situated between 47° 50' and 49° latitude north, the Alsatian vineyard area lies almost at the vine's cultivation limit; but it is precisely there, where ripening of the grapes is slow (and thus preserves the natural aromas endowing the wine with its fineness) that numerous crus are found.

Precipitation

Alsace, situated at the base of the Rhine graben, well protected by the Vosges mountain chain, is not shielded from oceanic influences, since all year round weather movements prevail from the west. These, however, are well moderated, for annual precipitation rarely exceeds 600 to 700 mm. in Alsace, whilst the summits of the Vosges receive 2 000 mm. of water. Maximum precipitation always occurs during the warmer months, in the spring and the frequent summer storms, bringing quite considerable soil erosion and risks of hail.

Temperature

The climate which is semi-continental, is manifested by cold winters (January average: 1.9 °C), but with only a fortnight or so going by without a thaw, and warm summers (July average: 20.1 °C), tempered by violent storms. The average annual temperature is between 10 and 11 °C, but two thermal characteristics of Alsace should be noted: rapid changes of temperature, with differences of 15 °C, and the phenomenon of temperature inversion, where masses of cold air stand over the plain with fog and cloud, while warmer air and clear, sunny weather bathes the Vosges foothills and mountains.

Sunshine

Sunshine, which partly determines the temperature, is measured in length: 1 500 to 1 800 hours per year in Alsace, concentrated over the summer period (72% between April and September) and during the final ripening of the grape in October which is a traditionally sunny month.

Microclimates

The Alsace vineyards occupy a privileged position in the Rhine Valley owing to the microclimate resulting from the concurrence of various climatic and topographical factors. Risks of freezing in a very cold winter, spring frosts, hygrometric degree of the air and autumn mists are a function of exposure, altitude, slope, air flow and even of the surface nature of the ground. In such a way, for example, a warm thermal belt has been noted on the flanks of and halfway up the hills, where the temperature is 1 to 1.5 °C higher than on the lower and upper slopes and where it drops less than anywhere else during the night; this thermal belt is not located exactly on the southern sides, but generally on the side with the steepest slope.

The vineyards of Alsace are tiered, then, at an altitude of between 150 and 350 m. (380 to 400 m being the upper limit for AOC demarcation); most favourable exposure is southerly with south-westerly exposure sometimes being marginally superior to the classic south-easterly exposure. In any case, exposure or orientation in relation to sunshine is not an adequate criterion in Alsace, because, according to the very variable nature of the soil, and in particular to its absorption and retention capacity or water, air and heat, one and the same orientation may be favourable or disadvantageous.

History of the Alsace vineyard area and its people

While the wild vine has no doubt always existed in the Rhine Valley, cultivation of the European vine (*Vitis vinifera*) dates back to the beginning of our era. With the particularly active settling of the Roman legions in the Rhine Valley, this population must also have brought with it its own varieties of vine. It is known that the Roman Emperor, Domitian, had vine plants uprooted between the years 91 and 95, fearing, no doubt, competition from Rhine production. It was only towards the years 272-282 that the Emperor Probus had wine growing reintroduced into Alsace. Germanic invasion (Alemans and Franks), in the 5th century, brought about a temporary decline in wine-growing, but it quickly picked up again and its importance grew under the rule of the Merovingians, the Carolingians, the bishops' palaces and the great abbeys founded in the seventh century which had bought up the Alsace vineyards or received them in donation. The vine was a source of wealth for the region, and a wine trade started up with central Europe, the Netherlands, England and Scandanavia. Nothing was to halt this expansion. From 119 wine-growing villages in the 9th century, it grew to 172 communes in the fourteenth century. Colmar was considered to be the wine-growing capital of Alsace; it grew rich from the trade in wine upon which its magistrates had imposed severe regulations regarding quality.

In the fifteenth and particularly the sixteenth century, the Alsace vineyard area seemed to have reached its apogee. From this period of prosperity of the wine-growing communes, date most of the magnificent half-timbered houses and fine wine cellars. The Société des Bourgeois d'Ammerschwihr (future Confrérie Saint-Étienne) was to gather, from the fifteenth century, the most competent people of the town to arbitrate the quality of all wines produced in the vineyards of the commune. A host of thriving towns, organized along the same democratic principle to rebel against the influence exerted by the nobility, controlled the cultivation of certain varieties of vine and their wine production. Soon, however, came the Thirty Year war which was particularly harsh in Alsace. Villages were ransacked and many disappeared, the population was decimated and the vineyards devastated; so that in 1648, five years after the accession to the throne of Louis XIV, its survivors weary of war, Alsace, with the aid of numerous immigrants, set about its reconstruction; vines were pulled up to plant wheat; and the small amount of wine was exchanged for food.

During the eighteenth century the vineyards were gradually restored but using mainly common varieties of vine and preferring the plain, to the detriment of the hillslopes. With the 1789 Revolution, the new masters totally abandoned quality wine in favour of ordinary, low quality wines selling cheaply. Quantity was the key word: in 1828 the vineyard area had grown from 23 000 to 30 000 hectares. But these high yielding vines were not resistant to the cryptogamic diseases which broke out in the nineteenth century. Then, in 1871, came the annexation of Alsace by Germany and with it new legislation authorizing the watering-down and sweetening of wine ("gallisation") which further reduced its quality.

With the passing of the 1914-1918 war, the wine growers of Alsace, aware of their feable impact on French wine production, decided instead to concentrate on quality and to replace the high yielding vines (various hybrids of *Vitis vinifera*) with specially selected vine stocks (riesling, (pinot, gewurztraminer), which had once made Alsatian wines famous. The vines were spaced out, and the method of training using distaffs with support from stakes, was replaced with wire fencing erected 90 cm. above the ground in order to avoid frost. The use of stock for grafting then became more common — different species to those of the high yielding vine stocks, but suited to the various varieties of vine and soils.

The elimination of badly situated vineyards reduced the area given over to vine cultivation from 25 000 hectares in 1903 to 9 500 hectares in 1948, but helped reestablish the reputation of Alsace wines. The honourable Confrérie Saint-Etienne, which had not existed since 1848, was revived in 1947 in Ammerschwihr, with its jurisdiction extending over the whole of the Alsace vineyard region.

Alsatian vines and the wines of Alsace

The classification of vine varieties

The great variety of vines planted in Alsace over the centuries is due no doubt to the great diversity of its soils, sometimes encountered in a single parcel given over to vine growing. The suitability of stock for grafting, to both the variety of vine and the pedo-geological nature of the terrain, is thus of primordial importance.

Nowadays, ten varieties of *Vitis vinifera* occupy the Alsace vineyards; they are harvested and converted into wine separately, for Alsace wines, contrary to other French wines denominated appellation d'origine, are traditionally characterized and designated according to the name of the vine from which they are produced and not according to their region, terrain or locality of origin. The bottle carries the name of a locality in the case of a cru of long-standing repute or of an appellation grand cru délimitée.

Whether the vines are of the white variety (chasselas, sylvaner, riesling, pinot blanc, muscat), red variety (tokay, pinot gris, gewurztraminer, pinot noir) or rosé variety (muscat rose, chasselas rose), they are all converted into white, with the exception of pinot noir which is generally converted into rosé.

Top of the range vine varieties are classified as gewurztraminer, riesling, muscat, tokay, pinot gris and pinot noir as distinct from bottom of the range vines including chasselas, sylvaner, pinot blanc, auxerrois and Edelzwicker denoting a wine produced from a blend of vines.

Within a demarcated area of production, these wines have a right to the appellation d'origine contrôlée "Vins d'Alsace" or "Alsace", and certain wines are entitled to the appellation "Alsace grand cru" with or without indication of locality. Annual production of Alsace wine (20% of French AOC white wines) totals on average 100 million litres, comprising about 140 million bottles, of which five million are bottles of AOC quality sparkling wine "Crémant d'Alsace". Out of total sales, 32% are exported, Alsace ranking notably after the wine-producing regions of Bordeaux, Champagne and Bourgogne.

Average yield fluctuates, according to the variety of vine, between 55 and 98 hectolitres per hectare; it is set by the legislator at 100hl/ha for all vines with the exception of the grands crus which are limited to 70hl/ha. Each year a committee of experts of the CRINAO sets the minimum and maximum alcohol percentage for each vine variety, as well as the commencing dates for wine harvesting.

We should also point out that, with effect from 1972, it is obligatory for all Alsace wines to be bottled in the area of production. It is the only region of France where this type of quality constraint is imposed, except, of course, for Champagne.

The wines of Alsace

Chasselas (315 hectares; 2.5%)[1]. This vine, which is said to have originated from certain oases in Egypt, appeared at the end of the eighteenth century, firstly in the Upper Rhine. It bears the name of the village of Saône-et-Loire from which it comes; it is also the vine of the Swiss Fendant and the German Gutedel. It is characterized by inconsistent cropping and very early ripening, no doubt the reason why its cultivation is in constant decline and will disappear before long. This vine produces a light, fresh, relatively bland wine, which is hardly ever found now under this appellation, but which goes into the making of Edelzwicker.

Sylvaner (2 523 hectares; 20.1%). This vine was introduced into Lower Alsace at the end of the eighteenth century and in the last century from Austria though it may have originated from Transylvania. It is called cilifanthi in Hungary and grande arvine in the Valais. In Alsace, it is the most commonly grown vine, especially in the Lower Rhine. It is of poor vigour, but is an excellent and consistent cropper. It is a later ripener and produces a light, fresh and fruity wine, with a semblance of sparkle. It is a wine for all occasions and very pleasant to drink. Where the vine profits from good exposure, however, (Zotzenberg/Mittelbergheim, for example), it develops into a nobler and finer, well-rounded wine, which ages well and compares with Pinot and Riesling wines.

Pinot blanc (Klevner) and **Auxerrois** (2 358 hectares; 18.7%). In Alsace, the first references to pinot date back to the sixteenth century. This is not the pinot blanc of Bourgogne, which is actually the chardonnay vine, but a Burgundian pinot vine, originating from the north of Italy. This pinot blanc is often vinified with another variety, auxerrois, which seems to have come from Lorraine and Luxemburg. Having few requirements, these átwo varieties of vine give excellent results in average situations. Although the auxerrois vine is a little more precocious and shows less

---

[1] Figures for 1985 supplied by the Comité interprofessionnel du vin d'Alsace (CIVA).

acidity than the pinot blanc vine, the two vines are blended together to make Pinot, a wine of certain class, better constructed than Sylvaner, well balanced but supple, delicately bouqueted and with a pleasant acidity.

Muscat (378 hectares; 3%). The muscat vine is mentioned as far back as 1510 in the records of the parish of Wolxheim. Nowadays, this vine, of eastern origin, includes two varieties: (1) the so-called Alsace muscat, an identical vine to the muscat of the Midi, and thus relatively late in the Rhine climate and which for this reason tends to be replaced with (2) the muscat ottonel vine, which is very precocious and therefore prone to flowering accidents; this variety with its admirable bouquet is very akin to the chasselas vine (perhaps chasselas x muscat de Saumur). The two muscat varieties are blended together in the making of the light wine which is the driest and the least structured of the top of the range wines. It is fruity, with a very characteristic musky taste and a strong, aromatic bouquet. All the flavour of the grape is restored to the wine, endowing it with special appeal, particularly as a light aperitif.

Riesling (2 606 hectares; 20.7%). This is the Rhine vine "par excellence", which produces the most noble and the finest Alsatian wine. Although introduced in the fifteenth century from the Rhineland, but originating from the Orléans region, the Alsatian riesling vine is different to its German counterpart and has nothing to do with the numerous rieslings which now appear all over the world. The vine which is late and a consistent and heavy cropper, has the distinctive characteristic of continuing to ripen under relatively low temperature conditions. Where it occupies the best situations and is harvested late, a dry wine will be obtained, of lively acidity and fine and racy, combining a delicate bouquet with exquisite fruitiness. The balance between acidity and fruit must be harmonious for this king of Alsace wines.

Tokay Pinot gris (618 hectares; 4.9%). While the name of tokay is connected with Hungary through legend (General Schwendi of the House of Austria, would have introduced it to his Alsace vineyards around 1565) this is actually a pinot of Burgundian origin which has existed in Alsace since the end of the seventeenth century. It is also the ruländer of the Baden region or the malmsey of the Vaud and Valais vineyards. Its ripens very early and its yield is uncertain, due to flowering difficulties. It produces a strong wine, sometimes luscious and vigorous, with a fresh, rich bouquet, but pronounced acidity, which ages admirably. Tokay is an exception among Alsace wines not least due to its reputation acquired in the vineyard area of Cléebourg, to the extreme north of Alsace, where the soils particular to that region comprise Tertiary conglomerates, the dominant elements of which are sand and clay.

Pinot noir (809 hectares; 6.4%). This was without doubt the first vine to be imported from Bourgogne, probably by virtue of the analogous topographical and climatic conditions of that area and Alsace. This prestigious red vine occupied an important place in the Middle Ages, but it subsequently disappeared, except in a few localities where red wine (continued to be enjoyed (Ottrott, Marlenheim, Rodern). Its vinification into ruby-coloured rosé wine, a recent phenomenon, has witnessed a growing success, so that the use of this variety of vine is constantly on the increase. Relatively late, this very heterogeneous variety is therefore used to make a rosé wine which is not very acidic, characterized by pleasant fruitiness and much appreciated for its originality. Its conversion into red wine, as in the olden times, is now reappearing, much to the delight of wine lovers.

Gewurztraminer (2 496 hectares; 19.8%). This comes from the particularly aromatic selection of the traminer or savignan rose vine, introduced from the Haut-Adige. The traminer vine is mentioned in Alsace in the *Kreuterbuch* of the botanist

Bock, in 1551. This vine lent itself, no doubt better than others, to the selection of particularly musky varieties which emerged in the nineteenth century, especially after 1870, when the gewurztraminer vine appeared in Alsace (litterally: spicy or musky traminer). Out of a generally more musky population than in times past, it was, nevertheless, a non-aromatic variety of savagnin rose which was to produce Klevner de Heiligenstein, the appellation designated to that commune. The transition from traminer to gewurztraminer was an Alsatian success, for it unquestionably attains optimum quality only in Alsace; this is because the environment of the Vosges foothills is propitious to this precocious vine which is sensitive to climatic irregularities and is a moderate cropper. It produces, therefore, a wine for savouring, rather than just for drinking, a wine of high class and fine thoroughbred which is robust and beautifully structured with a very characteristic, subtle and elegant bouquet. The great vintages endow it with a nice mellowmess. It ages well, retains its distinctive characteristics and its floral aroma. It is often through Gewurztraminer that one comes to appreciate Alsace wine.

Edelzwicker, blend of vines (495 hectares; 3.9%). Edelzwicker is a wine designation proper to Alsace; it is an assemblage of several vines of Alsatian Appellation Contrôlée wines, generally including chasselas, sylvaner, pinot blanc and auxerrois. It is a continuation of the ancient method of blending wines from several carefully selected vines, with a predominance of one which gave the blend its name. In fact, there were, and still are, mixed parcels of vineyard, planted with several types of vine. Nowadays, Edelzwicker is the only authorized name for these blends of which the producer is the sole judge.

Crémant d'Alsace. Crémant d'Alsace is made exclusively from pinot blanc or noir, riesling and tokay, which are discussed above. It is vinified according to the champagne method and strictly regulated. Its production is recognized and is on the increase; in 1985 it counted for 3% (25 000 hectolitres) of all Alsace appellation wine production.

Consumption of Alsace wines

Before Alsace wines can be offered to the consumer, they must all be tasted for approval. Their main characteristic being that of fruitiness, bottling takes place quickly, 8 to 10 months after harvesting in order to preserve the aromas emanating from the vine and vinification.

While traditionally it is said that Alsatian wines must be drunk while they are young, this depends on the type of vine and the geological nature of the soil it is produced from. Oenologists strongly advise never to drink Alsace wine too young, at least not until it is two years old. This age limit is equally valid for wines of an average vintage. On the other hand, wines of a good vintage take longer to develop and their peak is only attained after four, five years or more; furthermore, they keep well and do not age quickly. Years in which the grape ripens well provide wines for very long keeping, whatever the type of vine. It is Tokay Pinot Gris and Gewurztraminer, however, which age the best, irrespective of their vintage.

Alsace wines, whose bouquet must be sampled through the nose, and whose freshness savoured by the palate, must be served immediately upon opening in order to preserve all the aromas of the volatile elements, preferably not in an ice bucket (the shock of cold will ruin a wine), at a temperature of 8 °C for Crémant d'Alsace, 12 °C for white wines and Pinot rosé and 16 °C for red Pinot noir.

Itineraries

The itineraries propose to follow the Alsace wine trail (fig. 2) in a north-south direction. Along its way or by taking detours if need be, we will explore the essential features of the composition of the Alsace subsoil along the edge of the Vosges Mountains. From time to time, we will examine in detail the nature of the geological soils and their effect on the vine and the wine, without forgetting all the history attached to these regions (see the numerous leaflets issued by the tourist board and, in particular, the annual Guide on the vineyards of Alsace).

The Alsace wine trail in the Lower Rhine (fig. 2 and 4)

From Wissembourg to Cléebourg

On leaving Wissembourg, take the D 334 westbound, in the direction of Weiler. Behind the Chapel of N.-D. de Weiler, 200 m before the customs, a large quarry opens out ①[1]. The Palaeozoic of the Vosges basement is composed, here, of vertical beds of grey grauwackes. These are volcano- sedimentary sandstone and schistose deposits, interspersed with veins of effusive volcanic rocks rich in iron, dating from the end of the Devonian and the beginning of the Carboniferous. On the surface, this ground is gullied by fluvial and glacial deposits of the Quaternary.

Returning towards Wissembourg, the route intersects the Vosges Fault which brings into contact the Vosges basement rock with its Triassic cover (Vosgian Sandstone, Muschelkalk). The latter forms a small fracture zone which is traversed for a distance of 3.5 km before intersecting the Rhine Fault, bringing us out into marly terrain of the Tertiary.

Take the D 77, towards Rott, where we reach the northern pocket of the AOC vineyard area; but first we will examine the nature of the subsoil in the vicinity of four villages grouped together in a single wine-growing cooperative.

On entering Rott, the right-hand slope and the trough of the road ② show:

— at the base, greenish grey marls of the Pechelbronn Beds (Lower Oligocene) which constitute the Tertiary basement of the whole region;

— on top, clays, sands, layers of sandstone and conglomerate, containing Foraminifera and Oysters, characteristic of the Rupelian; the shingle is composed of Vosgian Sandstone and Muschelkalk; this is part of the Rott Conglomerate Formation, the littoral deposit of the arm of the sea which occupied the Rhine Graben in the Middle Oligocene; these conglomerates occupy all the slopes to the west of Rott, at the foot of the Vosgian Sandstone from which the material was derived.

On leaving Rott, take the D 240 to the left via Oberhoffen and Steinseltz, where the Tertiary hills are covered with loess and loam. At Riedseltz, turn left, then, at the northern exit, take the minor road to Altenstadt. After 1 km, on the right, the great sand pit of **Riedseltz** opens out ③.

Beneath a cover of loess, whitish sands, worked over an area of more than 10 m, are interspersed with brown or black, sometimes lignitic, clays. These are the sandy fluvial and marsh deposits, characteristic of the Pliocene throughout the Rhine Graben at the time when the Vosges began to thrust up. The numerous plant remains (*Nyssa, Tsuga, Magnolia*, etc,) indicate a warmer climate than that of today.

---

[1] Itinerary stopping point.

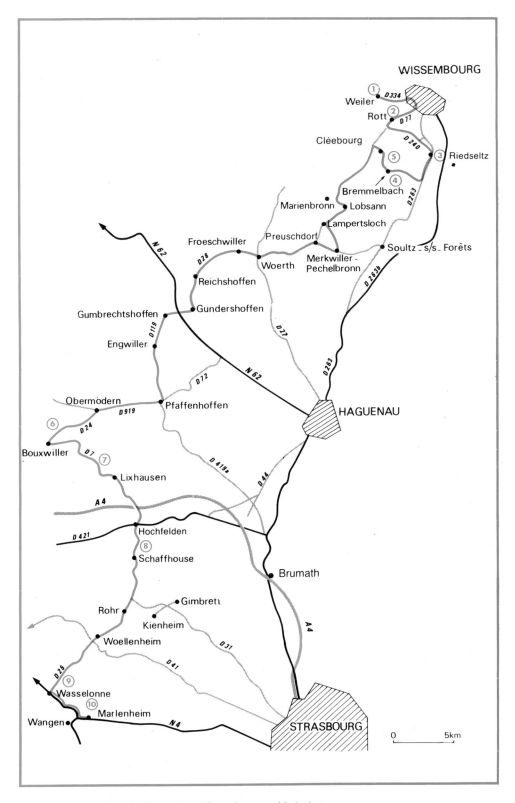

Fig. 2 — Itinerary through Alsace: from Wissembourg to Marlenheim

Return towards Riedseltz and Ingolsheim; at the top of the hill, turn right towards **Bremmelbach**. After approximately 2 km, take a mine track which leads to a moto-cross ground, formerly a clay pit ④. Exposed here on the surface is marly soil deposited by the sea of the Rupelian and contemporaneous with the Conglomerate of Rott.

Go through Bremmelbach and head for **Cléebourg** where at the wine cooperative's cellar ⑤, Alsatian wine specialities are offered, even on Saturdays and Sundays. There you can taste Auxerrois as well as Tokay Pinot Gris upon which this region has built its reputation, its predominantly sandy soils (Upper Rupelian, Pliocene, loess) not altogether unconnected with this success. Vintages which are the product of well balanced years, not too dry, provide a Tokay which is extremely fresh in the mouth, whose alcohol is discreet and which has a characteristic aroma that evokes, whilst being savoured, smells of the woods combined with the fragrance of lilies.

From Cléebourg to Marlenheim: the Saverne Fracture Zone

This journey intends to join up with the official start of the wine trail. Follow the D 77 which runs along the foot of the Hochwald Massif, practically along the line of the Rhine Fault, in a southerly direction towards Lobsann. This village is famous, because from 1818 to 1950 it supplied the whole of Europe with Lobsann asphalt for surfacing roads and for waterproofing. The asphaltic limestone was extracted by means of galleries, to the north-west of the location, in the upper part of the Pechelbronn Beds.

Continuing towards Merkwiller, then Woerth, one crosses a section of the oil field of Pechelbronn which is located in one of the highest geothermal gradient zones in the Rhine Graben. Visit the oil museum of Pechelbronn.

From Woerth (location of the only restaurant in France where neither alcohol nor tobacco are available, and where one can sample a natural fruit juice version of Sylvaner and Muscat, and excellent family dishes) continue to Froeschwiller and Reichshoffen; this is a pilgrimage to the heart of the battlefield of the 1870 war (numerous monuments); we will also enter the fracture zone contained between the Rhine Fault and the Vosges Fault. Map in hand, select your route via Gundershoffen, Pfaffenhoffen and Obermodern to **Bouxwiller**.

Bouxwiller Limestone is the continental Lutetian type, with its distinctive horizon of mammal fossils, discovered at the time of the Cuvier works of the nineteenth century (famous quarry behind the Catholic church) ⑥. Beneath this limestone, marl contains a layer of lignite, discovered in 1743 and worked by means of galleries from 1811 to 1881. These Eocene rocks, their fauna and flora reveal that the formation of marshes and the limestone lake of Bouxwiller corresponds to the very first subsidence movements of the Rhine Graben, forty-five million years ago.

Leave Bouxwiller by the Hochfelden road; after about 6.5 km, before **Lixhausen** ⑦, there appears, on the left-hand side of the road, a quarry where grey marl of the Lias is worked, marl with more or less ferruginous ovoid concretions (concentrated in pockets of Quaternary age, which in the past provided iron ore), rich in pyritic Ammonites of Pliensbachian age.

Continue on the D 25; between **Hochfelden** and **Schaffhouse**, on the side of the hill, to the left ⑧, appears the great quarry exposing marl and limestone with Gryphaea arcuata (Oysters very frequent) of the base of the Lias (Hettangian-Sinemurian) which is very rich in fossils. The road runs alongside the horst of Kochersberg, trending NE-SW, and keeping to the left-hand side. Older and older layers are thus traversed; at Rohr appears the varicoloured Marl of the Keuper (upon which an OAC vineyard area has been demarcated at Gimbrett and Kienheim); at Woellenheim clay and dolomite of the Lettenkohle can be observed, and imme-diately afterwards, one enters Muschelkalk where several quarries ⑨ open up along the left-hand side of the road and on entering **Wasselonne**. Here, turn left for Strasbourg (N 4); the road runs alongside the Mossig which has cut into the heart of the horst; this is the Kronthal, with its Vosgian Sandstone cliffs, crowned áwith the Sainte-Odile Conglomerate (several quarries on the left).

Marlenheim and its wine trail through limestone soil of the Muschelkalk

Marlenheim, a "bourg" town with an ancient history, and its vineyards which extend towards Nordheim, enjoy a sheltered situation provided by the relief of the Kronthal — Kochersberg horst (television transmitter). Here, alongside the N 4, a wine trail will take you on a walk of about two hours over the slopes on which the old village is built ⑩ .

The itinerary (fig. 3), signposted from the Town hall square (Place de la Mairie) provides a continually fine view of the hills and the Alsace plain. All along the path there are signs supplying information on the cultivation of the vine, the wine-making process and the distinctive characteristics of the Alsatian vines. With regard to the nature of the soil and subsoil of this terrain, it rightly deserves its name "Steinklotz" or "block of stone", being comprised of sandstone and dolomite of the Upper Muschelkalk and the Lettenkohle. The geological map shows the various stratigraphic levels and their position (south-easterly inclination) tilted towards the plain, due to faults cutting the edge of the horst.

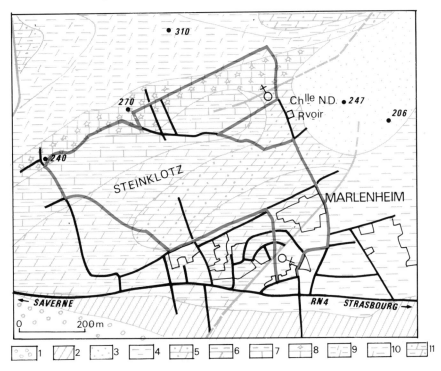

Fig. 3 — The Marlenheim wine trail through the limestone terrain of the Triassic: Muschelkalk and Lettenkohle (extract from geological map to the scale 1/50,000, sheet no. 233, Saverne).

1. Recent alluvial: 2. Slope-and valley bottom colluvium: 3. Scree: 4. Grypsiferous and saliferous grey marl (Lower Keuper): 5. Varicoloured marl and dolomite (Upper Lettenkohle): 6. Dolomite and limestone (Lower Lettenkohle): 7. Ammonoid limestone (Upper Muschelkalk): 8. Crinoidal limestone (Upper Muschelkalk): 9. Dolomite and fissile marl (Middle Muschelkalk): 10. Gypsiferous varicoloured marl (Middle Muschelkalk): 11.· Finely undulating dolomite (Lower Muschelkalk).

This area consists, then, of typical limestone and sandy limestone terrain with calcareous magnesite soils of the brown type of the rendzine group. Despite the variation in geological levels (and which one can identify along the trail by the limestone layers which jut out with respect to the marl), a certain uniformity emerges, not only in the type of surface soil, but also in the quite frequent erosion and landslide phenomena. Near the Chapel of N.-D. des Sept-Douleurs, of 1772, one can observe the faulted contact and the different nature of the terrain in this sector.

Marlenheim wines became famous for being vinified from pinot noir into red wine, and rosé wine from Marlenheim, which is light and embellished with a pleasant taste of cherry, has been made there for centuries. It is still appreciated as a wine to be consumed young for full enjoyment of its fruit. It was, in the past, personalized by certain wine-growers, by the name of Vorlauf.

Festival of the grape harvest: third Sunday of October. Re-enacting of the marriage of *Ami Fritz* (Erckmann-Chatrian): 14th and 15th August.

From Marlenheim to Molsheim: between Mossig and Bruche

Leave Marlenheim in the direction of Saverne and immediately take the road to the left to Molsheim (fig. 4). **Wangen** (festival of the Fountain of wine on the first

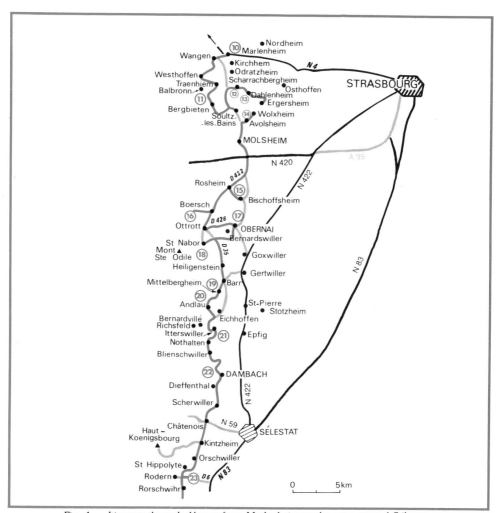

Fig. 4 — Itinerary through Alsace: from Marlenheim to the area around Sélestat.

Sunday of July) and **Westhoffen** have a long-standing reputation as fortified wine-growing 'bourg' towns. We are now in a low-lying region at the foot of the Kronthal Horst, the Balbronn Graben, for this depression, composed of the Upper Triassic (Keuper), and therefore essentially of varicoloured and gypsiferous grey marl, is also bounded to the east by the heights between Scharrachbergheim and Dangolsheim whose rocks are of Middle Triassic age (Upper Muschelkalk). The Balbronn rift valley constitutes, therefore, a veritable topographical trough in which the marly terrain easily eroded on the horsts on both sides, is preserved.

Crossing this graben, from **Traenheim** (visit its wine trail) to **Bergbieten**, the colours of the soils, distinctly reddish, greens or greys of the iridescent marl, leave no doubt as to the homogeneity of the soils of this sector (see the old gypsum mines at **Flexbourg** ⑪). These are, from time to time, water-logged soils, of the pseudoglei or vertisol type, especially suited to rieslings. The wine cellar of the Traenheim cooperative or the wine-growers of Bergbieten, for example, will recommend these to you (grand cru de l'Altenberg).

A detour via **Scharrachbergheim** is recommended, in order to take advantage of a magnificent panorama from the top of the Scharrach and to discover that the type of terrain is altogether different here ⑫ . It is composed of conglomerates of Jurassic limestone pebbles ('Grande Oolithe' visible in an abandoned quarry on the southern slope), slightly cemented by sandy clay. They bear witness to the destruction of a tectonic slope between the Vosges Mountains and the plain, which caused a torrential accumulation of material, torn away and shaped by rivers and streams near their outlets on the sea coast or in the lagoons which occupied the Rhine Graben during the Early Oligocene, thirty or thirty-five million years ago. The vineyards which cover this terrain profit from a marly limestone soil which is among the most favourable soils to the Alsatian vines, and especially to the delicious Gewurztraminer which one must make sure to sample in Scharrachbergheim.

Rejoin the N 422 bound for **Soultz-les-Bains**. At the intersection with the D 118, turn left and after 1 km on the right, you will come to the entrance to a quarry exposing the Upper Muschelkalk ⑬ . The alternation of limestone beds and marly layers demonstrates beautifully graded sequences. To the north you will notice, and may visit, a Jurassic quarry (Grande Oolithe) half-way up the Scharrach. Following the N 422 to Soultz-les-Bains, one enters the heart of the Mutzig-Soultz Horst, cut into the Buntsandstein, by the Mossig, as in the case of Kronthal. At the village centre, turn left towards **Wolxheim**. About 700 m after the level crossing, a track on the left leads across vineyards to the old Royal quarry ⑭ , opened in the seventeenth century by Vauban for the construction of the citadel of Strasbourg.

Here, the top of the varicoloured sandstone and the Lower Muschelkalk crop out in an enormous face, composed from top to bottom as follows:

Shelly, dolomitic and calcareous sandstone, yellowish in colour (the large concentric ellipsoids are sedimentary load structures) . . . . 10 m

Voltzia sandstone whose upper section (clayey sandstone) is an occasionally carbonate deposit with a marine fauna, while the lower section (millstone sandstone) forms beds of fine, pink sandstone (grey on the surface due to staining from the upper layers), separated by fine clayey lenses, green or red in colour, containing a brackish water fauna . . . . 12 m

One can rejoin the wine trail at **Avolsheim**, not forgetting to visit there the Dompeter church, consecrated in 1049 by the Alsatian Pope Léon IX.

Molsheim, ancient episcopal and university town, and centre of the Bugatti car industry, also possesses "AOC" vineyards which cling to the Muschelkalk slopes of the Mont de Mutzig, occupied by a military camp.

Regional wine festival: 1st May

The area around Obernai: from Rosheim to Saint-Nabor

Follow the N 422 towards **Rosheim**. As you enter the town, take the left-hand turn towards Bischoffsheim. After about 1 km, on the left, a track takes you to a large quarry at the foot of the Chapel of Bruderberg ⑮ . Limestone of the Middle Jurassic was once worked here to make lime. Above the layers of the 'Grande Oolithe' of the Bajocian, rich in Sea Urchin and Oyster fossils, which incline towards the south-east, marl and limestone of the Bathonian crop out. These limestones, and the numerous Tertiary slope conglomerates produced from this material, constitute more than half the wine-growing terrain of Alsace.

Return to Rosheim, where a visit must be paid to the churches of Saint-Pierre and Saint-Paul (jewel of twelfth century Rhine architecture) and the Roman house, or "Maison des Païens", of the same epoch. Take advantage of the proximity of Rosenwiller to visit a venerable Jewish cemetery, at the south-west exit of the village. You can get back to Rosheim on the D 604.

The D 35 then takes you to **Boersch**, going through a low-lying area, with Muschelkalk and Lettenkohle behind the beautiful hills of the Bischenberg and the Mont National (slope conglomerates covering the Jurassic). At the southern exit of Boersch, the D 216 which goes to Mollkirch or Klingenthal, penetrates into the Vosges Mountains and presents, for a distance of 2 to 3 km, a geological profile of the various layers from Buntsandstein, Vosgian Sandstone to shelly sandstone ⑯

Now we come to **Ottrott** which is dotted over the mountainside on a complex soil of faulted Muschelkalk and vast Quaternary scree slopes and veneers. It is one of three villages long renowned for their red wines produced from the pinot noir vine. The colour is not intense, but the cherry fruitiness which, in good years, resembles that of a cherry brandy, is a sign of a good wine for keeping; it is served at a temperature of around 15 °C, while it should be drunk nice and fresh when young.

The N 426 will take you to **Obernai**, the small metropolis of the fifteenth and sixteenth centuries, where the middle classes had the reputation of keeping the best wine for their own consumption. The town backs onto the Mont National ⑰ composed of Oligocene conglomerates. A visit to its vineyards is a must. Mini wine festival: weekend of 15th August; wine harvest festival: 3rd Sunday of October.

From Obernai take the D 109, which skirts Bernardswiller, to **Saint-Nabor**, with its little vineyard situated at the foot of the **Mont Saint-Odile** (764 m) of Vosgian Sandstone, crowned by conglomerate (highest point of Alsace where 6,000 years of history come together). Down below, the low-lying, faulted, marly region (Keuper and Lias), covered with a Quaternary veneer, is in contact, along the Vosges Fault, with Devonian grauwackes.

The great quarries of Saint-Nabor ⑱ exploit this volcano-sedimentary terrain of the Vosges basement: fine sandstone and very metamorphosed breccia and tuff.

Take the minor road to the Urlosenholtz Forest House; the road strictly follows the Vosges Fault; then come down on the D 35 to Heiligenstein.

From Heiligenstein to Mittelbergheim: the Barr Fracture Zone

Here, at the foot of the pseudoporphyritic Andlau Granite, nestles the small Barr Fracture Zone: Vosgian Sandstone, fallen away and preserved at the level of the Vosges Fault, intensely faulted Lias and Dogger, covered with Tertiary conglomerate and scree. This is expressed in the evolution of beautiful hills which adjoin the Vosges Massif – one of the most favourable situations for a vineyard. Also found here is a range of famous crus.

Heiligenstein, on the northern peak, presents a superb panorama over the plain. It is the only commune of Alsace authorized to plant a variety of traminer which is almost non-aromatic, a savagnin rose introduced in 1742, which produces Klevner de Heiligenstein. Unrivalled, this dry, subtle wine emits an aroma of incense and a rather spicy, flowery flavour which betrays the family ties of the vine.

The town of **Barr** is situated in the middle of the vineyards, of which the grand cru Kirchberg stands out. Among the varieties of vine which grow here, the gewurztraminer vine can be distinguised by its fullness, its smoothness, and its flavour of liquorice which it acquires with ageing. On the Kirchberg the sylvaner vine also achieves quite original expression which is almost resinous, which we will come across again on the southern side of the Zotzenberg, the hill between Barr and Mittelbergheim, for the nature of the subsoil is identical there: Dogger limestone covered with Oligocene conglomerate.

At Mittelbergheim, a soil/wine comparison can, in fact, be tried with the late sylvaner vine which grows on decidedly different soils ⑲ .

On the Zotzenberg, to the north-west of the village, the varied types of terrain of the fracture zone (Jurassic marls to the west, Dogger limestone and sandstone to the east) are partly covered with Tertiary limestone conglomerate which caps the hill. On the upper part of the side of the Zotzenberg, the soil, which is more stoney, provides a crisp and fruity Sylvaner, with a fullness and roundness which liken it to Riesling; it has the reputation of a grand cru which ages well. At the foot of the slope, fine colluvium deposits predominate and produce a less expressive wine.

The Stein, which forms the slopes immediately to the south of the village, is an excellent limestone soil provided by a solifluxion veneer. If vinified separately, Sylvaner ranks in richness with, or is even superior to that grown on the Zotzenberg.

The Forst, at the foot of the Crax Vosges Sandstone hill, to the west of Mittelbergheim, comprises a marly Jurassic subsoil, covered here by thick sandstone scree. This soil, which is permeable and poor in nutrients, retards the ripening of the sylvaner vine, so that the wine stays green and acidic (taste of sauvignon) and will only keep for two or three years.

On Wiebelsberg, immediately to the south-west of the previous area but in the commune of **Andlau** (D 62 road), we come across the same sandy soil. The south-westerly exposure being, however, better than that of the Forst, and with the soil warming up rapidly, Sylvaner wine from here acquired a certain reputation in the past, when wines were consumed quickly. Nowadays it is a grand cru area for Riesling which nevertheless suffers here in good years from poor expression of its distinguishing characteristics.

The other varieties of vine of Mittelbergheim provide, in good years, wines with a spicy, smoky and original tone, which really seems to be characteristic of the soil of the Barr Fracture Zone.

From Andlau to Dambach: the mountainside

We are now going to make our way along the D 62 to **Andlau** ⑳ , which is situated to the west of the Vosges Fault, but with no well defined escarpment. The Andlau vineyard area is thus one of the rare vineyard areas established on soils of the Vosges basement. Furthermore, at the entrance to the village, the two sides of the valley lie on different schistose soils. To the north, Steige Schist, hard and slatey, has been metamorphosed to hornfels at the contact point with the Andlau Granite, producing a stony and dark soil which is mixed with granitic sand from the upper part of the Kastelberg (grand cru). To the south, Villé Schist, which is more clayey, folded and shiny, provides a more friable and greyer soil. On both sides, then, the soils are siliceous, acid, but rich in mineral nutrients, stony, dark and relatively impermeable. These soils give, for example to Riesling, a very expressive musky taste, that some describe as bituminous, with an aroma of unroasted coffee.

The mountain vineyards of Bernardvillé and Reichsfeld close by, set on Villé Schist and on the volcano-sedimentary Permian, are worth the detour.

Continue to **Itterswiller** and stop at the carpark opposite the Arnold Winstub 21 . The panorama to the south-east presents two buttes, the locations of vineyards renowned in the past called Fronholz and Blettig. Their west sides are steep and consist of limestone molasse and Tertiary marl covered by 8 metres of clayey whitened Pliocene sand, surmounted by a formation of whitened sandstone blocks dating back to the beginning of the Quaternary. On Blettig, there are old quarries exposing these types of terrain which are traversed on the Epfig wine trail.

Carry on towards Nothalten and Blienschwiller, villages situated right on the Vosges Fault, which is marked in the relief, flanked by high veneers covering Tertiary marl of the Oligocene. In fact, in this sector between Andlau and Saint-Hippolyte, the Vosges Fault and the Rhine Fault are practically coincident; there are no fracture zones, nor isolated Vosges foothills.

Dambach-la-Ville and its wine trail through granite terrain

The fortified medieval city of **Dambach** deserves more than a quick visit to its old quarter and a few wine cellars 22 . The wine trail takes you on a lovely walk of one and a half to two hours through the vineyards, starting from the market place (Tourist information office); the trail is arrowed and provided with information boards as on other Alsace wine trails. The geological characteristic of this trail is that it presents a very homogeneous, granitic soil (fig. 5). The bare rock, the Dambach-Scherwiller two-mica granite, is rarely visible, since its weathering product, sand, and its acid colluvial soils are relatively thick at the slope bottoms and are consequently enriched with nutrients much to the advantage of the vine.

At the northern extremity of the wine trail, by taking the first track on the left which climbs the valley, towards hill 326, it is easy to reach the old Dambach mines where manganese ore (braunite) and iron ore (haematite) are found.

The twelfth century Chapel of Saint-Sébastien, with its seventeenth century sculptured baroque altar, nestles at the exit of a chestnut tree grove.

The Frankstein wine trail is named after the locality, to the south-west of Dambach, which produces a renowned cru, as is that of Bernstein (ruined château overlooking the vineyards). Here the main variety of vine grown in reisling (36% of the wine), but also the gewurztraminer vine whose distinctive characteristics emanate from the soil. The vineyards set on the covered plain favour the sylvaner vine (27% of wine), which is pleasant consumed young, and the pinot blanc vine (14%), deliciously vigorous, which is steadily being replaced by auxerrois. Over 5% of the harvest is converted into Crémant d'Alsace.

Wine celebration night: first Saturday of July. *Wine Festival*: second Sunday in August.

Continuing southwards, we follow the granitic massif from which the ruins of several châteaux stand out. Carrying on to Scherwiller (wine trail), then Châtenois, one observes that the vineyards are set on the broad alluvial cone of the Giessen, which dominates, from 20 m, the plain to the east of Sélestat. At Kintzheim, visit the eagles aviary and, further on, the 'Montagne des Singes', before stopping, at the limit of the Lower-Rhine, at the very beautiful restored Château du **Haut-Koenisgsbourg**, set on an outlier of Vosgian Sandstone.

At Sélestat: Grand procession of floral floats, second Sunday in August.

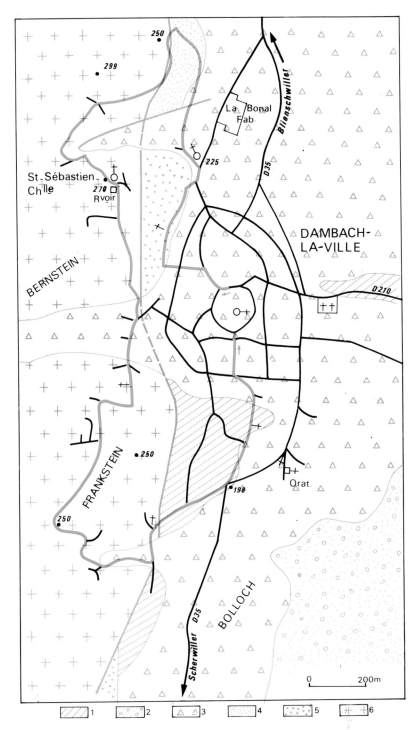

Fig. 5 — The wine trail at Dambach-la-Ville through granitic terrain (extract from Geological Map to scale 1/50,000, sheet no. 307, Sélestat).

1. Slope-and valley bottom colluvium; 2. Older alluvial (Würm); 3. Foot-of-slope soil cover (Riss): 4. Gypsiferous and saliferous grey marl (Lower Keuper); 5. Vosgian Sandstone (Middle Buntsandstein); 6. Dambach two-mica Granite.

The Alsace wine trail in the Upper Rhine (fig.6)

Saint-Hippolyte, at the northern extremity of the Ribeauvillé Fracture Zone

The merged Vosges and Rhine Faults (lead and zinc exploitation) cut Saint-Hippolyte in two: granite containing potassium feldspar to the west, and Tertiary marl covered with shingle to the east.

 An quarry exposing this grey, sandy marl of the Middle Oligocene is situated on the D 6, which goes from the **Rodern** crossroads to the N 83 (first road on the right) ㉓ . Here we have the 'Couches à Mélettes' (beds containing a type of small salt water fish) of the Rupelian, which fill the Rhine Graben for a depth of over 300 m.

 The vineyards of Rodern are situated entirely on granite upon which one finds to the south-west of the village, vast patches of coal-bearing ground (sandstone and shale showing plant imprints). The traditional wine of Rodern is Pinot rouge, delicious, fleshy, with that aroma of cherry or plum, and its length, while at Gloeckelberg, grand cru terrain, tokay pinot gris and gewurztraminer predominate.

At the Rodern crossroads, the Ribeauvillé Fracture Zone opens out, broadly extending towards the south, between the crystalline rocks of the mountains and the alluvium of the plain.

Bergheim and its wine trail through marly terrain of the Keuper

The Rhine Fault cuts Bergheim in two and relegates the vineyards to the west, on hillsides carved up into strips and compartments of varied terrain of the Buntsandstein, Muschelkalk, Keuper, Lias, Dogger and even Tertiary conglomerate and marl (fig. 7). The various stratigraphic levels of these formations are almost all represented here, but a large part of the surface is situated on the varicoloured or grey marl of the Lettenkohle and Lower Keuper. In the latter, gypsum is common and has been exploited for the manufacture of plaster and for soil fertilizer (old gypsum quarry to the north of Tempelhof).

 The vineyard of **Bergheim** thrives essentially on the marly clay soil of the hills, (grand cru Kanzlerberg) but also on marly limestone soils (grand cru Altenberg). It has been said of these wines that 'they are mostly of a haughty nature culminating in the bitterness of grande noblesse'. This can only be ascribed to the soil. With this in mind try a vigorous Sylvaner, or better still, a severe Gewurztraminer, but whose aroma becomes more accentuated with age, and compare the two soils.

Gewurztraminer festival: fourth Sunday of JulyFrom Ribeauvillé to Sigolsheim, Kientzheim, Kaysersberg

From Ribeauvillé to Sigolsheim, Kientzheim, Kaysersberg

 The vineyards of **Ribeauvillé** are hemmed in between the gneiss of the mountains and the alluvial cone of the Strengbach, and yet this commune is one of those containing the highest number of renowned cru localities. The marly soils are the same as those of Bergheim and, although the famous Carola mineral water spring emerges from the very same soils, it is the Tokays, Rieslings and Muscats of the grands crus Geisberg and Kirchberg which have made a name for themselves in this beautiful, very historic town. Don't miss *Pfifferday* on the first Sunday of September, the traditional festival of the strolling fiddlers' guild (wine flows from the public fountain).

St Hippolyte
Rodern
Rorschwihr
Bergheim
(23)
D 1b
Ribeauvillé
D 106
Hunawihr
Guémar
Riquewihr
Zellenberg
(24)
Beblenheim
Mittelwihr
Kientzheim
Bennwihr
D 1b
Kaysersberg
Sigolsheim
(25)
Ammerschwihr
N 83
Katzenthah
Niedermorschwihr
Ingersheim
Turckheim
(26)
COLMAR
(27)
D 417
Wintzenheim
Wettolsheim
D 14
Eguisheim
Husseren
Voegtlinshoffen
Herrlisheim
(28)
Hattstatt
Gueberschwihr
(29)
Pfaffenheim
Soultzmatt
(30)
Rouffach
Westhalten
Orschwihr
Bergholtzzell
N 83
Bergholtz
Guebwiller
Issenheim
Soultz
Jungholtz
Wuenheim
D5
Hartmannswiller
(31)
Wattwiller
D 430
Bitschwiller
Uffholtz
(32)
Cernay
Thann
N 83
N 66
0   5km

Fig. 6 — Itinerary through Alsace: the Upper Rhine

Follow the wine trail between **Hunawihr**, with its fourteenth century fortified church situated right among the vineyards (grand cru Rosacker on the Upper Muschelkalk), and Zellenberg, village perched on a patch of calcareous sandstone of the Aalenian surrounded by marls of the Toarcian.

Riquewihr has the reputation of being the most often visited 'bourg' town of Alsace, but you can avoid the crowds in the shelter of a good wine cellar and sample a Riesling, which receives unanimous approval here. Try to distinguish the two soils in specific crus renowned for centuries (24)

On Schoenenbourg, which dominates Riquewihr to the north (fig. 8), the iridescent and gypsiferous marl (gypsum quarry — firing range on northern rampart) of the Keuper are covered with sandy and stony scree derived from the Vosgian Sandstone situated to the west. The combination of a light, aerated soil and a clayey subsoil, rich in nutrients and with quite good water retention capacity, is, without doubt, at the origin of the excellent Riesling, the best in the region and produced on this hillside. The perfume of flowers or of angelica of the young wine turns into a characteristic petrolic aroma in a fine aged wine.

On Sporen, 1.5 km to the south-east of the locality, marls of the Lias (Pliensbachian with ferruginous nodules and Toarcian clayey limestone) are reworked into a surface cover. The clayey, colder soil, the lower altitude, the different orientation of Sporen in comparison with Schoenenbourg, explain the

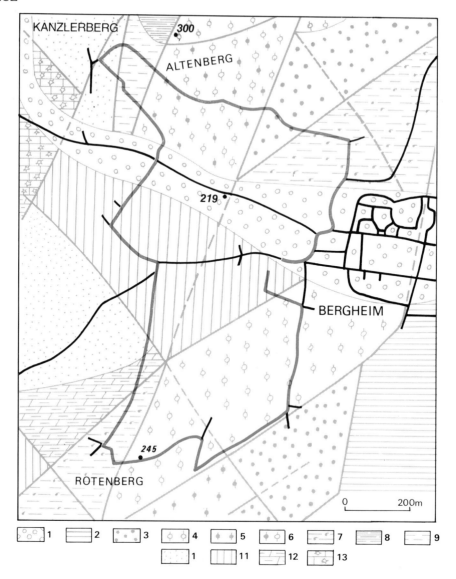

Fig. 7. — The Bergheim wine trail through the marly terrain of the Triassic (Keuper) and the Jurassic (Lias) — (extract of geological map to the scale 1/50,000, sheet no. 342, Colmar-Artolsheim).

1. Recent alluvial; 2. Slope-and valley bottom colluvium; 3. Scree; 4. Grypsiferous and saliferous grey marl (Lower Keuper); 5. Varicoloured marl and dolomite (Upper Lettenkohle); 6. Dolomite and limestone (Lower Lettenkohle); 7. Ammonoid limestone (Upper Muschelkalk); 8. Crinoidal limestone (Upper Muschelkalk); 9. Dolomite and fissile marl (Middle Muschelkalk); 10. Gypsiferous varicoloured marl (Middle Muschelkalk); 11. Finely undulating dolomite (Lower Muschelkalk).

quality, certainly well expressed in this Riesling, though less sought after nowadays for flawless ageing.

At Riquewihr, don't miss the PTT history museum and its special expositions from April to November. *Riesling festival*: penultimate week-end of July.

Beblenheim, Mittelwihr, Bennwihr are clustered together on the eastern edge of the hills covered with slope conglomerates of the Oligocene. This terrain ranks among the most favourable for the vineyard. Sample the two extremes here of Sylvaner, bouqueted and tender and Gewurztraminer with its balanced aroma.

Turn right on the D 1b, towards **Sigolsheim** (fine view from the military cemetery, to the north of the village) and **Kientzheim** (Château of the Confrérie Saint-Étienne and Alsace wine museum), to **Kaysersberg** (ruined château and birthplace of Doctor Albert Schweitzer). This route climbs the broad fan of the Weiss alluvial cone which covers the southern quarter of the Ribeauvillé Fracture Zone. Along with **Ammerschwihr** (where the Confrérie was founded in the fifteenth century), these villages, martyrs of the last war, have remained a Mecca of Alsace wine, totalling no less than a dozen renowned localities. All the same if you are one who enjoys Kaefferkopf, it should be mentioned that this Ammerschwihr cru does not, in fact, come from one particular soil at all, nor from one specific vine, for it can be made from pinot, riesling, muscat or gewurztraminer vines, a detail which is rarely indicated on the label.

The varied types of terrain, between Kaysersberg and Sigolsheim, allow a comparison between the nature of the soil and the distinctive features of the Gewurztraminer wines of Kientzheim ㉕ .

— The granitic terrain, on the side of the Bixkoepfel, between Kientzheim and Kaysersberg, provides mostly colluvial, sandy, silty, shallow, fertile soils but which have poor water retention capacity. Gewurztraminer grown on this acid soil takes quite a long time to mature; it is vigorous and has a certain fineness, but lacks body. In average, less sunny years, and therefore less dry, the wine is of even higher quality (Schlossberg grand cru).

— The alluvial terrain of the Weiss valley, with its clayey, sandy, poorly evolved soil on sand and granite shingle, is only moderately fertile but retains water well. This soil, as acid as the previous one, is suited to a Gewurztraminer which matures quickly, remains light, but fruity, and is good for rapid consumption.

— The limestone marl ground of the southern side of the Mont de Sigolsheim incorporates extremely diverse terrain, which is above all marly, of the Muschelkalk, Lias and Dogger, which merge together in the soil cover: they are magnesite limestone soils, since conglomerates of the Oligocene play a part here. This vineyard area produces a high quality Gewurztraminer, especially in good years; it is less precocious, but with time, it overtakes the previous crus in body, fruit, aroma and especially longevity (fig. 9b p. 43).

From Ammeschwihr to Turckheim: the southern extremity of the Ribeauvillé Fracture Zone

One should now leisurely make ones way along the minor roads to the west of the N 415, towards Katzenthal and Niedermorschwihr, through the hills that a series of faults separates visibly from the mountains. Thus, the Florimont or Letzenberg will show us the discordance between the Jurassic oolitic limestone (several quarries) and the Tertiary conglomerate covering it. This is all demonstrated in the wine trail at Turckheim.

From Ingersheim, a small road leads to the top of the Letzenberg (magnificent 360° panorama). Coming down, pass through Niedermorschwihr (grand cru of Sommerberg); then follow the D 10b through granite mountains to Turckheim. Bypass the old town, to the east, and head towards the new houses, to the north-east, until you come to the foot of the Letzenberg ㉖ .

A cliff of more than 50 metres allows one to study the Tertiary conglomerate accumulated there along the edge of the sea in the Lower Oligocene; the conglomerate beds are composed of well rounded pebbles of white oolitic limestone (Middle Jurassic), grey limestone (Muschelkalk) and ochre calcareous sandstone (Lower Jurassic). Note the imbrication of the pebbles, through the dissolution of areas of contact (imprinted pebbles). Towards the top, the red marly layers are of marine origin (Foraminifera, Mussels) and date the formation as Latdorfian.

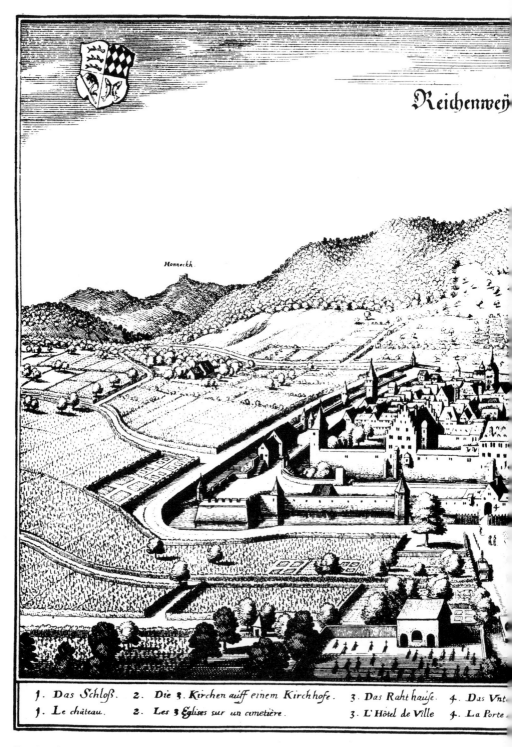

Reichenweÿ

Honneckh.

1. *Das Schloß.*   2. *Die* 3. *Kirchen auff einem Kirchhofe.*   3. *Das Rahthauſe.*   4. *Das Vnt*
1. *Le château.*   2. *Les* 3 *Eglises sur un cimetière.*   3. *L'Hôtel de Ville.*   4. *La Porte.*

Fig. 8 — Facsimile (extract from Topographia Alsatiae, by Matthieu Mérian, 1663) representing
the town of Riquewihr set amidst its vineyards; view towards the west and in particular of the
Schoenenbourg hill situated to the north of the town, fortified in the Middle Ages and in the
seventeenth century.

Riquewihr.

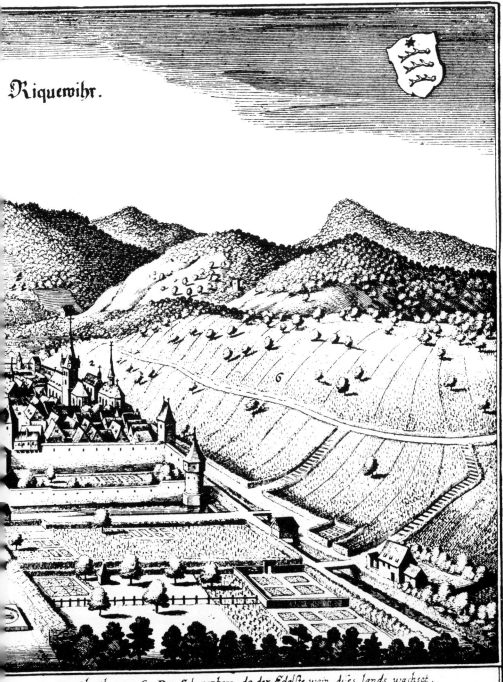

or . 5. Das Oberthor. 6. Der Schanenberg, da der Edelste wein dises lands wachset.

e. 5. La Porte Haute (Dolder). 6. Le Schoenenberg, où pousse le Vin le plus uable de ce Puys.

A comparison of Riesling wines from the Turckheim-Wintzenheim region is strongly recommended.

The king of Alsatian wines is made from a late vine which requires complete maturing of the grape for all its qualities to be brought out; the warming up of the soil at the end of autumn is thus absolutely essential for it. In this area ㉗ it grows:

— On granitic terrain, to the north of Turckheim (grand cru **Brand**); the colluvial and acid brown, sandy, silty soils are moderately fertile (rich in phosphate, but deficient in potash and magnesia). In a dry year they cause the vine to suffer, with the result that the Riesling of this area is very fine, subtle and very fruity, but lacks lively acidity and body. Consumed quickly, in the past, it acquired the reputation of the Brand de Turckheim. In an average or wet year, Riesling is much improved.

— On calcareous terrain, on the eastern side of the Brand **Schneckelsbourg**; Muschelkalk limestone is covered with granitic sand. Soil texture is very akin to that of the granitic terrain, but, without being really stony, the soils have a calcareous reaction and retain water quite well. Riesling produced from this terrain is more vigorous, but has less powerful fruit than that grown on granite; it needs three to four years therefore to acquire the incomparable body of a fine aged wine.

— On limestone marl terrain, on the south-west side of the Letzenberg **(Heimbourg)**; the vine grows on the calcareous conglomerate and marl of the Oligocene overlying Jurassic oolitic limestone. The magnesite limestone soils (rendzines) are both stony and only mildly permeable. A typical Riesling is harvested here, with its lively acidity, its mild taste of the limestone soil in the first year, then its vegetal and flowery fruit which is preserved for several years. It is thus a rival of the Riesling produced from the previous soil.

— On the alluvial terrain of the **Fecht** valley, where the argillaceous sand alluvial cone is lacking in limestone; the soils which are poorly evolved, composed of silicious stones, are not very fertile, but warm up quickly. Here the Riesling is light, expressive, with plenty of fruit from the beginning, but lacks body and must be consumed in the second or third year, especially if it is from a good vintage (dry year). In places, these alluvial deposits are covered with a thin layer of loess and silt; the soil is thus colder here, but produces, in good years, a Riesling with more lively acidity and more bouquet than that grown actually on the alluvial deposits.

Colmar – capital, for centuries, of the Alsace wine-growing region

Regional Alsace wine festival: week of 15th August. *Sauerkraut* and *regional produce shows*: last week-end of August and first week-end of September.

Nothing to say about Colmar — that is to say it is an absolute must to break ones journey here and, in passing, sample the crus of the Hardt, the vineyards of the plain, set on sands, clays and gravels of the Fecht alluvial cone (see above), to the north-west of the town, where you will also come across the Maison du vin d'Alsace (12, avenue de la Foire-aux-Vins), headquarters of the Comité interprofessionnel du vin d'Alsace (CIVA) and the Institut national des appellations d'origine des vins et eaux-de-vie (INAO Alsace and east).

It is also important to know that the AOC vineyard area extends up the Fecht valley beyond Wihr-au-Val, thriving at the slope bottoms of the Osouth-easterly facing crystalline massif.

From Wintzenheim to Gueberschwihr: the Rouffach-Guebwiller Fracture Zone

To the south of **Wintzenheim**, Tertiary conglomerate, at the edge of the Vosges Fault, forms the Rothenberg. The slope descending towards Wettolsheim forms the famous locality of the grand cru, Hengst (yardstick). The excellence of this soil will be confirmed when you taste an Auxerrois, with its perfume of verbena and citronella, or a Gewurztraminer, supple, but with a captivating bouquet; a blend of musk, smoke, rose and orange, in the great vintages.

Come off the N 83, so as not to miss **Eguisheim**, typical Alsatian village with its concentric layout, where in 1002, at the Château of Count Hugues IV, the future Pope Léon IX was born. Here, fault series also appear, to form the great Rouffach-Guebwiller Fracture Zone. The vineyards do not extend this far, as they do in the Ribeauvillé Fracture Zone, for the sandstone terrains of the Lower Triassic, cut up into a mosaic, are frequently over 500 m high and covered in forest. It is on the eastern, relatively rectilinear slope, at the foot of a major fault, that Jurassic limestone (rarely that of the Muschelkalk) appears under the slope scree, and is then covered again, to the east, by a broad fringe of Tertiary conglomerate deposits. It is on this terrain frequently composite and covered in turn by Quaternary loess, that the vineyards are planted (grand cru Eichberg).

At **Husseren**, the road providing access to the châteaux is cut out of the Vosges Sandstone topping the Wintzenheim Biotite Granite. From the Marbach tuberculosis sanatorium, it is possible to get to hill 576, near the Chalet farm, where there is an outcrop of Voegtlinshofen Basalt, a volcanic chimney of Miocene age, like the volcanic Kaiserstuhl Massif, in the Baden region opposite Colmar.

Continue along the D 1, to **Gueberschwihr**, then turn right towards Saint-Marc; the road crosses a stretch of oolitic limestone (grand cru Golder). At the western limit of the vineyard there is a large fault; here, at spot height 342, take the track on the right which goes up into the forest, to the silicified Vosgian Sandstone quarries ㉘ , worked at one time to make paving stones. The quarry face, surmounted by the main conglomerate, is over 30 m high (numerous sedimentological and tectonic features, magnificent striae of sinistral thrust faults which one wants to finger and understand, from the top of these sheer cliffs, the subsidence tectonics of the Rhine Graben).

Pfaffenheim and its wine trail through a terrain of surface formations on a limestone subsoil

The 300 hectares of vines are located between the village, at the foot of the slope cover, and the sandstone scree covered with forest, at the foot of the major fault of the fracture zone (fig. 9). Numerous faults, visible or implied, are expressed in the morphology of this soil, up to 80% lying on surficial or Quaternary formations. But a great many old quarries ㉙ all around **Pfaffenheim**, demonstrate that the limestone subsoil of the HMiddle Jurassic is not far away (less subsided parts). In a similar way, the Oligocene conglomerate of Vosgian sandstone shingles is covered with loess.

The soils of the Pfaffenheim vineyards are all of the brown calcareous type; rendzines or leached soils are rare. Here the conditions are favourable to the gewurztraminer vine, which occupies, moreover, the biggest areas and the smoothness of whose wine delights the taste buds, especially if it comes from the Schneckenberg: but this soil is equally suited to Pinot and Sylvaner, easy wines, embellished here with a touch of musk. Note the timid appearance of the appellation Crémant, particularly made from pinot blanc.

From Rouffach to Guebwiller: section of the fracture zone

Make your way to **Rouffach** and, at its north-west entrance, take the lane suitable for vehicles which, passing close to the Château d'Issembourg, climbs up through the vineyards to the Rouffach Sandstone quarries, under the summit of the **Strangenberg** ⑳

Here we find lovely examples of ochre-yellow calcareous sandstone, inter-stratified in the conglomerate formations of the Oligocene. These sandstones, of marine facies, contain a level of red clay, equivalent of the fossiliferous zone of the Latdorfian. Several historic monuments of the Upper Rhine (church of Saint-Martin of Colmar, collegiate church of Thann, etc.) were constructed using Rouffach Tertiary Sandstone.

Westhalten and **Soultzmatt** (mineral water) are situated in a small valley which intersects the central part of the fracture zone, which is raised up in a Vosgian Sandstone horst. The road continues towards Wintzfelden and Osenbach which are located in a very beautiful interior graben in Muschelkalk and Keuper. It is also an appendage of the AOC vineyard area.

From Soultzmatt continue to **Orschwihr-Bergholtzzell**. The last straight stretch of road follows a small valley through which passes the major fault of which we have admired the throw creating the Vosges Sandstone cliffs, though here the subsidence is more significant: the fault separates the Muschelkalk from the Tertiary conglome-rate. These last two types of geological terrain have brought prosperity to wine-growers throughout the region. The communes share the famous locality names such as Strangenberg, Bollenberg and Zinnkoepfle. To convince yourself, taste, amongst others at Westhalten, a Sylvaner and an Auxerrois, distinguished by a discreet smoky bouquet, and also an excellent Crémant rosé, and, in the Orschwihr region, you will be taken by a Riesling, fleshy and full of verdure, or a Muscat, fresh and fruity like the grape.

The road then passes via Bergholtz to **Guebwiller** and the opening out of the Valleé de la Lauch. This town also has a great wine-growing history, based on seven crus of renowned localities (thanks to the Schlumberger domains). On this terrain at the southern extremity of the fracture zone, the faults ÿpdraw in and deeper soils appear on the valley sides: grauwackes, tuffs and lavas of the Carboniferous.

The dark, stony, heavy soils find expression in the more opulent Riesling, Tokay and Gewurztraminer wines; but at the exit of the valley, where the soil is lighter and sandy, such as the celebrated Wanne, location of the grands crus Kitterle and Kessler, the wines are distinguished by their nutty taste. One should also observe the marly limestone soils on the way to Bergholtz, to the north (grands crus Spiegel and Saering), and to Soultz and Wuenheim, to the south, the extreme point of the fracture zone (grand cru Ollwiller).

At Guebwiller: *Wine festival* on Ascension Day at the old Dominican convent.

From Hartmannswiller to Thann: the Thann fracture zone

While, on the plain, the potash basin of Alsace, with its mine shafts and tips, stretches out to the left, the wine trail now links up patches of demarcated vinefields on subsoils of conglomerate, Alsatian molasse and loess. Turn right, towards **Wattwiller**, to see the magnificent fault breccia of Tertiary age, which, silicified and dislocated by erosion, forms rocks, for it is between 30 and 50 m thick (Hirtzenstein ruin, by road, 1 km to the west of Wattwiller, on the right, in the direction of the family house) ㉛

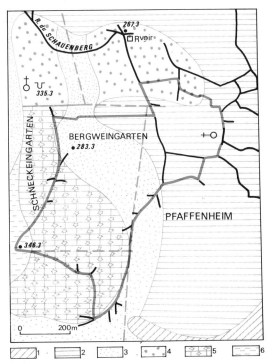

Fig. 9. — *The Pfaffenheim wine trail through a terrain of superficial formations: loess and scree on Jurassic limestone and Tertiary conglomerate (extract of geological map to scale 1/50,000, sheet no, 378, Neuf-Brisach-Obersassheim).*

1. Colluvium: 2. Loess; 3. Scree; 4. Conglomerates and marls (Lattorfian); 5. Limestones of the 'Grande Oolithe' (Upper Bajocian); 6. Argillaceous marls and limestones (Lower Bajocian).

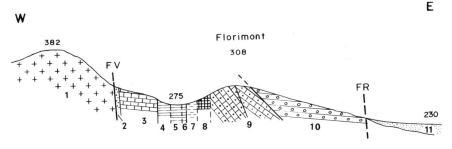

Soils of the Alsace vineyard region to the north-west of Colmar

1. Turckheim Granite; 2. Buntsandstein; 3. Muschelkalk; 4–6. Argillaceous-calcareous Lias (Sinemurian, Pliensbachian, Toarcian); 7. Sandy Dogger (Aalenian); 8. Marly Dogger (Middle Bajocian); 9. Oolitic calcareous Dogger (Upper Bajocian); 10. Conglomeratic Tertiary (Oligocene) discordant on Mesozoic; 11. Quaternary: older and recent alluvials.

The road skirts the hills which are dotted with vineyards, to the west of Cernay, and goes on to **Thann**. This is the end of the vineyard area, but a fine end with regard to the wine produced here. In fact, the vineyards boil down here to the renowned grand cru Rangen, revered for centuries, but especially its soil, composed of ancient volcanic rocks (Carboniferous), mean that the "best wines of the region are produced here". These Culm materials — grauwackes (fine sandstones with volcanic elements), ashy tuffs, various lavas — hardened by metamorphism, form a stony and fertile soil where the vine will suffer if the climate is too arid. The wine here is rich, expressive to the point of pungency, according to the type of vine. In the case of Riesling, for example, which has a lot of body and a musky taste, there is analogy with the Riesling from the Guebwiller and

Andlau valley; it is indubitably the substratum of the soil which is reflected in the wine.

We will finish with a geological study of this terrain, going back up the valley to see the quarry of the *"Petrified Forest"* of **Bitschwiller** ㉜ . At the war memorial, cross the Thur, and turn left for the immense worked quarries (shale, lavas, breccia, faults) or right, to discover, in vertical beds, traces of fossilized branches and trunks dating back more than 300 million years (Viséan).

The food and drink trail: The harmony of Alsace wines and the dishes of the region

Wandering through the vineyards of the Vosges foothills will have given you an appreciation of the region, its people and the fruits of their labour – the great variety of wines produced there, especially if you take a little time and enjoy sampling them in the full knowledge of their origins. The marriage of these wines with the dishes of the region, will, no doubt, also have tempted you, for Alsace is not lacking in good inns and "Winstubs". But while these gourmand combinations are a matter of personal taste, gastronomic traditions do exist even for light family meals.

Firstly the drinking of Alsace wines other than as a complement to meals. White wines are particularly suitable for drinking outside meal times, especially the dry and fruity types. At receptions, your guests will be pleasantly surprized by the refreshing blend of a Pinot Blanc or a Riesling with a strawberry, bilberry or blackcurrant cordial. A light Gewurztraminer or Muscat is the ideal traditional complement to a snack of "Kougelhopf". Keep some pretzels and other salted biscuits in for ÿaperitifs. These are always served with a first class Alsatian Muscat opening the appetite without overloading the stomach.

At any time of the day, you will be offered little specialities in the "Winstubs", — typical wine bars where you will not be surprized for long by the cordial atmosphere once you have washed down an onion tart, some knuckle of ham, smoked shoulder with horseradish (Schiffala), some wine- grower's pie ("tourte vigneronne") or Munster valley pie, a gruyère or saveloy salad, with a Sylvaner or a supple and elegant Pinot blanc. To accompany Alsace snails or a "tarte flambée" (Flam-mekeuche), you might try a lively Riesling, keeping the Pinot noir or the Tokay Pinot gris for the delicious hotpot of meats, potatoes and onions called Baeckeoffe. Don't forget to taste an Edelzwicker, which is often excellent in the Winstubs.

One last speciality you are recommended to taste outside meal times is the drink "Warmer-vin chaud-Win" (sic), described as fortifying on account of the red wines generally used; but try the recipé with a Pinot noir, or even a Pinot or Tokay Pinot gris white wine, which goes well with those Alsace gingerbread fingers covered with icing sugar.

Then we come to the wines from Alsace which make not an insignifi-cant contribution to the preparation of dishes. Whether in home cooking or haute cuisine, the aromatic constituents of Alsace wine and its dryness do wonders for sauces, court-bouillons, marinades, pâtés, hotpots and numerous regional dishes. It is Riesling, preferably aged, which best transmits its vegetal bouquet and its essential hint of acidity. As a general rule, Alsace wine is responsible for the typical flavour of numerous dishes, so very different from the same recipés of other gastronomic regions.

Finally there are the well-matched marriages of wines and regional dishes according to the mood of the moment or the advice of the head cook. It is Ofor you to choose.

With entrées and hors-d'oeuvre, comprising Alsace cooked meats or salt beef, served with small side salads and horseradish sauce, a light and fresh wine is advised:

Sylvaner, Pinot blanc or the Edelzwicker blend. Alsatian foie gras, on the other hand, which has traditionally already been steeped in an aged Alsatian wine, calls for a structured wine, not too rich, such as Tokay Pinot gris, if served at the beginning of the meal. An opulent Gewurztraminer is more suitable if the foie gras is to be eaten on its own or served after the meat.

All fish dishes, and in particular trout, pike-perch, pike or salmon, however they are prepared, preferably in a sauce, grilled or poached, are served exclusively with Riesling. Seafood, with its salty juices, is also set off best by the verdure of Riesling, although a blander Sylvaner, is also quite suitable. For lobster with an American sauce, a stronger tasting wine would be recommended, such as a robust, though not too robust, Gewurztraminer.

If the pìece de résistance is a sauerkraut, Riesling and Sylvaner are again the most suitable wines. With poultry or white meat, opinions differ; there are those who always extol Riesling, while others choose from the Pinot range, Pinot blanc or Auxerrois, preferably supple, Tokay Pinot gris, if one is looking for a more distinguished harmony, and Pinot noir, if one wants to be more original. Red meats, including lamb and game (Alsace pheasant, venison and wild boar) traditionally demand a good red wine; that might be the time to have a change from Alsace wine, though one could try a Pinot noir with nice fruit and a beautiful colour, or equally a well structured and heady Tokay. With ham, whether braised or otherwise, and salad, the last two wines are also recommended.

With cheese, again you are likely to turn to red wines from other provinces. However, the soft white cheeses (fromages frais) and cheese spreads harmonize well with Pinot blanc ou Edelzwicker, while the stronger tasting cheeses, and even Alsace 'Munster', go perfectly well with a fruity and powerful Gewurztraminer.

Finally for the desserts, or the last course, when we also arrive at the end of this progression through the aromatic characteristics of the wines, vital to any gastronomic enjoyment. Traditionally, the roundness and lusciousness of Gewurztraminer harmonizes the best with the unctuousness of pâtisserie, damson tarts, kirsch soufflés, etc. An opulent Tokay Pinot gris, of a good vintage, is also perfectly suitable. For iced desserts and sorbets, however, some would go for an Alsace Muscat; and, if you are served a "tarte au fromage blanc" (type of cheesecake), select a Pinot blanc-Auxerrois or a Riesling, depending on your taste.

Now you just need something to accompany your coffee and this requires serious thought. Alsace, being the region of white brandies, where all varieties of orchard fruits and forest berries are distilled, you will be presented with an almost unlimited choice; but don't forget the brandy "marc de Gewurztraminer", which Alfred de Vigny described as being of the pburning soul "of the Alsace soil"

Alsace, with its Confrérie Saint-Etienne (the oldest wine and food society of France) at the Château de Kientzheim, offers a fantastic field of study which allows you, upon due admittance, to rise from the status of apprentice to that of journeyman and master, through obedience to the statutes: love of good living, good eating and the wines of Alsace.

> FOR FURTHER
> INFORMATION

Geology:

Guide géologique: Vosges-Alsace, by J.-P. von Eller et coll. (2nd edition, 1984), published by Masson – see in particular itineraries 1, 4, 6, 7, 20, 25, 26.

Sittler C. (1969) — Le Fossé rhénan en Alsace. Aspect structural et histoire géologique. *Rev. Géogr. phys. Géol. Dynam.* (2), **11**, 5, pp. 465-494.

Sittler C. et al. (1982-1986) — In Encyclopédie de l'Alsace, published by Publitotal, Strasbourg – See headings: hills, Rhine Graben, Geology, Vineyards.

Oenology:

Delforge A. 1978). — 151 Winstub et tavernes pittoresques d'Alsace . . . (et les restaurants alsaciens de Paris et d'ailleurs). Published by Alsatia, Colmar 263 p.

Marocke R., Balthazard J. and Huglin P. (1977) — Données concernant les exportations en éléments fertilisants de la vigne et un essai de fumure. *Les vins d'Alsace*, **5**, pp. 3-7. Published by Alsatia, Colmar.

Renvoisé G. (1983). — Le guide des vins d'Alsace. Published by Solar. Coll. Solarama, Paris, 64p.

Schwartz J., Marocke R., Couturier A. and Ochsenbein G. (1974). — Kientzheim. Esquisse géologique, étude des sols, de la végétation, de la faune entomologique et des caractères viti-oenologiques de son terroir. *Bull. Soc. Hist. nat. Colmar*, **55**, pp. 127-149.

Sittler C. and Marocke R. (1981). — Géologie et oenologie en Alsace: sols et terroirs géologiques, cépages et spécificité des vins. *Bull. Sci. géol.*, **34** (3), pp. 147-182

Sittler C. (1983) — Le grand cru du Rangen de Thann. Fondements historique et géologique. *Bull. Soc. ind. Mulhouse*, **790**, pp. 61-70.

Sittler L. (1969). — La route du vin d'Alsace. SAEP pub., Colmar-Ingersheim, 171 p.

La gastronomie alsacienne (1969). – Coll. "Connaissance de l'Alsace", Saisons d'Alsace. Published by Istra, Strasbourg, 341 p.

Le vin d'Alsace (1978). Published by Montalba, Diff. Vilo, Paris, 216 p.

Le vin d'Alsace (1981), *Bull. Soc. ind. Mulhouse*, **780**, pp. 33-100.

Old well at
Riquewihr

Page 49: Bunch of Alsatian chasselas grapes (Photo CIVA – Colmar).

Above: Harvesting at Gueberschwihr. View looking south: vineyards set on slope cover over Jurassic limestone of the 'Grande Oolithe', grand cru Goldert (Photo CIVA – Colmar).

Below: Bunch of tokay pinot gris grapes (Photo CIVA – Colmar).

50

Above: The fortified church, to the south-west of Hunawihr, surrounded by vineyards set in very varied soils of the Trias and Lower Lias group. Taken from the middle of the Ribeauvillé Fracture Zone, this view facing north, shows the gneiss and granite mountainside (with the three Châteaux of Ribeauvillé) whose peak, Taennchel, is topped with Vosgian Sandstone; also shown is the grand cru Rosacker (Photo CIVA – Colmar).

Below: The vineyards on the mountainside, to the north of Kaysersberg where one can see the ruined castle, are set on migmatite granite — grand cru Schlossberg (Photo CIVA – Colmar).

51

The vineyard of Bar-sur-Aube, view from Voigny (Photo Laurain).

SEDIMENTARY ROCKS

a²	Recent Quaternary
a¹	Older Quaternary
	Oligocene
e² e	Middle and Upper Eocene Undifferentiated Eocene
e¹	Lower Eocene

c² c	Upper Cretaceous Undifferentiated Cretaceous
c¹	Lower Cretaceous Urgonian
J³	Upper Jurassic (Malm)
J² J	Middle Jurassic (Dogger) Undifferentiated Jurassic
J¹	Lower Jurassic (Lias)

DEMARCATIONS

Champagne

Chablis

Fig. 10. — Geological map and demarcation of vineyard areas of Champagne and Chablis (See Bourgogne).

Champagne

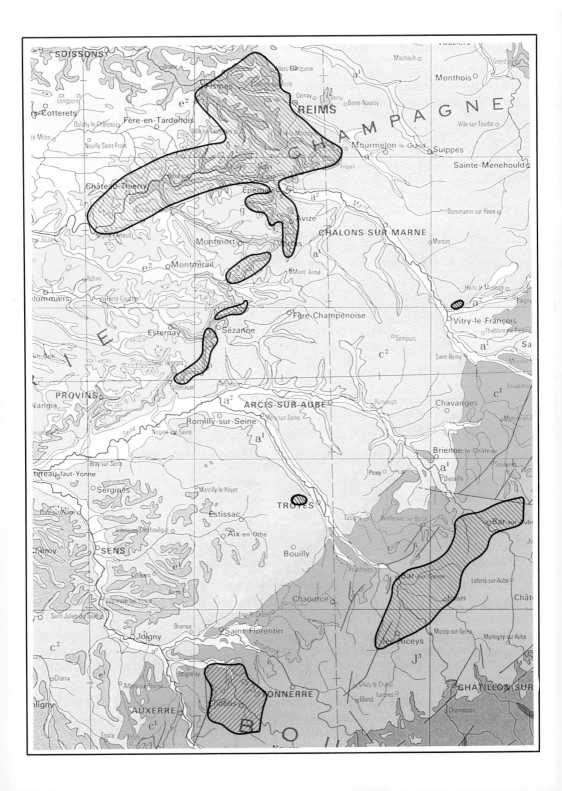

The vineyard area of Champagne is at the northern-most limit for cultivation of the vine. Consequently, maximum advantage must be taken of the sunshine and this is why it is essentially planted on well exposed slopes.

Though this area represents only 2.5% of French vineyards, it is spread over a vast area in the departments of the Marne, the Aisne and the Aube (fig. 10) as well as in certain communes in the Haute Marne and the Seine-et-Marne.

Three varieties of vine are authorized in Champagne: two black grape varieties, meunier and pinot noir, and one white, chardonnay. Except for the champagne Blanc de blancs (white wine produced from white grapes), the cuvées are composed, in varying proportions, of wines produced from these three vine varieties. Furthermore, as Dom Pérignon discovered, the blending of wines from different crus results in a superieur end product to that produced by the individual constituents.

The vineyard soils, rearranged through the centuries by man, have lost all their typical features. Normal pedological evolution produces brown soils on colluvium and rendzines on chalk. The deep penetration of the roots in the diaclases of the chalk assures the plant's water supply.

The vine and its soil

Vine planting

In Champagne, the preferred medium of the vine is chalk; the best crus are located on the slopes of the Montagne de Reims, planted with pinot noir and chardonnay, and on the Côte des Blancs, planted essentially with chardonnay.

Because of the generally west oriented inclination of the beds in this section of the Paris Basin, the slopes of the Marne and Vesle valleys are in fact composed of Tertiary terrain. The type of vine planted here varies in accordance with the changing substratum with the pinot noir and chardonnay varieties progressively giving way to the meunier vine.

Similarly, around Sézanne, the selection of vines is governed by the same substratum conditions: to the north, the meunier vine prevails while to the south, the predominant vine types are pinot noir and chardonnay.

The vineyards of Vitry-le François and Montgueux (Troyes) on chalk, recently reestablished to meet demand, have been planted with pinot noir and chardonnay.

Planted on Kimmeridgian marl, the vineyards of the Aube profit from an appreciably warmer climate. After a significant decline, caused by phylloxera, this region is again expanding rapidly. According to legal requirements, the gamay vine has been replaced by authorized champagne vine varieties, with a predominance of pinot noir.

These vineyards produce noticeably different wines to those of the Marne, and this can be attributed to climatic and soil-related conditions. The chardonnay vine contributes fineness and lightness to the cuvée, while pinot noir adds body and bouquet and meunier gives it the required freshness.

Climate

Champagne has an Atlantic climate, although continental influences are not insignificant here. The average annual temperature is in the region of 10 °C, with the vineyards of the Aube enjoying slightly more sunshine and summer temperatures which are higher by about 1 °C. The number of frosty days per year varies from 60 to 80. The most fearsome days strike in the spring, and on the plain can have the effect of shrivelling up the new growth. While the rainfall régime is identical on the plain and on the plateaux (rainfall spread over the whole year, with slightly higher rainfall in summer and autumn), it rains slightly more, nevertheless, on the plateaux and in the valleys (700 mm) than on the Champagne plain (600 mm). Summer storms can occasionally be violent and hail is particularly feared at this time.

Viticulture

"Chablis", "cordon de Royat", "Guyot" and "vallée de la Marne" are the only training methods authorized and are short and low to the ground, the aim of this being to limit yield and benefit ripening.

Varieties of stock for grafting have been selected for resistance to phylloxera and ferric chlorosis, a disease which causes leaves to turn yellow and is due to chlorophyl synthesis failure. In fact, the precipitation of iron in the calcareous soils prevents its production. An original means of combatting the chlorotic tendancy of chalk involves spreading the vinefields with Sparnacian lignite. This practice began shortly after the 1789 Revolution. The lignite is extracted essentially from the Reims Mountains, and is called locally ash or black mountain earth, and is worked in vast quarries called jauges or ash quarries. The pyrite from this Soissonnais lignite provides, after oxidization, iron necessary to the vines. In addition, the sand and clay associated with it improves the texture of the soil.

This practice is carried out in conjunction with that of spreading a type of manure over the ground made from household waste, which has undergone a certain sterilization process and which enriches the soil with organic matter.

Vinification

After an initial racking of the must, it is put into vats where primary fermentation lasts for two weeks. The white wine, left still, settles under the influence of natural or artificial low temperatures. In February-March, comes the bottling stage – the drawing off of the wine allowing secondary fermentation to take place within an enclosed environment and to trap the carbon dioxide produced in solution in the wine. This secondary fermentation is assisted by the addition of a cane sugar solution and yeasts and produces the bubbles. The bottles are put into storage horizontally, on racks, in the stillness of the wine cellars, and kept there for a year or more. The sediment formed is slowly directed down towards the bottle necks by gentle movement (the bottles, on racks, being gradually turned and tilted neck down by expert hands). Following this mass upright storage, the sediment is drawn from the bottle in readiness for its final maturing. The small amount of wine lost is replaced by some old cognac and Champagne liqueur, the amount of sugar added regulated according to the quality desired (brut, sec, or demi-sec). This vinification process takes place in cellars maintained at constant degrees of temperature and humidity. Around Reims and Épernay, this stability is assured by vast underground networks of galleries tunnelled into the chalk and which the great Champagne houses gladly open to the public.

History

While the vine existed sixty million years ago in Champagne, as proven by the imprints of vine leaves in the Thanetian travertine of Sézanne, its morphology was closer to the Virginia creeper variety than the cultivated vine.

Prior to the Roman conquest, the existence of a vineyard in the Montagne de Reims would have been highly probable, since, in the year 92, the Emperor Domitian prohibited the cultivation thereof. Two centuries later, an area of low relief, Porte Mars, in Reims, celebrated the authorization granted by Emperor Probus, for replanting.

Subsequently, Mediterranean cultivation of the vine was to survive. Ever since the ninth century, the vine has been supported by a low post and wire trellis, which is still a standard practice, exposing it to maximum warmth and limiting grape yield to ensure high quality.

The vineyard even extended to the chalky Champagne plain, so much so that, at the beginning of the eighteenth century, overproduction brought about misery for the wine growers. Wine produced then was red and had a sparkling tendency, caused by incomplete fermentation of the must.

At the end of the seventeenth century, Dom Pérignon, a monk at the Abbey of Hautvillers, experimented with fermentation in the spring to produce a sparkling wine by a process of trapping carbon dioxide in the bottle. The stopper had to be kept firmly in the bottle neck by means of wire or a muzzle.

This wine was soon appreciated at the court of Louis XV, for accompanying fine meals. The first commercial houses were founded in this era, at Épernay and Reims. Nevertheless it was not until the 1800's that champagne attained the perfect limpidity for which it is known today.

The production of sparkling white wine was, during the nineteenth century, to supplant that of red wine. Today, only a few communes still produce much sought-after, non-sparkling red wines (Bouzy, Ambonnay, Ay, Damery) or rosés (Les Riceys).

Just like all the French vineyard areas, Champagne suffered from the invasion of phylloxera which, breaking out in the Marne valley in 1891, caused notably reduced production. Stabilized at around 11 000 hectares by 1950, this vineyard region continued to expand, reaching, in 1985, over 25 000 hectares dedicated to vines. It is still expanding, notably in the Aube and the valley of the Marne.

Prestigious wine province, Champagne was always a stopping-off place, grievously hit by the wars. The old regional dialect of Champenois has disappeared, as well as many traditional customs. Among those which have survived, are the 'Feux de la Saint-Jean' (in the Marne valley especially) and the 'Fête du cochelet' which marks the end of the harvesting. Carrying on the dynamic tradition of the communes and associations, other festivities have been revived or initiated (cask rolling races in Bouzy and a champagne festival, held each year in a different village).

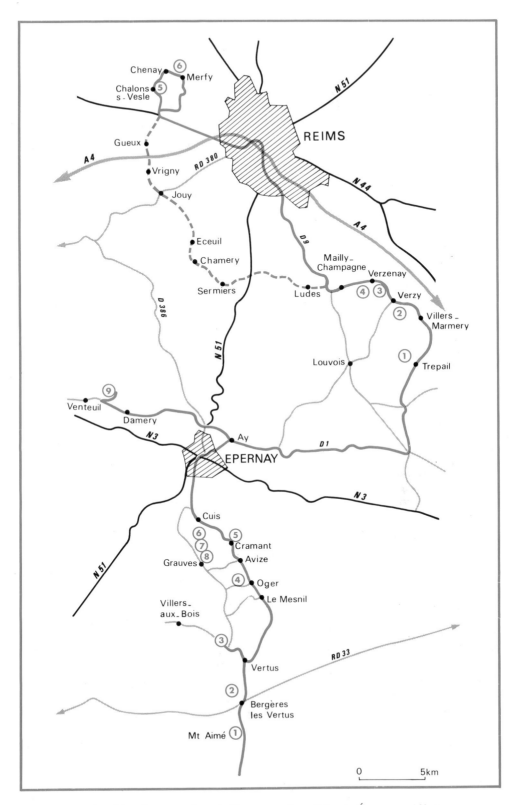

Fig. 11 — Itineraries through Champagne: from Reims to Épernay and Vertus.

Itineraries

La Montagne de Reims

Situated to the east of the Tertiary outcrops of the Paris Basin, the Montagne de Reims is a distinct area of higher relief of over 180 metres, dominating the Champagne plain. Composed of Tertiary terrain, this small patch of the Champagne Brie region, isolated to the north of the Marne, belongs to the cuesta of the Ile-de-France of which it constitutes the most easterly part. Geologically, this region has marked characteristics distinguishing it from the zone situated to the north-west by the absence of marine horizons and from the south-west area by the presence of a sedimentary series in which all the stages are represented.

The vineyard area of the Montagne de Reims is almost entirely set on slope formations accumulated on chalk and derived from regional Tertiary materials. In the lower area, the vineyard may lie on chalk, while, in the upper section, it reaches the sandy limestone of the Thanetian.

The Montagne de Reims is a structural plateau through whose surface, which is covered with Quaternary aeolian silt, appear the Sannoisian boulders acting as re-inforcement (fig. 12).

The edge of the cuesta exhibits the Oligocene and the Eocene which give heavy and wet terrain, covered, as is the silt of the plateau, in wood and forest. The bottom section of the talus and the area linking up with the Champagne plain show outcrops of the Paleocene and of Campanian chalk. The calcareous nature of these subsoils, their good drainage and the gentle slopes allow the development of high quality vineyards.

The Champagne plain, comprised entirely of chalk more or less covered with

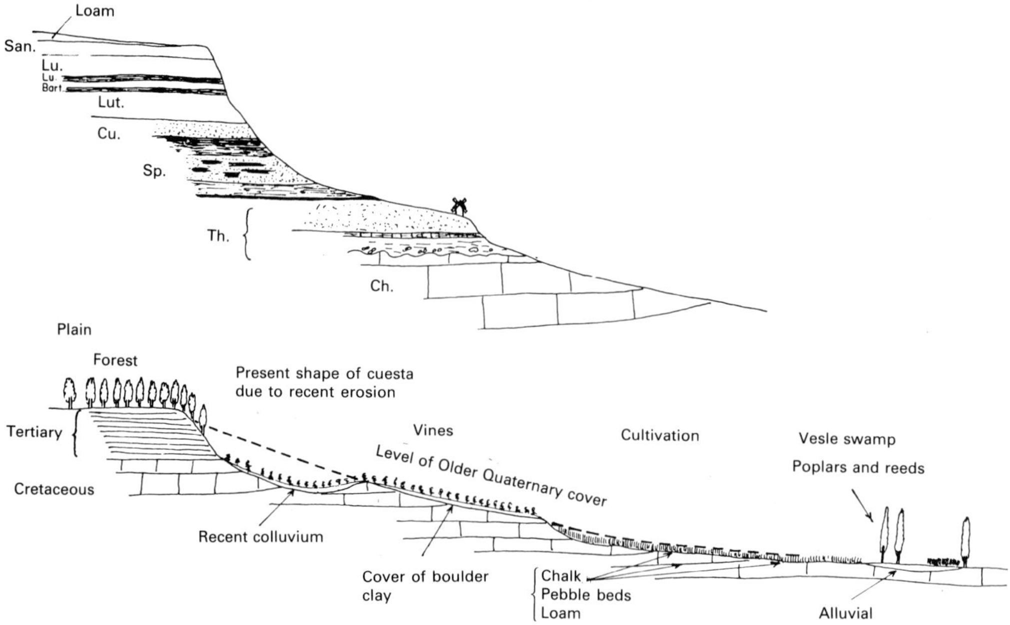

Fig. 12. — *Geological section of the Montagne de Reims, Geomorphological profile and utilization of soil from Reims to the Vesle.*

Ch. Chalk: Th. Thanetian: Sp. Sparnacian: Cu. Cuisian: Lut. Lutetian: Bart. Bartonian: Lu. Ludian: San. Sannoisian.

rendzines, gravel or loam, is a great cereal and beet cultivation region. Areas of most pronounced relief are occasionally planted with vines.

Go to Trépail ①, fig. 11, to the east of the Montagne de Reims. The slope of the sports ground, which backs onto the hills, is formed by white Campanian chalk, exposed over a height of 15 metres. Two types of profile, clearly visible but not easily accessible, show grey rendzines on chalk, and brown soil on more clayey colluvium. In the middle of the face, a subvertical band of slightly yellowed chalk, cut up into great blocks separated by crushed chalk and clayey streaks, marks a small fault. The chalk which is very white and very pure, is quite rich (for chalk!) in macrofossils (Pycnodonts, Spondyls, Chlamys, Sea Urchins, burrows and coprolites containing fish debris, etc). The outcrop shows surface fragmentation, cutting the rock up into blocks which become smaller the nearer they are to the surface, and subhorizontal fissures caused by the expansion of the rock. This breaking up was caused by freezing deep down, during the cold periods (glaciation) of the Quaternary.

Continuing along up the track to the left, through vineyards and woods, one follows a fine section in the surface formations: silt-laden colluvium and chalk solifluction (slope deposits). Shortly before the track becomes enclosed, the right-hand slope shows the passage from the Cretaceous to the Tertiary: the white chalk turns into a chalky mass, packed at the base with angular blocks of yellowed and indurated chalk which disappear within 1 to 2 metres. The matrix which is at first whitish and uniform, becomes lumpy and grey. Higher up, with the calcareous granules becoming more and more abundant, the material becomes hardened and takes on the appearance of a dark grey limestone, cut up into horizontal irregular tablets. Such a section may be directly compared with the pedological profiles of limestone crusts which occur in a hot and markedly dry climate.

Forming a thickness of some fifteen metres, *Microcodium* Sand crops out here and there along the track. At a small, dangerous underground quarry, the most indurated levels were once worked. This sand is composed of calcareous granules, derived from the weathering of the indurated chalk, the palaeopedological crust and isolated *Microcodium cells*. These airborne organisms, of uncertain taxonomic attribution, eat away at the limestones. In the oblique bedding of the base are intercalated beds of conglomerate containing calcareous components and levels rich in soft shingle.

The Trépail section is continued in a vast quarry in sand with lignite streaks, then by argillaceous lignite of Sparnacian age. Above, are 1 to 3 m of white, occasionally rubefied sand belonging to the Cuisian. Clay with millstone directly overlies the Cuisian, without a trace of the Middle and Upper Eocene.

Carry on from Trépail via Villers-Marmery to **Verzy**. One can see, on the northern slope of the Montagne de Reims, the pronounced asymmetry of the valleys. This would be caused by the influence of periglacial climates during the Quaternary (more precocious thawing on the well exposed slopes, allowing a longer erosion period). The prevailing winds, depositing silt on the slopes facing eastwards (to leeward), would have driven, by means of this process of sedimentation, the streams, rivers and waterways towards the east and caused a higher degree of erosion on the west-facing slopes.

The higher ground rising from the plain to the summit of the cuesta is covered with solifluction material, composed essentially of clay with millstones. It represents patches of dissection of an ancient cover linking the plateau to the Vesle valley (fig. 12). Observe the soil where the vines grow, composed of this colluvium.

From Verzy, join the plateau by the Louvois road. At the top of the hill, to the left, you will come to **Faux-de-Verzy** ②(beech trees with a twisted appearance, very likely suffering from a viral disease). In this remarkable and pleasant spot behind the Croix-Rouge, one comes across old quarries bearing millstone and rubefied argillaceous sand of Stampian age. The alluvium which covers the ground which is decalcified, leached on the surface and often water-logged, is rich in crust debris and ferruginous pisolites. To the right, below the **Mont-Sanaï** Observatory ③, the detachment surface of a huge land-slip offers a beautiful section in the Middle and Upper silicified Ludian; brown red clay and grey clay containing millstone blocks overlies brown green marl with rusty streaks, visible for 2 to 3 m.

Go through Verzenay, in the direction of **Mailly-Champagne**, past the windmill on the right (beautiful panorama). At the exit of the wood, take the road to the left and follow it until you come to the junction. To the left appears an outcrop of Campanian chalk. Both roads lead to the "ash" or "black earth" quarries, which are worked for enriching the vineyards ④. The lignite sand and clay supply the soil with organic matter and iron and combat the chlorotic tendancy of the chalk. The right-hand road provides a further view of the Cretaceous-Tertiary contact and the *Microcodium* sand.

The quarries expose, at their base, the Sparnacian, where sedimentation occurred in vast marshes, cut by channels, sometimes under marine influence. This sedimentation is characterized by pronounced horizontal and vertical variability of the facies.

The black clay at the base of the quarry contains, sporadically, marine fossils (Cyrena, Corbula, *Tympanotonus, Melanopsis*). It is overlain by more or less coarse reddish-brown and grey sand, passing laterally into finely laminated sediments composed of white sand and brown and grey clay. The Sparnacian ends with very black lignite clay, with wood and leaf imprints; the ceiling is marked by a strong ferruginous accumulation. The maximum thickness visible is of some fifteen metres.

The Cuisian is composed of white and greyish sands of about 4 to 5 m thick, which contain fine beds of grey clay and accumulations of desiccation pellicles. The upper section is very rich in carbonate.

The Lutetian is comprised of a group of marly clay beds, strongly coloured in beige, grey, green, rust and red hues. The associations of green, red and rust clay and the presence, in some beds, of calcite concretions, suggest a pedological evolution under wet conditions.

Above these, various limestone beds alternate with marly layers representing the Bartonian (1.5 to 2 m); the white, greyish, yellowish limestone, pierced with numerous twisted tubes, suggests paludal sedimentation which is confirmed by the fauna (Limnea, Planorbs, Cyclostomes, Bythinia) and the flora (gyroliths and stems of Characées).

The last Bartonian layer, 0.30 m thick and rich in Limnea, presents an irregular surface, penetrated in places by a yellow fine-grained limestone with irregular breaks. This limestone, which in places is very fossiliferous, contains fauna from a marine environment of variable salinity (Oysters, Pholadomya, Turritella, Cyrena, *Venus, Cardium*, etc.) Discontinuous and of varying thickness (0.40 m), this level represents the Ludian transgression. The Ludian continues as continental or lagoonal beds of soft marly limestone, marl and clay in decimetric beds. At the summit of the face, is an outcrop of brown clay with millstone pebbles, affected by solifluction and cryoturbation.

In order to contrast the geology of the Montagne de Reims with that of the vineyards of the Vesle Valley and of the hills, go via Reims or along the foot of the cuesta, to **Châlons-sur-Vesle**. On the road from Châlons-sur-Vesle to Mâco, is a vast quarry ⑤of greenish or yellowish white fine sand of some fifteen metres in thickness. This beach deposit shows cross stratification accentuated by numerous fossiliferous beds. The fauna, which is very varied, is unfortunately decalcified and fragile. Sedimentation is almost contemporaneous with the weathering of the chalk in the Montagne de Reims.

From Châlons-sur-Vesle, go to **Chenay**. The vineyards are set on calcareous sand overlying the Châlons-sur-Vesle sand and the Sparnacian and the Cuisian. At the exit of Chenay, towards Merfy, take the turning to the left opposite the War Memorial (lovely view over Reims), which leads to the plateau. After passing through cultivated land, the road becomes hemmed in by quarries ⑥ in marine Lutetian limestone. The layers which are irregular and separated by interbeds of calcareous sand, contain an abundant and varied fauna, preserved in the form of impressions or internal moulds.

The Côte des Blancs and the Valley of the Marne (fig. 11)

In the Côte des Blancs, the Tertiary layers are of a much reduced thickness and only crop out in the upper parts of the slopes. The vines, although planted on the top of the hillsides (100 to 200 m up) grow almost exclusively on the Cretaceous. In the Marne Valley, where the Eocene thickens and is inclined towards the west, the chalky part of the slopes quickly diminishes and so the vine grows on heavy soils, derived from the Tertiary levels.

To the south of the Côte des Blancs is the geological, geographical and historical site of the **Mont Aimé** ①, where one can observe fine quarries in the Montian limestone bed which forms its capping. Facing southwards they are accessible by numerous paths leading from the upper esplanade. From the top of the quarry face overhang, there is a fine view of the capture of the Somme by the Soude, to the detriment of the Petit Morin which, underfed, drains the Saint-Gond marsh. The quarry exposes 20 m of white cross-bedded limestone. While slightly sandy at the base, it becomes cavernous in the upper section, due to dissolution.

This formation crops out well at **Faloises** ② ("cliffs"), above the road from Bergères-lès-Vertus to Vertus. One can reach, by crossing the vineyards, under-ground workings and quarries, from which stone was used in the nineteenth century for the restoration of Reims Cathedral.

Above **Vertus**, on the road to Villers-aux-Bois, is a vast quarry ③ just down from the rubbish dump on the right-hand side, exposing the same very accessible levels.

Return to Vertus (beautiful view over the chalky plain of Champagne) and continue to **Oger** by the road which crosses the vineyards of the Côtes des Blancs. Continue up onto the plateau on the D 38 and take the first road on the right for a distance of 500 metres. A quarry ④, on the left, exposes the Upper Eocene. It is composed of massive, thick-bedded limestone, occasionally brecciated or recrystallized. In the upper section it is strongly silicified, with numerous chalcedony-clad cavities.

Continue on through **Cramant**, leaving it by the minor road which goes straight down to the D 19. At the exit of the village, at the location of a crossroads ⑤ hemmed in by steep ground, there is a vertical face in chalk. This chalk, which corresponds to the upper section of the Campanian, belongs to the *Magas pumillus* zone, small Brachiopods which can be collected quite easily.

Return to Cramant and follow the D 10 towards **Cuis**. Once level with the church, take the minor road which bears right and continues on the flat towards the vineyards. After one kilometre and past a copse, go up to the left alongside the adjacent plot of vines. The slope exposes clays and clayey faluns with *Tympanotonus* and *Cyrena* of the Sparnacian ⑥. Carrying on up the slope, one reaches another plot at the top of which there are outcrops of Unios and Teredine Sands of the Upper Cuisian ⑦. In the coarse, reddish-brown, slightly argillaceous sand there is bone debris of Reptiles (Tortoise and Crocodile), Fish (*Lepidosteus*) and Mammals, showing the fluviatile origin of the formation.

Continuing towards **Grauves**, on the left you will notice a great cliff ⑧ of massive, white limestone, at the base of which green and white streaky clay is exposed. This cliff marks the origin of major former landslides which are made evident not least by the presence in the vineyard of huge blocks, some of which are rich in Potamides lapidum. A landslide whith started in a small valley began moving again in 1988, taking road and vines with it.

Continue through **Épernay** and the Valley of the Marne to Cumières and Damery. Above **Damery**, on the road from Fleury to Venteuil, you will come across a small quarry ⑨ where calcareous sand has been worked and which is very rich in fossils (be careful! — This quarry is dangerous, due both to the fracturing of the limestone and the numerous excavations which have been carried out by thoughtless amateurs). The fauna which is abundant and varied and remarkably well preserved, corresponds to a littoral or infralittoral environment. This ancient beach is situated almost at the southeastern-most point of the marine Lutetian in the Paris Basin. The white and green marl above the quarry is equivalent to the limestone at Grauves, the lateral variations of the facies between the north and south sides of the Marne Valley being particularly significant and rapid.

The vineyards of the Aube

Many itineraries are possible for getting from the vineyards of the Marne to those of the Aube (fig. 13). The slowest, but the most pleasurable, passes through the Côte des Blancs, the marsh vineyards of Saint-Gond and the Côtes of Sézanne and Villenauxe. To the west of Troyes, the Montgueux butte supports the first vineyard of the Aube.

Situated on the Coniacian and Upper Turonian chalk, the vineyard is planted with pinot noir. On the outcrops behind the water tower, along the D 141, the white, dry, slightly resonant, very fissured (tectonically) chalk contains some fossils (Lamellibranchs including Inoceramus, and Brachiopods). From the summit of the butte, there is a fine view over the dry and humid parts of Champagne.

The vineyards of Bar-sur-Aube and Bar-sur-Seine grow at an altitude of between 200 and 300 m, on steep hillsides with a south-easterly aspect. As a result of wine-growing tradition, the vines are almost exclusively located on outcrops of the Upper Kimmeridgian. Only the vineyards of Trannes, on the Valanginian, and those of Mussy-sur-Seine, on the Upper Oxfordian, form an exception to the rule.

Bar-sur-Aube and Bar-sur-Seine are situated at the foot of the Côte des Bars, in a geologically uncomplicated region, the slope of which, dipping towards the centre of the Paris Basin, exposes outcrops of older and older layers going south-east. The surrounding relief, which is quite pronounced, is directly related to the geological structure (fig. 14); its configuration is due to the succession of a group of marly and marly-limestone layers (Upper and Middle Kimmeridgian) and a limestone formation (Portlandian). The hard limestone remains exposed on top by virtue of its arrangement and resistance to erosion and forms the structural surface of a vast plateau. The marly group, where laid bare by the disappearance of the limestone capping, is severely eroded and forms, in the landscape, a steep slope with a considerable difference in height.

The rocks, the slopes and the water supply control the agricultural utilization of the different landscapes; the limestone plateau, more or less covered with alluvium, is an area where the main cereal cultivation alternates with forest of mediocre quality. The upper part of the slope which is steeper, constitutes the privileged domain of the vine, while the lower section, corresponding to the more calcareous levels of the Kimmeridgian, supports mixed farming.

Where the valleys are quite deep (further up from Bar-sur-Aube), they cut into a fairly resistant level located beneath the marl and marly limestone of the Kimmeridgian. This, belonging to the Upper Oxfordian, influences the topography by creating a very distinct shelf, the ledge and slope of which are forested (forest of Clairvaux).

The area around Bar-sur-Seine

Take the D 17, from Mussy-sur-Seine to **Riceys**. Shortly after the village exit, there is a large quarry ① located behind some industrial buildings (Fruehof).

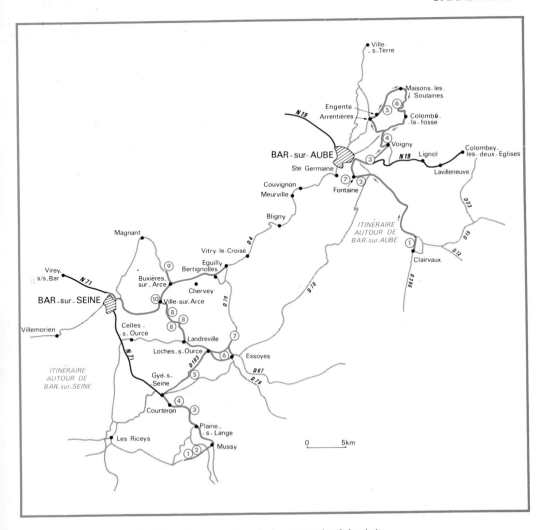

Fig. 13 — *Itineraries through the vineyards of the Aube*

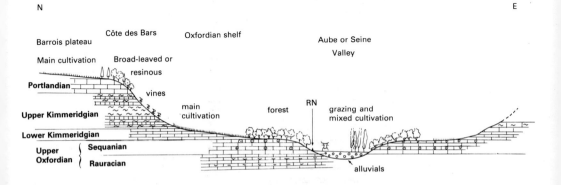

Fig. 14 – *Geomorphological profile of the regions of Bar-sur-Aube and Bar-sur-Seine.*

A section corresponding to this diagram can be followed to the south of Bar-sur-Aube, between hill 331 (to the east of Baroville) and the Molin farm (between Lignol-le-Château and Bar-sur-Aube). It can be viewed from the panorama of Voigny.

Approximately 1 km further on, a small outcrop ②shows, in collapsed limestone blocks, a rich Upper Oxfordian fauna. The quarry face, composed of cavernous limestone beds alternating with more marly horizons, is no longer very easy to decipher, though the arrangement is still quite apparent. The fauna consists of impressions of various Lamellibranchs (*Pinna*, *Lima*), of isolated or colonial Crinoids, Ammonites and Brachiopods. This formation, called Mussy "slaked Limestone", was mined by the cement works and supports the small vineyard of Mussy-sur-Seine.

Between **Plaine-Saint-Lange** and **Courteron**, opposite a dangerous parking place, a big outcrop ③exposes an assembly of grey limestones, the layers of which are interbedded with marly layers at the base of the outcrop and are contiguous towards the summit. Two thick beds occur in the middle part of the section. No macrofauna could be collected here. This group is situated at the boundary of the Mussy slaked Limestone and the Limestone of La Bellerée.

Carrying on towards Courteron, numerous disused quarries ④are partly hidden by a copse. The last one is accessible on the right, shortly before the Courteron deviation. The levels, which were worked for road metal and construction purposes, are part of the Limestone of La Bellerée (Upper Oxfordian or "Sequanian"). These quarries present a very varied biodetrital and bioclastic facies: gravelly or oolitic limestone, more or less coarse calcarenites, crinoidal limestone, but also chalky and compact limestone. In this deep and well-stirred environment, existed a thriving living world as evidenced by small Exogyra beds (*Nanogyra nana*), various *impressions or tests of Lamellibranchs — Pectinids, 'Ostréidés'' (Lopha)* and *Trigonias —* and Gastropods (in particular Nerinea), the radiola of Sea Urchins, Crinoids, etc.

Continue along the N 71, then take the D 103, from **Gyé-sur-Seine** to **Loches-sur-Ource**. At first the road follows a little valley bordered with woods and occupied by meadows and crops. Exploiting the favourable exposure, the bottom of the slopes of this valley are planted with pinot noir. After a couple of bends, a hollow ⑤on the right-hand side of the road corresponds to an old quarry, the face of which has partly collapsed. Among the grey marl several decimetric layers of grey marly limestone are intercalated. In this assembly, attributable to the Upper Kimmeridgian, there is a proliferation of *Exogyra virgula* constituting the bulk of the fauna remains. Although less common, numerous other Lamellibranchs can be collected, including Pholadomyas and Trigonias, Gastropods, Ammonites (*Aulacostephanus, Aspidoceras*) the tests of which occasionally show Exogyras and Serpulas.

Around **Essoyes**, a village which has retained a most particular and delightful charm, there are numerous quarries where the Oisellemont Limestone of the Lower Kimmeridgian was once worked. One of these quarries which is well preserved, is accessible via the D 67, between Loches-sur-Ource and Essoyes, along a track to the left, just before the bridge over the Ource ⑥.

The vast quarry face comprises chalky limestone in thick beds, at the base, and hard limestone, cut up into blocks and slabs, at the top. The chalky limestone is the more fossiliferous ('Ostréidés', including *Lopha*, Trigonias, Pholadomyas, Pinna, Nerinea, Pteroceras, Terebratulas, Rhynchonella, isolated or colonial Crinoids, Solenopores, etc).

The road from Landreville to **Ville-sur-Arce** climbs progressively, firstly through crops, then through an extensive vineyard interrupted, at the level of the pass, by a sparse wood set on Portlandian limestone. As soon as you leave this pass, a track to the right leads to a face ⑦which exposes the high levels of the Upper Kimmeridgian. Heading down towards Ville-sur-Arce, numerous fossiliferous outcrops appear among the vines. Leaving the valley bottom, at the lower boundary of the vineyards, the road cuts into stratigraphically lower layers of the Kimmeridgian, richer in limestone horizons and less propitious to viticulture.

From Ville-sur-Arce, carry on up via Buxières to **Magnant**. At the bottom of the little valley, level with the farm "La Bergerie", at the confluence of two small valleys, a small quarry ⑧exhibits the limestone facies of the Lower Portlandian. This limestone, called Barrois Limestone, is deposited here in layers between 0.10 and 0.25 m thick, separated by small beds. The surface is irregular, with perforations, burrows and tracks. The limestone, which is light beige and of a sublithographic appearance, is fragmented into angular blocks. Certain layers contain impressions of Lamellibranchs and have a surface crust of *Exogyra virgula*.

Coming back down towards Bar-sur-Seine, and level with Ville-sur-Arce, there is a fine quarry on the right ⑨ where scree is exploited for fill and road metal. This material, formed by the freezing that took place in the glacial periods and accumulated at the slope bottoms, is comprised mostly of Portlandian limestone. Very often, this scree covers the areas planted with vines; it provides good surface drainage, whilst the deep roots find the necessary water reserves by penetrating down into the Kimmeridgian marl.

The area around Bar-sur-Aube

At the location of **Le Four à Chaux** ①, on the D 396, slightly to the north of Clairvaux, there is a vast quarry behind some buildings. The greyish-beige, slightly clayey limestone, showing numerous traces of limonite, is arranged in beds several decimetres thick, separated by finer marly interlayers, constituting an elevated and quite dangerous quarry face. Amongst the collapsed blocks, the fauna is quite varied: Pholadomyas, Trigonias, *Gervillia*, 'Ostréidés', *Pinna*. This assemblage is attributed to the Upper Oxfordian.

At the crossroads of the D 70 and the N 396, take the D 13 in the direction of **Fontaine**. After a few hundred metres, you will find a quarry ② exposing Sequanian limestone. It is beige and in contiguous layers, showing numerous stylolitic elements, and is visible over an area of some 10 metres. The macrofauna is composed of various Lamellibranchs, including Trigonias, Gastropods (Nerinea), isolated Crinoids and Solenopores. The tops and bottoms of the beds show perforated surfaces and tracks.

Continue through Bar-sur-Aube taking the N 19 in the direction of Chaumont. Shortly after the Baralbin champagne tasting chalet, take the road to **Voigny**. Level with the first curve, to the left, the trough of the road ③ cuts into a fine example of oolitic and gravelly limestone at the base of the Kimmeridgian. Fossils are plentiful here (Lamellibranchs, Nerinea, etc.)

From Voigny to **Colombé-la-Fosse**, the road traverses vineyards, then climbs up towards a Portlandian butte covered with woods. On the left bend, take the right-hand track; within a few dozen metres climbing up through the vines, there is an *excellent panorama* ④ depicting the relationship between the geology, the morphology and the use of the soil.

Continue via Arrentières to Engente. At the exit of this village, at the boundary of the forest located on the edge of the Portlandian plateau, slopes planted with vines ⑤ on the right and left-hand sides of the road incise the very fine fossiliferous Upper Kimmeridgian.

Join the D 74. Between Maison-lès-Soulaines and Colombé-la-Fosse, at the location of the sharp bends above Colombé-la-Fosse, there is a large quarry ⑥ serving as a depot for the Highways Department, set in the base of the Portlandian. Here, Barrois Limestone, light in colour and sublithographic, is arranged in small contiguous beds.

In the upper section of the quarry face, erosion has disturbed the beds and cryoturbation is responsible for the reorientation of the fragments. The limestone itself is not particularly fossiliferous, but the interlayers show encrustments of *Exogyra virgula*, of tracks and burrows. In the collapsed blocks of the quarry, all the intermediary elements are in evidence inbetween the beds perforated by burrows and the bioturbation breccia levels.

Returning to Bar-sur-Aube, go to the site of **Sainte-Germaine** (7). Along the Bar-sur-Seine road there is a fine view of a vine-covered hillside, which is particularly steep and whose boundary follows the Kimmeridgian-Portlandian contact.

Going towards the Sainte-Germaine chapel, the road leads along the edge of an old wooded embankment, crosses some agricultural land, then weaves through a succession of five overgrown slopes. The horizontal surface, called the Roman Camp, is in fact a blocked spur of which the embankments form adapted protection and the natural defences correspond to the edges of the Portlandian cuesta. From the eastern extremity of these embankments, there is a beautiful panorama over the countryside and the Bar-sur-Aube vineyards, as far as Colombey-les-Deux-Églises. The development of this site dates back to the Iron Age.

The gastronomy and wines of Champagne

While the Champagne region is highly renowned for its wines, it is much less famous for its cuisine. Nevertheless the latter does show a certain originality and is not just confined to cooking with champagne, far from it in fact.

The regions embraced in the province of Champagne, each with its own geological, human and agricultural identity, possess distinctly different culinary traditions. The cuisine of the wine-growing areas was, more often than not, simple, with dishes that could be left on the stove all day while work was being done. Traditional fare would consist of soups ranging from a simple hotpot broth, served with slices of bread, to elaborate dishes: onion soup au champagne, "gratinée au champagne" (onion soup au gratin made with champagne) or Dom Pérignon hotpot.

Champagne cooked pork meats ("charcuterie") varies according to region and includes some famous specialities: Sainte-Menehould pig's trotters, "andouillettes de Troyes" (small sausages made of chitterlings), "boudin blanc de Rethel" (white pudding), Ardennes ham and thrush pâté, Reims ham and pâté. This selection of charcuterie is one of the main ingredients of Champagne hotpots, the numerous variations of which always consist of simmering fat bacon, pork belly, ham, salt pork, sometimes some stewing sausage, with haricot beans, carrots, turnips, celeriac, potatoes and green cabbage.

Meat dishes, often cooked in champagne or local wine and spirits, go very nicely with a red Champagne wine (Bouzy, Ambonnay, Les Riceys, etc.) There is also a culinary tradition which centres around lamb and game, of which Champagne has long been a great producer. Game dishes include quail, casserole of partridge cooked in champagne, casserole of pheasant, rabbit and hare "à la champenoise", etc.

It was a particular tradition of Chalons-sur-Marne, Baye, Les Riceys, etc. to make "ashen" cheeses (kept in riddled wood ash). Then there are the products which have a nationwide reputation: "marolles", "langres", "Brie de Meaux", "chaource" and very local cheeses which are becoming difficult to find: "trappiste d'Igny", "délices" and "carrés de Saint-Cyr", "éclance", etc.

Characteristic of the vineyard areas is "tarte aux raisins". Reims has also become famous for its biscuits ("biscuits roses", "biscuits au champagne", "croquignolles", "nonettes", "massepains") and its pâtisserie ("pavés de Reims", "délices de Reims", "flan au champagne", "rabotte champenoise", 'sabayon au champagne '(zabaglione) and darioles, only made on Saint Remi's Day.

As an accompaniment to celebration meals, champagne should be chilled on ice, but not iced (9 to 10 °C). Although traditionally brought on with the dessert, the "champenois" will happily drink it either as an aperitif (perhaps the best time for really appreciating a good champagne) or, on occasions, right through the meal.

The various stages of a meal may be accompanied by drinks selected from a wide range of products: ratafia (sweet wine blended with marc brandy) as an aperitif, white, rosé or red "Coteaux champenois" (non-sparkling Champagne wines), champagne, or grands crus red wines to be selected depending on the menu. The dessert may be accompanied by a champagne and the coffee followed by a liqueur brandy (une 'fine') or a champagne brandy ('marc de champagne').

FOR FURTHER
INFORMATION

Geology

Guide géologique: Bassin de Paris, by Ch. Pomerol and L. Feugueur (3rd edition, 1986), published by Masson — See in particular itinerary 12, from Provins to Reims.

Guide géologique: Lorraine-Champagne, by J. Hilly, B. Haguenauer et coll. (1979), published by Masson — See in particular itineraries 15,16 and 17 relative to Champagne.

Oenology

Bonal F. (1984). — Champagne. Published by Grand-Pont, Lausanne.

Dovaz M. (1984). — L'encyclopédie des vins de Champagne, published by Julliard.

Comité interprofessionnel du vin de Champagne (1968). — Champagne, vin de France. Published by Lallemand.

Chambre de commerce et d'industrie de Reims (1982). — Le vin de Champagne.

Etudes champenoises. (1988). — Vignerons et vins de Champagne et d'ailleurs XVIIe–XXe sièle—Published by Centre d'Etudes Champenoises, Departement d'Histoire d L'Université de Reims.

Page facing Foreword: Mailly-Champagne vineyard in autumn (Photo. Laurain).

Above: Mailly-Champagne vineyard in spring (Photo Laurain).
Below: Verzenay windmill (Photo Laurain).

Next page: Bourgogne: Vineyards of Vougeot, at the foot of a crinoidal limestone ledge of the Bajocian where, at the same place, the Vouge re-emerges.

SEDIMENTARY ROCKS

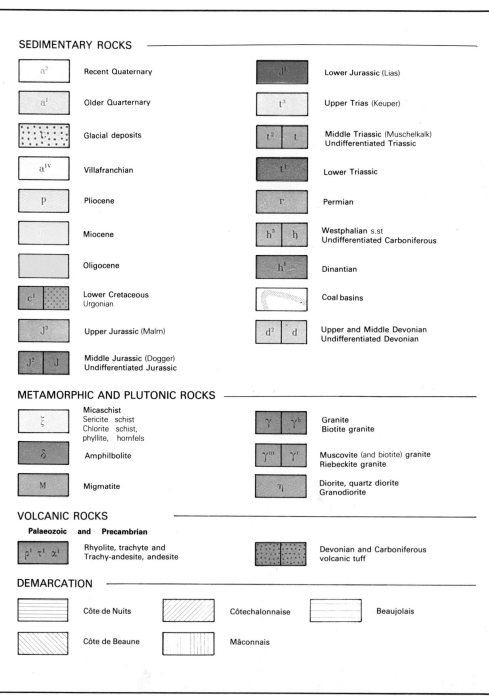

a^2	Recent Quaternary
a^1	Older Quarternary
t	Glacial deposits
a^{IV}	Villafranchian
p	Pliocene
m	Miocene
	Oligocene
c^1	Lower Cretaceous Urgonian
J^3	Upper Jurassic (Malm)
J^2 J	Middle Jurassic (Dogger) Undifferentiated Jurassic

J^l	Lower Jurassic (Lias)
t^3	Upper Trias (Keuper)
t^2 t	Middle Triassic (Muschelkalk) Undifferentiated Triassic
t^l	Lower Triassic
r	Permian
h^3 h	Westphalian s.st Undifferentiated Carboniferous
h^l	Dinantian
	Coal basins
d^2 d	Upper and Middle Devonian Undifferentiated Devonian

METAMORPHIC AND PLUTONIC ROCKS

ξ	Micaschist Sericite schist Chlorite schist, phyllite, hornfels
δ	Amphilbolite
M	Migmatite

γ $γ^b$	Granite Biotite granite
$γ^m$ $γ^r$	Muscovite (and biotite) granite Riebeckite granite
η	Diorite, quartz diorite Granodiorite

VOLCANIC ROCKS

Palaeozoic and Precambrian

$ρ^l$ $τ^l$ $α^l$	Rhyolite, trachyte and Trachy-andesite, andesite

	Devonian and Carboniferous volcanic tuff

DEMARCATION

	Côte de Nuits		Côtechalonnaise		Beaujolais
	Côte de Beaune		Mâconnais		

Fig. 15. — *Geological map with demarcation of Burgundian vineyard area (Bourgogne and Beaujolais).*

Bourgogne Beaujolais

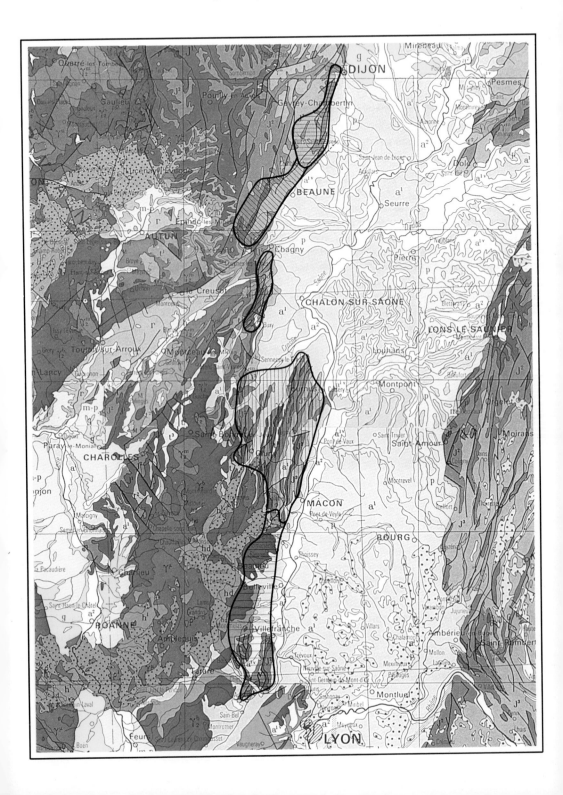

The first appearance of vineyards in the Côte de Bourgogne very probably dates back to the Gallo-Roman epoch, as maintained by G. Roupnel (1932); 'the analysis of Gallo-Roman remains found particularly in the Bolards excavations around Nuits-Saint-Georges, confirms this.'

After various historic upheavals, including the barbarian invasions of the early centuries, the planting restrictions imposed by the Roman colonizers, the diseases incurred by the vine, etc., the vineyards of Bourgogne were to experience a new boom towards the twelfth century through the impetus given by the monks of Cluny and Cîteaux.

The wines of the Côte-d'Or acquired a prestige comparable to that of the Gallo-Roman era, but they were a "rich race" of wine, and tended to be exported outside their area of production, despite the difficulties and expense of transportation at that time.

The cultivated varieties of vine, pinot noir and chardonnay for the big red and white wines and gamay and aligoté for the "grand ordinaire" wines, all appear, on several accounts, to be native to Bourgogne in spite of certain controversial affirmations. The expansion, in the fourteenth century, of gamay, a high yielding and low quality vine on this limestone terrain, very nearly compromised the good name of the red wine of the Côte; but severe measures, announced by a famous edict of Philippe II le Hardi, in 1395, to banish the 'disloyal plant' and the bad cultivation practices oriented towards high yield at the expense of quality, progressively restored the confidence of Beaune wine drinkers.

The vine and its soil

Relief, exposure and geology

In Bourgogne (fig. 15), the role of exposure in relation to sunshine is of primordial importance. Geology firstly intervenes by providing such exposure, by virtue of its structures (fault relief) or by the uneven resistance of terrains to erosion (hill and slope relief, in the geomorphological sense). Then the shaping brought about by rivers comes into play, by creating, for example, south-facing slopes in an east-facing fault or cuesta façade. It is also important, of course, in understanding the vineyards of Bourgogne, to consider the nature of the terrain: granites of the Hercynian basement, argillaceous and limestone secondary cover and stony or sandy clay deposits of the Tertiary and the Quaternary.

Bearing in mind these various elements and their geographical distribution, the vineyard areas of Bourgogne can be divided into two large groups: the faulted eastern façade, the high ground of the Massif Central and the Burgundian limestone plateaux, running in an almost straight line from Beaujolais to the Côte de Nuits, and the Côte (cuesta) of the Upper Jurassic in Lower Bourgogne (vineyards of Chablis and also of Pouilly-sur-Loire which are situated very close here to the vineyards of the Sancerrois).

The eastern façade of the Massif Central and the Burgundian plateaux

From Lyon and its suburbs to the environs of Dijon, a distance of some 200 km, vineyards spread out almost uninterruptedly, strung out along the eastern face of the Massif Central or the plateaux bordering it. It is a façade of tectonic origin, caused by the fault system along which, in the Tertiary Period, the Saône rift valley (Bresse graben) subsided, and which is nowadays shaped by erosion and dissected by the rivers flowing down to the Saône.

But this tectonic and quite sudden contact, between the granitic or limestone high ground to the west, and the plain resulting from the sedimentary filling of the Bresse graben to the east, alters, as the difference in height tapers off, from south to north.

In Beaujolais, the crystalline basement contact coincides with the plain.

The Mâconnais region is dissected into a series of parallel blocks, sloping towards the Saône, which have each retained part of their sedimentary cover of Triassic and Jurassic age. This has given rise to a series of limestone crests and very jagged slopes, but aligned parallel over a distance of some fifty kilometres from Pouilly-Fuissé to north of Tournus.

The Côte Chalonnaise which is less rigorously organized, is also composed of panels with a limestone structure of Jurassic age; the southern section plunges down to the west, opposite the secondary mountain ranges of the Mâconnais on the other side of the Grosne Valley, while the northern part slopes down towards the plain, encircling, in an almost periclinal fashion, the north-eastern extremity of the crystalline horst of Mont-Saint-Vincent.

As regards the Côte, (Côte de Beaune followed by Côte de Nuits) this is a fault scarp which runs almost as straight as a die; it is the major fault line between the limestone plateaux (Middle or Upper Jurassic) and the Bresse graben.

The south-east facing cuesta of Lower Bourgogne

An extension of what, in the east of the Paris Basin, is known as the Côte des Bars, the Côte du Chablisois and de l'Auxerrois is the result of the slight incline of the terrain towards the centre of the Paris Basin, that is towards the north-west, and of the superposition of two distinct geological formations: the *Exogyra virgula marl* and marly limestone of the Kimmeridgian, and the Barrois Limestone of the Portlandian (latest Jurassic). Limestone forms the uppermost, resistant section of the high ground while marl constitutes the lower slopes. In this area of high relief, trending NE-SW, the Yonne and its tributaries, flowing towards Paris to the north-west, have gouged out great notches which have considerably increased the surface area of the vine-growing slopes, by providing a variety of aspects.

In the Châtillonnais area, the Massingy vineyards are found in totally analagous conditions, but on older levels; marl and marly limestone of the Oxfordian, capped with Tonnerrois Limestone of Oxfordo-Kimmeridgian age.

Climate

Climatic factors are essential for the growth of the vine and the final ripening of the grapes, irrespective of other environmental conditions.

Rainfall and humidity

The average annual rainfall of 700 mm on the Côte may vary from about 450 to 950 mm; it is spread over 160 days with maximum precipitation generally occurring in May-June and minimum rainfall in February-March and in the autumn (September-October), with July and August being an unpredictable period.

The low rainfall of February and March minimizes the risk of the soil becoming water-logged and helps it to warm up during the spring, thus reducing the risk of freezing.

The high amount of rainfall in June is beneficial to plant growth, but may be detrimental to successful flowering (a condition known as 'coulure') and produce, in very particular instances, a lowering of the temperature with an accompanying risk of freezing, or cause considerable erosion in vineyards planted on particularly steep hillsides.

The reduced rainfall in September and October gives the vine a better chance for ripening and the halting of rot and can, on occasion, save harvests jeopardized in August.

The Côte-d'Or region seems, in spite of certain hazards, to be relatively privileged in comparison with the southern sectors (Chalonnais, Mâconnais and Beaujolais) which are rather more subject to storms from the southsouth-west.

Temperature and sunshine

Decennial annual averages show that the region receives 2 000 hours of sunshine per annum, of which roughly three quarters is spread over the April to September period (1 200 to 1 750 hours representing the extreme variations thereof). Average sunshine is therefore a little less than half the theoretical length of 4 476 hours, or 45.6%, with the sunniest years receiving 55 to 60%. Sunshine has a major influence on the thermal régime of this east-south-east facing wine-growing area.

Varieties of vine

Red vines: *Pinot noir*, (or "noirien") produces the big red wines of the Côte; it is distinguished by short, cylindrical bunches of slightly ovoid grapes with soft, thin, bluish black skin, containing a white juice pulp.

This variety of vine is very fond of limestone soils on well drained hillslopes and, in a temperate climate like that of' Bourgogne, it produces its best wines which are bouqueted, tasty, robust, have a beautiful ruby colour and plenty of finesse. In places, at a height of between 380 and 425 m, sometimes in shallow soils, the pinot noir vine produces wines of a lighter colour and less fully matured. On the other hand, in deep and wetter silty clay at the contact of the foothills and the plain, the wines have more body but lack bouquet and finesse.

Yield is low; less than 228 litres per 1/24 of a hectare. These are wines for keeping and can take from ten to twenty years, according to the soil they are grown on and the climate of their vintage, to reach their peak.

The gamay vine is the producer of red wines grown on the granitic soil of Beaujolais which enjoy a world-wide reputation, even the new wines which are consumed as early as mid-November.

In the other vineyards set in limestone soil of the Mâconnais, Chalonnais, the Côte and the Hautes-Côtes, this vine produces wines which are very popular as vins de tables, classified as "grand ordinaire" or "passetoutgrain", when made from a blend of gamay and pinot noir. It is more supple and loses that harshness which is often associated with it when produced from a limestone soil.

The gamay vine is characterized by average sized clusters of oval, deep black grapes containing white juice; it is early and vulnerable to spring frosts, though it may fruit again after the frost. There are certain varieties of the gamay grape which contain a coloured juice and are called "teinturiers" (dyers), but these are not particularly popular. The Côte-d'Or provides the best conditions for the gamay vine, in deep, clayey, occasionally decarbonated soils, which run along the foothills adjoining the plain and in which it does better than the pinot noir vine.

The wine may be light, with a very pleasant fruit. Grown in certain vineyards in Beaujolais, such as Morgon and Moulin-à-Vent, it can occasionally be an excellent wine for keeping.

White vines: *Chardonnay* is, par excellence, the white Burgundy grape. It produces small-sized clusters of golden grapes which are less tightly bunched than those of the pinot noir vine. Being a later ripener than the latter, it is generally harvested a few days later and being more resistant to rot, can better withstand rain at the end of the season.

The type of terrain preferred by the chardonnay vine is calcareous, on a hillside location, on marly, sometimes very clayey soil, whether it be the Kimmeridgian marl of Chablis, the Oxfordian marl of Corton-Charlemagne or that of Meursault, Puligny and Chassagne, where the wine-growers describe their Chardonnays as 'the best white wines in the world', which is no doubt true.

The aligoté vine is a white, vigorous, consistent cropping variety, producing an average quality wine, called "Bourgogne aligoté". The clusters are plentiful, but small, with equally small, spherical grapes which take on a greyish pink shade when fully ripened, on the faces exposed to the sun. This vine is very susceptible to grey rot and spring frosts; it does better on the plateaux and the top of the slopes than at the bottom. It produces a very fruity white wine which is drunk young as it quickly loses its characteristic crispness.

Itineraries

Beaujolais

Beaujolais is distinguished by the following features;

The Hercynian basement, forming the eastern extremity of the Massif Central and rising to 1,000 m in the hinterland, while the Saône is at an altitude of only 170 metres, is composed of acid rocks (granite, microgranite or rhyolite and tuf) and also of schist of Carboniferous age, often metamorphosed. Weathering has reduced most of these rocks to sand which disguises the deep subsoil, fills up the areas of high relief and has provided the material which the little rivers and streams running down to the Saône, have accumulated at their contact with the plain. The high ground is croup shaped with convex slopes which, seen from the plain, emerge progressively from the alluvials (See Guide géologique Lyonnais-Vallée du Rhône).

Sedimentary rocks which comprise two sorts: Some, clayey or calcareous, form the terrain of the older cover (Triassic, Lias and Middle Jurassic), of marine origin,

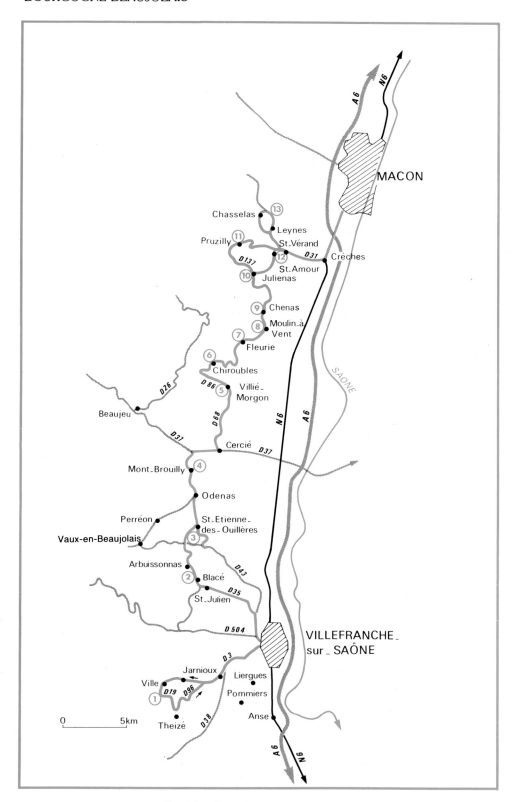

Fig. 16 — Itinerary through Beaujolais

deposited over the basement during the Mesozoic. The latter was preserved, collapsed and carved up by a series of faults, at the foot of the crystalline high ground in Lower Beaujolais (to the west and the south of Villefranche-sur-Saône). The other sedimentary terrain is composed of Pliocene or Older Quaternary sand and gravel, produced partly by the erosion of the Hercynian basement and accumulated at the slope bottoms in a sort of alluvial cover which the rivers coming down from the crystalline Beaujolais then carved up into long croups.

In order to fully appreciate this itinerary (fig. 16), one should call to mind certain characteristics of the Beaujolais vineyards whose wines will vary right through the journey. To begin with, the only vine grown here is the gamay noir vine, the white juice of which takes on those beautiful red colours with fermentation, 'cuvaison'. This same gamay plant also produces different wines, essentially according to the substratum of the particular vineyard. We will begin with the region of Bas-Beaujolais (Lower Beaujolais) or 'Mesozoic, limestone-clay, sedimentary Beaujolais', where the wines are less alcoholic and quite acid like, for example, the very good, young and light table and bar wines which are served in Lyon in the 46 centilitre "pots" [1].

These wines are often drunk nowadays in preference to the much more robust wines, which is sometimes a shame. The nine Beaujolais grands crus are produced from the same gamay vine, but are grown either on weathered granite or schist. Being more fleshy and more robust, they tend to keep longer — even for 10 years and more in the case of Morgon for example, or Moulin-à-Vent, which are said to 'morgonner' with age and take on a particular aroma and taste resembling sherry, like certain wines from the Côte de Beaune. We will be crossing the grands crus vineyards at the end of the itinerary.

It is advisable here to consider the regulation of the appellations d'origine contrôlée (AOC) du Beaujolais, which can be summarized as follows:

In order of quality, there are firstly the nine "crus or appellations communales": gamay vine and granitic or schistose substratum. Then come the 'Beaujolais-Villages' which have the right to the appellation Beaujolais followed by the name of the village, but which, for the sake of simplification, are more commonly called Beaujolais-Villages. This category embraces around forty villages, with the same production characteristics as the "crus": gamay vine and granitic or schistose substratum and all located in the north of Beaujolais. It is a medium quality wine, good for early drinking when grown on light soil and a wine for ageing when grown on firmer soil. Finally come the "Beaujolais simples" or "Beaujolais-Beaujolais", the vineyards of which are very extensive, especially in the south of Beaujolais, and are planted on what may be sedimentary terrain, but always with the same gamay vine.

Leaving **Villefranche-sur-Saône**, take the D 38, then, at Liergues, the D 116. You now start to cross *sedimentary Beaujolais*, or Bas-Beaujolais, which stretches to the south-west of Villefranche-sur-Saône to the Valley of l'Azergues. From Villefranche-sur-Saône, built on the alluvium of the Saône and at an altitude of 179 m, you will climb steadily in a south-westerly direction towards the village of Theizé (450 m). The sedimentary sequence (Triassic, Lias and Dogger), which covers the crystallophyllitic basement, is in turn capped with a thick continental Upper Pliocene detritic succession: Frontenas-Alix gravel, quite a coarse quartzo-ferruginous rock with crystalline and crystallophyllitic elements of local origin. From Villefranche-sur-Saône to Liergues, we follow, on the right, a little hill fortified with Dogger limestone. Behind, to the east, appears the high ground of the eastern part of Pommiers, at the base of which is an outcrop of the metamorphic basement (throw of some 200 m). We drive over the Pliocene until we reach the village of Les Essards.

We carry on to Jarnioux, then **Ville-sur-Jarnioux**, after which we will come across the Cruiz quarry ①on the D 19 which goes to Theizé. This quarry provides a good illustration as to why Bas-Beaujolais is called "region of golden stones". In fact,

---

[1] Nearly half of Beaujolais wine production (some 500 000 hectolitres), is exported and consumed all over the world, from Tokyo to Los Angelès, in the days following its sale (the third Thursday of November), thanks to the extraordinary advertising success of the slogan 'Le Beaujolais nouveau est arrivé'.

the Aalenian limestone, of which there are substantial outcrops, is fawn-coloured and makes a nice building stone; it is a crinoidal limestone showing oblique stratification.

The sections of the Cruiz quarry exhibit fine examples of disintegration of the crinoidal limestone and one can recognize all the rock types of Bas-Beaujolais in the landscape. The soil of this region is fresh and often quite deep. The vineyards here produce wine akin to the real 'Beaujolais lyonnais': light, 'gouleyant', cherry-coloured, slightly acid taste, to be drunk cool to satisfy a great thirst.

After returning to the suburbs of Villefranche-sur-Saône, the itinerary will link up with the so-called Beaujolais wine trail as we take the D 43 and D 35 for Saint-Julien. Between Villefranche and Saint-Julien, we go over the Pleistocene alluvial fill of the west bank of the Saône. This fill is distributed in a system of interlocking terraces: 18-20 m terrace in the town of Villefranche, 55-60 m terrace from Ouilly to La Rigodière, 90-100 m terrace at Saint-Julien.

Between Saint-Julien and Blacé we cross the main boundary fault of the Bresse graben. It brings the conglomerate and red marl of the Upper Oligocene (left slope of the graben, a short distance past Saint-Julien) into direct contact with the metamorphic basement or the first members of the sedimentary cover: Triassic or Sinemurian (the latter forming the basement of the village of Blacé). The throw is in excess here of 250 metres.

We are thus about to leave the sedimentary terrain and enter the *crystalline and metamorphic Beaujolais* area, and examine the outcrops of the rocks which comprise it, bearing in mind that they are often weathered. The granitic or gneissic sand is called locally 'gore' and the weathered schist and andesite is called "morgon".

Stop ②at the view point of **Salles-Arbuissonnas-en-Beaujolais**, after Blacé; you will observe, amidst the rolling vine-covered hills, the little village of Salles. with its very characteristic Beaujolais architecture, where some buildings have been preserved belonging to a priory founded in the tenth century by the monks of Cluny.

We should also mention here **Vaux-en-Beaujolais**, located close by, to the west. This is the famous village that inspired the novelist G. Chevallier in his work "Clochemerle", in which he described, with great humour, the colourful, quaint, country life of a village held under the spell of its wine; Beaujolais.

At **Pont-Mathivet** ③, a quarry exposes intrusive Odenas granite. This granite, of Early Carboniferous age, cuts the metamorphics of the Monts du Lyonnais (gneiss) and Brévenne (schist) and causes contact metamorphism in the volcano-sedimentary rocks.

After Pont-Mathivet, the road stays on Odenas Granite. From Saint-Étienne-des-Ouillères follow the D 43, still on granite, to the village of **Brouilly**. The wine from this region, appellation grand cru "Brouilly", tender, vinous and gay, is called the wine of love. The substratum is either granitic or schistose.

Take the minor road on the right which climbs up the **Mont Brouilly**. It is at the foot of this mountain that one of the Beaujolais grands crus is grown. We are now on Lower Viséan (Carboniferous) andesite, metamorphosed by the Odenas granite. From the Mont Brouilly (500 m) ④, the view extends to the west over the Haut-Beaujolais, with an average height of 700-800 m; this high ground is composed of rocks of the Lower Devono-Carboniferous or, as in the foreground, of granitic terrains. To the east, a magnificent panorama over the Bresse plain shows, in clear weather, the Mont Blanc massif in the background. Quite close to us, 1.5 km to the east of Mont Brouilly, a major fault brings the Viséan and the Upper Oligocene overlying limestone of the Upper Oxfordian, into contact. At this point, subsidence of over 400 metres is estimated.

The wine produced from the Mont Brouilly vineyards bears the appellation "Côte de Brouilly" and has the reputation of a fine, elegant, rich and flavoursome wine with a grapey taste.

We now cross the vineyards of the Beaujolais grands crus. Get back onto the D 43 northbound (by turning right), which will take you up to the D 37. Turn right here so that you are now heading eastward. This is the Vallée de l'Ardières, a tributary of the Saône and an important east-west communication route controlled by Beaujeu, a small town which gave its name to the region and the vineyards.

As you come into Cercié turn left onto the D 68 towards Villié-Morgon. Before advancing onto Morgon grand cru terrain, you will go through vineyards set on slope bottom colluvial soils which gradually merge with the older stony and silt-laden terraces of the Saône plain. These soils are often leached, occasionally water-logged and are reserved for the 'communale' or 'régionale' appellation vineyards.

Follow the route along the D 68 until you come to **Villié-Morgon** ⑤, home of the first small wine-cellar to be established in Beaujolais. This cellar is located in a seventeenth century château opposite the church, and Oyou will be able to obtain documentation here as well as sample some wines. Wine with the appellation "Morgon" comes from a vineyard set on "morgon", which is the result of weathered schist also called 'la terre pourrie' (rotted earth). The wine is generous, fleshy, robust, with an intense colour and a taste of sherry which it acquires with ageing, for in good years, this makes a good wine for keeping.

From Villié-Morgon, take the D 86 and continue on to **Chiroubles** ⑥, set on its own natural terrace with one of the finest panoramas in France. It is the earliest cru of the Beaujolais range, embodying, for the real wine lover, the body, fruit, countenance and tenderness of a prestige wine. The substratum is granitic and the vines grow at the highest altitude. Chiroubles is reputed to be the favourite among female palates. It is also said that, in order for it to be enjoyed by women, it must be men who drink it.

Carry on via the D 119 and then the D 68 to **Fleurie** ⑦ with its vineyards still on granitic sand. This is the domain of the fruity, light and fragrant wine, par excellence.

Proceed along the D 68 to **Moulin-à-Vent** ⑧, set on the hillock of the Poncier, in the hamlet of Thorins, and visit the mill constructed on an outcrop of granite. The vineyards grow on shallow, friable, pink soil of granitic sand; this is typical "gore" (or "gorrhe"). From the mill, the view over the Bresse opens out below with the relief caused by the main boundary fault of the Bresse graben, which is associated with manganese mineralization. There is an old mine below Romanèche-Thorins. The soil of Moulin-à-Vent is said to be influenced by the manganese, though this will always remain difficult either to prove or invalidate. It must play a part, nevertheless, in the production of a very robust cru, tender in its youth, fleshy in its adolescence, elegant and thoroughbred with maturity and a wine for keeping comparable with the Bourgognes.

The vineyard of **Chenas** ⑨ is nearby to the north-west, and set on granitic sand. It was once an ancient oak forest, hence the name ("chêne" meaning oak). The Chenas cru is a robust and generous wine which produces excellent bottles with an aroma of peony.

Carry on, on the D 68, to **Juliénas** ⑩ where the vine grows on both granite and schist and gives a fruity, well-constructed, robust cru, which can be aged for five years.

From here take the D 137 to **Pruzilly** ⑪, the location of a big quarry exposing once again the sound rock and the numerous facies illustrating the variety of the rock types of this sector (microgranite and rhyolite).

We now return to the grands crus and **Saint-Amour** ⑫, on the D 469. The name would seem to come from the fact that at one time the vineyards belonged to the canons of the chapter Saint-Vincent of Mâcon, who, amongst other feudal prerogatives, had the *"droit de cuissage"* (a certain sexual right over the young ladies of the vineyard!). This cru, grown on granitic soil, is renowned for its body enveloped in a sparkling ruby colour, its finesse and delicacy. It has a great following among wine lovers who like Odrinking it either young, when it is supple and very pleasant in the mouth, or when, after three or four years, it is better balanced and has acquired race and distinction and its characteristic ruby colour.

Having observed the last of the grand cru vineyards of Beaujolais, the final stopping place of our itinerary, and one which concludes it most appropriately, is reached by going via Saint-Vérand to the northern exit of **Leynes** ⑬ . The road is set on Lower Bajocian limestone, while to the left one can see the contact with the Palaeozoic basement and rocks of the Triassic and Lias; the Arlois valley is incised into the marl of the Lias. We are now, therefore, at the geologically defined boundary separating Beaujolais, to the south, and Mâconnais, to the north.

You can now get back to Mâcon by returning to Saint-Vérand and joining the N 6 at Crèches-sur-Saône, from where Mâcon is a distance of 6 km to the north. Alternatively, from Leynes, you can make straight for the start of the Mâconnais itinerary at Saint-Vérand since the first stop is no. 13 of the Beaujolais itinerary. From here you may contemplate both the end of Beaujolais and the beginning of Mâconnais.

Mâconnais

A group of secondary mountain chains trending consistently NNE-SSW, controlled by a system of parallel faults, and terrain inclined approximately 200 to the east, are the distinguishing features of the landscape of the Mâconnais mountains. Well demarcated to the east and to the west by the two valleys (two grabens) of the Saône and Grosne, they disappear to the north, near Sennecey-le-Grand, below the

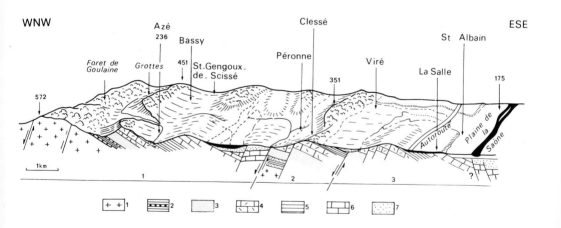

Fig. 17. — Structures, forms and vineyards of the Mâconnais.

The difference in resistance of the terrains to erosion has caused the alternation of relief and depressions. G. Granite: Tr. Triassic (sandstone and clay): L. Clayey Lias: Jc. Limestone of the Middle Jurassic: M. Marl and calcareous marls (Callovian-Oxfordian): Js. Limestone of the Upper Jurassic.

More recent rocks have contributed to the thickening of the lower sections. T. Sandy clay rock (Plio-Quaternary): a. River and stream alluvium.

The repetition of blocks (1,2 and 3), bordered by faults and tilted to the east, produces an alternate system of secondary ranges which are almost all severe and wooded, and long sheltered depressions where the vines can grow on the sunny slopes.

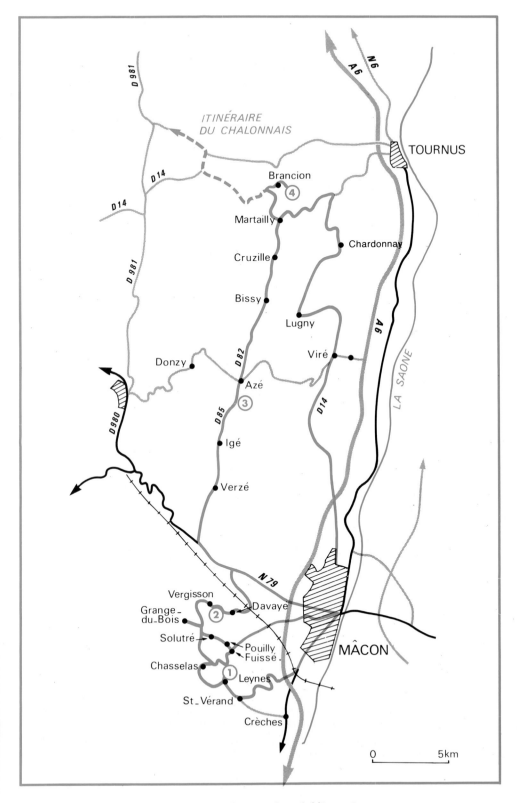

Fig. 18. — Itinerary through Mâconnais

Bresse Tertiary and come to an end south of Pouilly-Fuissé, where the cover of Jurassic terrain is entirely stripped, exposing the granite of Beaujolais. The mountains cover a distance of some fifty kilometres from north to south, but are only some fifteen kilometres wide.

In the types of terrain which reoccur from west to east due to the faults which are opposed to the general downward slope to the Saône, three resistant elements take turns in forming crests which command the landscape (See Guide Géologique Bourgogne):

— the crystalline basement (Mont Saint-Romain, signal de la Mère Boitier), occasionally reinforced with Triassic sandstone;

— limestone of the Middle Jurassic, shaped into cuestas or spurs, above marl slopes of the Lias (Brancion, Vergisson and Solutré rocks).

— limestone of the Upper Jurassic, less steep, above marl of the Callovo-Oxfordian.

The removal of Liassic and Oxfordian marl by erosion has produced long monoclinal asymmetrical depressions (dip slope facing east, face slope facing west) of which the best developed is surely the one we follow from Cruzille to Verzé. These monoclinal depressions are shaped in a succession of ledges and low sections by the valleys of rivers which, descending by and large towards the east, cut the mountain chains into vigorous transverse valleys and create south-facing slopes: for example the Bissy-Lugny-Montbellet line, where the Saint-Oyen river flows, and that of Azé — Saint Maurice-de-Satonnay — Laizé, with the river Mouge (fig. 17).

The Triassic and Jurassic series, represented by varicoloured clay, sandstone, hard limestone, marly limestone, marl and clay, will, in fact, determine the distribution of the soil types, whether on the west-facing slopes, overlain by a hard limestone capping, as in the case of Vergisson or Solutré, or on the east-facing and south-east-facing slopes.

There are two distinguishable types of terrain in Mâconnais:

Limestone or calcitic terrain (rendzines, calcareous brown soil, calcitic brown soil) with a pH in the region of 7 or more, on which the white vine, chardonnay is planted (provided that exposure and altitude are favourable), giving originality and quality to the AOC white wines destined for keeping;

Siliceous, clayey or sandy terrain, frequently associated with silicified sandstone shingle or "chailles", the pH of which is acid, but moderately so, (values of 5 to 6), and which corresponds to zones producing the early white wines or is reserved for the red vines of the 'grand ordinaire' category, such as gamay.

We can either commence from **Mâcon** southbound, and come off the N 6 at the town exit, and head for Loché, Vinzelles and Saint-Vérand (fig. 18) or, having completed the Beaujolais trail, start straight from Saint-Vérand where the two itineraries merge.

Travelling from Saint-Vérand to Leynes, we leave the Carboniferous schist (Viséan) and come onto the Mesozoic. Leaving **Leynes** on the north exit, the first stopping place (1), is the same as (13) on the Beaujolais trail and for this reason should be referred back to.

Next, go and see Chasselas, where you will enter the limestone and marly limestone levels of the Upper Bajocian-Bathonian, with easterly dips. Then continue to Fuissé, where, going down into the village, we will observe the very clear contrast between the Saint-Léger hill, to the east, consisting of Palaeozoic granite and tuf covered by transgressive Triassic sandstone, and *la cuvette de Fuissé-Pouilly*, (basin of Fuissé-Pouilly), set in limestone and marly deposits of the Dogger and Oxfordian. An area of uneven ground, accentuated by a small stream, separates these two compartments.

We should recall just here that the majority of the Mâconnais vineyard area produces its white wines with only the chardonnay vine, on sedimentary terrain. The brown limestone and calcitic soils produce the most renowned crus — wines which age well, especially those from Pouilly-Fuissé, grown on the well-exposed, very sunny slopes of the hills of Pouilly, Solutré and Vergisson. Another appellation, Saint-Veran, is produced at Leynes, Chasselas, Crèches, Davaye and Prissé. The vineyards lower down which are not so well exposed and often comprised of silt-laden soils with 'chailles', produce the Mâcon-Village or the "AOC régionale" wines.

From Pouilly go to Solutré, either directly, or by paying a visit to Grange-du-Bois and the Solutré excavations.

La roche de Solutré ②forms a famous profile of the Bajocian escarpment (Aalenian to Middle Bajocian) lying on marl of the Upper Lias covered with limestone scree. The cliff stands out so well due to the presence of a very resistant coral reef limestone (Fig. 19). The village has given its name to a stone age period, the Solutréan (15 000 to 12 000 b.c.), on account of the existence, on the escarpment scree, of a famous prehistoric deposit which has not only yielded flints very finely moulded into laurel leaves, but also an ossuary of almost one hectare containing an accumulation of horse bones in a layer of more than a metre thick (approximately 1 000 skeletons), at the location of Le Crot du Charnier. In addition, there is an exhibition at the museum of neolithic and Bronze Age skeletons, ceramics and pottery.

The itinerary then takes us through Vergisson (D 177), Davayé, onto the D 89 and N 79 to Roche-Vineuse. Between this locality and Mâcon is the anticlinal of the Grosne with easterly dips of the Mesozoic formations, dissected by longitudinal faults, outlining successive secondary mountain chains.

From La Roche-Vineuse, the road follows the most important of these chains as far as Brancion, following the furrow made in the marl dominated to the right (east) by the limestone cuesta.

The village of **Azé** ③is known for its caves and and tiered galleries, one containing a prehistoric deposit (Bear and Rhinoceros remains; stone-chip industry).

Throughout this region, the vineyards are scattered and appear wherever the soil, slope and exposure are favourable; amid grazing land, crops and forests. The region receives more sunshine than the Côte-d'Or. The villages are typical, with Roman churches and houses constructed in gallery style, with cellars underneath. Passing leisurely through these villages, you will come across some beautiful examples.

Gamay and pinot make fruity wines which are nice drunk young; white wines made from aligoté and chardonnay are "robust and rustic" and should be drunk while they still have all their crispness. The white wines of Lugny and Viré are the most popular.

Continuing through Bissy, Cruzille and Martilly, we come to Brancion on the D 16. This is an old feudal "bourg" whose Roman church, constructed with yellow 'chailles' limestone of the Aalenian-Bajocian, is founded on the coral limestone of the Bajocian. The village settles on the softest level, forming a ledge of marly limestone (Upper Bajocian). Above, oolitic and bioclastic limestone of the Bathonian support the château. From the side of the cuesta, towards the west, we can see the talus of the Lias, then the sandstone of the base of the Triassic supporting La Chapelle-sous-Brancion. The view opens out over the Grosne graben, some secondary mountain chains of the Jurassic and, beyond, over the crystalline Charolais.

The village of **Brancion** ④which is presently undergoing restoration, possesses alley-ways and streets lined with medieval style houses. There are also the imposing remains of a château dating back to the beginning of the tenth century, converted in the fourteenth century by Duke Philippe le Hardi, with a dwelling where the dukes of

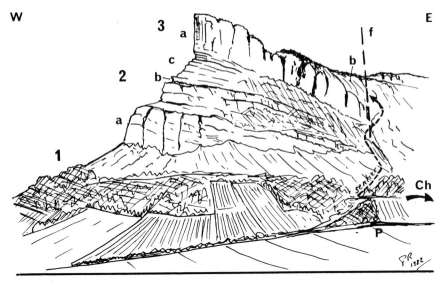

Fig. 19. — Rock and vineyard of Solutré.

1. Basement of Liassic marl, weathered, slid down to a varying degree and covered with limestone scree accommodating the vineyard. The prehistoric deposit, called Crot du Charnier (Ch), is located to the right, in the scree beds, on marl deformed by the deposits.

2. Limestone sequence formed by the accumulation, in a shallow marine environment, of detritus comprised of debris of benthonic organisms, in particular Crinoids (sea lilies):

a. Frequent cross-bedded strata indicating the existence of currents having accumulated the bioclastic detritus (conchiferous debris of Lamellibranchs, Brachiopods, Crinoids, encrustations of Foraminifera (Nubecular), etc. At the summit, there are finer levels of a calmer environment (of Sponge spicules, clayey streaks) containing some Ammonites (Graphoceras) giving an Aalenian age;

b. Brecciated levels containing purplish-blue argillaceous-micritic gangue and numerous organisms (Bryozoa, Lamellibranchs, Gastropods, Brachiopods, sponge spicules, Rhynchonella, etc);

c. Crinoidal limestone, the product of the cementation of a coarse detritus resulting from the breaking-up of dense Crinoid populations.

3. Compact, white, saccharoid mass built up by corals, forming the tip of the rock. The coral lens (a. bioherm, patch reef) is intercalated between crinoidal accumulations; it gets thinner towards the east, and is covered, and partially replaced laterally by grey, stratified limestone (3b), containing Corals and crinoids. Age: Bajocian.

f. Fault; P. carparks.

Bourgogne resided, a fifteenth century market and a squat looking Roman church with a twelfth century square tower.

From Brancion, you can get back to Mâcon on the D 14, going via Chardonnay from where the vine probably originated and Lugny where you are recommended to sample the white wine (likewise at Viré and Clessé). Take the D 463, 163, 56, 55, 106 and 103 to Sennecey and Mâcon. The landscape and the geological features are similar to those on the road from La Roche-Vineuse to Brancion.

Alternatively, from Brancion you can get onto the D 981, by taking the D 146 and D 215, to join the Chalonnais itinerary.

La Côte chalonnaise

The Côte chalonnaise, known particularly for its wine from Mercurey, Rully, Givry and Montagny, stretches from the locality of Saint-Gengoux-le-National, in the south, to the valley of the Dheune river, in the north, this river twisting round the northern tip of the region at Chagny. The Côte does not have the structural regularity of the Mâconnais mountains.

It is composed of Triassic and Jurassic terrains which are underlain by the crystalline spur of the Charolais, to the west, in particular by the dome of Mont-Saint-Vincent. The Palaeozoic structures were rejuvenated after the deposition of the Mesozoic cover which had to adapt to the fault compartments of the underlying basement.

The soil types of the Chalonnais are thus essentially a product of a limestone-or limestone-clay, occasionally dolomitic clay substratum which excludes a priori the brown and acid brown soils. The leached soils are able to evolve on the 'chaille' silt, the Triassic sandstone and even the granite, as at Bissey, to the north of Buxy; granite and sandstone create a very clear distinction in this vine-growing region.

The search for quality soils, for planting the chardonnay vine, producer of the fine white wines including those of Montagny and Rully, is carried out in terrain of a predominantly clayey limestone texture, well exposed to the east, south-east and south, at an altitude of between 220 and 350 m.

With regard to the planting of the red vine, pinot, at Rully, Mercurey and Givrey for the premiers crus, and in other communes which are the domains of the 'AOC régionales de Bourgogne', the vines are also planted on brown limestone or calcitic soil, but of a less clayey texture. The clayey soils of the Triassic and Lias are, in fact, absent from the northern section of the Côte chalonnaise, with the exception of Saint-Désert and Moroges.

Mercurey and Givry produce frank, robust and bouqueted red wines; on the other hand, the white wines of Rully are particularly popular, with plenty of finesse while the wines of Montagny, the favourites of the monks of Cluny, are said to 'keep the mouth fresh and the head clear'.

Itinerary

Coming from Mâcon, take the A 6 motorway or the N 6 to Tournus, then take the D 215, via Mancey, Sercy, Santilly and Saint-Boil. Crossing over the Grosne, a short distance before Sercy, one passes from the mountains of Mâconnais into Chalonnais (fig. 20).

The Côte Chalonnaise which stretches north-south and is trailed by the main Saint-Gengouxle-National — Rully road, is comprised of Triassic and Jurassic rocks, dispersed in the south around Saint-Boil and more concentrated in the Montagny — Buxy — Saint-Vallerin region, the domain of the renowned appellation Montagny Blanc, and particularly in the communes of Mercurey and Rully, the meeting place of red and white wines.

Ask at **Saint-Boil** for a minor road on the left which leads to a Gallo-Roman quarry ①. This exposes soft oolitic Kimmeridgian limestone or the "Corallian Oolite" with its chalky facies, so-called by earlier authors. The limestone with a NNW-facing dip of approximately 10°, is affected by sizeable diaclases which were utilized during quarrying works and the devidence of which is still very fresh (broken and unfinished objects, etc.).

Return to Saint-Boil and continue along the D 981, just to the north of the village, to **Les Filetières** ②, where a cutting on the left-hand side of Pthe road presents a beautiful section of red clay with flintstone. It overlies Upper Oxfordian or Kimmeridgian limestone. It is a residual formation partially derived from Cretaceous units and is formed from rubefied clay and sand, generally accompanied by flintstone.

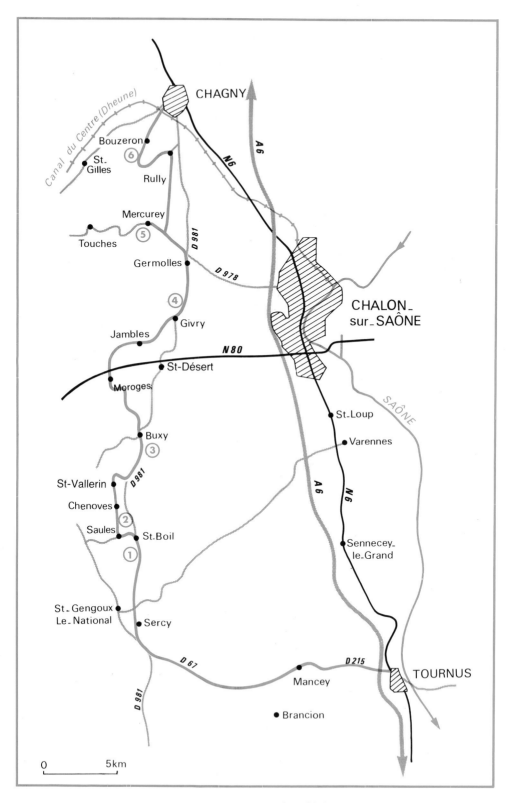

Fig. 20. — Itinerary through the Côte Chalonnaise

Return to Saint-Boil and continue via Saules, Chenoves and Saint-Vallerin, where the most concentrated vineyard area is found. Rejoin the D 981 for **Buxy** ③, where Lower Triassic sandstone, which appears in outcrops in the village, is in contact with Upper Kimmeridgian limestone along a fault with a throw of 400 m. Pay a visit to the Buxy wine cellar and be sure to sample the marvellous Montagny blanc.

From Buxy, head north and bear left for Bissey, then Moroges, which you pass on the right before crossing the N 80 and continuing to Jambles (D 170). The N 80 runs alongside a large fault, trending 70° N, which cuts deep into the Côte Chalonnaise. The ground with its sedimentary cover, which, up until here, inclined westwards, now slopes eastwards towards the Bresse Graben. This fault makes contact with the southern border fault of the dome of Mont-Saint-Vincent.

Leaving Jambles, continue along the D 170 to Givry whose wines, grown on limestone soil, were, according to the villagers, much enjoyed by King Henri IV. It is also said that his favourite possessed a vineyard here too.

Leaving **Givry**, one observes, along the D 981, huge quarries in red limestone ④. Of late Oxfordian age, this limestone is oolitic and biodetrital, with coarse levels containing oncolite and limestone gravel, punctuating the rock with light patches, and streaks of beige lithographic limestone. The formation is well bedded with the base showing horizontal stratification, with small beds occasionally separated by clayey joints, and oblique and cross bedding higher up. Fossils are abundant but poorly preserved.

Continue northwards, on the D 981, to Germolles, where you cross the Orbise flowing along a flexure. Then bear left on the D 981 for **Touches**. From this little village, situated immediately south of Mercurey, there is a magnificent panorama northwards, over the vineyards of the Val d'Or ⑤. Vineyards occupy all the terrain suitable for cultivation, consisting mainly of marl and marly Oxfordian limestone. On the other side of the valley, on the slope opposite and to the right (east), the wooded limestone overlying marl, gives an idea of the quite simple, monoclinal and faulted structure. To the left (west), the different levels of the Jurassic sequence follow each other; the wooded croup of the last slope belongs in fact to the crystalline basement overlain by Triassic sandstone.

From Touches, you can drive through the vineyards of Mercurey followed by those of **Rully**. In both these places, red and white wines are grown with bouquets which resemble the wines of the Côte de Beaune, a fact which will not surprise the geologist, since the substratum is comparable.

After Rully, you climb up onto the high ground situated to the west, on a minor road which takes you to **Bouzeron**, where aligoté enjoys an excellent reputation. From the summit ⑥, you can see *la trouée de la Dheune* (the Dheune gap), to the north. It is a major fault, an extension of the northern tectonic edge of the Blanzy Graben. It is manifested in places, by the abrupt transition from a monoclinal attitude, which we have been following for 120 km (through Beaujolais, Mâconnais and Chalonnais), to a horizontal attitude which predominates northwards, to Dijon, some 50 km away, and beyond.

Next go to **Chagny**, where the Chalonnais itinerary terminates, and then on to Beaune, from whence the itinerary of the Côtes commences.

The Côte d'Or

The Côte, or Côte d'Or, embracing the vineyards of the Côte de Beaune and the Côte de Nuits, covers, from south to north, the eastern edge of the Burgundian plateaux, from the Dheune valley to the Ouche valley, in a SSW-NNE direction from Santenay to Nuits and in an almost S-N direction from Nuits to Dijon.

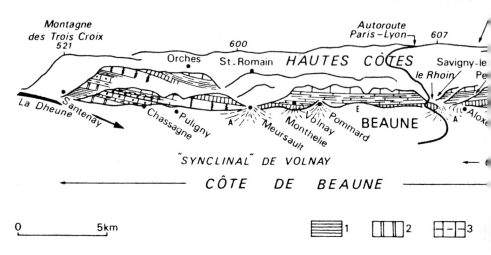

Fig. 21. — *The Côte. Terrain, structure and distribution of the vineyards.*

In the foreground, the façade of the Côte presents an 'S' shape, produced by two transverse undulations (Gevrey Anticline, Volnay Syncline). The bottom of the slope is more or less covered with limestone debris, slipped or spread by run-off (E); at the outlets of the combes, indentations of the Côte, there are older alluvial cones, of which the main ones are indicated (A).

In the middle distance are the buttes and limestone mesas (Oxfordian) of the Hautes-Côtes.

In the background is the profile of the Mountain compartment, around 600 m high on limestone of the Middle Jurassic; Comblanchien limestone worked at an altitude of approximately 280 m. on the Côte, reaches 641 m. in the mountain compartment uplifted along faults.

The soil of the Côte

The structure and morphology of the Côte differ from that of the Mâconnais or Chalonnais for two main reasons (fig. 21):

• The Jurassic layers which are monoclinal up to here, become horizontal;

• The boundary of these Jurassic layers with the Tertiary formations of the Bresse is still a fault contact, with a large throw (600 to 1100 m). The monoclinal structures, which plunged regularly under the older alluvials, are replaced by steps with subvertical fault planes. The Côte, with its steep fault slopes, consistently dominates the Bresse plain from 150 to 200 m.

This morphology will determine where the vineyards are sited i.e. confined to the slopes and piedmont of the Côte, especially those facing east, south-east and south, at altitudes of between 225 and 300 m, whilst the vineyards of the Mâconnais and Chalonnais are more dispersed, sometimes facing south-west and west, and are often discontinuous.

The plateaux situated to the west of the Côte, from Dijon to Chagny, form two steps. To the west, the highest so-called 'Mountain' compartment (500 to 600 m), is stratigraphically reduced in comparison with the Palaeozoic Morvan and the peripheral Liassic depression of the Auxois; it does not support any vineyards due to its altitude and harsher climate.

On the other hand, the eastern compartment, or **l'arrière-côte** (rear côte), which is at an altitude of 400 to 500 m and which is sunken relative to the mountain compartment, supports the vineyards known as the Hautes Côtes de Nuits and de Beaune, on the south and south-east facing slopes and at altitudes of between 300

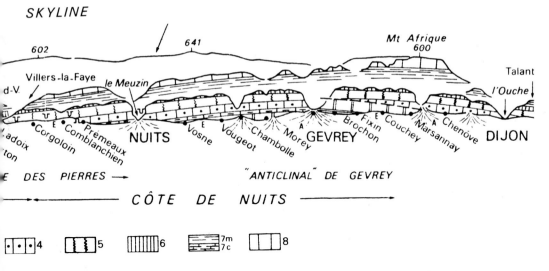

1. *Summit of Liassic marl, cropping out in the vineyards at the heart of the Gevrey Fold and near Santenay, due to the uplifting of the south side of the Volnay Syncline; 2. Crinoidal limestone (older Brochon Stone; Bajocian); 3. Prémeaux Stone; 4. White Oolite (Middle Bathonian); 5. Comblanchien limestone containing intercalated marly levels, to the south (Middle Bathonian); 6. Oolitic and bioclastic limestone, usually termed 'Dalle nacrée' (pearly slab) (Upper Bathonian-Callovian); 7. Limestone marl (7m), Argovian facies (slopes of Mt. Afrique, Butte de Corton) or flaggy limestone (7c), near Beaune (Oxfordian); 8. Limestone or dolomite forming the capping of the buttes.*

and 425 m; this topographical situation places a climatic restraint on the maturation of the vine and the ripening of the grapes so that these vines are eight to fifteen days behind the vineyards of the Côte.

Another very important tectonic aspect relates to the Côte (fig. 22). The latter shows, in fact, two transverse undulations; one, which is synclinal, brings the Upper Jurassic down to the level of the Bresse in the Côte de Beaune (so-called Volnay Syncline), where the grands crus vineyards are set, particularly on the Callovian and the Middle and Upper Oxfordian; the other, which is anticlinal, lifts up the Middle Jurassic, even exposing the Upper Lias, to the north of Gevrey-Chambertin, in the Côte de Nuits, where the majority of the quality vineyards thrive on the Middle Jurassic (crinoidal limestone and marl with Oysters of the Bajocian).

These different orientations of the substratum, and its stratigraphic and petrographic variability, are not without influence on the originality of the crus of the **Côte de Nuits** in comparison with those of the **Côte de Beaune**.

A particular mention should be made to the communes of Comblanchien, Prémeaux and Corgoloin, where opencast mining is carried out in marble limestone called 'Comblanchien' (Bathonian). The excavation of this creates imposing "cavaliers" disturbing the morphology of the landscape of the Côte; this sector, halfway between the Côte de Nuits and the Côte de Beaune, has acquired, on the part of those familiar with the local geology, the name of **Côte des Pierres**.

Marly Bajocian limestone (marl with Ostrea acuminata), overlying hard crinoidal limestone of the same stage, constitute the substratum of the soils of the grands crus vineyards of the Côte de Nuits; but the brown calcitic or limestone soils on this substratum can be disturbed by Bathonian limestone gravel scree, derived from the uphill slopes.

Marly limestone and marl of Middle and Late Oxfordian age (Argovian facies), overlying ferruginous oolite and hard limestone of "Dalle nacrée" (pearly slab)

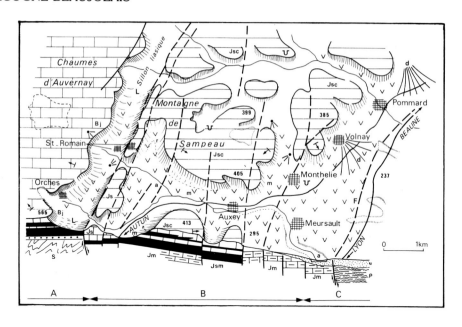

Fig. 22. — Geological and morphological setting of the Côte and the Hautes-Côtes to the south of Beaune.

Structure of the landscape: S. Hercynian basement; L. Triassic and Liassic, predominantly marly succession (Saint-Romain Trough); B. crinoidal Bajocian limestone (Saint-Romain and Orches cliffs); Jm. Middle Jurassic limestone (Comblanchien Limestone and oolitic variants, 'Dalle nacrée' — pearly slab); Js. Upper Jurassic marl and limestone (m. Pommard and Auxey Marl; r. Saint-Romain Marl; c. limestone and dolomite).

Recent terrain: P. marl and clay of the Bresse Graben (Plio-Pleistocene); e. Slope bottom enrichment, with main alluvial cones (d); a. River alluvials.

Structure: F. Main fault of the Côte; A. mountain compartment (Chaumes-d'Auvernay Syncline); B. 'arrière-côte' (rear-côte) compartment; C. Bresse Graben.

Vineyards: V. main locations.

(CallovianOxfordian layers), form the substratum of the soils of the Côte de Beaune vineyards; they are similar brown calcitic or brown limestone soils, the coarse texture of which may be disturbed by scree or gravelly colluvials derived from hard coral, oolitic and organo-detrital Upper Oxfordian limestones (Rauracian facies), which dominate the landscape and are generally covered with broad-leaved or coniferous woods.

Alluvial cones, derived from the combes of the Côte and consisting of stony alluvials several metres thick, run along the foot of the hills. The good drainage of these older or recent stony alluvial cones permits the cultivated area of the AOC Villages vineyards to be extended to the lower section of the piedmont, up to the borders of the Dijon-Lyon railway line.

Characteristics of the environment and "appellations d'origine" of the Côte

The ideal environment (soil and microclimate) for obtaining a high quality wine is one in which the best pysical conditoins for progressive ripening occur; an environment which will guarantee a balance of those elements in the wine which constitute its "body" and which will preserve the substances responsible for its 'bouquet'. Various hypotheses have been formulated concerning the role of certain environmental chemical elements, such as potassium, for example, or manganese and magnesium, but these have never been proven, other than with regard to their influence on the physiological development of the vine and its productivity, but with no evidence of their effect on the type or quality of the wine.

Nevertheless, between the upper, often wooded limits of the vine-growing hillsides and the lower and wetter areas of the plain suited to cereal growing or grazing, a whole range of AOC quality wines are grown: AOC Grand cru, AOC Premier cru, AOC Villages and AOC régionales Bourgogne for the pinot noir and chardonnay vine varieties, AOC Bourgogne grand ordinaire rouge with the addition of gamay, and Bourgogne aligoté for the vine aligoté, the only example in Bourgogne of an appellation which is not geographic.

In the soils of the villages of the Côte, a certain number of physical characteristics (slope, "stoniness", total limestone and clay content) have been analysed and related to quality levels (fig. 23).

Values corresponding to these characteristics are always concentrated at the level of AOC Grand Cru and Premier Cru, whereas there is often a spread of values among AOC Villages and régionales Bourgogne.

AOC Bourgogne vineyards are generally situated on piedmont terrain usually with a gradient of less than 2 %, while the AOC Villages and Cru thrive on gradients of 3 to 5 %, and even up to 20 %, as, for example, in the grands crus of Corton.

"Stoniness", for which values fluctuate between 5 and 40 % in the AOC Villages and Crus while is normally less than 5 % in the AOC Bourgogne soils, is very important. It is essential in determining the level of quality because of the role it plays in the water régime of the soil, that is by facilitating drainage and limiting excess retention water. As for clay content (the fraction smaller than 2 microns, expressed as a percentage of the soil finer than 2 mm), the optimum, for all vineyard terrain, seems to be in the region of 30 to 45 % in calcimorph soils, whether stony or not.

Total limestone content, which varies from 0 to 50 % in fine soil, is found in all the vineyard terrain, but low values (less than 10 %) are most frequent in the AOC régionales vineyards of the lower areas, where hard- packed soils occasionally appear, totally decarbonated in the upper horizons.

All these criteria, slopes, "stoniness", clay and limestone content, have been selected for their intervention in the drainage potential of the soil. The distribution of the values measured for these criteria confirms that the soils which produce the fine wines must possess the best properties facilitating the internal drainage of the soil and expelling any excess water during the vine's growing period and the ripening period of the grapes, in an optimum climatic context.

The Hautes Côtes

To the west of the Côte, the vineyards are spread out unevenly in the closest and most open valleys, providing favourable southerly, south-easterly and south-westerly aspects, such as the Meuzin valley or the valley (before the Dheune) du ruisseau des Clous (Saint-Romain – Auxey) and the Dheune valley itself; but the vineyards also extend across those plateaux with the best exposure, at altitudes reaching a maximum of 425 m.

These sites already spell more difficult microclimatic conditions than those to which the vineyards of the Hautes Côtes de Beaune/de Nuits are subjected: risks of spring frosts and ripening difficulties in the autumn.

The majority of these vineyards occupy soils on Jurassic substratum, with, nonetheless, a more diversified substratum than in the Chalonnais or Mâconnais.

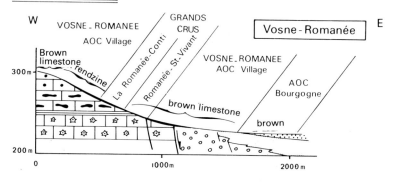

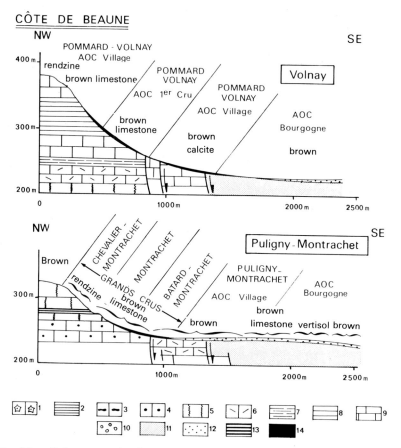

Fig. 23. – Soil-type as related to underlying lithology in the AOC vineyards of the Côte (according to S. Mériaux, J. Chrétien, P. Vermi and N. Leneuf. Bull. sci. Bourgogne, 1981, t. 34, adapted).

The Jurassic structure of the Côte: 1. crinoidal limestone (Bajocian); 2. Ostrea acuminata marl (Upper Bajocian); 3. Prémeaux Stone; 4. white Oolite, oolitic and bioclastic limestone (Middle Bathonian); 5. Comblanchien Limestone with, in the south (b), Pholadomya bellona marl (Middle Bathonian); 6. Dalle nacrée (pearly slab) (Callovian); 7. limestone marl 'ÿand Pernand Marl (Middle Oxfordian); 8. Pommard Marl (Upper Oxfordian); 9. Nantoux Limestone (Upper Oxfordian); 13. marly intercalations between 4 and 5.

Infilling of the Bresse Graben: 10. conglomerate, limestone and clay (Oligocene); 11. marl, sand and gravel (Plio-Pleistocene).

Cover: 12. alluvials and silt-cover; 14. colluvials, limestone scree.

Itinerary through the Côte and the Hautes Côtes

The preceding itineraries have covered soils which, from the crus of Beaujolais on crystalline or crystallophyllic substratum, are, along with the Mâconnais and then the Chalonnais, on sedimentary rocks, usually Jurassic. After the quite complex morphology through many faulted and dislocated compartments in the Mâconnais, the Chalonnais becomes more simple and, in the north, around Mercurey, the geological conditions are the very ones which will prevail in the Côte or Côte d'Or. Thus, for the sake of continuity, we will pick up again in the extreme south, immediately after crossing the Dheune gap described above.

If, however, you only wish to study the Côte at this stage, deferring the rest of the Burgundian vineyards until later, we can point out an equally practical approach and one which has the advantage of going from the simplest site, in terms of geology and geomorphology, to the more complex sites. Starting from Beaune and immediately heading north, go to stop no. ⑦and observe the hill of **Corton**. Having seen, from this classic example with its great bacchic simplicity, what constitute the fundamental elements of viticulture in the Côte, return to **Puligny-Montrachet** and go to stop no. ①(fig. 24).

Continue on then, from Chagny or Beaune, to the western exit of the village of Puligny-Montrachet ①and observe, southwards, the transition from the Côte de Beaune to the Côte chalonnaise and the structural differentiation which occurs at the level of the Dheune gap.

Beneath our feet, one of the faults contributing to the faulted complex at the foot of the côte passes between Puligny and the raised part. In the village of Chassagne this fault brings the base of the Bathonian into contact with the top of the Argovian marl (throw of approximately 80 m).

Puligny-Montrachet figures among the communes which produce the best white wines of Bourgogne. Its hillside is dominated by the Upper Bathonian oolitic facies. Below, Middle Bathonian marly horizons are mostly covered with scree of unadulterated, angular material, of barely worn kidney-shaped concretions derived from subjacent limestone mixed with silt and clay. At the foot of the hillside, older alluvials spread out, covering Pliocene or Quaternary deposits of the Bressan Basin.

This stop provides a suitable opportunity for finding out a few basic facts relating to the pedology of the Côte vineyards. Calcareous, gravelly and stony scree, and marl, also rich in limestone gravel on the well exposed slopes, are the soil types which produce the finest grand cru and premier cru wines.

More clayey, deep, only slightly stony soils, which may or may not be calcareous and are occasionally markedly water-logged, characterize the vineyards from the simple appellation communale to those of the regional level.

From Puligny-Montrachet go to La Rochepot on the D 33. We will be crossing the compartment of the rear côte ('l'arrière-côte). The plateau, which reaches a height of 500 m, is formed, to the north, by Malm (Middle to Upper Oxfordian, with marly and limestone facies), and, to the south, by Dogger (Bathonian and Callovian limestone). These two parts are separated by a flexure subparallel to the Dheune gap, which is followed by the road.

Shortly before La Rochepot, on the D 33, the itinerary crosses the fracture zone. Beyond, the landscape changes completely, on approaching the Mountain compartment.

At **La Rochepot**, you can visit the château, originally dating back to the eleventh century, then converted in the fifteenth century and rebuilt by Sadi Carnot, son of the President. You can also visit the pittoresque village of Gamay which gave its name to the lesser Burgundian vine, held in contempt by Philippe le Hardi who, in 1395, described it as 'highly injurious to humans', but which now prevails in

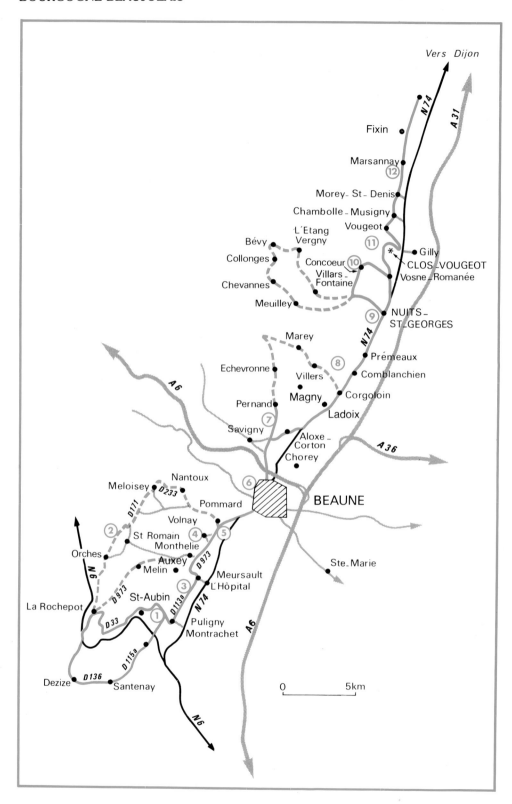

Fig. 24. – Itinerary through the Côte-d'Or.

Beaujolais. You may also go to Santenay, the most southerly vine-growing location, with its luscious reds which age well and smell of both almond and strawberry.

From La Rochepot, we will take the D 171, to stop shortly before rejoining the D 17, above Saint-Romain. As you make your way, take advantage of the beautiful view over the Saint-Romain Fault sectioning off the Oxfordian limestone of the rear côte, to the east, which dominates a small Liassic trough (basement of the Mountain compartment). The throw here is of the order of 300 metres. We pass through this combe until we come to Évelle H(note the church tower, of "lava"), then we climb up the Dogger cliff at Orches (reddish brown limestone in oblique bedding of the Bajocian).

Now go to the cliff edge on the right-hand side of the road ②: we are on cliffs of Bajocian rocks (crinoidal limestone with oblique bedding, visible to the right). The Mountain plateau is cultivated owing to the marly level containing Upper Bajocian *Liostrea acuminata*. Immediately below the plateau, the Liassic trough is cluttered with scree; further down, one can make out the Domerian rise followed by that of Sinemurian limestone.

Beyond the fault, the plateau of the "rear côte", reinforced with a resistant, mainly limestone series, (Upper Oxfordian) comprises three terms:

1) resistant limestone at the summit;
2) so-called Saint-Romain Marl, which produces excellent white wines;
3) oolitic and marly limestone at the base.

Saint-Romain is situated on the upper limestone; to the rear, one can distinguish the different levels indicated, according to the land use determined by man.

From the structural and morphological point of view, we will note that the Mountain compartment clearly dominates (550 m on average) that of the "rear côte" (450 to 380 m, from west to east) and that the throw separating the two steps is of several hundred metres. We will also observe that the Liassic trough, morphologically in a hollow, belongs to the structurally uplifted compartment.

To reach the vineyards of the Hautes Côtes, go from Saint-Romain to Pommard, via Meloisey and Nantoux. There is a co-operative of the Hautes Côtes on the southern approach road into Beaune.

Return to the Côte through the valley of the Saint-Romain stream, with its aluvial-colluvial bottom, sunk into Argovian marl. At Auxey, the Dogger limestone is uplifted by the fault.

On your way, visit **Meursault** ③, with its white wine which is both dry and luscious, with an aroma of ripe grapes and a nutty flavour. The cellars of the château, which one can visit, are impressive, and the church is beautiful. The red wine of **Volnay** ④ has a large following among wine-lovers for it has all the qualities of finesse, lightness and fragrance. Philippe IV de Valois enjoyed it, as early back as his coronation in 1328, and, when he visited Eudes VI at the château de Volnay, in 1336, "the wine valet had his work cut out".

Victor Hugo preferred the Clos des Épenots, of **Pommard** ⑤. The vineyards here produce powerful, very bouqueted red wines, which go well with game.

At **Beaune** ⑥, in addition to the Hospices, (the general hospital and the Museum) and the church of Notre-Dame, "fille de Cluny" (daughter of Cluny), you are recommended to visit the Wine Museum of Bourgogne, located in the former mansion of the dukes of Bourgogne, a building dating back to the fifteenth and sixteenth centuries, and the fourteenth century winery with its magnificent wine-presses and vats. The history of the vineyards and the cultivation of the vine is tastefully and skilfully presented here. The thirteenth century church of Saint-Nicolas is the church of the wine growers' quarter. It has a Roman tower, a fine stone spire, a fifteenth century porch with a tiled roof and a twelfth century portal. Just opposite the church, take the Savigny-lès-Beaune road, then the D 18, until you are in the vicinity and south of **Pernand-Vergelesses**. This is a most important stop ⑦ by virtue of the classic observations which it allows.

At the level of the hill of **Corton**, the classic section of the Côte de Beaune ⑦ comprises, from top to bottom:

1) oolitic and bioclastic limestone, with Rauracian facies and sparse brown calcitic soils which are very often wooded as in the case of the Corton butte;

2) a marl slope with Argovian facies, covered with rendzine type soils, which are very calcareous and propitious to the cultivation of the chardonnay vine, producing renowned white wines (Corton-Charlemagne);

3) a more resistant limestone level, revealed by a topographic rise or a simple slope break, with grey marly limestone in decimetric beds, at the base of the Argovian facies (Middle Oxfordian), then a thin metric level of nodular yellow or red limestone with ferruginous oolites and abundant Ammonites (Middle Oxfordian) overlying yellowish Callovian and Upper Bathonian limestone.

These limestone levels, which occupy the middle section and the foot of the slope, are partly covered with clayey-stony scree which have evolved into rendzines or brown limestone soils according to their depth, which is linked to the localized erosive action brought about by run-off. These soils bear the most prestigious red wines of the commune of **Aloxe-Corton** (grands crus and premiers crus, on the south and south-east slopes of the hill).

In the bottom of the valley line, continuing from the dry valley of Pernand, the occasionally deeper soils are formed from coarse limestone alluvials and colluvials, associated with limestone clay silt. The Jurassic substratum (Bathonian) is located nearby; the soils, of the brown limestone type, support the vines of the appellation d'origine communale (Aloxe-Corton). Further down, in the vicinity of the Beaune-Dijon road, the same valley line shows deeper clayey silt, partially decarbonated and with no limestone gravel content. Debris from siliceous concretions partly originating from certain Argovian limestone levels, reappears in the south-east piedmont of the Corton hill (location of Les Chaillots).

You may like to try an experiment involving a well-planned wine-tasting excursion round the vineyards growing on these soils. Begin with Aloxe-Corton, the most muscular, most robust wine of the Côte de Beaune. Pernand-Vergelesses resembles it, though is less robust and has a flavour of raspberries or cherries. Savigny-Vergelesses starts off with a more pronounced flavour of cherries, which is very characteristic of Savigny. You will have been admiring, from stop no. ⑦, the panorama which ÿstretches from the Aloxe-Corton vineyards set on the slope bottoms and goes from right (ENE) to left (WSW), to the vineyards of Pernand-Vergelesses, then to Vergelesses de Savigny and finally to the vineyards of Savigny, still on the slope bottoms, and at the same altitude. The vineyards which continue to the south-east and which, after the N 74, assume the appellations of Chorey-lès-Beaune, are the most vigorous in the north-east and have a flavour of cherry in the south-west. This is a good illustration of the relationship between the geology and the soil, with the elements eroded from the high ground above continuing to play a role in the aromas and flavours of the wines produced further downhill.

The morphology of the Côte de Beaune, with great outcrops of soft marly Middle Oxfordian limestone (Argovian facies), is somewhat less pronounced than that of the Côte de Nuits, reinforced at its summit by the resistant Bathonian limestone (Comblanchien facies) which overhangs the landscape in the form of cliffs, especially in the combes.

For those interested in the Hautes Côtes, take the D 18 at Pernand going via Échevronne, Changey, Marey (where the Maison des Hautes Côtes provides an opportunity to sample the wines and savour "la gastronomie bourguignonne"), and Villers-la-Faye, and rejoin the Côte at Corgoloin.

So we have now left the Côte de Beaune and, before embarking on the Côte de Nuits itinerary, we come to the Côte des Pierres, the centre of which is Comblanchien ⑧.

This is a real quarry centre employing several hundreds of workers. The Middle Bathonian level which is quarried here is not very thick. Its development, dating back to the Second Empire, has to do with the fact that the limestone can be sawn up into rather thin lamina or slabs. Comblanchien is a very compact limestone with a porosity value of between 0.2 and 0.9 %, and a specific weight of 2.65, nearing that of calcite (2.71); it is generally beige in colour, with pinkish streaks (dolomite). Thanks to recent studies, the environment in which it was formed is well known (shallow sheltered sea water in the intertidal zone). The lovely smoothness and hard quality of the rock have made it a much valued material for floor covering and it is used in the construction of many buildings both in France and abroad.

Next go to Prémeaux, where pinkish limestone with concretionary horizons (Lower Bathonian) is quarried by means of galleries and similarly at **Nuits-Saint-Georges**, where we will be stopping ⑨. The wines from this town were recommended to Louis XIV by his doctor, Fagon, who prescribed Nuits and Romanée as remedies. Thus his whole court came to drink the wines from a vineyard whichs date back at least to the year one thousand.

From Nuits-Saint-Georges, take the D 25 which penetrates into the Hautes Côtes, passing through Meuilley, Chevannes, Collonges, Bévy, L'Étang-Vergy and Villars-Fontaine. As you rejoin the D 25, bear left towards Concoeur, on a road which climbs up into limestones, some of which are quarried to the west.

To the south, shortly before coming onto the plateau, a small quarry ⑩ exposes the Oxfordian, in Argovian facies, in the form of fine limestone in small decimetric layers, alternating with foliated marly limestone. Not far from here, one can see 'Dalle nacrée' (pearly slab) limestone (Callovian) and some rather poor evidence of ferruginous Oolite.

We then go back down to **Vosne-Romanée** through a combe incised into the Callovian resistant limestone. The valley narrows at the passage of the Bathonian and opens out into the vineyards, with a very fine view over the Bressan plain. We are now back in the Côte de Nuits with, as far as Gevrey-Chambertin, more vigorous relief than that of the Côte de Beaune. The slope connecting with the Bresse is shorter, meaning that the expanse of the vineyards is more restricted here. These diverse characteristics, which are related, result from the fact that the cuesta is formed by the total thickness of resistant Comblanchien Limestone. Not only is the Bathonian entirely exposed, but also the Bajocian crops out in the lower, scree-strewn section of the slope.

You are recommended to visit the château du **Clos de Vougeot** ⑪ . An estate belonging to the abbey of Cîteaux from the twelfth century to the Revolution, le Clos de Vougeot (approximately 50 hectares) is one of the most famous vineyards of the Côte de Nuits. Its vines belong nowadays to numerous growers. At the time of the first geographical classification of the Burgundian crus, in 1860, it was said that it would be impossible to split up properties which were seemingly identical and which all had an indisputable reputation, and that the wine produced would be all the more commendable the more uniform and least fragmented the estate was; in other words that viticulture and vinification play a determining role. The case of Clos Vougeot shows, however, that this affirmation was unwarranted and that the subsoil and soil have retained every bit of their importance, because, in spite of the 50 hectares being divided up amongst over 50 owners, the wine of Clos Vougeot with its robustness and aroma of truffle and violets, continues to be consistently finer and more delicate from the higher ground and heavier from the slope bottom.

The château, comprising a twelfth century cellar, a thirteenth century winery with four gigantic wine presses installed by the monks, and a Renaissance building, has been in the possession of the *Confrérie des chevaliers du Tastevin* since 1944.

This body organizes, each year, numerous chapters; over five hundred guests attend dinners where new knights are enthroned whose gastronomic and oenophilic attributes have been recognized by the Great council of the Order.

Above Clos Vougeot, there is a predominance of grands crus, including the great names, at Vosne-Romanée and Vougeot, and going from south to north the greatest names include: *Romanée*, with under one hectare and 25 hectolitres per year, *Romanée Conti*, with less than two hectares and 50 hectolitres – these wines are perfectly balanced and keep exceptionally well. They are named after the prince of Conti who purchased the estate, at a very high cost, in 1760, in competition with 'la Pompadour'. Further north, there are the wines of Richebourg, Échezeaux, Musigny and many others.

From Vougeot, go to Chambolle-Musigny, then Morey-Saint-Denis, paying tribute, in passing, to the grands crus of Bonnes mares, then stop between Morey and **Gevrey-Chambertin** ⑫ . Here, on the left-hand side of the road, an old quarry (now occupied by vines), incised into the Lower Bajocian, exposes the rocky substratum of the grands crus of Gevrey-Chambertin (clos de Bèze-Chambertin). It presents a characteristic facies of crinoidal limestone, with its usual oblique stratification.

The soils are frequently shallow, occasionally with outcrops of rock. But the majority of the vineyards lies on varied scree covering a third, two-thirds or in particular instances, the whole of the slope.

The grand cru here is Chambertin, which, for Roupnel, combines grace with vigour, firmness with strength and finesse with delicacy, opposite qualities which endow it with the wonderful synthesis of unique generosity and complete virtue.

The vineyard area of the Côte de Nuits is found then on terrain of a different and older age than that of the Côte de Beaune, which is at the top of the Middle Jurassic or at the base of the Upper Jurassic. The marly limestone environments are quite similar to each other, but, nevertheless, have quite a few slight differences, making wine from Nuits more robust and fuller than that from Beaune.

Chablis

The vineyards of Chablis, located at the northern extremity of Bourgogne, were at one time part of an important wine growing area, with Tonnerois, Avallonnais, Joigny and Les Riceys, which surplied the capital in particular with red and rosé wines, by virtue of the means of transport provided by the Yonne and the Seine (see in fig. 10 the demarcation of the Chablis vineyard area).

At the end of the nineteenth century, the disastrous phylloxera disease destroyed the majority of these vineyards, with the exception of those of the Côtes de Chablis, where the limestone-clay type of terrain and the good exposure were propitious to the planting of chardonnay, the noble vine called here 'le beaunois' — producer of fine wines. "Chablis is a limpid, fragrant, lively and light white wine, whose name has become synonomous, outside France, with great dry white wine". (Poupon and Forgeot, 1969).

According to sites and exposure, the vineyards offer an array of qualities of white wine ranging from **Petit Chablis**, wine from the plateau of which most classic is that of Lignorelles, to **Chablis**, wine from the well exposed hill slopes, spread through the commune of Chablis and the outlying communes, such as Beine, Maligny, Fleys, Chichée and so on; and finally the **Chablis grands crus** and premiers crus which are confined to the best soils concentrated around the town of Chablis.

There is also a small vineyard area producing red wines which has survived in

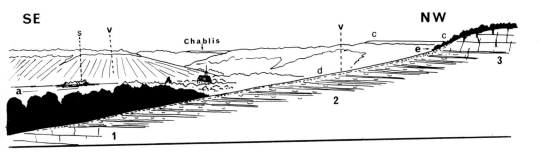

Fig. 25. — Structure and morphology of the vineyards of Chablis.

Structure of the landscape: 1. Astartes limestone; 2. alternation of marl and limestone with Exogyra virgula, the main support of the vineyards; 3. Barrois Limestone base, fissured, karstified and dry on the surface.

Surface terrain and relief forms: C. Côte (cuesta) des Bars, produced by the inclination of the terrain to the north-west and to the difference of resistance of the limestone and marl to erosion; V. regular, very flat slope of the vineyards, covered with limestone debris which slipped down hS0136Tthe slope (d); it is a 'settled' slope, the shaping of which no doubt dates back to the periglacial climates of the Quaternary; S. Serein valley and alluvials (a), undercutting the cuesta and forming, as a result, a very wide funnel-shaped breach (e), giving rise to extensive development of the well exposed slopes.

certain communes of the Auxerrois, such as Irancy, Saint-Bris-le-Vineux and Vincelottes, where pinot noir is grown, and is also associated with the chardonnay and aligoté vine varieties which may be used to enhance the Bourgogne AOC wines.

Geologically, all these vineyards form part of the south-east margin of the Paris Basin, having been sited on the fringe of the Upper Jurassic (Kimmeridgian and Portlandian) and possibly on the base of the Cretaceous (Hauterivian).

The Jurassic beds slope in a monoclinal fashion towards the centre of the Paris Basin; they crop out either in gently sloping structural surfaces trending northwards, or in sometimes steeply sloping cuestas, which are well exposed to the south, south-east and south-west, dominating the Serein valley at an altitude of 100 to 150 m in the region of Chablis.

The vineyards are situated on these well exposed slopes, along the Serein valley and the sometimes narrow tributary valleys. The slopes are sometimes very steep (15 to 20 %) and sometimes very gentle; vineyards are even found on the plateaux, at an altitude of 200 to 250 metres.

The lithological series of the Chablis region is as follows, going from bottom to top (fig. 25):

1) The chalky Tonnerrois limestone and the fine Astartes limestone of Early Kimmeridgian age, form the base on which the town of Chablis is built and the Serein valley bottom; but they can support vineyards, as at Chemilly and Viviers.

2) Limestone and marl with Exogyra virgula of Middle and Late Kimmeridgian age and about 80 m thick, composed of alternating marly limestone and either grey clayey marl with shellbeds (approximately one third) in the case of the thicker ones, or dark blue clayey marl, in thin layers of a few metres. This formation supports all the most renowned vineyards, particularly those of Chablis. These layers constitute the broad slope connecting the valley bottoms and the plateau.

3) Barrois Limestone of Portlandian age forms the plateau; it is occasionally covered with younger, basal Lower Cretaceous limestone.

The Portlandian is composed of more compact and finer sublithographic limestone, showing numerous clay and marl intercalations at its base and forming a transition zone recalling the Upper Kimmeridgian, specific to the AOC Chablis vineyards. This basal assembly crops out in escarpments of 6 to 7 metres high, before the typical limestone of the Portlandian.

A complex of calcimorphic soils, overlying stoney clay colluvials, covers almost the entirety of the the vine-growing slopes, the morphology of which is conditioned by limestone of the Portlandian at the summit of the cuesta, and marly formations of the Kimmeridgian, on the slopes.

On the plateaux and along the edge of the plateaux, in a horizontal position, a hard limestone (sublithographic facies of the Portlandian, Spatangue Limestone of the Hauterivian) underlies quite shallow soil (less than 0.30 m) or 'petites terres'. Erosion, the absence of colluvial cover, explains its thinness. The soils which are covered with forest are decarbonated and are called "petites aubues"; the cultivated soils are recarbonated. Most of this terrain represents the domain of the appellation Petit Chablis.

The soils formed on the marly facies of the Upper and Middle Kimmeridgian and on the marly base of the Portlandian, in particular on the marly shell beds with *Exogyra virgula*, constitute the privileged domain of the Chablis grands crus and premiers crus. These soils can be thick, directly overlying the marly substratum, or in the form of an almost continuous blanket of colluvials of variable thickness (0.40 to 2 m), with gravel often of Portlandian origin.

Chablis grand cru is confined to the slope situated to the north-east of the town on limestone and marl with *Exogyra virgula*.

Wines and gastronomy

Bourgogne, by virtue of its geographical location, is fortunate enough to be a natural crossroads of Europe. Nature and man have taken advantage of this position and as a result, its wines, renowned worldwide, as well as its cuisine, bring us unrivalled and continually renewed pleasure[1].

Wine from Bourgogne is made primarily to be enjoyed around the table and all dishes go well with it, but for three exceptions: onion-based "potage bourguignon" (Burgundian soup) from Auxonne, the marvellous wine grower's salad and all vinaigrette specialities, and finally desserts, though for these some gourmets do succumb to an excellent Crémant de Bourgogne méthode champenoise (high quality sparkling wine made according to the champagne method).

Before sitting down at the table, you can't miss trying a "vin blanc cassis" (white wine and blackcurrant), more commonly known as "kir", after the colourful canon Kir, who was mayor of Dijon and deputy of the Côte d'Or. The blackcurrant comes from the Hautes Côtes and the nice dry white wine will invariably be a Bourgogne aligoté also from the Hautes Côtes or a Mâcon-Villages; add more or less of the crème de cassis (19° proof) to suit your taste. Try some small fresh "gougères" (cheese and cabbage pies) which will prepare your palate perfectly and sharpen the appetite.

You will then be given the choice of 'jambon persillé bourguignon' or 'dijonnais' (Burgundy/Dijon ham sprinkled with chopped parsley), or Burgundy snails, nicely accompanied by a Rully or a Pouilly-Fuissé.

In actual fact, you will need numerous occasions on which to experience all these delights. You might like, one tranquil summer evening, to stop off along the Saône and order a Saône fried or poached fish dish, delightfully combining pike, carp, tench and eel, and accompany it with a bottle of Montigny.

Alternatively you may prefer "truite de l'abbaye de Fontenay à la Bristol," (a trout dish), prepared with a white wine court-bouillon, or perhaps "écrevisses à la marinière" (crayfish), cooked in a Chablis wine. For either of these dishes you would naturally select a nice dry Chablis.

Bourgogne, which is a wholesome region imbued with the good solid common sense of its country folk, has created for itself a type of cuisine which has become incompatible with the rat race of today when time is no longer taken to savour life. The cuisine of Bourgogne requires time, both in its preparation and in its eating. So, at our leisure, let's enjoy some "oeufs en meurette", consisting of eggs poached in a red wine sauce and served with bits of bacon and slightly garlicky croutons.

A wine from Fixin will do nicely for this and will provide a perfect introduction to "poulet (from Bresse) Gaston Gérard" — a chicken dish in which the essential flavours will have been delicately brought out and transformed by a good Dijon mustard. A Savigny-lès-Beaune or a Volnay will be a perfect complement to this dish.

If you should happen to visit our region during the grape harvest, the dish 'caille aux baies de cassis' (quail with blackcurrants) is not to be missed. The quails have been fed on grapes which they peck off the vines and this gives them a very distinctive flavour. For this occasion, a fragrant and delicate Chambolle-Musigny will delight the most intransigent of palates.

Beef from the neighbouring Charolais forms an integral part of many classic regional dishes, for example "boeuf à la mode", which is served with the same white wine that goes into its marinade, 'filet de boeuf mariné' (marinated fillet of beef) or venison cooked in Brouilly with its flavoursome and very distinct fresh grapey taste.

It would of course be a crime not to include "boeuf bourguignon" here, although this is a dish found all over France and a term all too often misused. Select your inn carefully and try it with a fine bottle of Nuits-Saint-Georges.

When the hunting season is in full swing, a whole range of game recipes can be concocted (jugged hare, boar, venison) and this is the moment of glory for Corton wines, whose great qualities are best expressed accompanying these types of game dishes.

Bourgogne keeps scrutiny over its appellations and cannot be accused of misleading advertising; thus, "coq au Chambertin" is rechristened "coq au vin de Bourgogne" or "coq à la bourguignonne", in view of the fact that we do not marinate our chickens in Chambertin (we may be gourmets but we are not fools!) but rather in a nice robust red wine. Accompany your meal with a bottle of Gevrey-Chambertin (preferably older than the chicken!) and you will still be able to tell your friends: 'Yes, I have really eaten "coq au Chambertin!"

In this region blessed with gourmets, it is commonly said that "a meal without cheese, is like a beautiful woman with only one eye". A whole selection of regional cheeses is there to tempt you but you would be wise to avoid those with rather too strong a taste, out of respect for the wine carefully chosen at the start of, or better still, before the meal.

"Le cîteaux" (made by the monks of the abbey of the same name) and "l'époisse" are our first choice and, if you have a huge appetite, fill your plate with a selection of cheeses including some "soumaintrain" made with cow's milk, some "charolais", a "bouton de culotte" or "trouser button" (that's its name!) made with goat's milk, and, last but not least, some "cancoillotte", which is now only produced locally on the Saône plain.

Some nice fresh bread "aux noix" (type of bread made with nuts) will greatly add to the enjoyment of your meal and a whole range of wines are likely to have you in extasy!: Vosne-Romanée, Morey-Saint-Denis, Beaune, etc.

---

[1] This chapter was written by L.-M. Chevignard of the Confrérie des Chevaliers de Tastevin.

Why not finish your meal with some delicious, delicate, though increasingly hard to find "pêches de vigne" (bush peaches) or a "crème à la feuille de pêcher" (peach leaf cream dessert) which will really make people jealous! If you want to keep to the more classic dessert, and be equally thrilled, sample some "tarte aux poires", tart made with pears cooked in wine and blackcurrants. After your coffee, a glass of "prunelle" (sloe gin) or perhaps some fine champagne or marc de Bourgogne (brandy) will elevate your soul!

FOR FURTHER
INFORMATION

Geology

Guide géologique Bourgogne-Morvan (1984), by P. Rat et coll., 2nd edition, published by Masson, Paris (see in particular the introduction and itineraries 4, 5 and 11).

Guide géologique Lyonnais-Vallée du Rhône (1973), by G. Demarcq et coll., published by Masson, Paris (see in particular itinerary 2: Beaujolais).

Leneuf N. and Gélard J.-P. (1980). — Géologie des vins de France. Excursion no. 210 C, XXVIe Cong. géol. inter., Paris. Published by BRGM, Orléans.

La terre et la vigne. A la découverte du vignoble beaujolais. Brochure, 40 p., CCST, place Saint-Laurent, Grenoble.

Oenology:

Bréjoux P. (1978). — Les vins de Bourgogne. Revue des vins de France. Coll. *Atlas de la France viticole*; published by L. Larmat., 275 p.

Gadille R. (1967). — Le vignoble de la Côte bourguignonne. Fondements physiques et humains d'une viticulture de haute qualité. Thèse doct., 688 p., published by Les Belles lettres, 35, boulevard Raspail, Paris.

Lavalle J. (1855). — Histoire et statistique des grands vins de la Côte d'Or. Paris, second edition Fondation Geisweiller, 1972.

Poupon P. and Forgeot P. (1969). — Les vins de Bourgogne. PUF, Paris, 5th edition.

Above: Château de Rully (thirteenth and fifteenth century) and its vineyards where the fine wines of the Côte chalonnaise are grown on Middle and Upper Jurassic limestone, constituting the substratum of the three hillsides of AOC Rully. This château belonged, in the last century, to the family of Fernand Montessus de Ballore, graduate of the 'École hS0136Tpoly- technique' and seismologist responsible for the first world earthquake census (Photo Leneuf).

Below: Grape-pickers in the vineyards of the great wines of Gevrey- Chambertin (Côte de Nuits) on Bajocian crinoidal limestone (Photo Leneuf).

103

Above: Photograph taken in Beaujolais of the vineyards of the Mont de Brouilly, the substratum of which is composed, at the base, of granite-derived sand, and more clayey soil on Palaeozoic andesitic tuf, half-way up the slope (Photo Leneuf).

Below: Vineyards of the Mâconnais in the appellation area of Pouilly-Fuissé set on Middle Jurassic limestone and Liassic marly limestone, at the foot of the famous Solutré rock (Photo Leneuf).

The glistening colours of autumn leaves in the grands crus vineyards of Morey-Saint Denis (Clos de Tart and Clos de la Roche) on crinoidal limestone and marl with Ostrea acuminata of Bajocian age (Photo Leneuf).

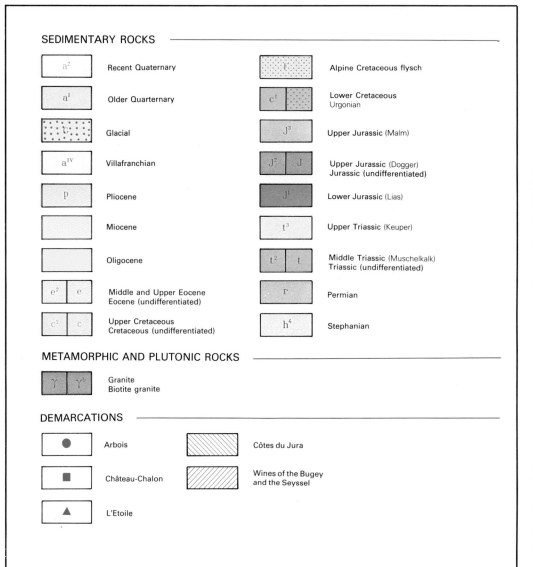

SEDIMENTARY ROCKS

a² — Recent Quaternary

a¹ — Older Quarternary

t — Glacial

a^IV — Villafranchian

p — Pliocene

Miocene

Oligocene

e² | e — Middle and Upper Eocene
Eocene (undifferentiated)

c² | c — Upper Cretaceous
Cretaceous (undifferentiated)

f — Alpine Cretaceous flysch

c¹ — Lower Cretaceous
Urgonian

J³ — Upper Jurassic (Malm)

J² | J — Upper Jurassic (Dogger)
Jurassic (undifferentiated)

J¹ — Lower Jurassic (Lias)

t³ — Upper Triassic (Keuper)

t² | t — Middle Triassic (Muschelkalk)
Triassic (undifferentiated)

r — Permian

h⁴ — Stephanian

METAMORPHIC AND PLUTONIC ROCKS

γ | γ^b — Granite
Biotite granite

DEMARCATIONS

● — Arbois

■ — Château-Chalon

▲ — L'Etoile

Côtes du Jura

Wines of the Bugey
and the Seyssel

Fig 26 — Geological map and demarcations of the winegrowing districts of the Jura.

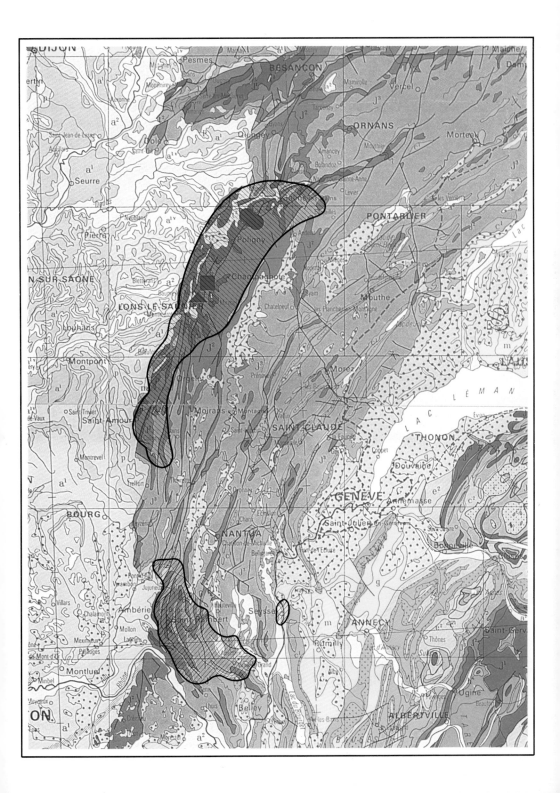

The vineyards of the Jura lie in the centre and the south of the chain. In the central portion there are the Côtes du Jura, between the regions of Arbois and Lons-le-Saunier; in the south there are the vineyards of Bugey.

THE CÔTES DU JURA

On the eastern border of the Rhône-Saône Trough the first slopes of the Jurassic plateaus bear the vineyards of the Côtes du Jura, the most extensive and best known of which lie in the region of Arbois and Château-Chalon, to the north of Lons-le-Saunier (fig. 26).

The wine-growing district and its soil

At first sight the Jura district is a mirror image of the Côte-d'Or district on the other side of the Rhône-Saône Trough. In fact the structures and rocks are very different, like the resulting morphology.

The structures? The wine-growing district is located on the outer folded belt of the Jura (the Ledonian Belt) and on the edge of the plateau, the fault contact between the outer folds of the Ledonian Belt and the Table Jura.

The rocks? Instead of the limestones and marly limestones of the Middle and Upper Jurassic, here it is predominantly Triassic and Liassic clays

which underlie the wine-growing district, with Middle Jurassic limestones capping it or forming the top of the slope on the edge of the plateau.

The nature of the relief? The Jura wine-growing district is again a "tectonic" district. The faulted edge of the plateau provides a slope with a favourable aspect, but in this case facing west. Another difference with the Côte d'Or winegrowing district is that the Triassic and Liassic clays are shaped into gentle hills onto which the vines have moved out in front of the edge of the plateau.

The vines of the Jura

The traditional varieties consist essentially of savagnin blanc, poulsard and trousseau, to which must be added the two Burgundian varieties, pinot noir and chardonnay.

Savagnin blanc is a variety with a fairly low productivity, with compact bunches of small grapes. It is harvested late, as late as the first frosts, and yields a wine with bouquet, which ages well to provide the famous amber wines with a nutty taste.

The poulsard, or Arbois vine, is a red variety, with loose spreading bunches, and purple or pink oval grapes having a white juice. It accounts for 80% of the red varieties in the Jura. It is sensitive to spring frosts because the buds open early. It yields a wine with little colour, more rosé than red, with freshness and bouquet.

Trousseau is a vigorous very productive red variety with small tight bunches yielding a well coloured astringent wine which keeps well, but lacks quality.

Soils

The Triassic-Liassic series of the Montchauvrot can be considered to be very representative of the winegrowing districts of the Côtes du Jura and Arbois.

Dark in colour, it formerly gave the Triassic-Liassic terrain the name of the "Black Jura". The series includes, from bottom to top: the Upper Keuper, consisting of marls, or rather iridescent, wine-coloured and greenish dolomitic clays, and dolomite; the Rhaetian, with dark clays, marly limestones with shell banks of *Avicula contorta* and sandstone horizons; the Hettangian and Sinemurian with limestones containing Gryphea and ammonites; finally the marly Middle and Upper Lias.

On its Bajocian limestone crag downthrown between two faults, the site of **Château-Chalon** dominates the valley of the Seille. It forms a notch in the edge of the Ledonian plateau with a small offset, precisely on the tectonic boundary separating the fold belt to the west from the plateau to the east. The plateau consists of the reddish/brown limestones of the Aalenian and Bajocian which overlie the marls of the Middle and Upper Lias. A projection half way up the slope marks the Upper Domerian (the Banc de Roc).

From the heights of the village of Château-Chalon there is a magnificent view over Ménétru-le-Vignoble, Voiteur and the valley of the Seille, villages which form part of the area bearing the Côtes du Jura label, and in particular Château-Chalon.

Four main sedimentary assemblages can be identified in this winegrowing district of the Jura, which are well represented on the hillsides:

1) At the base, *the Triassic formations* which are best represented near Arbois. These consist of a very variable succession of clays and iridescent marls associated with thin bands of dolomitic limestone.

These rocks give rise to heavy clay soils, which are decarbonated and sometimes decalcified at the surface. The structure of these soils remains stable, because of their high iron content, and water reserves are always sufficient to supply the vines. These are the black or wine-red coloured soils which are perfect for the poulsard variety.

2) *The marly limestone Liassic* series provides a terrain which is particularly suitable for growing vines. The greyish coloured soils which represent the unaltered marls at outcrop are the preferred locations for quality vineyards if the aspect is to the west or south west.

3) *The hard limestones of the Middle Jurassic* (Bajocian) plateau can occur as screes in the winegrowing areas. Frost-shattered limestone fragments, red decalcified clays and flinty silts are often mixed with and cover outcrops of the Upper Lias or Toarcian. The screes, which have sometimes been subjected to solifluxion, are generally thin. They yield a brown to dark brown soil which favours vines in locations with a good aspect, and vines providing a good alcohol content. However these soils are not always included under the most prestigious Château-Chalon label, as this wine is more specific to the grey marls of the Lias.

4) At the base of the slopes and in the valleys alluvials frequently occur as fluvioglacial outwash fans. The suitability of the ground varies considerably depending on the depth of the water table, and requires drainage.

Vine growing in the Jura is seen at its best on Triassic and above all on Liassic hillslopes which have a good southwesterly aspect. The effect of the Bajocian-Aalenian flints, frequently associated with Liassic marls in surface screes, mixed with the star-shaped segments of silicified crinoids (the L'Étoile vineyard), has been held to be responsible for the amber taste specific to the white wines of the Jura, which "sometimes combine the taste of gunflint with the fragrance of flowering blackberry, with an after-taste of walnut and hazel" (Dumay, 1967). However all of this has yet to be demonstrated by soil chemistry.

Appellations d'origine

The regional Côtes du Jura appellation has been granted to specific vineyards lying from north of Arbois as far as Saint-Amour-Cuiseaux, on steeply sloping sites having a good aspect, and on the piedmont slopes.

More restricted Appellations d'origine contrôlleé have been granted to the best vineyards. These are:

— **Arbois** and **Arbois-Pupillin**, very fine red, rosé, white, and yellow rosé wines which age well.

— **L'Étoile**, a label known for its white wines and also for its amber and straw wines. The latter are made from chardonnay and savagnin grapes, dried on straw hurdles and made into wine at the beginning of winter. The straw wines have a high alcohol content (17 — 22°), are liqueur-like and have bouquet.

— **Château-Chalon**, a large area of amber wines obtained from savagnin blanc, which is harvested at the time of the first frosts. The wine from this must remain in the cask for at least six years, without ullaging, covered and developing an amber wine through the effect of a film of specific yeasts. Château-Chalon is only obtained from particular acreages in Château-Chalon, Méétru-le-Vignoble, Nevy and Domblans.

Itinerary

From Dole to Arbois

Leave Dole by the D 475 (fig. 27). Go to Sellières where you will enter what geologists know as the Jura. The rocks underlying the district belong

to the Trias and Lias (Black Jura), as can be seen alongside the road at **Montchauvrot** ①.

Continue along the N 83 for 10 km as far as **Plainoiseau** and then turn to the right onto **L'Étoile**, where the vineyards have clung to the hillslopes ② for over 700 years and produce dry white wine from pinot-chardonnay, poulsard and savagnin. Some amber wine and also the best sparkling wines of the Jura are made here.

Turn north again, as far as Saint-Germain, to visit **Arlay**, its chateau and vineyards ③. This is the fife of the counts of Chalon Arlay. Very typical delicate whites, reds, ambers and rosés are produced from the usual varieties, including chardonnay, which was imported here more than a thousand years ago, and is locally known as the melon d'Arlay ou gamay blanc.

Go by the D 120 to **Saint-Germain, Domblans and Voiteur**, and then **Nevy-sur- Seille** by the D 70 ④. From here one can see the Château-Chalon vineyards from the banks of the Seille not far from its source in the hollow of *Baume-les-Messieurs*, with its abbey (fig. 28).

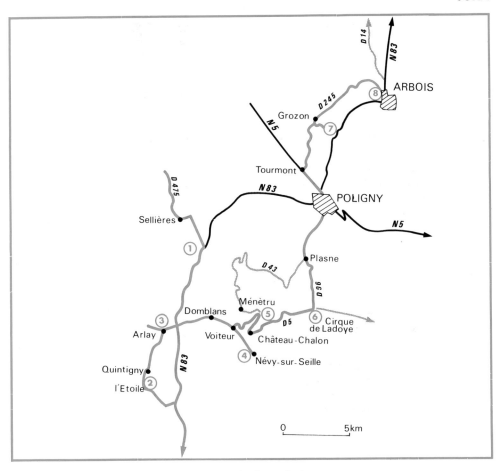

Fig. 27. Itinerary through the Côtes du Jura.

Return to Voiteur and climb to **Château-Chalon** (5). Here is the soil which produces the very special king of the amber wines, from a very late harvested at savagnin, which is left in the casks for at least six years. A film of specific yeasts forms on top of the wine and protects it indefinitely in cellars dug into the rock. The amber wine then develops its special rather dark amber colour. It has a strength of between 12 and 15° and its bouquet and flavour are reminiscent of walnut and plum. It is sold in bottles, called clavelins, containing 62 centilitres. Its flavour is so penetrating and special that it should not be drunk with other wines, whose merits it would overshadow. Not everybody appreciates it, but a meal with this wine alone and a main dish cooked in amber wine is an experience worth trying.

In passing, a word on the "straw wines", which should not be confused with the amber wine. These are wines from a "frozen" must, made into wine in February with grapes harvested in November and kept warm on straw. They are kept for 10 to 20 years in small oak casks and are sold in half- clavelins. It is very difficult to find these wines available commercially.

From Château-Chalon there is a magnificent view over the vineyards of Ménétru, Voiteur and the valley of the Seille, typical of the Côtes du Jura, in the Liassic Series and the Bajocian screes (fig. 28).

Take the D 5 to the east, as far as Granges-de-Ladoye, and a little further on there is a viewpoint on the right at the crossroads with the D 96 (6). The view over the **Cirque de Ladoye**, which is an offshoot from the famous blind valley of Baume-les-Messieurs, reveals a deep valley which cuts into the Bajocian limestone and the

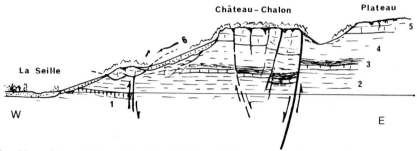

Fig. 28. — Interpretation of the site of Château-Chalon; a downthrown wedge between two parallel faults on the edge of the Jura plateau.

1. Limestones containing Gryphaea (Lower Lias); 2. Micaceous clays (Middle Lias); 3. "The Rock Bench", calcarenite (top of the Middle Lias); 4. Marls with limestone cobbles (Upper Lias); 5. Crinoidal limestones forming the resistant cap to the outlying butte of Château-Chalon and the plateau; 6. Limestone scree cover on the marly slopes.

Liassic marls. The straightness of the eastern wall suggests that it is controlled by a fault.

Take the D 96 to the north of Plasne. Several well-marked depressions can be seen along side the road; these are sink holes resulting from dissolution of the limestone (karst features).

Go down towards Poligny and leave the town westwards by the N 5. At Tourmont take the D 245 to the right as far as **Grozon** (fine Franche Comté houses) where there is a gypsum quarry 500 m to the south east ⑦. The gypsum is worked in almost horizontal galleries. An exposure provides a good section of the top of the Keuper (with gypsum bands and the "Two Metre Dolomite"), and of the Rhaetian containing Avicula contorta (a small lamellibranch similar to a mussel).

Return to Grozon and go as far as **Arbois**, by Vilette. The location of the Arbois district ⑧ is similar to that of Château-Chalon. The underlying geology consists of clayey marl formations of the Keuper and Lias, which are mixed at the foot of the slope with Bajocian limestone screes.

Wines of Côtes du Jura and gastronomy

The wines of the Jura are not only red, white, sparkling and rosé, but also amber and grey. A rainbow to make your mouth water, from early in the morning. Yield to the temptation of a fat Morteau sausage, washed down with a chardonnay d'Arbois white, after taking the precaution to choose an amber one. The day will seem all the better for it.

The marked character of the Jura whites comes from a typical vine of the region, savagnin, which is suitable for a whole range of dishes. This is the least known wine, but undeservedly so. White Arbois goes excellently with the regional Morbier cheese, which can be recognised by anybody because of its stripe.

There would seem to be some confusion between the rosé and the red wines of the Jura. In fact the variety used for the red wines of the Jura is poulsard, which itself has a light pink skin. Mixed with pinot, it acquires body and goes marvellously with grilled or even roast meat. As far as the rosé as such is concerned, it goes very well with a good Bresse chicken, nicely roasted under a crust of salt, or white meat.

You must not visit the Jura and Château-Chalon without meeting its famous amber wine, unique because no-one makes a better one, unique in its bouquet and flavour. The things which have been said about it! One good piece of advice, never have it served with foie gras, an all too frequent mistake. Avoid serving it cold and it will blend harmoniously with mushrooms or dishes with a sauce armoricaine. It is particularly flattered by lobster and sea and freshwater crayfish. Its extraordinary culinary qualities should be mentioned, particularly with reference to "coq au vin jaune".

And if you have the chance to be on the banks of the Loue in autumn, enjoy the intense and simple pleasure of gathering a few walnuts and buying a piece of one year old Comté cheese; you will know perfect happiness.

Above all do not make the mistake of leaving Arbois and its region without tasting that elixir of the Jura, the straw wine, which you will find in half bottles. Like a Sauternes, it should be served chilled, equally well as an apéritif in small glasses, or with roquefort or a dessert. Perhaps you would prefer a macvin, the ratafia of the Jura, as an apéritif — it goes marvellously with a chilled melon at the start of a meal.

BUGEY

The district and its soils

The Bugey is a natural unit, consisting of the southern part of the Jura chain. It is bounded on the west by the Ain, from Meximieux to Poncin, to the south by the transverse steep-sided valley of the Rhône, from Lagnieu, and on the east by its upper valley as far as Seyssel. It thus forms the southern point of the Jura and the south-eastern point of the département of Ain. Vines are scattered throughout the perimeter, seeking the best aspects at the foot of the hills. In the interior these quickly gain height, climbing to over 1 000 m, mainly because of the Upper Jurassic limestones, the summit of the Bugey being the Montagne de la Raie (1 217 m). Only the Cerdon district is well defined, but the label is shared by several other communes. The hills are mainly formed by marls, marly limestones and limestones of the Jurassic Series, from the Lias to the Tithonian, folded in a NW-SE direction in the central portion, and almost N-S in the north. Included with these are the edges of the alluvial terraces and molasse formations, particularly in the east.

The wines of the Bugey are wines from soils which differ appreciably from one another not only through the variety of the underlying geology itself, but also through the use of vines, aspect, method of wine-making, nature of the soil (in situ, slumped, slipped, its heterogeneity or lack of it, varying permeability, etc.), slope, and finally through the extent to which the soil has evolved. In addition to this the vines are very scattered and in the final analysis it is difficult to find one specific route through all the communes, of which there are a few dozen.

These wines, made from gamay and sometimes mondeuse, are mainly red wines with a strength of 9.5° and sometimes 10°, sometimes having a Villages label, and go well with the chicken with truffles of Valromey. There are also rosés, made from poulsard, gamay, pinot and mondeuse, which are light and also carry the Villages label with more than 9.5° (Virieu-le-Grand, Montagnieu, Manicle, Machuraz, Cerdon). The best known are the compliant dry white wines made with very ripe grapes, as at Seyssel, using only the roussette vine and a soil to which the fragrance of violets is attributed, the "Roussette du Bugey", or even sometimes a sparkling wine like "Cerdon".

Itinerary

To visit this region, coming from Lyon (fig. 29) take the Geneva road (N 84) as far as Meximieux (30 km). From there the climb to the nearby medieval village of **Pérouges** ①should not be missed. The wines of Bugey can be sampled here, at the Saint-Vincent vaults, but to enter the winegrowing area one must cross the Ain and go as far as **Ambérieu-en-Bugey** (13 km), which with several neighbouring communes produces typical whites, but above all reds.

We will retrace our steps, because it will first be necessary to make a detour towards the north, again by the Geneva road, to reach the village of **Cerdon** (20 km), which nestles among the first spurs of the Jura. There is a fine view of the area ②from the hairpin bend on the way up to the monument to the members of the Resistance, then on to Labalme, and, leaving the main road a little before Moulin-Chabaud, the village of Cerdon can be regained by the CD 11 which passes through

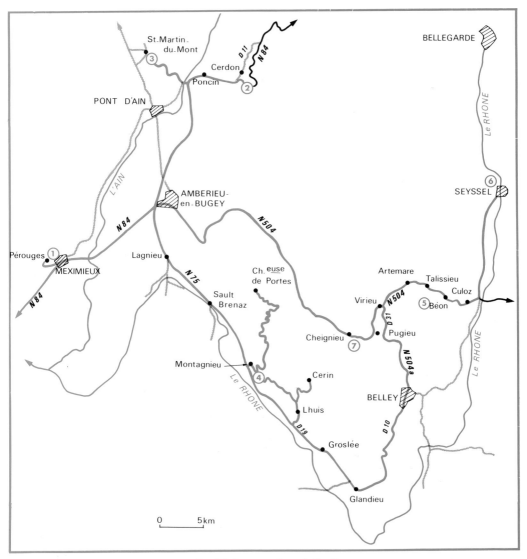

Fig. 29. Itinerary through the Bugey.

the terraced vines. Several varieties are used, but mècle dominates. The wines are white, but there are rosés too, with a pleasant hint of sparkle, which should be drunk chilled. They are much appreciated at Lyon, but sometimes do not travel well.

Returning towards Ambérieu, we can leave the main road after Poncin, for Neuville-sur-Ain and **Saint-Martin-du-Mont** ③. A sparkling white wine known by the name of "Gravelles" is made in this commune on the gentler slopes of the western foothills of the Jura.

From Ambérieu, at the Saint-Jean-de-Paris crossroads, take the Grenoble road (N 75), and the D 19 at Sault-Brénaz. This pretty route then follows the transverse steep sided valley (cluse) between the Rhône and the backs of the Bugey hills. Pass through **Montagnieu** ④, where light dry white wines, some of them sparkling, are produced together with the red Bugey wines at locations scattered all over the slope. As an alternative route, on leaving Montagnieu climb the western flank of the Bugey, through the woods and forest, to visit the site of Chartreuse-de-Portes, or, as a geological alternative, cross the folded relief of the Jurassic Series, reaching Lhuis and then **Cerin**, the French Solenhofen (excavations by the *Department of Earth Sciences at Lyon*. Late Jurassic fauna; permission required).

At Glandieu (41 km from Ambérieu) take the D 10 for Belley, to reach Pugieu and Virieu-le-Grand, and then Talissieu, Artemare and Culoz by the N 504. In this region ⑤, which has a southerly aspect, at the foot of the Valromey, the vines are scattered among other crops and provide the light dry "Bugey blanc" white wines from roussette, pinot and chardonnay grapes and the "Roussette du Bugey", mainly from roussette and altesse grapes.

Red wines however are also produced and the vines for these are scattered not only among the communes in the area but also throughout many other communes in the Bugey. The red "Vins du Bugey" are produced from gamay vines, and also rarely from mondeuse. These are lively light wines, with little colour, whose flavour used to be compared to that of some Bordeaux, although they have less subtlety. At the present time they are more reminiscent of some Beaujolais.

From there press on to **Seyssel** ⑥, 13 km from Culoz, where a valued Roussette is made from roussette vines, which are well suited by the brown soils of the fluvioglacial alluvium. The sandy slopes of the Tertiary molasse, which here rests against the heights of the Jura (Valromey and the eastern limb of the Grand Colombier Anticline), suit the molette vine, which with some chasselas (fendant or bon blanc), completes the range of varieties (see the Savoie itineraries).

To return, go back to Virieu-le-Grand and take the N 504. A **Cheignieu-la-Balme** ⑦ vines which were particularly famous in the past can be seen, because this is the homeland of Brillat-Savarin, whose sunny vineyard lies above Cheignieu-la-Balme, at the hamlet of Manicle-en-Valromey. Its growers, using old gamay, chardonnay and even pinot varieties, made a whole range of reds, rosés and whites, which "sparkled" in the glass. Manicle was praised by Martial and Pliny and it is known that the rich patricians of Rome had it sent to them in amphorae by the Roman occupants. Valromey means Valley of the Romans. Brillat-Savarin, the master epicure, treated his friends to "filet de boeuf clouté de truffes noires" sprinkled with his red or white Manicle, with the bouquet of violets, in the family house at Vieu in September.

The road then leads by the Cluse des Hôpitaux to Ambérieu-en-Bugey (33 km).

Wines and gastronomy

The Bugey is the homeland of the gastronome Brillat-Savarin, who wrote "to maintain that one should not have a change of wines is heresy; the tongue becomes saturated and after the third glass even the best wine evokes no more than a blunted sensation" (*in Publ. Syndicat des Vins du Bugey*, Belley, Ain). The whites of the Bugey, vital and fragrant, are drunk chilled, at the beginning of a meal or on their own. The thoroughbred chardonnay variety may be associated with altesse to yield the often mellow Roussette, which is pleasant for all occasions. The sparkling wines including Cerdon and some Montagnieu, are best appreciated before a meal rather than after it, and above all at receptions and functions. Gamay, fruity and light, is drunk rather cold, on all occasions. Pinot, fine and full bodied, ages well.

The Gamay of the Coteaux du Lyonnais, the Bugey and other localities in the region may, in addition to what has been said already, be used like Beaujolais, and for the same reason, for cooking sausage or meat "à la lyonnaise", following whispered recipes and notes which all would like to own.

Geology

Guide géologique Jura (Geological guide to the Jura) (1975), by P. Chauve et coll, Masson éd., Paris (*see* in particular the introduction and routes 2, 3 and 9). Caire A. (1978). Bajocian flints and the wines of the Jura. ASAC, 4, p. 32-35.

Oenology

Callot G. et Labau G. (1977). Geological study of the Revermont winegrowing district, Poligny-Arbois sector (Jura). *Inst. nat. Rech. agr. Serv. Sols. Montpellier*, 57 pp. appendices and maps.

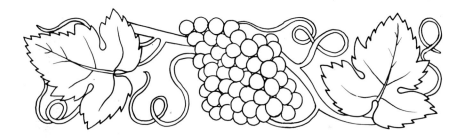

SEDIMENTARY ROCKS

a²	Recent Quaternary
a¹	Older Quarternary
t	Glacial deposits
p	Pliocene
	Miocene
	Oligocene
e² e	Middle and Upper Eocene Eocene (undifferentiated)
c² c	Upper Cretaceous Cretaceous (undifferentiated)
c¹	Lower Cretaceous Urgonian

S	Silky shale
J³	Upper Jurassic (Malm)
J² J	Middle Jurassic (Dogger) Jurassic (undifferentiated)
Jˡ	Lower Jurassic (Lias)
t² t	Middle Triassic (Muschelkalk) Triassic (undifferentiated)
r	Permian
h⁴	Stephanian
h³ h	Westphalian (sensu stricto) Carboniferous (undifferentiated)

METAMORPHIC AND PLUTONIC ROCKS

ζ ζζ	Gneiss Undifferentiated crystalline schists
γ γᵇ	Granite Biotite granite

OPHIOLITIC ROCKS

Mesozoic

σ ω	Alpine ophiolites Pyrenean ophiolites

DEMARCATIONS

⧄	Vins de Savoie

Fig. 30. Geological map and demarcations of the winegrowing districts in Savoie.

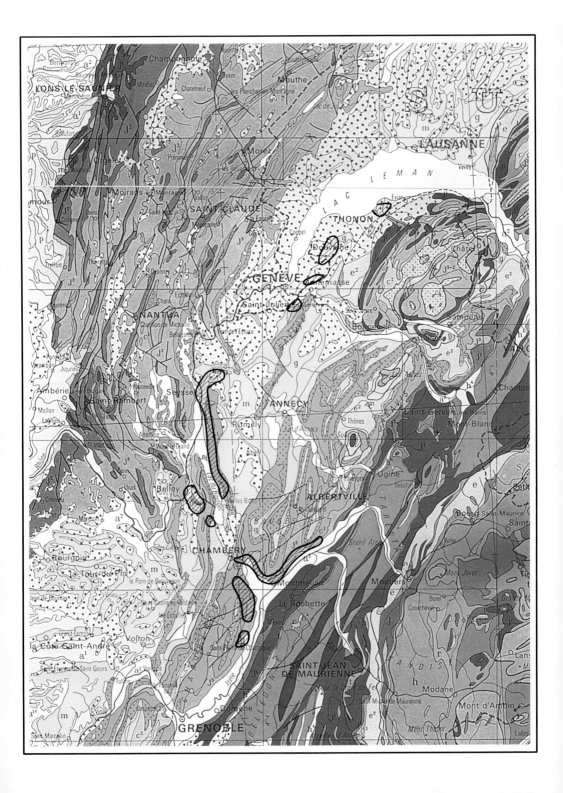

Since the Roman period, when the vines and wines of Allobrogia were already valued at Rome, and particularly since the Middle Ages, vines have been a part of the agricultural landscape of Savoie. Lovingly grown, these are found on all sunny well protected slopes at low and medium altitudes.

We will only consider here the winegrowing areas which have given rise, since 1973, to the Appellations d'origine contrôlées "Vin de Savoie" and "Roussette de Savoie", which are dominated by dry white wines, and the wines of Seyssel and Crépy, which received their classification at an earlier date. These labels extend over the départements of Savoie, Haute- Savoie and a small fringe in the départements of Ain and Isère (fig. 30).

Forming "islands" or "strips" they lie from north to south, from Lake Geneva to the valley of the Isère:

— the winegrowing districts of the lower Chablais (Ripaille, Marignan, Crépy),
— the winegrowing districts of the Arve valley (Bonneville, Ayze),
— the winegrowing districts of the Alpine foreland, or the Rhone valley (Frangy, Seyssel, the Chautagne region, Marestel, Monthoux, etc),
— the winegrowing districts of the Cluse de Chambéry, Combe de Savoie and north Grésivaudan (Apremont, Monterminod, Chignin, Arbin, Cruet, Sainte-Marie-d'Alloix, etc.)

Elsewhere vineyards go well up the valleys of the Tarentaise and Maurienne, where small winegrowing areas, "balancing" on slopes exposed to the sun, yield wines which are more appreciated for the tradition which they represent than for their intrinsic quality.

This applies for example to the winegrowing districts of the lower Tarentaise, including that of Cevins, pressed against the southern slope of a glacial bar. It also applies to the winegrowing districts on the banks of the Arc, in the middle Maurienne, the regions of Saint-Avre, Châtel d'Hermillon, Pontamafrey, Saint-Julien, and even Orelle, located on the outwash fans of torrents and screes, where the vines are disappearing as a result of fluoride pollution of the valley and accelerated desertification of the estates.

Vineyards and their soils

Major geological units and their relief

The winegrowing area of Savoie girdles the Alpine chain. On the geological map we can distinguish:

— *the Alpine foreland* (still called the Jura), consisting of anticlinal chains of Jurassic and Cretaceous limestones (Salèves, Mandallaz, Montagne d'Age, Vuache, Gros Foug, Mont du Chat, etc), separated by enormous synclines of Tertiary molasse (the continental "red molasse" of broadly Oligocene age, the marine conglomeratic gravelly-sandy molasse of the Middle to Upper Miocene), with the anticlines overthrusting the synclines towards the west,

— *the sub-Alpine chains*, including, from north to south, the massifs of Haut-Giffre, Bornes, Bauges and Chartreuse, stratigraphically equivalent to the Dauphiné-Helvetic group thrusted onto the foreland,

— *the Chablais Pre-Alps*, resulting from the piling up of internal nappes.

The geomorphology is linked with both lithology and the nature of the tectonics. Thus the Alpine foreland shows primary relief, where the competent limestones of the Upper Jurasic and Lower Cretaceous form characteristic anticlinal arches, often box folded (Gros Foug, Mont du Chat), which dominate the gently undulating country of the molasse synclines. In the sub-Alpine massifs, relief is primary to the west, where the Neocomian marly limestones are poorly developed. To the east on the other hand, where the marly limestones thicken, the relief is inverted, with perched synclines, like those of the Dent d' Arclusaz and the Granier, on the edge of the Combe de Savoie, standing out among the gentle Lower to Middle Jurassic terrains in front of the crystalline massif of Belledonne-Grand Arc.

Glaciers have left a strong imprint, opening up major valleys (Rhône, Arve, Isère, Arc), excavating steep-sided transverse valleys (cluses) (Chambéry, Annecy) and overdeepening lake basins (Lakes Geneva, Annecy, Bourget, Aiguebelette). These erosional features are associated with sedimentary phenomena which have resulted in major Quaternary deposits which play a part in the geomorphology and the nature of the soils.

The winegrowing districts have developed mainly on the light well-drained soils of the limestone-rich Quaternary formations. These are predominantly interglacial (Frangy) to postglacial (Ripaille) fluviatile alluvials, leached pebbly tills (Crépy, Seyssel), limestone to marly-limestone screes (Combe de Savoie, the foot of the Mont du Chat massif), and weathered molasse sand (Seyssel, Chautagne, Ayze). In many cases the subsoil of the slopes is heterogeneous, with a mixture of surface formations.

Calcium particularly favours jacquère vines and the keeping qualities of wines originating from altesse and red mondeuse.

Climate and insolation

Savoie has a continental climate with strong oceanic influences. Precipitation is abundant, particularly on the high ground to the west, between 1 200 and 2 200 mm of rain per year, and the mean temperatures are low, although with a hot indian summer, the severity of the climate increasing with altitude. These conditions are fundamentally unfavourable to the ripening of grapes, and we are on the limits of the area in which vines can be cultivated.

Nevertheless, because of the barrier of the mountain chains of the foreland which form a screen against precipitation, the orientation of some valleys, which offers optimum exposure to the sun on one slope, the thermal regulator of the major lakes, and valley breezes which prevent excessive cloud cover, there are regions with a rainfall of less than 1 100 mm in an altitude range between 250 and 500 m where annual insolation is of the order of 1 600 hours. Here selected winegrowing areas have developed, particularly on slopes with a good aspect where the sun reaches from the morning onwards. A southerly and south-easterly orientation is the best, but the western face of some spurs can yield remarkable wines such as Chautagne, on the western bank of Lake Bourget, to the north of Brison-les-Oliviers.

Vines, vineyards and wines

At the present time the winegrowing district occupies some 8 600 hectares, with an overall output of 450 000 hectolitres of wine, including 1 200 hectares of AOC Vins de Savoie (70 hectares at Seyssel and 85 hectares at Crépy), equivalent to 73 000 hectolitres of classified wines.

Savoyard peasants have always wanted to have their own plots of vines and the mountain people therefore came down to cultivate their acreage in the valleys, sheltering for a few hours or a few days in their "sartos" (huts in the vineyards), like the "baujus" of the Bauges massif, on the slopes of the Combe de Savoie. These days the winegrowing area is still divided up into a large number of plots and more than 50% of Savoie wines are made in private cellars and are sold by the growers who have mastered the technique of growing and wine making while maintaining traditions: "A la sinta Gueta, la man a la gogueta" (To Saint Agatha[1], billhook in hand).

Vine varieties

— Red varieties

• *mondeuse rouge*, still known as the Savoy Vine or Savoie Vine, which probably originated locally, (Allobrogia). This is a vigorous variety which grows well on limestone scree,

• *gamay noir*, with a white juice. Originally from the Beaujolais, it is mainly used in Chautagne, yielding full-bodied wines,

• *étraire*, from Saint-Ismier (Isère); A vigorous variety, still used in the Grésivaudan.

— White varieties

• *jacquère*, still called the vine of the Abymes de Myans, following its planting on the Granier rock slide after 1248. This is a vigorous rustic variety perfectly suited to a harsh climate and cold soils. It is by far the most widely cultivated, and is spreading.

• *altesse*, also called roussette, a variety which legend has it is a tokay- furmin brought back from Cyprus on the marriage Anne of Lusignan, the daughter of the King of Cyprus, to Louis, Duke of Savoy in 1432. With poor productivity and a liking for sloping ground, altesse yields quality wines with a high alcohol content.

• *mondeuse blanche*, or roussette d'Ayze, a slope-loving variety, which yields sugar-rich musts,

• *gringet*, used only in the Arve valley. This vine, of the traminer family, is the basis of the semi-sparkling and sparkling Ayze wines. It is supposed to have been brought back from Italy by Savoyard bishops returning from a council,

---

[1] A Sicilian saint, the patron of wine growers, celebrated on the 5th of February.

• *roussanne*, also called *barbin de Savoie*, a variety originating from Drôme (l'Hermitage vineyard), which yields the Bergeron de la Combe de Savoie, with a high alcohol content,

• *chasselas*, also known as "fendant roux" or "vert" or "bon blanc", precocious and strong, used on the shores of Lake Geneva, both in France and Switzerland.

Finally mention should be made of the use of the chardonnay or petite Sainte-Marie, molette, aligoté, malvoisie or velteliner rosé, pinot noir, cabernet, persan (prinsens or beccu) etc., varieties in small areas.

Winegrowing districts: their history, soils, wines and dishes

The lower Chablais winegrowing district (altitude: 390 to 550 m)

Since the 13th century the monks of the abbey of Notre-Dame-de-Filly, near Sciez, have cultivated vines on Mont Crépy, making wine on the equisite Crépy "fine lees". Also, according to a tradition, which is probably fallacious, the Duke of Savoy, Amadeo VIII, a hermit and future anti-pope (Felix V), when in retirement at the Château de Ripaille between 1434 and 1439 greatly appreciated the local wine, which gave rise to the expression "faire ripaille" (to have a good blowout), used by La Fontaine and Voltaire.

The winegrowing district spreads over the south bank of Lake Geneva, from Évian to Annemasse. It consists of isolated units, of small overall surface area in view of the mediocre climatic conditions, which are, however tempered by the proximity of the lake. The vineyards, which are only planted with chasselas, are located on medium to steep slopes, facing north west and west of the Würm plateau, where the leached till is pebbly. This applies to the vineyards in the communes of Publier and Marin, on the south west edge of the Gavot plateau, Sciez (Hameau de Marignan), Massongy, Ballaison-Douvaine-Loisin (Crépy winegrowing district), the northern, western and south western edges of the molasse dome of Mont de Boisy, Ville-la-Grand, on the Swiss frontier, alongside the late Würm channel borrowed by the Foron, and Bossey, against the brow of the Salève, in contact with the limestones screes of the Geneva moraines.

As far as the Château Ripaille district is concerned, this is located close to the lake, on the 10 m pebbly fluviolacustrine terrace of the Dranse delta.

The wines produced are white:
— AOC Vin de Savoie: light, a little heady, lively and vigorous;
— AOC Vin de Sa voie, cru Ripaille: quiet, easy-going, having the flavour of sweet almonds;
— AOC Vin de Savoie, cru Marignan: dry, fruity, with a taste of gunflint and hazel nut;
— AOC Crépy: dry, exquisite, with the fragrance of May blossom and the flavour of hazel nut and gunflint.

All these light and diuretic wines go perfectly with fish from the lake (bass, fry, etc.) and seafood.

The Arve valley winegrowing district (altitude: 470 to 700 m)

Planted from the Middle Ages onwards, this is located on the right bank of the Arve, on the bastions of the Chablais Pre-Alps. With a southerly aspect, the district lies partly on molasse and partly on the better drained tills and small outwash fans.

The AOC are restricted to the communes of Marignier, Ayze, Bonneville and Côte-d'Hyot. Gringet (70%) and mondeuse blanche varieties are planted together.

The AOC Vin de Savoie, cru Ayze, is limited to the slopes of better aspect. It is a light, naturally semi-sparkling, extra-dry white wine obtained either by spontaneous fermentation or by a second fermentation, gringet bringing flavour, freshness and character, and mondeuse blanche colour and versatility. AOC Vins de Savoie are produced on the lower slopes.

Of great value as aperitifs, these wines go pleasantly with fry from the lakes and fondue savoyarde.

The winegrowing districts of the alpine foreland or Rhône valley

These correspond to the Jura and molasse formations of Savoie.

• **The Usses valley winegrowing district** (altitude: 350 to 450 m). It is very ancient (a charter from the abbey of Cluny mentions it in 1039), and is highly valued, as emphasised by J. J. Rousseau in his "Confessions", when he paid a visit on the 14 March 1728 to M. de Fontverre, the curé of Confignon, ". . . part of Savoy two leagues from Geneva . . . and its excellent Frangy wine which it seemed to me spoke so irresistibly for him that I durst not quieten such a good host . . .". Likewise, early in the 18th century, Saint Francois de Sales requested that in payment for a sermon given at Seyssel he should be "given a cask of Desingy wine . . ."

The winegrowing area, which is of little extent but very scattered, is located in the communes of Bassy, Challonges, Chaumont, Chassenaz, Clarafond, Desingy, Franclens, Frangy, Musièges, Usinens and Vanzy. There the thick Würm tills (the plateaux of the Semine to the north and Desingy to the south) cover Miocene molasse and alluvials of the Riss-Würm interglacial preserved in deep channels. The steep slopes of the Usses valley and the adjacent streams, facing south, at heights below 500 m bear classified vineyards producing:

— The AOC Roussette de Savoie, cru Frangy, which comes almost exclusively from altesse vines growing on the interglacial alluvials; ". . . of a clear amber colour, Roussette in time gives off a remarkable aroma, a mixture of hazel nuts, violets, honey and almonds",

— The AOC Vin de Savoie and Roussette, corresponding to vines located on the well-drained less clayey tills.

• **The Seyssel winegrowing district** (altitude: 260 to 400 m): well developed since the 14th century through the efforts of the monks, the winegrowing district extends over both banks of the Rhône and the AOC are located in the communes of Corbonod (Ain), Seyssel (Ain) and Seyssel (Haute-Savoie). The underlying rock consists of the Miocene marine Molasse of the Seyssel Syncline covered by weathered sands, the Würm till and recent alluvium from the Rhône and Fier. These produce:

— The AOC Seyssel or Roussette de Seyssel, produced from altesse vines. This is a gentle accommodating thoroughbred wine having the fragrance of violets and the taste of bergamot, of a fine straw yellow colour.

— The AOC Seyssel mousseux, produced by the Champagne method from must obtained from altesse (at least 10%) and molette grapes, growing on sandy molasse: amber and bright, with a hint of violets, this sparkling wine is available in brut, extra dry and demi-sec.

● **The Chautagne winegrowing district** (altitude: 250 to 450 m). "There is in iSavoie a small corner of ground which could hold its own for fertility with any which we possess in France. This is the Chautagne . . . '', says the Count of Resie in his "Voyage to Chambéry and the Waters of Aix" in 1847.

This region, which has a favourable climate, extends from the confluence of the Fier and the Rhône to the north, to the north-eastern shore of Lake Bourget (communes of Chindrieux, Ruffieux, Motz, Serrières).

This forms the front of the Gros Foug Anticline whose limestones of the Malm and Lower Cretaceous overthrust the Miocenes molasses of the Seyssel Syncline. The vines are located either on the limestone screes at the foot of the hills (Chindrieux), or on the molasse (Ruffieux, Serrières), or on the lateral moraines above the marshy alluvial plain of the Rhône (Motz, Serrières), or again on the alluvials of the Fier. The aspect is fully to the west. This is the domain of the red wines grouped under the AOC Vin de Savoie, cru Chautagne. The main vine is gamay, giving rich purplish-ruby wines, full bodied, with substance, warmth, a flowery bouquet and a fruity flavour which goes perfectly with meat and game and the local cheeses.

● **The winegrowing district of the western side of the Mont du Chat spur**, within the borders of Savoie and the Bugey (altitude: 250 to 560 m). The winegrowing district around Lucey has been famous since the 14th and 15th centuries. Belonging to the suzerainty of the Counts of Savoy and managed by the castellan of Pierre-Châtel (Cluse d'Yenne), this princely district yielded wines which were exclusively reserved for the tables of sovereigns, whence their popular name as "their Highnesses' (altesses) white wines", and the name of the variety brought from Cyprus.

The vineyards are to be found in the communes of Saint-Jean-de-Chevelu, Billième, Jongieux, Lucey and Yenne. These form the western limb of the Jurassic Mont Landard — Mont de la Charve — Mont du Chat Anticline, with a faulted Jurassic core, which is upended or overturned and overthrusts the Miocene molasses of the Yenne-Novalaise Molasse Syncline. These structures are partly masked upslope by screes of the Dogger and Malm, and downslope by Würm tills. They are of a predominantly westerly aspect. This, par excellence, is the domain of the altesse variety. The following wines are produced:

— The AOC Roussette de Savoie, crus Marestel and Monthoux: restricted to steep slopes covered by limestone scree the vineyards, which are planted with altesse, have a very low productivity (25 hl/ha), yield remarkable wines, with a natural alcohol content (11 to 13°), aristocratic, full, harmonious, with a flavour which develops with age: hazel nuts, violets, honey, walnuts;

— The AOC Roussette de Savoie and Vin de Savoie, located on well-drained screes and pebbly tills. These are white wines from altesse, mondeuse blanche and chardonnay (50% maximum) vines, or red wines from gamay and mondeuse rouge (Monthoux) vines.

Altesse wines go well with freshwater fish dishes (pollan, trout, char, lake fry, etc.).

The winegrowing districts of the Cluse de Chambéry, Combe de Savoie and North Grésivaudan

• **The winegrowing district associated with the Granier rock slide** (altitude: 290 — 500 m): In the night of the 24 November 1248 the northern flank of Mont Granier, the northern end of the eastern Chartreuse Syncline, collapsed. This catastrophe swallowed up five parishes, including that of Saint-André, comprising sixteen villages and hamlets, and caused the death of more than 5,000 people.

This gigantic collapse involved the Urgonian limestone cliff, the Hauterivian marl and Valanginian limestone, all carried along on a vast landslide of underlying water-saturated Valanginian marls. The result was a 12 km2 mud flow which came to a halt against the drumlins along the axis of Cluse de Chambéry (Wïrm drumlins of Myans). This chaotic deposit, the Abymes de Myans, in which limestone blocks of all sizes are enclosed in a marly-limestone matrix, covers the edge of the Alpine trough, from the Neocomian to the Malm, and Quaternary tills and outwash fans.

The winegrowing district is located on the slide and in its immediate vicinity (communes of Apremont, Les Marches, Saint-Badolph, Myans and Chapareillan). The main vine used is jacquère. It yields very clear, light and diuretic dry white wines, with the taste of gunflint which must be drunk young. Treatment on fine lees may make them exquisite. The AOC depend on the nature of the ground, aspect and altitude. These are:

— The AOC Vin de Savoie, cru Abymes, with an easterly aspect, on the most chaotic lower part of the rock slide,

— The AOC Vin de Savoie, cru Apremont, located on the slopes below an altitude of 500 m, with an easterly and south easterly aspect, and a steep slope corresponding to the upper part of the slide and adjacent Neocomian formations more or less in situ,

— The AOC Vin de Savoie, comprising all the rest of the area having a favourable aspect and predominantly underlain by well-drained tills.

• **The winegrowing districts of Combe de Savoie and the north slope of the Cluse de Chambéry** (altitude: 290 to 500 m). The Cluse de Chambéry has always been a preferred route between the countries of France and Italy, and vines have been planted there since Roman times. The Monterminod (Mons esmeraldi) vineyard is mentioned as early as 11th century in a charter for a land grant to the venerable Odilo, abbot of Cluny, so as to "give comfort and pleasure" to the good monks of that abbey, who had just founded a daughter house on the banks of Lacus castellionis (Lake Bourget).

Likewise the *Mons amelioratus* (Montmélian) vineyard is mentioned in 1180, and the Counts of Savoy have obtained wine from there since the Middle Ages, having their vines at the foot of the castle in the place called Cornavin.

These days the winegrowing district extends from Fréterive, in the northeast, to Saint-Alban-Leysse, in the southwest, girdling the southern end of the Bauges. Located at the bottom of the slopes, on well-drained steep hillsides, it faces south. The underlying rock consists of the limestone and marly limestone screes of the Malm cliffs (the Chignin and Montmélian vineyards, at the foot of the Savoyarde, for example), particularly upslope. Further down the screes change into Würm tills and the outwash fans from torrents (Saint-Pierre-d'Albigny, Saint-Alban- Leysse).

This is the domain of the white wines obtained from jacquère and altesse, for Roussette de Monterminod, and roussanne for Bergeron, as well as the red wines obtained mainly from the local mondeuse rouge vine. There are numerous AOC and the localities correspond to the various communes. Thus there are:

— The AOC Vin de Savoie, crus Saint-Jeoire-Prieuré, Chignin, Montmélian, Arbin, Cruet, Saint-Jean-de-la-Porte, where the soils are mainly derived from screes;
— The AOC Vin de Savoie, applying to all the communes, with different aspects and till or alluvial soils;
— The AOC Roussette de Savoie, cru Monterminod, located on the leached tills which rest on the Berriasian marly limestones of the Saint-Alban-Leysse heights;
— The AOC Vin de Savoie, cru Chignin-Bergeron or Bergeron, restricted to the very steep south-facing limestone screes of the communes of Chignin, Francin and Montmélian.

Some of these wines are very well known; we would mention as an example:

— Chignin, a dry white wine, of a brilliant transparent amber colour, the flavour of hazel nuts, light and compliant, to be drunk straight away, exquisite if prepared on fine lees;
— Bergeron, or Roussanne white, dry and generous, having a high natural alcohol content (11 — 13°), a delicious bouquet, and a distinction worthy of the great wines of France;
— Mondeuse, the best localities for which are at Arbin and Saint-Jean-de- la-Porte, on the screes containing more limestone. With a purple colour Mondeuse has a special bouquet in which the fragrance of strawberries, raspberries and violets mingle as it ages.

As a result of their diversity, these wines from the Combe de Savoie can accompany a whole meal: dry white wines obtained from jacquère served as an aperitif, then with seafood, fish, fondue savoyarde and "diots" (Savoyard sausages), Mondeuse goes with meat, game and cheeses, particularly Tome, Beaufort and Reblochon, and finally Bergeron is equally well appreciated with the entrée as with the dessert.

Itineraries

A few route descriptions will aid discovery of the wines of Savoie and the soils which give them birth. The complex geological contexts and the large number of isolated areas make it necessary to consider three itineraries. Routes 1 and 3 are similar to those recommended in the already published regional geological guides for the Dauphiné Alps and the Savoy Alps, and in the future guide to Alemanian Switzerland and the Chablais. In addition to this there is in Savoie a route which is marked by the name " Route des Vins" which can be used to travel among the vineyards; routes 2 and 3 attempt to keep to this as closely as possible.

Route 1: From Annecy to Thonon: the vineyards of the Arve Valley and of the Bas Chablais (Fig. 31)

Take the A 41 motorway in the direction of Geneva-Chamonix, or the N 203 towards Bonneville. There the roads follow the molasse area lying between the Jura spurs of Mandallaz and Salève to the west, and the overthrust of the Bornes subalpine massif to the east, marked by the frontal swells of the Parmelan and the

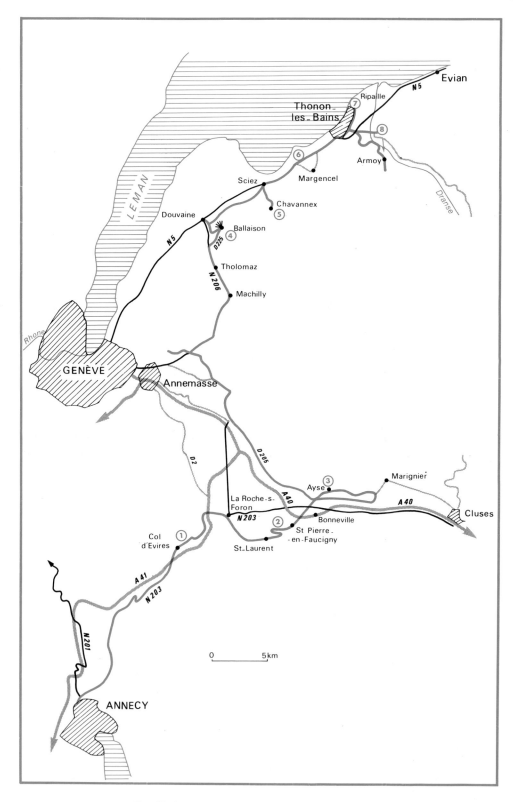

Fig. 31. Itinerary in Savoie, from Annecy to Thonon.

Sous-Dine plateau. The continental Oligocene marly sandstone molasse can be seen on the slopes, partly obscured by boulder clays. All of this is unstable, whence the great number of drainage works.

After passing the Col d'Evires (810 m) the view spreads over the Arve valley and the Chablais Pre-Alps which cut off the horizon ①. **At La-Roche-sur-Foron** the D 27 leads to Saint-Laurent, in a moraine landscape. When dropping down towards **Saint-Pierre-en-Faucigny**, stop at the first large hairpin for a view to the north ②, which includes the Ayze winegrowing district[1].

From west to east one can see the front of the lower Pre-Alps, with the wooded ridge of the Voirons Flysch, the hills of Faucigny, consisting of ultra-Helvetic flysch containing enormous schuppen forming the chaotic (Jurassic and Cretaceous) cliffs which overlook Bonneville, the Môle massif, corresponding to the median Pre-Alps (complex folding, particularly in the Jurassic). All this is thrusted over the sub-alpine flysch, the Oligocene grey molasse (Bonneville Grit) and the red molasse, which form the base for the relief and are masked to a greater or lesser extent by screes and till. Here is located the winegrowing district which extends to the east as far as the outwash fan of the Giffre. In this direction the syncline of the La Brèche nappe (Pointe de Marcelly) can be seen in the background.

At Bonneville, take the D 19 as far as Marignier and return to the west by the D 6 and by **Aize** ③. Observe the large numbers of small vines terraced on the autochthonous molasse, and taste the Roussette d'Ayze on the owners' premises. Return to Findrol by the N 205.

Go in the direction of Thonon, via Bonne. In this way one reaches the lower Chablais plateau, which is covered by Würm moraines from the Rhône glacier. For a little while after La Bergue the road follows the late-Würm Cranves-Sales channel cut by meltwater.

The N 206 and D 150 lead to Ville-la-Grand, the eastern suburb of Annemasse, located at the mouth of a second channel which rises towards Machilly. The D 15, towards Juvigny, follows the Swiss frontier, marked by boundary stones dating from 1816, and can be used to cross the winegrowing area on pebbly tills resting on the north bank of the channel, which is crossed again before reaching Saint-Cergues, dominated to the east by the Voirons.

Take the N 206 as far as Tholomaz, then the D 225 to Ballaison. Here we enter the **Crépy** winegrowing district ④. The pebbly till containing scattered erratic blocks covers the south west end of Mont de Boisy. Descend towards Douvaine. Before visiting the estate of the Grande Cave de Crépy and tasting the Crépy Goutte d'Or there is a panoramic view: to to north and northwest over the high Jura chain and the Swiss molasse plain in which the lake is set; to the west and the southwest, over Geneva and, further away, over the Rhône gap at Fort-l'Écluse, between Vuache and Crêt-d'Eau; to the south and southeast, over Salève, the Bornes molasse plateau and the subalpine front and finally, to the east, over the Voirons ridge.

Go in the direction of Chilly, Massongy and Sciez at the foot of Mont de Boisy. Stop at Marignan to taste the wine on the growers' premises. Go 1 km along the D 1 towards **Chavannex**: at the first bends observe the outcrop of coarse sandy molasse ⑤.

Return to Sciez and take the N 5. On the edge of Cinq-Chemins a quarry demonstrates the cross-bedded alluvials of the Thonon terraces, disturbed by a small tillite channel due to glacial readvance (crystalline erratic blocks can be seen at the entrance to the workings).

---

[1] A more complete view can be obtained from Mont Saxonnex. See the Guide des Alpes (Savoie-Dauphiné), éd. Masson, p. 49.

At **Margencel** crossroads[1] ⑥, there is a view over the Allinges dome, the eastern end of the Voirons unit, the Médianes front, with the Mont Hermone fold, and in the far distance the Dent d'Oche and Pic de Mémise.

On entering **Thonon** take Boulevard Le Corsent to the left towards the port. The road follows the 30 m terrace and then descends to the port before arriving opposite **Château de Ripaille** on the 10 m terrace ⑦. Visit the chateau and the vineyard, taste the Cru Ripaille. There is a view to the south east: in the foreground the 30 m terrace, in the middle ground the moraine plateau of the Gavot country, and on the horizon the median Pre- Alps with the Dent d'Oche.

The D 902 towards Châtel can be used to climb the fan of the Dranse, and then to enter the gorges between the Gavot and Ormoy plateaux. At the bridge there is a fine view of the Demoiselles, capped earth pillars in the tillite. The Dranse conglomerate, corresponding to Riss-Würm interglacial alluvial overlying the Riss blue boulder clays, can be seen at the Thonon 6 km kilometer stone.

Return to the edge of Thonon and take the D 26 towards Armoy. The road rises over the Thonon alluvial terraces which form a staircase and are worked in several quarries.

There is a scenic stop at a height of 556 m, with a view over the Dranse delta and over the *Marin et Publier vineyard* located on the leached tillites of the Gavot country ⑧.

The D 35 towards Le Lyaud and the GR 5 lead to the kettle of the Vua Bénit. The water level in this deep depression corresponds to the level of the water table in the alluvials and is made use of downslope, at Les Blaves and the La Versoie hot spring.

Return to Annecy going behind the Allinges dome, through Bons et Findrol.

Route 2. From Annecy to Chambéry: the vineyards of the Alpine foreland (Frangy, Seyssel, Chautagne, Marestel, etc) (fig. 32)

Leave Annecy by the N 508 in the direction of Bellegarde. After having crossed the Fier, which is set into the Continental molasse, one reaches the late-glacial Meythet plain.

At Chaumontet the road enters between the Mandallaz spurs to the north and the Montagne d'Age spurs to the south, displaced sinistrally by the major Vuache transcurrent fault. Carry on towards Frangy, following the valleys of the Petites et Grandes Usses. The Würm till masks the molasse in which Riss-Würm interglacial alluvials are embedded at Sallenôves (quarries). At the Douattes bridge, the Usses cut the Le Mont Urgonian, separated from the Vuache by the transcurrent fault, into gorges. At Frangy take the D 310 as far as Planaz where the Roussette de Frangy from the vineyard planted on the gravels of the Riss-Würm interglacial can be tasted ①.

Going via Desingy and Clermont (D 310 and D 31) and the western flank of the Rumilly Molasse Syncline (Miocene marine coarse sandy molasse) one reaches the cluse which cuts into the Gros Foug anticline at Saint-André- Val-de-Fier. The section, along the D 14, shows a box-type structure, the vertical dip of the western limb with stretched strata and the stratigraphical sequence of Jura facies, from the Oxfordian to the Urgonian ②. This can be investigated quickly at the western end (parking in the entrance to the EDF roadway). Here, from west to east there are:

---

[1] The conglomeratic flysch facies can be seen in the quarry of the Aérospatiale holiday camp by making a detour to the edge of Allinges.

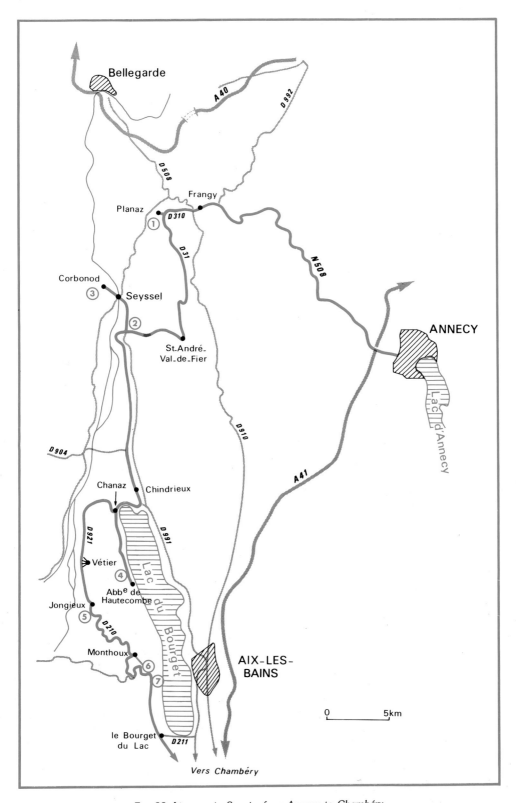

Fig. 32. Itinerary in Savoie, from Annecy to Chambéry.

— a first barrier, Urgonian sub-reefal limestone of Barremian-Aptian age (first tunnel);

— a depression: limestones containing flint, sometimes glauconitic and marly limestones containing cobbles, of Hauterivian age;

— a second barrier: reddish bioclastic limestones containing Alectryonia sp., of Valanginian age (second tunnel);

— a second depression: bedded clay limestones and multiply folded coal— bearing marls corresponding to marine littoral deposits or laguno-lacustrine deposits, representing the Upper Berriasian (Vions Formation);

— a third barrier bounding a large quarry to the west: fine limestones of "false marble" facies (Middle Berriasian);

— a third depression, passing eastwards into the quarry face: these are pale limestones with red and green marly seams and joints, containing breccia fragments and small black pebbles belonging to the Purbeckian (here the Lower Berriasian), an regressive facies marked by marine, brackish and lacustrine horizons. To the east the more massive benches correspond to marine limestones of the Portlandian, which are often dolomitic;

— a fourth very massive barrier: dolomitic reef limestones of Late Kimmeridgian age; an EDF dam has its foundations in these which, overturned and more vertical, bend over the road to form the anticlinal arch;

— a widening of the cluse: bedded, sublithographic, multiply folded limestones of Early Kimmeridgian and Oxfordian age containing ammonites.

Return to the western mouth of the cluse. The Urgonian cliff dominates a scree zone which masks its relationships with a small outcrop which can be seen to the right of the EDF roadway. These are Limnea limestones, passing into reddish and greenish sandstones and marls with recurrent limestones. This, upended and with a westerly dip, corresponds to the base of the continental Oligocene molasse which rests comformably on the Urgonian further to the north.

Going further to the west a retaining wall masks the outcrops for 100 metres, and then glauconitic sands with small pebbles appear at a housing estate. This is marine Burdigalian, with thickening banks and increasing coarseness to the west, as the dip decreases.

We leave at the confluence of the Fier and the Rhône, along the axis of the Seyssel Syncline overthrusted by the Gros Foug Anticline (a shear feature at depth), dominated to the west by the limestone mass of the Grand Colombier. Going north, towards **Seyssel** (Haute-Savoie and Ain) and Corbonod, a visit may be made to the vineyard located on the molasse and tillites to taste the Roussettes and Mousseux on the owners' premises ③.

Take the D 991 to the south, following the left bank of the Rhône (hydrological corrective work by the *Compagnie Nationale du Rhône*). We thus enter the Chautagne, lying in front of the Gros Foug. The serried vines climb the slope (screes, molasses, tills). At Ruffieux (Saumont crossroads) the Chautagne cooperative vaults allow tasting of the local wines, including Gamay.

At the southern exit from Chindrieux the D 914 follows the northern shore of Lake Bourget. The rocky islet of Châtillon in the middle of the Chautagne marsh is a monoclinal outcrop of the Neocomian. At Portou, after crossing the Savières canal, the outflow from the lake, we reach the eastern side of the Mont du Chat chain. A spur to the south along the edge of the lake leads to the Cistercian abbey of Hautecombe, founded in 1139 and restored in the 19th century. Occupied by the Benedictines of Solesmes, it is built on the Burdigalian molasse which dips towards the lake ④.

Return to Portou and go round the chain by the north and west (D 18 and D 921). The road cuts through all the members of the Mont Lindard monocline, from the Urgonian to the limestones and marly-limestones of the Dogger, which are followed alongside the Rhône for a long way, as far as Lucey.

To the south of this locality take the D 210 towards Billième. The road climbs the western overturned flank of the chain (Mont Lierre). At Jongieux we enter the winegrowing district which is planted on limestone screes upslope, and pebbly tills downslope.

On the hairpin bends above the village of **Jongieux** there is a view to the north over the winegrowing district and the Mont Lindard Monocline, emphasised by the Malm and Middle Berriasian strike scarps of Saint-Pierre- de-Curtille. On the horizon, beyond the Rhône, there is the chain of the Grand Colombier, above Culoz ⑤.

Tasting at several winegrowers in Jongieux, Billième, Monthoux and Saint-Jean-de-Chevelu.

Thus we reach the front of the Mont du Chat chain sensu stricto at the entrance to the Chat tunnel where the Burdigalian marine molasse can be seen plastered against the Neocomian limestone of the very upright western limb.

Take the road from the **Col du Chat** (D 914A). Stop at the crossroads with the road leading to the De La Source restaurant over the vertical Berriasian limestones of the western limb. A hundred meters further the secondary road crosses a mylonitic zone corresponding to the strike fault, and then reaches the bedded Aalenian limestones of the descending eastern limb of the anticline ⑥. Returning to the crossroads a 180° view shows from south to north, above the till of the anticlinal valley in which the restaurant lies:
— the eastern limb, culminating in the rocky Upper Kimmeridgian mass and the Dent du Chat;
— the western subvertical limb on which Upper Malm and Berriasian outcrop. A hand band of the latter faces us, — on the west, the Yenne Molasse Syncline closed on the horizon by the Mont Tournier chain, itself cut by cluse of Pierre Châtel;
— below, the glacial lakes of Chevelu and the hills of a rock slide
— to the north, the anticlinal valley of Billième, covered with vines bounded to the west by the overturned series of Mont Lierre.

From the Col du Chat (638 m) as far as the Conjux crossroads the road cuts through easterly dipping Dogger and Malm. There then begins the descent to the **Lac du Bourget**, the road cutting several times into the Hauterivian marly limestones and the Urgonians limestones which dip steeply towards the lake.

Make a stop in a large hairpin, close to a small bar, for one of the most majestic views in the outer Alps ⑦:
— in the foreground, Lake Bourget, glacially overdeepened in the molasse;
— in the middle ground, to the north, the periclinial southern end of the Gros Foug Anticline (Chambotte) in the Valanginian limestones which are buried beneath the Sierroz fan at Brison-Saint-Innocent. There are scattered vineyards here and there;
— in the centre the molasse hill of Tresserve, a feature left behind by the ice;
— towards the south, the Holocene Leysse Plain, with the airport, bounded on the east by the overthrusting Urgonian Voglans stump and the Sonnaz interglacial gravels;
— in the background, the overthrust of the Bauges subalpine massif, from the Revard in the north, to the Croix du Nivolet in the South, emphasised by Tithonian, Valanginian and Urgonian rock bands. To the south, past the notch of the Cluse de Chambéry, where one sees the jagged ridge of the crystalline rocks of Belledonne, the subalpine massif of the Chartreuse in profile with the Table du Granier and the Bec du Corbelet, sculpted in the Urgonian;
— turning to the west there is a depression which rises towards the Col du Chat; this is the line of the transverse Chat Fault, with a sinistral slip, which is still active because it moved in a recent earthquake (1956).

The road descends to the N 504 cutting through Neocomian limestone. Take the road to Bourdeau immediately on the left and then the road to Bourget- du-lac, along the lake shore (Amours woods). The basal conglomerate of the transgression by the Burdigalian molasse onto the Urgonian can be seen on leaving Bourdeau. Numerous pebbles bored by piddocks are embedded in a coarse sandy glauconitic matrix. Further on admire the size of the blocks and the progressive transition below the road into coarse sandy molasse containing *Pecten* and sharks teeth.

Then go via the Leysse plain towards Chambéry. To the west there is the alluvial terrace of Servolex bearing the Charpignat winegrowing area at the very north.

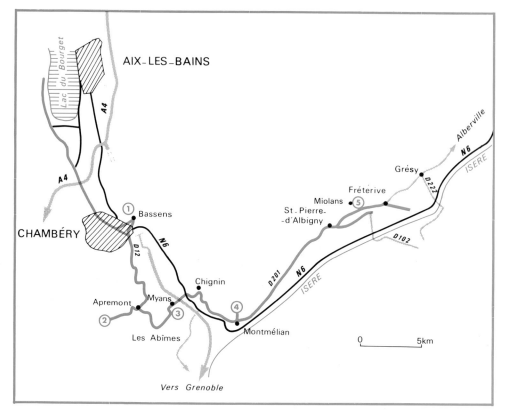

AIX-LES-BAINS

Lac du Bourget

A4

A4

CHAMBÉRY

① Bassens

D12

N6

Chignin

Myans

Apremont

② ③

④

Les Abîmes

Montmélian

Vers Grenoble

Miolans ⑤
St.Pierre-
-d'Albigny
Fréterive

Grésy

Alberville

N6

ISÈRE

D222

D102

D201

N6

ISÈRE

0   5km

Fig. 33. Itinerary in Savoie, from Chambéry to Pont-Royal.

Route 3. From Chambéry to Pont Royal: The Combe de Savoie and the Granier rock slide winegrowing districts (fig. 33).

This route largely coincides with the one shown in the *Guide gélogique des Alpes de Savoie* (p. 24 to 28), to which we would refer the reader.

At **Chambéry** take the D 512 as far as Bassens. There is a good view to the north from the supermarket car park over the Nivolet massif ①. From here can be seen, from west to east, beyond the doubled Tithonian cornices giving rise to the anticlinal valley of Verel-Pragondran:
— the line of the Berriasian limestones of Montbasin, producing downslope the slopes of Saint-Alban and Monterminod where the vines are grown on a cover of till;
— the Valanginian cornice of Lovettaz;
— finally the Hauterivian line crowned by the Urgonian cliff of Nivolet and Peney.

Going by the La Trousse crossroads and La Ravoire join the D 201 at Saint-Badolph and follow it as far as Apremont following the Cluse du Chambéry, which is cluttered with moraines. To the south west the first vines appear on the Berriasian limestones and marly limestones of the bastions of the Chartreuse.

At **Apremont** the road enters the **Granier rock slide** which can be seen in silhouette from the south (fig. 34). The 1248 fall is particularly obvious, accentuated with recent more limited rock falls. A small track through the heart of the chaos, both downslope towards Pierre-Hachée, and upslope, will reveal the Abymes and Apremont winegrowing areas, and one can enjoy tasting the wines produced from jacquère grapes. Note the enormous embedded blocks of Urgonian ②.

134

Fig. 34. — Mont Granier (Urgonian limestone cliff) and the scar of 1248. At its foot the winegrowing district of Abymes de Myans, on the slide.

Myans and its drumlin, the edge of the catastrophe, crowned by the venerated gilded Virgin, is reached by les Marches. A stop near the sanctuary or the cemetery reveals a general view over the Saint-Jeoire- Prieuré and Chignin districts to the north ③. From the north west to the south east there can be seen:
— in the far distance, the Nivolet and the Peney;
— closer by, the complex Curienne Anticline with the Mont Saint-Michel Monocline (Kimmeridgian) continuing as Mont Ronjou and the hill of Saint-Anthelme and La Tour de la Biguerne (Sequanian). These hills are separated from the overthrusts of Mont Gelas and the Savoyard scarps (Malm limestones and marly limestones) by the Mont Levin-Chignin depression, which is covered with screes and tills which underlie the main winegrowing district;
— finally, to the east, there is the valley of the Isère, dominated by the crystalline massif of Belledonne and wooded Liassic hills.

Go to Chignin to taste the wines, including Bergeron.

 Go to **Montmélian** by the N 6, then climb the rock accommodating the platform of the old fort (Upper Kimméridgian limestones). Here there is a panoramic view over the Combe de Savoie, the north Grésivaudan, the Cluse de Chambéry and the north Chartreuse (the Granier and the rock slide) ④.

To the north the rocky outcrop of the Savoyard overlooks the town. To the north-east one can see the wine districts of Arbin, de Cruet etc, located on the screes and the tillite terrace at the foot of the heights of the subalpine rim, marked in the distance by the perched syncline of the Dent d'Arclusaz. Along the axis of the valley of the Isère, Mont-Blanc shuts off the horizon, with an extension towards us named the Grand Arc Massif.

After visiting the cooperative vaults at Montmélian follow the northern edge of the anticlinal valley by the Route des Vins (D 201). Take the time to appreciate the wines, in particular Mondeuse, on the makers' premises or at the cooperative vaults at **Cruet**.

After passing the *outwash fan of Saint-Pierre-d'Albigny*, the excursion may stop at Fréterive, below the Dent d'Arclusaz, after a visit to **Château de Miolans**, perched on the Tithonian cliff where the Marquis de Sade was imprisoned in 1773 ⑤.

Return to Chambéry by the N 6 which follows the main course of the Isère and the cluse.

FOR FURTHER
INFORMATION

Geology

Geological guides (published by Masson):
— Alpes (Savoie et Dauphiné) (1970), by J. Debelmas et al. (particularly for the Chablais).
— Alpes de Savoie (1982), by J. Debelmas et al.
— Alpes du Dauphiné (1983), by J. Debelmas et al.

Debelmas J. (1979). Découverte géologique des Alpes du Nord. (Geological exploration of the Northern Alps). BRGM publications.

Delaunay G. and Rampnoux J.-P. (1981). Deformation of the fronts of the Bornes and Bauges massifs. Analysis of the fracture tectonics of the Savoyard foreland. *Bull. Soc. géol. Fr. 7*, **23**, (2) p. 203-212.

Gidon P. (1963). Géologie chambérienne (The geology of Chambéry). *Ann. C. E. sup. Chambéry*, Individual memoir, 176 pp.

Goguel J. and Pachoud A. (1972). Geology of the Mont Granier rock slide in the Chartreuse massif in 1248. *Bull. BRGM Fr.* sect. III, no 1, p. 29-38.

Oenology

Much information on the nature of the winegrowing districts, vine varieties and the taste and olfactory qualities of the wines has been taken from the documents mentioned below:

Connaissance des vins de Savoie (A study of the wines of Savoie) (1981), by G. Culas, a technical adviser to the *Institut technique du vin.*

Vins de Savoie en AOC, (AOC wines of Savoie), published by the *Syndicat régional des Vins de Savoie,*

1982 report of the commission responsible for the boundaries of the AOC Vin de Savoie and Roussette de Savoie, written by J. Caillet, J. Germain, G. Nicoud and R. Rivoire.

Top: The middle Maurienne district near Hermillon and Le Châtel (Rampnoux photo)

Bottom: Château de Ripaille and its vineyard (Rampnoux photo)

Top: Le Granier, an imposing cliff of Urgonian limestone which dominates the Abymes de Myan (Thomas photo)

Below: The Abymes vineyard, Savoie (Rampnoux photo)

Châteauneuf-du-Pape: Occupying a very ancient terrace of the Rhône composed of heavy quartzite pebbles, the vineyard spreads out over vast undivided areas, all bearing high quality wines. In the background lies the market gardening plain of Comtat Venaissin with the Mont-Ventoux barring the horizon with a fine silhouette (Photo Truc).

SEDIMENTARY ROCKS

a^2 — Recent Quarternary	c^1 — Lower Cretaceous Urgonian
a^1 — Older Quarternary	J^3 — Upper Jurassic (Malm)
Glacial deposits	J^2 J — Middle Jurassic (Dogger) Undifferentiated Jurassic
a^{IV} — Villafranchian	J^1 — Lower Jurassic (Lias)
p — Pliocene	t^3 — Upper Triassic (Keuper)
Miocene	t^2 t — Middle Triassic (Muschelkalk) Undifferentiated Triassic
Oligocene	t^1 — Lower Triassic
e^2 e — Middle and Upper Eocene Undifferentiated Eocene	h^4 — Stephanian
e^1 — Lower Eocene	h^1 — Dinantian
c^2 c — Upper Cretaceous Undifferentiated Cretaceous	

METAMORPHIC AND PLUTONIC ROCKS

ζ^2 — Micáschist Anatectic granite Sericite schist Chlorite schist, phyllite, hornfelse	γ^A — Granites d'anatexie
ζ $\zeta\zeta$ — Gneiss Undifferentiated crystalline schist	γ γ^b — Granite Biotite granite
δ — Amphibolite	γ^m γ^r — Muscovite and biotite granite Riebeckite granite Migmatites Gabbro
M — Migmatites	θ — Gabbros

VOLCANIC ROCKS

Quarternary	Tertiary
Basalt and labradorite	Phonolite

DEMARCATIONS

Northern Côtes du Rhône	Tavel and Lirac	Châteauneuf-du-Pape
Southern Côtes du Rhône	Diois	Gigondas and Beaumes de Venise
Ve – Côtes du Ventoux	Vi – Côtes du Vivarais	T – Coteaux du Tricastin

Fig. 35. Geological map and boundaries of the winegrowing districts of the Côtes-du-Rhône and the Diois.

Côtes du Rhône et Diois

THE NORTHERN CÔTES DU RHÔNE

Imprints of vine leaves and grape pips dating from the end of the Miocene (approximately 7 million years ago) have been reported to occur in the region by many authors, for example beneath the Coirons rock fall, 30 km to the south west of Saint-Péray (E. Samuel, personal communication), and in the early Pliocene of Pérouges (5 million years ago, the Meximieux Tuffs). Grape pips have been found in the recent Quaternary at several prehistoric sites in the region, proving that grapes were gathered, but not necessarily grown or fermented.

Documents mentioning vines and wine are however numerous from the Roman period onwards. Of the monuments which feature them we would mention the pulpitum of the theatre at Lugdunum and the mosaic in the Museum of Antiquities at Lyon which shows a grape pressing scene. The spread of vines beyond Gallia Narbonensis dates from the imperial period. The Rhône valley and the Lyonnais were not slow to see the cultivation of the allobrogica, obtained from Vienne-la-Vineuse.

In the Lyonnais vines became established very patchily. The oldest foundation is probably the Côte-Rôtie winegrowing district, dating from the second century BC, and several Latin poets in the first century AD praised its "Vienne wine".

Cultivation of the vine reached Lyon, the favourite town of Marcus Aurelius, in the second century, but not the Beaujolais. In 1573 Nicolas de Nicolaÿ counted seventy seven parishes growing vines in the Lyonnais, as against only eight in the Beaujolais. The winegrowing districts of Bugey, perhaps already cultivated in the Roman period, where extended by the monks in the Middle Ages. Winegrowing spread almost everywhere, particularly between Vienne and Valence (fig. 35).

Côte-Rôtie and Château-Grillet

The Côte-Rôtie winegrowing district is so called because it is "roasted" by the sun, for two reasons: the main area between Verenay and Semons (Rhône), downstream from Vienne, is on a south-easterly facing hillslope; the steep pebbly terraces are bare and fully exposed.

This area can be reached either by taking the N 86 to Givors, Condrieu or Serrières, or by leaving the A 7 motorway at Vienne-north or Vienne-south and taking the road for Condrieu (fig. 36). Coming from the north, for example, the N 86 through Saint-Cyr-sur-le-Rhône leads to the hamlet of Verenay (commune of **Ampuis**), whence a small road climbs onto the plateau in the direction of Lacquat and the Muny ridge. It cuts through irregular rocky outcrops of mica schists ①, frequently masked by screes. These are the oldest formations of this eastern spur of the Massif Central (Carboniferous metamorphism): see the Guide géologique Lyonnais-Vallée du Rhône).

Likewise climbing the slope through the vines, but this time above Ampuis itself ②, or towards Le Rosier, or towards Champin, or again towards Tartara, the very fine crumpled grey-brown two-mica schists are encountered sooner and extend further. At Ampuis the two types of rocks form a hard acid soil containing abundant stones, with a thin coarse sandy weathered cover on which only vines, or almost only vines, can become established. From Ampuis, the "capital" of the Côte-Rôtie, many roads lead through the vines.

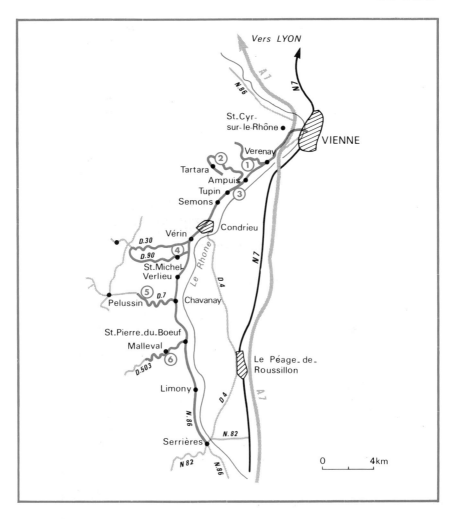

Fig. 36. Itinerary through the northern Côtes du Rhône: Côte-Rôtie and Château-Grillet

Admire the construction of the terraces from gathered pieces of schist with their patinated brownish hues, balanced on the slope without slipping. The soil is sandy, dry, lean, acid, but well drained at depth, meticulously worked, with proper retention of the slope.

Mainly syrah vines, which are said to be of Syrian origin (whence the name) are planted, and the earliest plantations are Roman, like the nearby city of Vienne. The vines yield a heady full-bodied red wine, which is nevertheless fine, has bouquet, and is generous and graceful. A proportion of viognier sometimes lightens its colour, making it more delicate and lighter, while syrah alone perhaps makes it harsher, but gives it a better colour.

The Côte-Rôtie winegrowing district currently covers 120 hectares. From the centre of this tiered cultivation, where everything seems to be the work of man, look across towards the other slope ③. Note the deep notch of the Rhône, an inheritance from the Pliocene valley, and the steep slope of the other bank, which, facing north west, is by contrast wooded and bears no vines.

The Côte-Rôtie label applies to the communes of Saint-Cyr-sur-le-Rhône, Ampuis and **Tupin-Semons**. It is continued southwards by the **Condrieu label**, which covers the communes of Condrieu, Vérin, Verlieux, Chavanay and extends as far as Saint-Pierre-de-Boeuf, thus extending along the entire border of the département of the Loire. It even extends into the corner of the département of Ardèche, in the commune of Limony. To the west the vineyards climb the hills in the direction of Chuyer and Pélussin.

In the north corner of the département of the Loire the **Château-Grillet label** straddles the communes of Vérin and Saint-Michel-sur-Rhône. It covers only 3 hectares, at an altitude of between approximately 165 and 250 m.

The Condrieu district is planted with viognier, like Château-Grillet. There is no more syrah. Thus both yield white wines. The **Condrieu** winegrowing district, although scattered over some 16 km of hill slopes alongside the Rhône, currently only covers 16 hectares, soon to be 20, but it has scope for further expansion. Being spread out in this way it has agreeable individual features associated with particular slopes, particular terraces, particular growers. It yields full-bodied white wines, full of aromatic savour and bouquet, which are fine and light. The Château- Grillet are held to be among the best white wines of France, having great quality and being lighter than the Ermitage blanc which we will meet later on.

As the wines differ in comparison with the Côte-Rôtie, so too does the geology. Here we enter a granite massif, the different facies of which can be observed by taking the D 30 between Vérin and Chuyer ④, or the D 7 between Chavanay and Pélussin ⑤, as well as in the Malleval gorges via the D 503 ⑥. A large area (Vérin, Saint-Michel-sur-Rhône) consists of biotite granite. Along the routes mentioned one meets outcrops of different granites, sometimes coarse-grained, sometimes preferentially oriented, particularly in the Malleval gorges. These rocks break up more readily than the mica schists of Ampuis which yield a coarser clay and sand, whence a more moulded, varied and more open relief. At the same time the slopes are less steep, allowing vines to alternate with other crops, interspersed with coppices, hedges and clumps of trees. The soil is sandy and coarse, well leached, light grey to pinkish to russet-red, drained by a well developed sand of irregular thickness and still mixed with some weathered granite clasts.

The winegrowing districts of Tournon, Ermitage and Saint-Péray

All along the Rhône valley, as an extension of the foregoing area, many vineyards are scattered on the outer slopes of the Massif Central in the Ardèche region from Serrières to Saint-Péray, and even spread onto the left bank of the Rhône in Drôme, in the Tain-l'Hermitage area (fig. 37).

We will therefore continue along the previous route towards the south, along the N 86, from Serrières to Tournon. The terrain is essentially metamorphic, with migmatites and gneisses, and locally, orbicular granite. These are locally covered by patches of loess. A fairly indistinct system of NE-SW orientated faults, some of which having a considerable throw, marks this boundary.

The first vineyards can be seen on the slope where Serrières is located, taking the first few kilometres of the N 519 to Annonay ①, where small roads climb up onto the plateau and serve the villages and hamlets. Outcrops of foliated granites can be observed, mixed locally with heterogeneous gneisses, to the east of Peyraud. The vineyards are scattered, seeking the best aspects.

A detour can then be made through Saint-Désirat to return to **Andance** via the N 82. There loess masks a depression filled with Pliocene marls ②. The vines are scattered on the lower slopes of these areas of high ground. At Saint-Désirat, not far

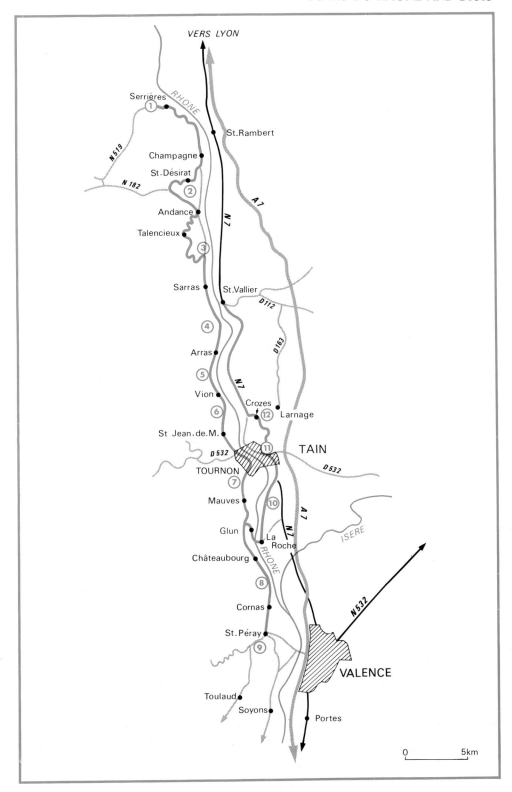

Fig. 37. Itinerary through the northern Côtes du Rhône: Tournon, Ermitage and Saint-Péry

from the N 82, cooperative vaults have already announced the cru Saint-Joseph label. These are full-bodied quality red wines, with colour and bouquet, which are produced as far as Saint-Jean-de- Muzols and Mauves, to the south of **Tournon**. There is also a white Saint-Joseph, mainly produced further to the south.

The Saint-Joseph wines are scattered within the vast domain of the Tournon wines. These cover the districts of Serrières, Tournon and the eastern part of the Annonay district. Thus by going along the small roads along the hillside (Talencieux for example), but also even alongside the N 86 as far as **Sarras** ③, one can see vines planted at the base of the high ground on light-coloured granites or, further towards the interior, on heterogeneous biotite granites and their screes. They are frequently scattered between orchards.

The winegrowing district continues further to the south, but here, from Sarras to **Arras** ④, on dark granites, and further towards the interior and to the south, from Arras as far as **Vion** ⑤, on gneisses containing granite sills. The vines are always scattered near the base of the slope, where there is a good aspect, alternating with orchards and gardens. There are even a few plots where vines can be seen to climb up the trunks of fruit trees. As before, the vines are essentially of the syrah variety. There is virtually no more gamay. As to the area occupied by the Tournon wine growing district, it is very difficult to estimate it because it is so scattered.

From Vion to **Saint-Jean-de-Muzols** ⑥ the rock again consists of various granitic rocks because of another major fault. From Tournon to Mauves, where yet another fault corresponds to the valley of the Doux, the hillside consists of the coarsely crystalline Tournon Granite, with an appreciable accumulation of sand at the base of the slope ⑦. All these rocks give a generally lean soil in situ on the outcrop and a little less lean, but heterogeneous soil on the scree slopes.

In all this sector there are two special labels in addition to the general label of **Vins de Tournon**. One is the **Saint-Joseph**. This covers Mauves and Saint-Jean-de-Muzols, but also Vion and beyond towards the north, as we have seen. In addition to the red wines, white wines are also produced in this Saint-Joseph district from marsanne grapes together with a little roussanne. These wines are fine and have bouquet. The other label is **Cornas**, on the territory of the commune of the same name, 12 km to the south of Tournon, along the N 86. The Cornas are full-bodied strongly coloured highly valued red wines, with a bouquet similar to those of l'Ermitage (see below) in their envelope and mellowness. There from Châteaubourg to Cornas ⑧ the granitic and gneissic edge of the Massif Central comes into faulted contact with sedimentary terrains. These are above all the Upper Jurassic (Kimmeridgian) limestones and marly limestones. They also give rise to rocky ground, to sometimes steep and rocky slopes, and a thin and variable soil, which in this case is basic. Vines thus grow on the lower slopes of these limestones, but above all, to the east of Cornas itself, on the granites and their screes.

From here go to **Saint-Péray** ⑨. The former Pliocene valley isolated the Jurassic relief of the Montagne de Crussol and passed to the west of the present Rhône via the depression leading to Toulaud and Charmes-sur- Rhône. Saint-Péray is located at the mouth of this old fossil valley, lying between granites and marly limestones, shaped by alluvials, screes and loess. The Saint-Péray vineyards produce famous white wines from vines which are similar to the tournons blancs, particularly marsanne. The vines are scattered among the crops over the hillsides of always gentle relief and a golden hue of a sometimes almost Provençal character. They yield a light fine wine with bouquet, which is however very lively, and unlike Tokays very good for arthritis and gout. Sparkling wines, which have a high alcohol content and are sometimes heady, and a few rosés are also produced.

From Saint-Péray it is suggested that a return north should be made via the N 86 as far as Glun, reaching La Roche-sur-Glun past the site of the Rhône dam, to the outcrop of the last Jurassic limestone rock in a northerly direction, in the very bed of the Rhône. Here we reach the department of Drôme where vast terraces of recent Quaternary pebbly alluvium spread out at the confluence of the Rhône and the Isère.

These are crossed reaching the N 7 by country lanes ⑩ . The vines are mixed with various crops on flat gravelly alluvial soils which are well drained to some depth. This is the district of the **l'Ermitage** (or Hermitage) **wines**, which continues north beyond Tain. Excellent red and white wines which should be offered together are made. The vineyards from which they originate climb the granite spur of Tain in the north in spectacular walled and revetted terraces which face due south ⑪ . Laterally towards the east they extend over the slopes and shoulders covered with loess. Between Tain and Crozes they penetrate the massif as far as the shore of the Miocene molasse sea. The soils are sandy, often coarse, arenitic, and sun-baked at Tain, more developed towards Crozes. Seen from far off or close by, and as exposed to the sun as it is to the visitor, the hillside of Tain displays an apron of unbroken vineyards. The red wines of Tain-l'Hermitage are renowned: delicate but generous, richly coloured and fairly full-bodied, often mellow, they are reminiscent of some Châteauneuf, perhaps without the substance, but superior to them in fineness. Tain-l'Hermitage whites are also produced, and these are similar to those of Crozes.

Les Crozes-Ermitage ⑫ effectively extend these to the north, with comparable and lighter reds. However the vine varieties (marsanne, roussette) yield a majority of excellent full-bodied, dry, delicate white wines with bouquet. The vines grow on the same geological formations as at Tain, but better defined, and continue as far as Larnage, from where one can return to Saint-Vallier and the N 7.

Wines and gastronomy

The red wines of Côte-Rôtie, Tournon, Cornas, Saint-Joseph, Ermitage and Crozes-Ermitage provide a masterly accompaniment to large meals, some being more heavy, but each having authority. The white wines of Condrieu, Château-Grillet, Saint-Joseph, Tournon, Ermitage, Crozes-Ermitage and Saint-Péry are better drunk with meals than on their own. They go well not only with shellfish and fish, when they are dry, but, frequently having a bouquet, they can compliment a sweet or a delicate meat. The fruitier wines form a pleasant addition to a dessert.

THE SOUTHERN CÔTES DU RHÔNE

In his *Natural History* Pliny mentioned a winegrowing district around Gigondas, and there is no doubt that many Vaucluse hills were already covered with a thick mantle of good vines in his lifetime.

Their existence is confirmed in the Middle Ages, but it was in the 14th century, when the Pope resided at Avignon, that some villages experienced a considerable development of their vineyards. It should be remembered that at that time the influence of the papal town extended over the whole of Europe, that trade followed in its footsteps and large quantities of wine were drunk there, without counting exports. There is no doubt that Châteauneuf-du-Pape owes its present renown to this.

At the heart of the district within the confines of the Tricastin, close to the village of Donzère (N 7), there have recently been discovered " . . . the largest and oldest wine-making vaults of the Roman period (early 1st century). More than 600 dolia for

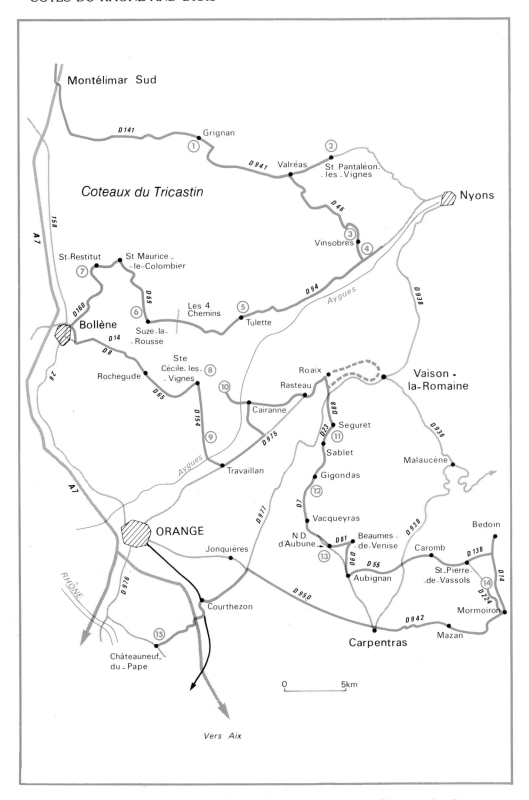

Fig. 38. Itinerary through the southern Côtes du Rhône, from Grignan to Châteauneuf-du-Pape

wine, miscellaneous equipment and objects indicate what facilities were required for processing the harvest of a 50 hectare estate . . ." (communication from M. Lasfargues, the Director of Historical Antiquities at Lyon).

The vineyards and their soils

The most widely cultivated variety is grenache. It provides a wine with tannin, body, alcohol and full flavour. Syrah brings a typical fragrance, the capacity to age and roundness. Cinsault brings fineness, delicacy and lightness; its presence is essential. Other minor varieties are of some importance locally, in particular in Châteauneauf-du-Pape.

The Vaucluse lies immediately above a trough which was very active during the Mesozoic, because 9 000 m of sediments are stacked up beneath the surface of the county. All the massifs which emerge from the deep basin thus offer the enthusiast either blue marls containing ammonites and belemnites or fine limestones with ammonites or very thick reef limestones (Urgonian facies) formed to the south of Mont Ventoux.

What a land of contrasts! So many distinctly different landscapes within a single département! Here there are the banks of the Rhône, the God of rivers, now so tranquil, with lush vegetation full of the chatter of insects, its spreading apple orchards and its fields of cereals. Avignon, the city of Popes, lively and ringing with bells, overlooks the flow of the river, the people and the produce from this land. Further to the east and northeast Comtat Venaissin and Haut Cimtat spread out their plains dominated by crops of early vegetables, cereals and fruit. Wherever the slightest hill or the smallest plateau rises up, there there is a vineyard of luxuriant or modest proportions!

Finally the mountains throw up solid barriers, which bear the names, from north to south, of La Lance, a dormant monster which bars the north, Mont Ventoux, the uncontested sovereign of the area, the harmonious long-drawn-out lines of the Vaucluse mountains, an immense limestone plateau punctuated by chasms and sink holes, and Mont Luberon which boldly marks the south with its unbroken line. A traveller coming from the north should be aware that near Grignan or Saint-Paul-Trois-Châteaux he crosses a climatic boundary which has been pointed out on several occasions.

Whereas the northern Côtes du Rhône grow on a relatively uniform ground (granite or gneiss) and each wine comes from a single variety (syrah, viognier, marsanne or roussanne), the southern Côtes du Rhône grow on a highly variable soil and are obtained from a number of varieties (23 for the region of the Côtes du Rhône label!). The Côteaux du Tricastin (AOC) on the left bank of the Rhône (limestone or gravelly red clay soils), and opposite them the Côtes du Vivarais (VDQS) on the limestone soils of the right bank, provide a transition to the southern Côte du Rhône (fig. 35).

Itineraries

From Grignan to Saint-Cécile-les-Vignes

Leave the N 7 or the A 7 motorway at Montélimar and then go off at an angle bearing steadily southeast in the direction of **Grignan**, crowned by its fine chateau which belonged to the daughter of Mme de Sévigné, Chantal de Bussy-Rabutin ①(fig. 38).

Immediately after crossing the small col between Grignan and Grillon one enters the Miocene **Valréas** Basin, one of the largest and best studied. Fossils are numerous where the base of the Miocene crops out, and take the form of lamellibranch shells, urchin fragments and numerous sharks' teeth. At Valréras go east via the D 941 as far as **Saint-Pantaléon-les-Vignes**, with its fruity red wine ②.

Return to Valréas and climb up onto the **Vinsobres** plateau to see the fields of lavender mixed with vines, and then to the village itself, the Aygues valley with its terraces bearing fine plots which will be described in a section of their own.

A tour of some forty kilometres, from Vinsobres to Travaillan in the Aygues valley[1] will show the different geological formations on which the Aygues valley winegrowing district stands.

From above the village of **Vinsobres** ③there is a fine view towards Mont Ventoux far off to the southeast and, in the foreground, over the Aygues valley. The village lies at a height of 280 m on Upper Pliocene with marls and pebble beds, but in the west it is in contact with the continental Upper Miocene consisting of sandy marls and conglomerates. The D 190 on the way to Valréas gives good sections through these formations.

To the south of and below Vinsobres one can see Quaternary terraces on which the greater part of the winegrowing district through which we shall be passing ④, stands.

These separate terraces, which are tiered on the right bank of the Aygues, offer a favoured site which, because of the SW-NE orientation of the valley and the height, over 450 m, of the Miocene-Pliocene plateau to the north, offer a favoured site which is sheltered from the mistral and which has a good exposure to the sun.

Go to the village of **Tulette** via the D 94. A good section through the intermediate terraces ⑤can be seen at the crossroads with the D 20.

Carry on as far as **Suze-la-Rousse** ⑥where the medieval chateau houses a new and already famous University of Wine. It is from Suze that one can travel the Tricastin loop. Take the D 59 to the north and pass through Saint-Maurice-le-Colombier taking the D 218 towards **Saint-Restitut** hill, which must not be missed ⑦. Splendid quarries for dressed stone (Lower Miocene), partly underground, will soon house an ageing cellar (go to the end of the viewpoint path). Carry on to Bollène, and taking the D 8 go through Rochegude and, in particular, Lagarde-Paréol (Fonsalette estate) which will give you a very pleasant surprise. Carry on to **Sainte-Cécile-les-Vignes**, a village which is true to its name because this commune alone produces one tenth of the AOC Côtes-du-Rhône label.

The village and the northern part of the commune lie on an ancient terrace which overlooks the present course of the Aygues from a height of some 10 m. To

---

[1] Itinerary written by A. Gauthier.

the south of the commune a large portion of the district is located on an even older terrace. The boundary between the two formations is emphasised by a band of "saffre" (yellow sand with irregular gravels of Helvetian age).

A quarry to the northeast of the village (Charbonneaux district) ⑧ provides a good section through these alluvials. To reach it follow the small road called Chemin vieux, which connects the D 576 to D 193, for about 2.5 km.

The alluvial deposit consists of small light grey predominantly limestone pebbles embedded in a greyish or yellowish sandy-marly sediment which is sometimes consolidated into a whitish conglomerate. Some sandy clay bands which undoubtedly come from the breakdown of the Helvetian molasse by river currents, will also be noted. This terrace has been mapped as dating from the Würm.

A section through the older terrace is provided by the gravel pit located some 6 km to the south of the village, alongside the D 154, 800 m from Aygues ⑨. The alluvium consists of the same pebbles as before, in this case bound in a sandy clay matrix which acts as a reservoir for water. The various features of this terrace provide a good base for the vineyards.

After having passed through Aygues, the same terrace reappears beyond the village of Travaillan forming the Plan de Dieu and the Bois des Dames region. The D 975 from Travaillan to Rasteau passes through this until close to the village. Before this, however, turn left towards the north at the crossroads with the D 8 in the direction of Cairanne.

From Sainte-Cécile-les-Vignes to Beaumes-de-Venise

This is a small region standing on the Lafare-Suzette massif to the east which produces excellent wines and reveals a very disturbed geology because of the uplift of a salt dome which has brought the red marls and gypsum worked at Beaumes to the surface.

From Cairanne return towards Sainte-Cécile-les-Vignes. Very fossiliferous (*Pecten*, Turritellas) Miocene blue marls crop out along the Aygues 2 km to the northwest of the village ⑩ .

The very beautiful slopes of **Cairanne**, which produce wines with a fine bouquet, run into those of **Rasteau**, a village famous for its natural sweet wine. The vineyards in these two communes stand partly on the underlying Miocene and partly on the alluvial terraces of the Aygues and the Ouvèze. At Rasteau an ancient terrace, with a red clay matrix, is very rich in rounded quartz and limestone pebbles.

The variety of aspects, the stoniness of the soil and the drainage lead to a great variety of wines which can be discovered both in the excellently equipped cellars of the cooperative vaults and in the more welcoming family-run vaults of the many private growers. Go to Roaix and take the D 7 and then D 88 south unless you decide to take a detour to **Vaison-la-Romaine** and its ruins.

The beauty of the Crèche de Séguret ⑪ , Sablet and Vacqueyras, clinging to almost vertical Miocene slabs, or to rounded hills of yellow "saffre" covered with fine vineyards is followed by the attractions of **Gigondas**, where the Florentine cypresses and the high wall of the Dentelles de Montmirail (vertical Jurassic limestones) form an unforgettable setting for this jewel of a village ⑫ .

And what can one say about its wines! The aromatic savour of these esteemed French wines, associated with a well developed gamy fragrance in some years, a rare breed, as subtle and vibrant as a Genevoix novel, make these the flower of all the wines in this part of the Rhône valley.

Let us tear ourselves away from these delights to go to **Beaumes-de-Venise**, without omitting a visit to the site of the Romanesque chapel of Notre-Dame-d'Aubune with its square bell tower ⑬ .

Highly appreciated Côtes du Rhône and Côtes du Ventoux are once again obtained from Miocene terrain. The very delicate rosés and full-flavoured reds are accompanied by an excellent muscat, a natural sweet wine, whose existence is due to the praiseworthy efforts of local growers and wine makers.

From Aubignan to Mazan

A string of villages perched on the southern flank of Mont Ventoux produce excellent wines known everywhere, of a good character and colour at Caromb, more accommodating at Bédoin and often light at Mormoiron. Table grapes are one of the riches of the area.

A visit to the sand and ochre quarries, whose colours are so bright that it is hard to believe they are natural, is not to be missed, neither is the collecting of fine gypsum crystals at Mormoiron in the white hills (fibrous gypsum, particularly along the road from Mormoiron to Saint-Pierre-de- Vassols) ⑭ .

Châteauneuf-du-Pape ⑮

There is little further to be said about the prestige of this, one of the country's front ranking wines, so esteemed are its strength, its flavour and its body, its unfailing breeding, and its keeping qualities.

Most of the harvest is obtained from very special alluvial ground — a pebbly soil with very large quartzite clasts in a red clay matrix brought down by the furious Rhône during the Early Quaternary. The pebbles can be seen everywhere, and everywhere they capture the heat of the sun to impart it to the luxuriant vines during the night.

Like the cooperative vaults, many private cellars offer a full range of young and old Châteauneuf-du-Pape. From Châteauneauf-du-Pape one may go on towards Tavel after crossing the Rhône.

Marriages of wines and dishes

The range of experiences offered to all wine lovers and connoisseurs is so rich that it is not possible to describe combinations in detail. Nevertheless here are a few main guidelines.

All the wines of the Haut Comtat Venaissin and adjacent Drôme (Valréas, Visan, Vinsobres, Saint-Maurice, Tulette, villages du Tricastin) are generally low in tannin, scented and vary in character, flavour and aromaticity. They go well with simple dishes (grilled meats, small game, or cheeses).

The wines of Sainte-Cécile-les-Vignes are sober, full of body, like those of Vacqueyras, Cairanne and Rasteau. Most meats and meats in sauce set them off well. Séguret, Sablet, Aubignan, Caromb, Bédoin and Mormoiron offer greater subtlety.

Beaumes-de-Venise is lighter and paves the way for delicate compliments: a mixed green salad with hot chicken's liver, an ice cream or a burbot form an elegant accompaniment to a rosé. For an aperitif a (small) glass of muscat makes way for the feast.

Gigondas, in your case my pen would run away with itself — but there is not enough room and how can one translate feelings which lead directly to the spirit in sufficiently evocative words?

One principle to begin with: any dish of partridges, thrushes, larks, pigeons, leverets and wild rabbit, everything with the smell of the forest, should be allied with the contents of a bottle of Gigondas which has been carefully aged (5 to 10 years).

Another principle: no truffles, no pâté, no pheasant, no ribs of venison lightly coated with gravy should be served without this wine.

After such delights even the finding of a beautiful fossil pales into insignificance.

Châteauneuf-du-Pape: the wine for boar, buck, all strong venison, beef steeped in sauce, dry goats' cheeses, veined blue cheeses like "picodons", for example. His Majesty Châteauneuf will always find its place on the tables of a high culinary tradition.

THE RIGHT BANK OF THE RHÔNE DOWNSTREAM OF THE CONFLUENCE WITH THE CÈZE: THE LAST CÔTES DU RHÔNE, TAVEL AND LIRAC, THE COSTIÈRES DU GARD

The Côtes du Rhône label keeps its quality features in the lower valley of the river, and the red wines of Domazan, between Avignon and Remoulin- Pont du Gard, for example, are excellent. In this area the limestone heights of the "garrigues" are drowned beneath Pliocene blue marls or directly beneath the alluvials of the Rhône and its tributaries. Here and there rocky outcrops form tectonically produced features: The E-W Roquemaure Fault to the north, the Villeneuve-lès-Avignon narrows, the Aramon Sill, and finally the Beaucaire Sill beyond which lies the river's recent delta.

Itinerary

Do not miss seeing the geological curiosities of the area: the slickensides of the Roquemaure Fault ①(3 km to the south of the locality), the lake shore "roads" of ancient Lake Pujaut (to the north of Villeneuve-lès-Avignon), and finally the Fosses de Fournès, a curious maze of ravines in fossiliferous Pliocene marls (fig. 39).

The great name of **Tavel**, "the premier rosé wine of France" (and therefore of the world . . .), rather overshadows the other quality products of the region. In fact it is for its rosé alone that this area, centred on the village of Tavel, only 14 km to the northwest of Avignon, has an AOC classification ②. Unlike the above there is nothing special about the geological context. Tavel is located between Roquemaure and Pujaut, on the eastern limit of the "garrigues". The classified vineyards stand on pebbly soils resulting from ancient frost shattering of the limestone. The wine has a strong colour and a noble mien. Although strong, it can be drunk in large draughts if desired. Drunk well chilled and without caution on hot days it will have a few surprises in store! Because of this it is to the rosé and the right bank what its

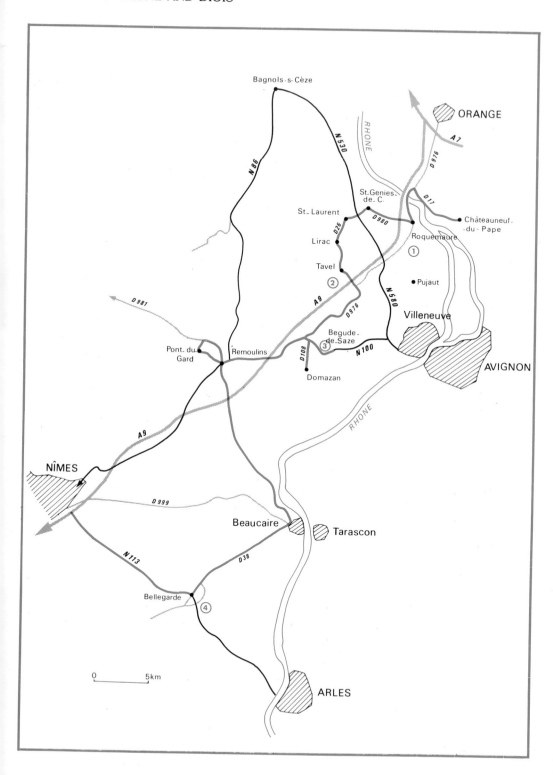

Fig. 39. Itinerary through the southern Côtes du Rhône: Tavel, Lirac and Costières du Gard

neighbour on the other side of the Rhône, Châteauneuf-du-Pape, is to the reds — even more so, because no one would contest its royalty!

In its making grenache dominates many other varieties: cinsault, white and red clairettes, picpoul, bourboulenc and carignan. Finally the exceptional red wines produced bear the name Côtes du Rhône.

The **Lirac** district, 3 km to the north of Tavel, is not essentially different. It specialises almost equally in rosés, which are excellent and are similar to the above in quality, and in the varieties authorised, to which are added white ugni and maccabéo. The label covers worthy red wines and a fairly rare clairette white. The dry pebbly limestone hillsides extend to the north of Tavel in the communes of Lirac, Saint-Laurent-des-Arbres, Saint-Geniès-de-Comolas and Roquemaure.

Finally, **the Région des Costières** extends from Beaucaire to close to Montpellier. It bears the classical varieties of the Midi and the Côtes du Rhône which provide wines classified as AOC. The label applies to 24 communes in Gard and two in Hérault, the district being essentially located on the Costière proper, that is on the very high (Villafranchian) terraces of the Rhône. The silica pebble gravels bear lateritic soils, formed at the expense of the clayey sand and loess matrix, with extensive loss of carbonate. It will be noted that ice wedge cracks dating from the Early Quaternary have been described. These cut through the gravels and are filled with loess. A visit outside Costières, to the Bégude-de-Saze cutting on the Avignon to Nîmes road, will reveal fluviatile deposits from the Rhône overlying the fans and marls of the marine Pliocene ③. The north west border of the Costière lies along a recently active fault, the Vauvert Fault, which together with the parallel Nîmes Fault (NE-SW) bounds the Vistre Graben. In the area on the boundary of Hérault part of the district is located on similar ground, but outside the geographical boundaries of Costière.

The label covers very well known and very pleasant rosés wines, reds reinforced by varieties giving colour, and whites made from clairette, grenache blanc, maccabéo and malvoisie in particular. The quality of the wines produced has been very much improved by the total elimination of aramon since 1968, and by more careful selection. Clairette de Bellegarde is produced between Arles and Nîmes, on the eastern edge of the Costière ④.

CLAIRETTE DE DIE AND CHATILLON-EN-DIOIS

It is from the famous writer Pliny (*Natural History* Book XIV, Chapter 9, 13) that we have the first mention of Clairette de Die, followed by high praise because the writer contrasts this "truly natural sweet wine" with sweet wines "adulterated" by the addition of honey, heated must, and various resins and berries, as was the practice among the ancients.

He describes how the Voconci, whose capital Dea Augusta became the modern town of Die, obtained their "aigleucos", a sweet wine which remains sparkling. "To prevent it from frothing (fermenting), and consequently from changing into a true wine, the must drawn from the vat was placed in casks which were immersed in the cold water of rivers until the winter solstice, that is until it was freezing hard ..."

The wine makers among the Voconci thus successfully used the method which their descendants still use today, cooling the musts in a cellar, accompanied by various filtration processes which are designed to remove yeasts and block fermentation.

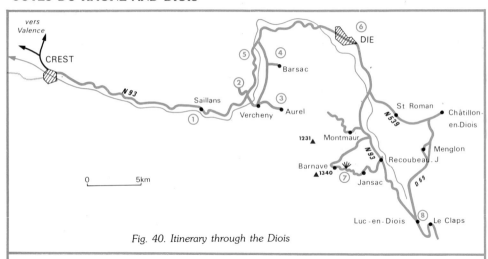

Fig. 40. Itinerary through the Diois

Fig. 41. The stepped terraces of the Drôme near Vercheny

*1. Middle terrace, 2. Fragment of the Upper terrace, 3. Alternation of Jurassic limestones and "black earths"
In the background, the dip slope of the Tithonian scarp*

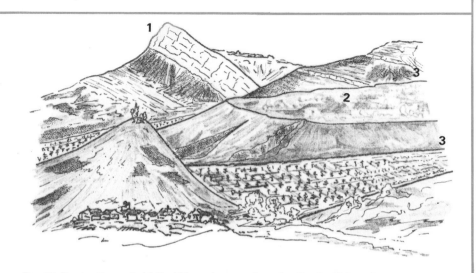

Fig. 42. Barsac: the conical hill of Mareyches seen from the Combe Noire col

1. Tithonian scarp, 2. Quaternary cover, 3. Alternation of Jurassic limestones and "black earths"

The winegrowing district and its soils

It is almost certain that the Voconci already had a muscat vine, which has a very characteristic sensitivity to rot. Since these remote times the vine stocks have been subjected to many changes, but it is felt that Clairette de Die owes its essential quality to muscat, the clairette variety only being used to lighten the flavour of the muscat, whose heaviness would be unpleasantly apparent if the wine were only to be made from those grapes.

For the winemaker the problem is one of obtaining a product with the delicate fragrance of muscat, which is light and not heady, as sometimes happens in the only direct competitor of Clairette du Die, namely Asti Spumante.

Geology has its part to play in the choice of vines. The heavy soils containing few stones derived from the Jurassic marls (black earths) are perfectly suited to muscat, whose vigour and vitality are well known, to the extent that many plants were able to withstand the great phylloxera crisis.

Finally it should be noted that the Châtillonnais district offers a variety of vines which can be used to produce very light red wines and "still" (non-sparkling) white wines.

If the factors or parameters which govern the growing of vines in those parts of this region of tormented complex relief which have historically been devoted to that purpose are investigated, one undeniable fact becomes apparent: the existence of microclimates, which remain a fundamental factor and govern the existence, establishment and development of vines throughout the Diois. These are the result of a combination of many factors, some of which are difficult to identify, such as orientation (a light or shady aspect), altitude in relation to major watercourses (risk of frost in the deepest parts), hours of sunshine (the screening effects of some rock masses), morphology (ridges, hollows, etc.), the nature of the underlying rock and its hydraulic properties (drainage and drying-out; the problem of heavy soils).

Itinerary

From Crest to Die; the Bas Diois

Starting from **Crest**, proudly dominated by its precipitous castle, go directly to the target and find the first representatives of the district which are called **Saillans** (1), Vercheny, Aurel and Barsac (fig. 40).

At **Vercheny**, climb up to the old village, to the place known as the Temple (2) and follow a track which goes due north through a magnificent vineyard with a southeasterly aspect. From there you will see the Upper Jurassic limestone carapace which is emphasised by the great anticlinal arches and which recedes to give the Drôme the opportunity to cut massive narrow gorges (fig. 41).

The village of **Aurel** (3) is nested, in the true sense of the word, in a sunlit bowl illuminated by rocks which rise above the dark marls forming the famous Jurassic "black earths". Don't hesitate to follow the road which leads to Viopis and from there to **Barsac**, two places which are steeped harmoniously in the spirit of wine, with a rich past which has left them full of poise and substance (4) (fig. 42).

Medieval **Pontaix** controls the passage. Here you are at Sainte-Croix, a small parcel of land perched in such a way as to get the best benefit from the sun. A detour to **Ponet and Saint-Auban** ⑤ will show you a small, rather cool and dry valley where the vines have chosen the better side, for the glory of Clairette.

Die welcomes you. So too do its cooperative vaults ⑥. Excellently equipped, here a uniform product is produced which you may taste at your leisure. Local winemakers could offer you a thousand variants in all the villages between Saillans and the capital of Clairette.

From Die to Châtillon-en-Diois and Luc-en-Diois; the Haut Diois and the Châtillonnais

A very dense patchwork of plots scattered among woods and cereals awaits you. Do not miss **Barnave** ⑦ and its sheltered hillslope. To the north rises the **Serre Chauvière** and its limestone scarp below which is a good example of slumping. This village is almost entirely devoted to vine growing.

One of the most striking views can be seen from the summit of this Serre Chauvière mountain, which is reached by taking the forest road which begins at Montmaur-en-Diois.

To the east the hollow of Châtillon-en-Diois is dominated by Tithonian limestone strata, faulted locally or sharply folded. The winegrowing district carpets the scree slope beneath. Further beyond rises the enormous (Urgonian) limestone monument of the Montagne de Glandasse, on which the play of the setting summer sun should be watched for a long time. All the vineyards spread out at your feet in a chequerboard of contrasting greens.

Go to **Luc-en-Diois**. 3 km beyond, a fantastic landslide caused by slip on a marly band at the base of the Tithonian limestones (Upper Jurassic), the Claps, has dammed the valley of the Drôme, which crosses it in a waterfall ⑧. From Luc-en-Diois the D 69 leads to **Châtillon-en-Diois** where the "black earths" crop out in the hills which emerge from the terraces of the Bez.

On returning the tour is not complete without an extended run through the elongated plots which stretch on either side of the road going from **Châtillon-en-Diois** to Saint-Roman.

The wines and their drinking

Clairette de Die can be drunk as an aperitif. It can also be drunk with a dessert. Opening a bottle among friends towards 10 or 5 o'clock is not to be recommended, as the palate is not very receptive at those times. My experience would lead me to advise you to begin a meal with a thimble-full of this semi-sparkling wine, and then to continue with it, provided that the dishes go harmoniously with it: lukewarm oysters, lightly salted, and white leeks, followed by freshwater fish in hot butter, steamed vegetables, slightly crisp (small steamed potatoes and beans) or julienne, or sugared petits pois cooked on a base of lettuce fit admirably into this alliance.

The flavours of goats' cheese are made stronger, which never ceases to surprise. With a view to the better management of their vineyards the growers of the Côtes-du-Rhône requested the Bureau de Recherches Gélogiques et Minières (BRGM) to map the territory of the commune of Buisson (Vaucluse). The use of existing topographical and geological data and some investigation in the field produced a satisfactory summary illustrated in an atlas of cadastral, topographical, hydrographical and simple geological maps on the scale of 1/5000. A detour via Buisson, quite close to the itinerary, 10 km to the northwest of Vaison-la-Romaine, and a visit to the Syndicat de Vignerons will enable those interested in the problem to see the amount of interest which has been raised by this study. The basic data used to prepare the document were processed by computer and may in the near future be supplemented, modified and consulted via a small console. Using the same equipment these technical data may be associated with annual data on management of the vineyards, so that the communal association of winegrowers will have an easily handled tool and probably as yet unsuspected resources, including the means to take geological and pedological facts into consideration when managing their vineyards (NDLR).

FOR FURTHER INFORMATION

Geology

Regional geological guides (Masson editeur, Paris).
— Lyonnais-Vallée du Rhône (1973), by G. Demarcq et al. (See in particular the introduction and most of the routes).
— Alpes: Savoie et Dauphiné (1983), by J. Debelmas et al.

Oenology

Bailly R. (1978). — Histoire de la vigne et des grands vins des Côtes du Rhône. (History of winegrowing and the great wines of the Côtes du Rhône). Orta Impr., Avignon.
Brunel G. (1981). — Guide des vignobles et des caves des Côtes du Rhône. (Guide to the winegrowing districts and vaults of the Côtes du Rhône). Lattès Édit., Paris.
Charnay P. (1985). — Vignobles et vins des Côtes du Rhône. (The winegrowing district and wines of the Côtes du Rhône). Aubanal édit., Avignon.
Durand G. (1979). — Vin, vigne et vignerons en Lyonnais et Beaujolais. (Wines, vines and winegrowers in the Lyonnais and Beaujolais). Presses Univ. Lyon, 540 pp., 58 tables.

Top: Tain. Hillside, village and wooded hill. Vines are grown in terraces on the gueiss slope and lower down on the screes which merge with the pebbly alluvial terrace more than 20 meters high (Demarcq photo).

Bottom: Vines at Crozes-Hermitage. Terraces and walls on the gueiss hill. At the foot vines are grown on the scree slopes (Demarcq photo).

Top: The Barsac district in the heart of the winegrowing Diois offers good examples of methodical planting of the limestone-rich outwash fans. At the base the Jurassic marls are deeply dissected by erosion (Truc. photo).

Bottom: Aurel, a splendid village with an abundance of sunlit vines shows slopes shaped a few thousand years ago by the last Quaternary glaciation now deeply dissected by run-off. In the foreground a fine outwash fan completely covered with vines (Truc. photo).

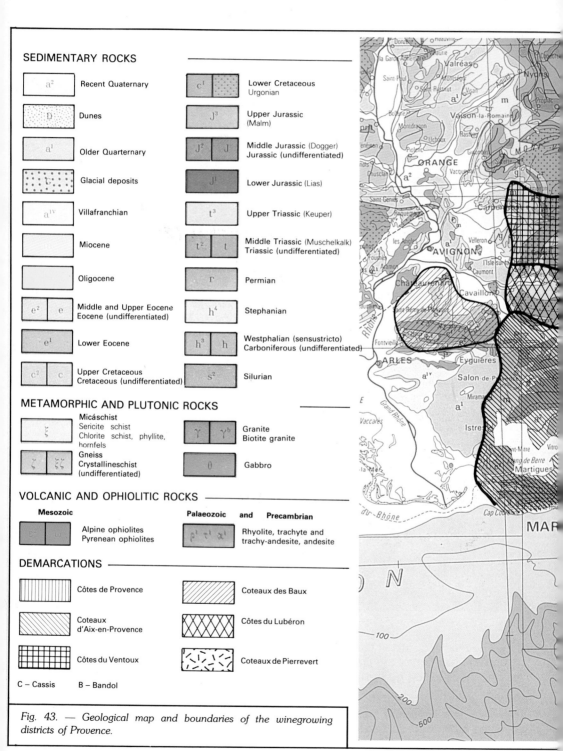

SEDIMENTARY ROCKS

a^2	Recent Quaternary	c^1	Lower Cretaceous Urgonian
D	Dunes	J^3	Upper Jurassic (Malm)
a^1	Older Quarternary	J^2 J	Middle Jurassic (Dogger) Jurassic (undifferentiated)
v	Glacial deposits	J^1	Lower Jurassic (Lias)
a^{IV}	Villafranchian	t^3	Upper Triassic (Keuper)
	Miocene	t^2 t	Middle Triassic (Muschelkalk) Triassic (undifferentiated)
	Oligocene	r	Permian
e^2 e	Middle and Upper Eocene Eocene (undifferentiated)	h^4	Stephanian
e^1	Lower Eocene	h^3 h	Westphalian (sensustricto) Carboniferous (undifferentiated)
c^2 c	Upper Cretaceous Cretaceous (undifferentiated)	s^2	Silurian

METAMORPHIC AND PLUTONIC ROCKS

ξ	Micáschist Sericite schist Chlorite schist, phyllite, hornfels	γ γ^b	Granite Biotite granite
ζ $\xi\xi$	Gneiss Crystallineschist (undifferentiated)	θ	Gabbro

VOLCANIC AND OPHIOLITIC ROCKS

Mesozoic		**Palaeozoic and Precambrian**	
s^2 ω	Alpine ophiolites Pyrenean ophiolites	ρ^1 τ^1 α^1	Rhyolite, trachyte and trachy-andesite, andesite

DEMARCATIONS

	Côtes de Provence		Coteaux des Baux
	Coteaux d'Aix-en-Provence		Côtes du Lubéron
	Côtes du Ventoux		Coteaux de Pierrevert

C – Cassis   B – Bandol

Fig. 43. — Geological map and boundaries of the winegrowing districts of Provence.

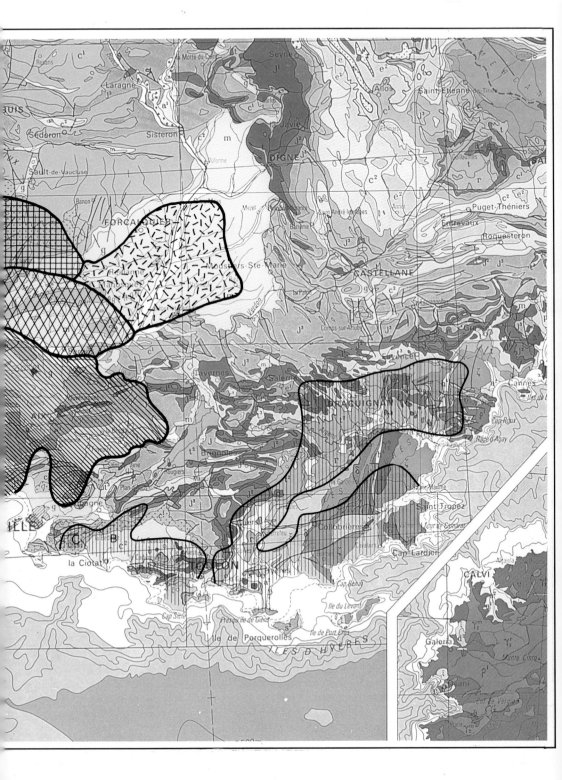

In his preface to R. Dumay's "Guide du Vin", P. Townsend, after having described the most famous rivers of France through the vineyards reflected in their waters adds: "... But the rivers which I love most are those ancient pebbly rivers of Provence, the Durance, Arc and Argens. It was the soil of Provence which received the first vines, and which was the first to yield wine in France". Nevertheless R. Dumay reminds us that "equipment has been found at the abbey of Thoronet which would prove that the growing of vines was practiced by Cistercian monks". The Provençal wine growing district was improved before the Roman conquest by the introduction of new varieties by the Greeks. Curiously the present reputation of the region is very low in comparison with that of the Bordelais, Bourgogne and Champagne. Perhaps this is due to the excessive distribution of mediocre "little Provençal rosés"?

To come to Provence, and to taste its wines and climate without the feverishness of holidays is to change the way one looks at life.

Vines and their soils

Geographical reminder

Winegrowing Provence includes vast areas in some natural regions: the Toulon depression at Saint-Raphael, the Arc Basin, the middle Var hills etc., but above all small to medium-sized pieces of land locked within the fragmented and tormented relief which is characteristic of the area. The first stony or forested hills, often at the mercy of fires, rise from the sea, limestones from Martigues to Sanary, sandstones or shales to the east, as far as Saint-Raphael. Close to Nice there are the Vallauris plateaux, the valley of the Var, and then the bastions of the Maritime Alps which border the shoreline. The red peaks and crags of Estérel strike a colourful note between Saint-Raphael and Cannes.

In the hinterland there is the elongated plain which isolates the Maures, drained to the south west by the Gapeau and to the east by the Argens. Then there is a country of hills of varying size, sometimes interspersed with low altitude plateaux, dominated by mountain chains rising to over 1000 metres: the Sainte-Baume, which is both massive and long, the Sainte- Victoire, which is more craggy and rocky. On the whole the high ground is aligned east-west, producing low zones having the same orientation, which are dominated by slopes of contrasting aspect.

The highest ground is to the east of the line joining Meyrargues, on the Durance, with the northern districts of Marseilles. To the west starts a region of low plateaux (200 m) and plains: the Crau, which provides a transition to the Rhône valley, the Camargue and the Bas-Languedoc. Only the Alpilles, with a height of almost 500 m, like a projection of the Lubéron, isolated between the Durance and Rhône, form the Costes which modestly supplement the southern edge of the valley of the Durance, between Salon and Meyrargues.

To the north west the Grand Lubéron and the Petit Lubéron form a marked barrier between the lower Durance and the Apt valley, a barrier which is incompletely cut by the Combe de Lourmarin (which is in fact a cross valley). Beyond the very wide synclinal depression of Apt and Calavon there rise the mountains and plateaux of Vaucluse, separated from Mont Ventoux (1902 m) to the NW by the Nesque gorge and the Aurel Trough. Ventoux and the western edge of Vaucluse form a vast amphitheatre facing Carpentras and the Rhône.

To the north east, hills cut by the Durance in the Mirabeau gorge separate the Digne-Valensole Basin and the Manosque hills from Basse-Provence. Here we are already in the Haute-Provence of Giono, with wide horizons dominated by high mountains. From the vines of Pierrevert, in the heat of a fine afternoon, the eyes are bewildered to see the snows of Cheval-Blanc and the Trois-Éve✷és, and the tall silhouette of the Tête-de-l'Estrop.

Geology of Provence

The structure of Provence (fig. 43) is very complex in detail. We will only subdivide the area into three units: the Hercynian basement, the tegument and the Alpine cover.

The basement outcrops in the hills to the south west of Toulon, at Hyères, particularly in the Maures and in the Tanneron. It consists of metamorphic siliceous schist roughly arranged in north-south bands. The valleys, hollowed in less resistant rocks following the same trend, are connected together by major erosional tracts which follow the dominant east-west fracturing. To the east of the Maures and in the Tanneron the rocks are more massive and granites (particularly Plan-de-la-Tour) and diorites intruding the gneisses can be seen.

The fracturing of the basement extends without change into the three units of the **tégument** which directly overlie it. At the base the Carboniferous is reduced to two southerly basins, forming a depression in the Maures, at Plan-de-la-Tour, in the Tanneron and along the Reyran and Biancon. The rocks are sandstones, acid or mixed volcanic rocks, rarely coal-bearing shales. The Permian consists of sandstones and conglomerates, but in particular fairly well-compacted wine-coloured pelites hollowed out by the Toulon depression at Saint-Raphael and red rhyolitic lavas which protect the high ground of l'Estérel and the Colle-du-Rouet. It is overlain by the indurated grits of the base of Trias, outcropping in a continuous ring at the northern edge of the depression, from Sanary to Muy, and then directly covering the base of the Tanneron.

The cover is compositionally and structurally very much more complex. It should be remembered that it is almost entirely made up of rocks containing an appreciable proportion of calcium carbonate. These include above all limestones, forming the bulk of the high ground, and marls with a greater or lesser sand content which outcrop in the depressions. Argillites with a lesser carbonate content are associated with gypsum in the lower levels (Trias), which form the region of Draguignan in particular. They are found again at the end of the Mesozoic and in the Tertiary of the Bandol Basin (Oligocene), the Marseilles-Aubagne Basin (Oligocene), the Aix-en-Provence Basin (Upper Cretaceous to Oligocene), and the Manosque and the Mormoiron Basins. Gravels and conglomerates which are consolidated to a greater or lesser extent, and always have a high carbonate content, form the terraces of the Durance, the Crau and the Tertiary deposits of the Valensole. The screes and colluvials which are of great importance to winegrowing generally consist of limestone clasts, even on the northern edge of the Permian depression. Only isolated silica-containing ranges (Sicié, the Maures, Estérel, south Tanneron) and the south of the depression contain exclusively siliceous colluvials.

Finally there are **four basaltic volcanic peaks** lying outside the Hercynian domain in the wider sense: Evenos, near Toulon, Rougiers and Beaulieu. The latter two bear vines, and their light and well drained soil is very kind to them. A fourth minute outcrop outside the winegrowing area is the Lubéron near Peypin d'Aygues.

The major subdivisions of the winegrowing area and the varieties planted

On the whole very much the same varieties and two dominant groups, one for Vin délimité de qualité supérieure (VDQS), the other recently for Appellation d'origine contrôlée (AOC), are characteristic of Provence, despite its geological diversity. The sun, which causes soils to dry out equally well over limestone, shale or volcanic rock, is undoubtedly the common factor. The four "old" appellations contrôlées still dominate quality output despite the considerable efforts made to improve this. Here time is in its favour and this very ancient producing region is becoming rejuvenated to justify and reinforce its reputation.

For red wines and rosés the varieties used are mainly cinsault, grenache and mourvèdre, generally with syrah and carignan, sometimes barbaroux and tibouren, or cabernet sauvignon. White wines are provided by clairette and ugni blanc, with bourboulenc and sauvignon. The proportions of the main and secondary varieties and their diversity contribute to the diversity of the output.

In addition to the VDQS and AOC qualities, Provence produces often pleasant local wines whose aereal limits follow the caprices of the topography. Here the southern sun arranges matters rather well: Along the Alpine Durance vines grow at over 700 m at Rémollon, and at up to 1100 m on the sunny slope at Réottier in the Hautes-Alpes!

The Camargue produces the **"Vins de Pays des Sables du Golfe du Lion"**, only on the sands of the coastal dunes, and of these the Listel of Salins-du- Midi is the best known, in red, rosé or white, and also the very clear light Gris de gris. The "Vins de pays de la Petite-Crau" are produced to the north of the Alpilles.

On the eastern side of the Rhône valley the **Côtes du Ventoux** (AOC) winegrowing area borders the high ground to the east of Carpentras. Its red wines are of a fine clear ruby colour and are strongly scented. The rosés are pleasant, the rarer whites are mainly made from clairette and bourboulenc.

A little further to the south the **Côtes du Lubéron** (AOC) surround the mountains in the lower Durance (south) and the Apt valley (north). The vine varieties are the same as in Ventoux, with a dominance of grenache, syrah, cinsault, mourvèdre and carignan for the reds, clairette and bourboulenc for the whites. The reds are lively and pleasant when drunk young, some however age well.

Going to the east one meets the **"Coteaux d'Aix-en-Provence — Coteaux des Baux-de-Provence"** which adorn the centre and the southern slope of the Alpilles. With the **"Coteaux d'Aix-en-Provence"**, which extend over forty eight communes in Bouches-du-Rhône and over two in the Var, these districts produce wines with the AOC classification. The underlying rock is essentially limestone in the form of cryoclastic colluvials as at Mas- de-la-Dame, near Baux. Cabernet sauvignon may represent up to 60% of the varieties accepted for red and rosés wines. It is very important in the production of Château-Vignelaure, near Rians. The wines must have a strength of at least 11°. The vineyards extend along the southern slope of the Durance valley, over the low plateaus between Salon and Aix, the hillsides in the Arc bassin, at the foot of Sainte-Victoire and to the east penetrate the low hills on the boundary between Var and Bouches-du-Rhône.

However, quite close to Aix-en-Provence, a small district of great quality has been distinguished with an appellation contrôlée, namely **Palette**, with Château-Simone vines, on the left bank of the Arc, on lacustrine limestone scree on a north slope. The remarkable reds should not make one forget the fruity and compliant blancs de blancs.

Near Marseilles the Côte des Calanques shelters the Cassis district (AOC), which is famous for its white wines. The vineyards lie with variable aspects (south, west and northwest) in the amphitheatre overlooking Cassis, on the scree slopes of the limestone hills. It also produces reds and rosés.

Appellation contrôlée **Bandol** extends over eight communes around the town. The land consists of hills of moderate relief, crowned by pine woods sorely tried by fires, of which the lower slopes bear the vines. The soil consists of limestone and silica, sometimes moderately influenced by Triassic gypsum. Vineyards have grown here since 600 BC, when the wine produced was put in amphorae and carried away in ships. The trade in reds, which fear almost no climate, began in the 18th century and went as far as Brazil and the Indies. The whites are mainly located around Sanary.

Since 1977 **Côtes-de-Provence** have had an AOC classification. This recent change in category has resulted in a gradual change in the varieties used. These are the conventional varieties, but in the case of whites vermentino and sémillon must be added. The wine must have a strength of at least 11°, and a classification of the vintages has been in existence since 1955. The soils vary greatly: from the limestone hillsides of Correns or La Ciotat to the shaly slopes of La Londe and Saint-Tropez, or again to the good soils of the Permian, well drained on the slopes and topographical crests which yield the excellent reds of Pierrefeu, Cuers or Les Arcs, and the rosés of Vidauban.

To the north of the Côtes-de-Provence, numerous communes in Var produce the wines of the **"Coteaux varois"**, which have recently acquired the VDQS classification. The growing district is often highly fragmented, except on the slopes which spread beneath the sun at Tavernes, Brignoles, Brue-Auriac or Saint-Maximim. The subsoil is limestone throughout the producing area.

To remain in Basse-Provence, mention should also be made of the Bellet district, around and above Nice, which provides wine with an AOC classification. This minuscule district occupies steep slopes on limestone scree and produces original reds and rosés thanks to two special grapes: folle noire and braquet, in addition to cinsault. The very pleasant whites are made from rolle, roussan and mayorquin.

Finally near Manosque the middle Durance region includes the **"Coteaux de Pierrevert"**, which extend over forty communes. With a good aspect these hills of moderate relief provide reds and rosés from conventional Provenal varieties. They also yield whites, a clairet and a very agreeable sparkling wine. The soil is a scree soil, originating from the Tertiary limestones and conglomerates.

The climates of the Provençal region and the lower Rhône valley

The Mediterranean climate, with hot dry summers and low rainfall, is typical here, but there are a few variations which are not without influence on vines and wines.

The Rhône valley, right bank (southern Côtes-du-Rhône, Tavel, Lirac, Costières du Gard, Vins des Sables du Golfe du Lion): A climate marked by long bouts of mistral, which dries the atmosphere, even in spring and autumn, and cools the winters to the point where frost occurs, despite the low altitude and a low rainfall, of the order of 500 mm, even lower in the Camargue.

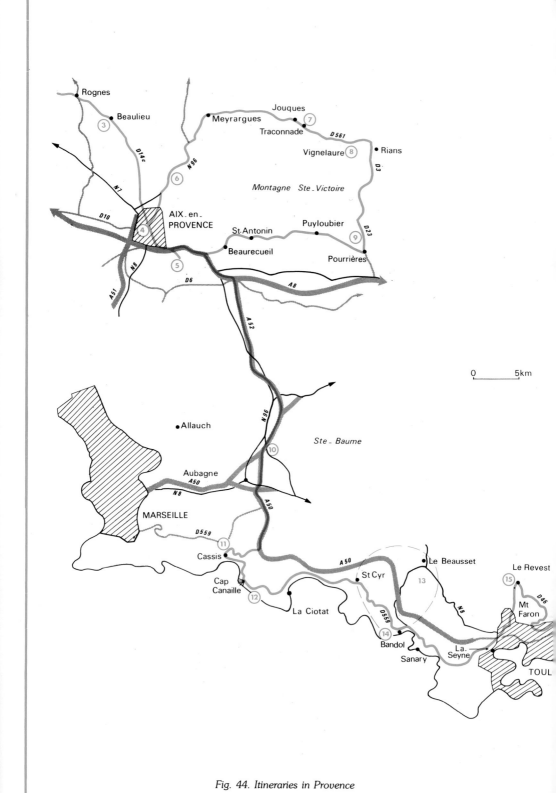

Fig. 44. Itineraries in Provence

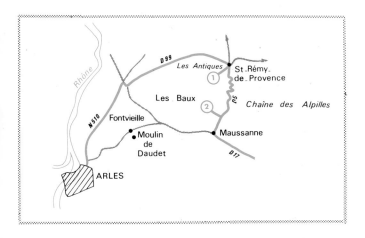

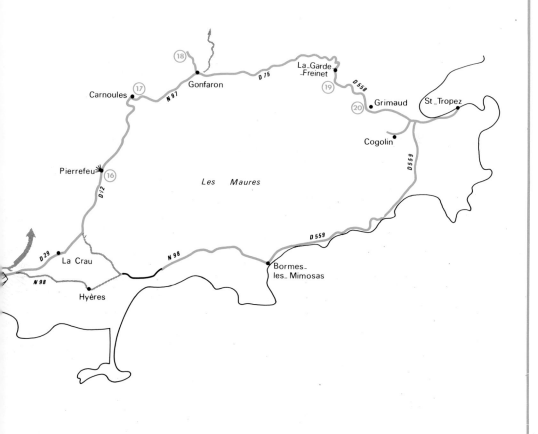

Coteaux d'Aix-en-Provence — *Coteaux des Baux-de-Provence*: a region showing similar tendencies, but attenuated by a higher altitude and higher rainfall.

Coteaux d'Aix-en-Provence sensu stricto and *Côtes de Provence*: areas where the influence of the mistral decreases progressively and rapidly to give way towards the east and southeast (Tour des Maures) to an easterly and southeasterly wind which brings heavy rain in winter, many storms in summer, and increases the rainfall towards the east (800 to 900 mm). The Coteaux of Varois are drier and cooler.

Palette has the same tendencies, but its topographical situation on a north slope, on limestone scree, relatively sheltered from the mistral, modifies the general picture. Winter frosts are a little more severe. The limestone scree, well areated and well drained, does not heat too much in summer here.

Cassis and Bandol are maritime districts, affected by fogs, in the medium rainfall zone of Provence. The mistral, which occurs at Cassis, is very moderate at Bandol. Aspects are variable, the limestone screes of the north slope are somewhat more favoured.

The Nice region has higher summer temperatures, but contrasts are softened by the sea. It can however snow in winter, as the mountains are close. Humidity and rainfall are fairly high (800 to 1000 mm).

The Pierrevert area shows an appreciable continental deviation from the Provençal climate. The mistral still plays an important part. Dry hot summers, cold winters, very low rainfall, an area with a marked rainfall minimum being centred a little to the south over Cadarache, with less than 500 millimetres.

Itinerary

From Arles to Saint-Tropez, via Aix-en-Provence, Cassis, Bandol and Pierrefeu

This route can be done in one day (rapid overview, a few stops, no tasting), but it is preferable to take three days over it (fig. 44).

From Arles to Salon-de-Provence via Baux-de-Provence

Leave Arles by the N 570 and then take the D 99 in the direction of **Saint-Rémy**. This far one travels along the northern foothills of the Alpilles, in the area dear to Van Gogh. The Urgonian and Hauterivian limestones dip northwards beneath the periglacial colluvials on which the road is built. Before reaching Saint-Rémy, note ahead and to the left the raised plateau of the Petite-Crau, an old terrace of the Rhône planted with vines (local wines).

At Saint-Rémy take the D 5 towards **Les Baux**. This passes through the area mined by the ancients (Roman remains) ①. Park on the right and cross the road to examine a geological section which shows a transgression of the Burdigalian (white molasse, to the north, with a slight northerly dip) over the Upper Cretaceous (grey limestone marls with freshwater fossils and a steeper dip). The Alpilles massif is an elongated WNW-ESE anticline marked by several stages of deformation. The road first climbs its northern flank, rising towards the col (240 m), and then descends a sinuous valley towards the south. Note the Hauterivian limestones with a slight northerly dip. An area of low ground is entered suddenly on crossing the Les Baux Fault. In front on the left there are workings of very red bauxite (an aluminium mineral originating from tropical weathering in Mid Cretaceous time).

On the right the depression is lined with thick well-drained limestone colluvials bearing the vineyards of Mas-de-la-Dame. The old village of Les Baux, rising on a promontory of Burdigalian molasse ②can be reached via the D 27A. There is a magnificent view over the marshes of Les Baux, Crau and the Camargue, to the south and southwest, the Alpilles and the Coteaux-des-Baux winegrowing district in the immediate vicinity.

Leave Les Baux by the D 5, which touches Maussane. The D 17 then leads to **Mouriès** (note the Rognacian limestone rocks, emerging from the alluvial plain). The hills to the north of Mouriès show Jurassic dolomites displaced over the Upper Cretaceous of the Maussane Syncline. The D 5 then scales the edge of the Crau, and descends towards the N 113 which leads to Salon.

From Salon-de-Provence to Aix-en-Provence via Lambese and Beaulieu

Take the D 572, and then, at Pélissanne, the D 15 which takes you along an alluvial depression on the Miocene between the limestone massif of Les Costes to the north and Barben to the south. After Lambesc the countryside becomes more pleasant and the reddish tints of the "belle peire de Rognes", a Middle Miocene molasse which rests on the Hauterivian of Les Costes at Rognes, will be noted. This lies in the Trévaresse seismic zone, where an earthquake in 1909 ruined the old villages from Lambesc to Venelles.

From Rognes the D 14C crosses the wooded massif of La Trévaresse and provides an opportunity to visit the **Beaulieu** winegrowing district ③(VDQS Coteaux d'Aix-en-Provence) which stands on Miocene colluvials and on basalt gravels from the old worn down volcano. The site is pleasant, surrounded by forested slopes on the limestones of La Trévaresse. The D 14C climbs these giving views over the Durance valley and the Lubéron which borders it to the north. Rejoin the D 14 and cross the agricultural Puyricard plateau on Oligocene and Miocene marls, to descend to Aix-en-Provence.

The town of **Aix-en-Provence** ④stands on a major NNE-SSW fault belt which provides a passage to the surface for the calcium carbonate containing hydrothermal waters (40 °C) which make the town a spa. The Romans occupied the site. Middle Miocene blue marls containing oysters and gastropods can be seen in the town near the psychiatric hospital. To the east begin the plateaux which shelter Lake Bimont and enclose the Montagne Sainte- Victorie, the Cézannian jewel of the Aix country.

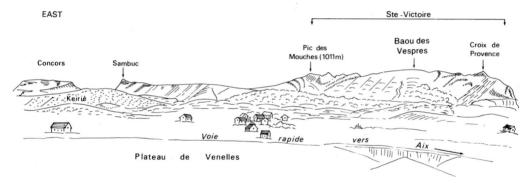

Fig. 45. View (looking east) from the butte de Venelles

From Aix-en-Provence to Rians. Palette and Chateau Vignelaure

Leave Aix by the N 7 going towards Nice and at Les Trois-Sautets bridge take the D 58H to Meyreuil. After crossing the Arc the minor road climbs the limestones of Montaiguet. At the end of the straight on the left lies the road to **Château Simone**, another jewel of the Aix country ⑤. From quality vines, a very favourable topographic and climatic situation and ageing caves cut in the rock in the 16th century by the Carmelites the chateau produces and improves exceptional wines which benefit from the appellation contrôlée "Palette". Depending on one's taste, one may prefer the dark, generous red wine, or the blanc de blancs, the rosé being less original for the region.

Returning to Aix outcrops of the Montaiguet limestones, the lignite levels which have yielded a rich reptilian fauna, can be examined on the road to the chateau.

Take the N 96, known as the Route des Alpes, which climbs the northern edge of the Aix bowl, and then cross the **Venelles** plateau ⑥. To the right a clear view of Montagne Sainte-Victoire (1011 m) flanked to the north by the Ubacs and Concors (fig. 45). These massifs of Mesozoic limestone meet the valley of the Durance at Meyrargues. Leave the N 96 at the Peyrolles turn-off and take the D 561 to the right. On passing notice the site of **Jouques**, a Provençal village tucked away in a cool and relatively damp valley ⑦. Tufa causes the stream to fall in cascades (similar tufas on the downstream side of the bridge, with traces of plants). The russet Miocene marine molasse crowns the heights around the village, above the grey Hauterivian limestone. Fossil marine shells and Helix (gastropods) can be found in the molasse, together with some ammonites in the Hauterivian limestone.

After Jouques the road passes close to the karstic spring of Traconnade, used by the Romans to contribute to the water supplies of the town of Aix. It is now used to supply drinking water to Jouques. The Hauterivian limestones and marls are capped by red Upper Cretaceous conglomerates underlying clay sandstones, and then the thick band of the Rognacian limestones. The road crosses this formation of lacustrine origin following the steep sided valley of the Jouques stream. Note the bridge over the Provence Canal (Bimont branch). At the start of the red argillites of the Rians Basin (Eocene), the road to **Château de Vignelaure** ⑧ lies on the right. This is an estate which produces a "Coteaux d'Aix-en-Provence" wine which is notable for its quality due to well-exposed limestone ground and very careful wine making from noble varieties, in particular cabernet sauvignon.

The Rians Syncline forms a W-E orientated depression between the Jurassic limestone massifs of the Ubacs (south) and Vautubière (north). At Rians itself the eastern extension of the syncline is marked by a transverse band of Trias (gypsum, cavernous dolomite), in a displaced position, which has subsequently slumped. The pebbly slopes are occupied by vines cultivated on "bancaous" (terraces with dry stone walling).

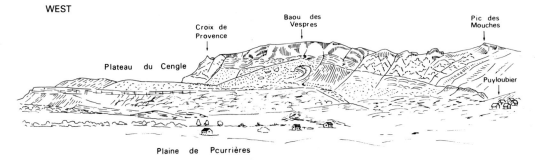

Fig. 46. Sainte-Victoire seen from the road to the south of Pourrière.

Note the flattened heights in the middle distance and the Baou des Vespres (remains of a Miocene erosion platform)

From Rians to Cassis via Puyloubier and La Barque

The D 3 leaves Rians towards the south. After 3.5 km take the D 23 to the right. Cross the austere massif of La Gardiole whose brooding oak groves form the setting for "Récits de la Demi-Brigade" by J. Giono. At Puits-de-Rians, a limestone and bauxitic breccia is covered by the clay limestones of the Fuvélian, with a characteristic lacustrine fauna. The road passes close to the unique feature of the Pain de Munition, then winds into a dry gorge in the direction of **Pourrières**. A little before this village one reaches the northern edge of the vast Arc Syncline, containing Upper Cretaceous and Tertiary strata ⑨.

The vines of Coteaux d'Aix-en-Provence occupy the pebbly piedmont of the Montagne Sainte-Victoire (fig. 46), whose cliffs dominate the landscape above Puyloubier. The D 17 and the D 58 run along the very foot of the mountain, in a remarkably colourful setting, through Saint-Antonin-sur- Bayon and Beaurecueil. Rejoin the motorway at Barque, and go towards Toulon. In this way one gets through the semi-urban area of La Bouilladisse and Aubagne without difficulty while enjoying excellent views over the chaotic hills which overlook them.

The motorway first rises on the northern monoclinal slope of the Regagnas (Fuvelian outcrops, with lignite), the summit of which (716 m) stands out in profile to the southeast. It then fairly quickly descends the faulted southern flank of the same massif. The tabular Allauch massif will be noted on the right, and forward to the left the bastions of Saint-Baume, here dominated by the limestone cliffs of Roussargue and Bassan (749 m), and in the background Bertagne (1041 m) and the high ridge (1147 m). At the Pont-de-l'Étoile ⑩ the motorway enters the small Oligocene basin of Aubagne. To the right the summit of Garlaban, dear to M. Pagnol, dominates the cliffs of the Allauch massif whose eastern border is fault bounded. In front is the less spectacular mass of the Douard which is crossed using a dry valley in the Urgonian limestones.

These pale rocks are followed at La Bédoule by the Aptian grey limestones and dark marls, overlain by a cornice of Cenomanian (sandstones, then limestones) and by Turonian at the Pas d'Ouillier cutting. At this point one enters the Upper Cretaceous Beausset Basin. On the right of the roadway an esplanade provides the opportunity to admire the view over the Bay of Cassis.

Leave the motorway at the Cassis spur and descend towards the town. The road passes through hairpin bends on the northeast slope of the Saoupe. The very fine AOC Cassis district ⑪ can be examined. This is located on the limestone screes which overlook the bay and benefit from exceptional exposure to the sun. Gastronomy and geology can be combined by tasting grilled fish or bouillabaisse with a local white on the port quay in front of the splendid cliff of Cap Canaille, in which russet bands of coarse sandstones run from south to north offsetting the white limestones containing rudists (Turonian). It provides a striking example of a lateral change in facies. It is then recommended that one follows the pedestrian promenade along the shore towards Arène to enjoy the seaside and examine the fossiliferous facies of the Cenomanian and the marly Lower Turonian.

From Cassis to Toulon via Bandol

If the fire prevention regulations permit it, chose to go to La Ciotat via the road running along the crest of Cap Canaille, which offers splendid views over the creeks to the west, Sainte-Baume to the north east and the Beausset Basin to the east. This will provide an overall view of the winegrowing districts of Saint-Cyr, La Cadière and Le Beausset, which are associated into the district of **Bandol** ⑫ . Descending towards La Ciotat note the alternating limestones, sandstones and conglomerates, and in particular, on the left, the site of the Pont-Naturel quarry. The D 559 leads pleasantly from La Ciotat to Saint-Cyr-sur-Mer at the edge of sea. The Senonian sandstone slabs outcrop intermittently. The winegrowing district forms part of the Côtes de Provence.

To examine the very special Bandol district it is preferable to take the network of small roads between Saint-Cyr, Le Beausset and Bandol which thread through the small hills with wine-coloured flanks and overshadowing forested summits ⑬ . In passing one can taste and then buy some of these full-bodied reds or an incomparable blanc de blanc to accompany grilled sea perch, for example at Baumelles (St-Cyr) or La Laidière (Evenos), which also yields a rosé with a remarkable fragrance.

At Bandol, at the end of the quay, examine a Tertiary conglomerate containing enormous basalt boulders from the flows of Evenos ⑭ . The Sanary road runs along the bay then crosses a wooded hill. Sanary leads directly into Toulon. Note on the right the Six-Fours fort, built on very resistant quartz-phyllites which form part of the Sicié massif, and in front, the limestone hills framing Toulon, including Mont Faron (542 m) and Mont Caume (801 m) further to the northwest. Part of the town of Toulon is built on Permian, the sandstones of which form the Saint-Mandrier peninsula to the south of the roadstead. Here therefore we have the three units, basement, tegument and cover within a traverse of a kilometre or so.

From Toulon to Saint-Tropez via Pierrefeu and La Garde-Freinet

The Toulon conurbation can be largely avoided by taking the D 46 which goes round the Faron massif. One might also examine Mont Caume, the site of the **Revest** ⑮ (red bauxite, between Urgonian limestone in the face and a cap of Cenomanian) and Mont Coudon (702 m) which overlooks the Permian Gapeau depression to the east. At Valette we rejoin the red Permian soils and enter the ring-shaped plain which borders Les Maures to the north west from Toulon to Saint-Raphael. The D 29 passes through the horticultural plain of La Crau and rejoins the D 12, which should be taken to the left.

This road runs along a piedmont of schist screes originating from the western edge of the Maures (chlorite schists). Competing with the well- drained hill tops on the Permian this piedmont bears the vineyards of Pierrefeu, one of the flowers of the Côtes de Provence. In fact some enthusiasts would only recognise the "reds of Pierrefeu, the rosés of Vidauban and the whites of Correns" as meriting this label. Many other places are however famous, and the classification of wines established in 1955 for example could be used.

At **Pierrefeu** ⑯ the cooperative vaults and an estate like l'Aumerade provide an opportunity to see whether one prefers the strong and coloured red, or the rosé, which is more treacherous to the legs, without forgetting a very pleasant white. A stay in this area would provide the opportunity to branch out towards the districts of Hyères and La Londe- les-Maures to the south, Cuers and Puget-ville to the north west and Carnoules to the north.

Take the D 13 which crosses the schist hills and arrives opposite Canoules, facing the strike scarp of the limestone Provence ⑰ . This is much more marked to the east, towards **Gonfaron**, where the D 39, to the left of N 97 on going through the village, provides a good section through the Palaeozoic-Mesozoic boundary ⑱ . The red Permian phyllites are conformably overlain by the pinker sandstones of the Lower Trias, themselves overlain by Muschelkalk limestones, here little deformed on the slip plane which separates them from the sandstones. Vines grow on Permian hills with a good aspect, partly covered by Triassic sandstone and limestone colluvials.

From Gonfaron the D 75 and then the D 558 can be taken to return to La **Garde-Freinet**. The austere rocky schist landscape of the Maures gives way to pine forest in the southern part of the Permian depression. After La Garde there are old workings on the right of the road where quartz and black tourmaline can be collected ⑲ .

At **Grimaud** ⑳ the road crosses the southern end of the Plan-de-la-Tour Granite and then descends into the Môle valley, going towards the Gulf of Saint-Tropez. The piedmonts of Grimaud, Cogolin, Saint-Tropez bear vineyards of the Côtes de Provence (in particular Château Minuty, Bourrian, etc).

From **Saint-Tropez**, the southern coastline of the Maures can be visited from Saint-Tropez to Bormes-les-Mimosas (Clos Mistinguett, Brégancon), to the more austere Cap Nègre where the mica schists yield garnets, kyanite and staurolite at Londe-les-Maures (clos Mireille, La Jeannette, Les Mauvannes, etc), and the valleys of the interior towards Croix-Valmer (La Croix) and Grimaud (cooperative vaults).

Thus, in the wild Maures or on their coastal edge, illuminated by the sea and the mimosas, we end our consideration of the relationships between sun, soils and wines in Provence which began in the glare of a mistral day at Les Baux.

Wines and gastronomy

Whether dealing with the produce of the land or the produce of the sea Provençal cooking makes use of two typical and standard additives: olive oil and garlic. With these naturally go tomatoes, occasionally peppers, and a varied palette of fines herbs (thyme, savoury, fennel, basil, etc.) offers many refinements. Specifically Provençal dishes are however a rarity: bouillabaisse, bourride, pistou soupe (basil), aôli and guinea fowl stuffed with black peppers and savoury are the highlights. The daubes, grillades and other recipes only represent local variations on more widespread themes.

Garlic, like cod, makes it difficult to find an ideal accompaniment for aôli. The least harm is done with a well chosen Provençal rosé (Vidauban, Saint-Tropez, some Pierrefeus) or a Listel Gris de Gris. The best rosés, with Bandol, Château Simone or a Beaulieu (Côteaux d'Aix), blend their slightly spicy flavour pleasantly with that of bouillabaisse, or fish soup, which if often rich in fragrances, or bourride, in which aôli melts in the rich cream of the fish broth.

With pieds-et-paquets, dear to the inhabitants of Marseilles, one may enjoy white Bandol or Cassis, or the magnificent blanc de blancs of Château Simone. Likewise fish grilled or flambé with fennel, sea perch, sea bream or even mullet, so estimable when fresh from the sea, and red mullet, grilled without being gutted, go well with the whites of the Côte Cassis or Bandol. The combinations of Bandol with fish and of Cassis with shellfish are probably best.

Grilled meats can be washed down with various reds: Pierrefeu, Saint-Tropez, Château Simone. Like a Bandol, the latter accompany meats in sauce, or game, for example the late autumn thrushes of the Valensole plateau. Just one rosé can compete with them and goes well with everything except fish: Tavel. We would however recommend one exception, the combination of Tavel or Bandol rosé with red mullet, the game of the sea.

FOR FURTHER
INFORMATION

Geology

Guide géologique Provence 2nd edition (1979) by C. Gouvernet, G. Guieu and C. Rousset. Masson édit., Paris. See in particular routes 4, 10, 11, 12, 13, 14.

Guide géologique Alpes-Maritimes-Maures-Esterel (1975) by R. Campredon et M. Boucarut. Masson édit. Paris. See in particular routes 1, 2 and 3.

Top: Château-Simone (AOC Palette), the chateau and the vineyards stand on the Lutetian lacustrine limestones of Montaiguet (Rousset photo)

Bottom: The Pierrevert vineyards on limestone scree and Tertiary conglomerate soils. In the background, from left to right, the hill of Toutes Aures, the hill of Mont d'Or de Manosque, the valley of the Durance and in the background the massif of the Tête de l'Estrop and Le Pelat (Rousset photo)

Opposite page: AOC Bandol. The Château des Baumelles at Saint-Cyr-les- Lecques. In the background the Upper Cretaceous monocline of le Camp (Rousset photo).

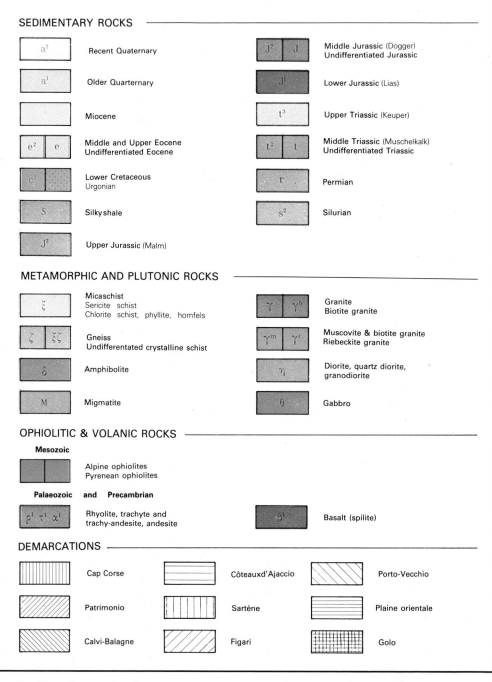

SEDIMENTARY ROCKS

a^2 Recent Quaternary	J^2 J Middle Jurassic (Dogger) Undifferentiated Jurassic
a^1 Older Quarternary	J^1 Lower Jurassic (Lias)
Miocene	t^3 Upper Triassic (Keuper)
e^2 e Middle and Upper Eocene Undifferentiated Eocene	t^2 t Middle Triassic (Muschelkalk) Undifferentiated Triassic
c^1 Lower Cretaceous Urgonian	r Permian
S Silky shale	s^2 Silurian
J^3 Upper Jurassic (Malm)	

METAMORPHIC AND PLUTONIC ROCKS

ξ Micaschist Sericite schist Chlorite schist, phyllite, hornfels	γ γ^b Granite Biotite granite
ζ $\xi\zeta$ Gneiss Undifferentated crystalline schist	γ^m γ^r Muscovite & biotite granite Riebeckite granite
δ Amphibolite	η Diorite, quartz diorite, granodiorite
M Migmatite	θ Gabbro

OPHIOLITIC & VOLANIC ROCKS

Mesozoic

Alpine ophiolites
Pyrenean ophiolites

Palaeozoic and Precambrian

ρ^1 τ^1 α^1 Rhyolite, trachyte and trachy-andesite, andesite

β^1 Basalt (spilite)

DEMARCATIONS

Cap Corse	Côteauxd'Ajaccio	Porto-Vecchio
Patrimonio	Sartène	Plaine orientale
Calvi-Balagne	Figari	Golo

Fig. 47. — Geological map and vineyard demarcations of Corsica.

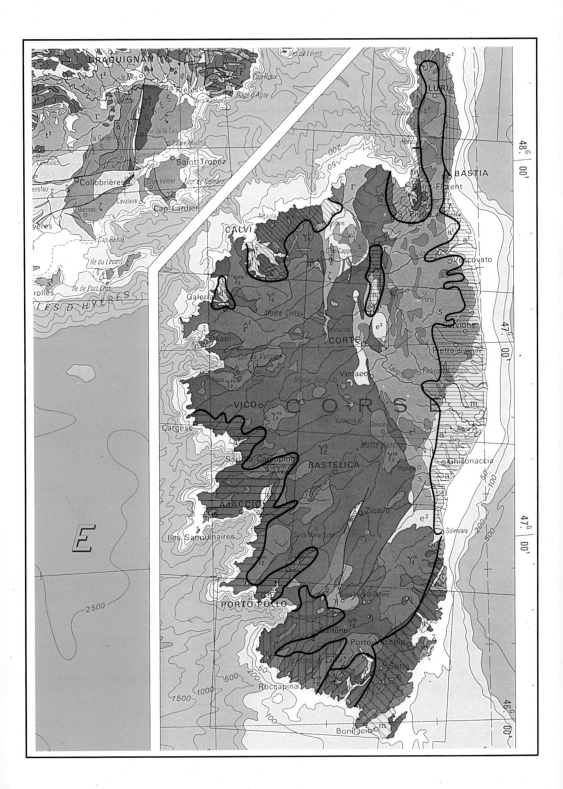

Vineyards have spread to different parts of Corsica at greatly varying rates over the years. It is hard to say who first brought vines into the island and when, but there was already mention of them by the Roman authors Strabo and Diodorus Siculus. It seems likely that vines were first introduced into Corsica by the Greeks or the Roman Legionaries.

The Genoese encouraged vine-growing in the Middle Ages, partly to ensure an adequate supply for themselves, and partly to control common grazing rights. Much later, in 1752, there was even a decree compelling every landowner to plant four vines. Vineyards are therefore as common on slopes as on level ground, and may be close to villages but are just as likely to be out among scrub and moorland, where they are always carefully enclosed by walls.

Planting methods remained outdated right into the 19th century. The land was worked with mattocks and the young vines were planted in trenches. Wine-making techniques were just as antiquated, and Corsican wine gained a reputation for not keeping.

With the opening up of the eastern plain the total area under vineyards in Corsica had risen to 30 000 hectares by 1976. Latest statistics show that in 1982 vineyard cultivation had fallen to 20 000 hectares, giving an annual production of slightly over 1 500 000 hectolitres.

Vines and soils

Geology

The traditional distinction is between eastern Corsica and the areas to the west. The soils in the eastern part of the island are identical to certain soils found in the Alps, which is why the region is known as Alpine Corsica. Similarly, the soils to the west have counterparts in the Maures and Estérel mountains, an ancient Palaeozoic basement area in southern France, and the region is known as Ancient or Hercynian Corsica (fig.47).

Western Corsica and Sardinia are formed by and large of the same rocks. A geologist sees both islands as a single entity. The rocks of western Corsica are for the most part granitic, but volcanic and metamorphic rocks are also found, as are occasional sediments. Eastern Corsica is composed mainly of various shale types and associated greenschists.

The junction of eastern and western Corsica is marked by the "central depression". This joins the mouth of the Regino, west of Ile-Rousse, with the mouth of the Solenzara, and is nowhere more than 600 metres high. The eastern plains are formed of recent sedimentary rocks.

The two large structural features mentioned above can clearly be seen when the geographical map and the geological map are compared. The island has four main geographical areas: western Corsica, the central depression, eastern Corsica and the plains. This is explained by four large geological units known as granitic Corsica, shaly Corsica, the structurally complex central lowlands and the sedimentary plains (A. Gauthier: *Roches et paysages de la Corse*, 1983).

Climate

"Its latitude and its position at the very heart of the Gulf of Genoa make Corsica a natural and integral part of the Mediterranean climatic zone, with both sub-tropical and temperate affinities..." (Simi, 1981).

"Corsica is a mountain surrounded by sea. Winds bring in moist air which is obstructed by the mountains and condenses..." (Ratzel).

These two quotations sum up the island's climatic conditions perfectly. The very hot summers and the mild lowland winters are part of Corsica's attractions. Rainfall is directly related to the prevailing winds. On western hillside slopes, the Libeccio is responsible for most of the rain. Precipitation on the eastern hill-slopes is affected by the Sirocco, which blows from the southeast. These rains are generally irregular with two peaks. The largest is in November-December, with a weaker one in February-March. There are about 2 750 hours of sunshine annually, one of the best records in France.

Soil

Corsica has a wide variety of rocks and a complex structure, giving it very varied soils.

Those derived from granitic rock (tours 1, 2 and 5) are often mixed with sand and may show different stages of development. Soil formed from recent erosion is a mixture of sand and gravel, usually shallow, grey and rocky, or else brown on the surface. Brown, lateritic soils may be found, resulting from ancient erosion.

The soils of the eastern plains (tours 3 and 4) were formed on the Miocene or alluvial deposits. The Miocene produces light to heavy, acid soils. On the ancient, leached alluvials the soils are very pebbly, acid and low in nutrients.

The red soils are relatively pebble-free with a silty texture. They are reasonably well provided with nutrient elements. Brown terrace soils are a light, acid, sand-loam mixture with a high proportion of pebbles. Recent alluvial deposits are rich in nutrient elements and very varied in texture.

In general, the soils of the maquis had reached a state of balance and were not particularly acid. Once cleared and cultivated, however, this balance was disturbed by harvesting, the leaching effect of irrigation and the use of acidifying fertilizers. Except in the somewhat rare calcareous areas, all the soils are acid. This can lead to problems with vine nutrition, and growers therefore use considerable amounts of lime and phosphoric acid to correct the situation.

Vine varieties

A diagram would show that there are two types of vineyard in Corsica:

• *Those on hill-slopes and in traditional areas,* sited around villages below the 300 to 350 metres contour (Sartène, Ajaccio, Balagne, Nebbio, Cape Corse), and also on certain slopes in the eastern plain, are in general planted with varieties of the twenty-six local strains.

Three main varieties unquestionably stand out from the rest. A white grape, the vermentino or Corsican malvasia (malmsey), is picked just before it is fully ripe, giving a very high quality wine with a lovely greeny-yellow colour, good acidity, a fairly high alcohol content (12 to 13.5°) and a distinctive aroma. There are also two red grapes.

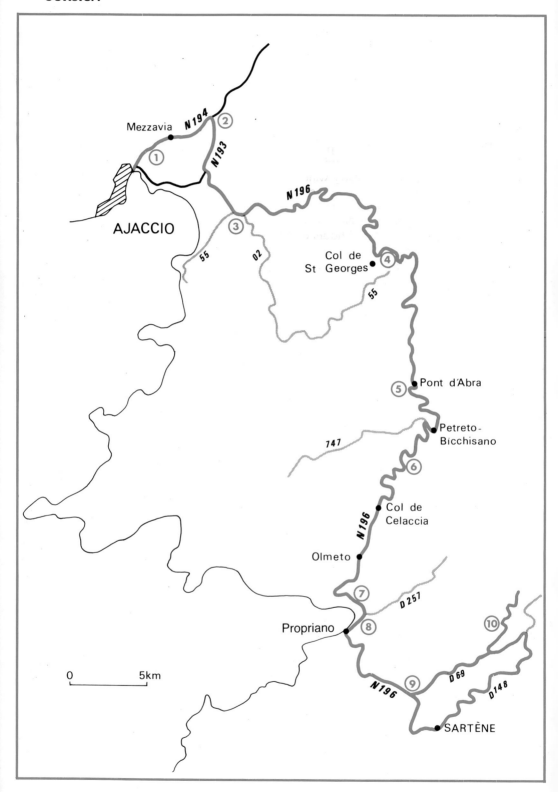

Fig. 48. — Tour 1, Ajaccio to Sartène

The nielluccio is the base for the Patrimonio red wines, which are high in colour, rich in bouquet, well-structured and plump, with over-tones of grenache, cinsault and vermentino. The other is the sciaccarello, the grape "which crunches when you bite it". It makes a red wine which is sometimes a little short on colour, but with its peppery bouquet and its robust, well-knit structure it is an incomparable base for red and rosé wines.

Provided the wine-making has gone well this type of vineyard produces high quality wines, and since 1972 they are all within the AOC (appellation d'origine controlée) area. Yield is nevertheless sometimes fairly low (20 to 40 or 45 hectolitres per hectare) and there are local outbreaks in Marana-Casinca and Nebbio of golden mildew, a fungal disease transmitted by a variety of leaf-hopper.

• *The vine-growing areas of the great alluvial plains,* especially the eastern plain, have large estates and a vine selection dominated by varieties from Provence (grenache, cinsault, carignan). The vineyards have châteaux where building regulations permit, and produce wines for everyday drinking which are also intended for blending. A small part of the production comes from recommended varieties of grape, yielding wine of good quality when harvested from the ancient Quaternary alluvia.

Itineraries

The regions of Ajaccio and Sartène are traditional wine districts with a long-established reputation. With their well chosen grape varieties (the vermentino, or Corsican malmsey, and sciaccarello) these vineyards have been producing noted wines for a long time.

The Ortolo valley, in the south of the region, also saw the birth of modern vine-growing techniques in Corsica when the island's first industrial vineyard was founded at the end of the 19th century.

In the last twenty years a new wine district has grown up in the Navara and Ortolo valleys and the Sotta-Figari lowlands.

The stops on tours 1 and 2 will allow the traveller to find the main igneous rocks:

— granodiorites with potassium feldspar, plagioclase (also known as soda-lime feldspar), dark mica (biotite), amphibole (hornblende) and quartz;

— monzonites, with a higher potassium feldspar content, often found in association with basic rocks (diorites and gabbros);

— leucocratic granites, so called because of their lighter colour, with a high feldspar and quartz content, and containing light coloured mica.

— alkaline granites which, like the leucocratic granites, form escarpments.

Ajaccio to Sartène

The Ajaccio region:

Leave Ajaccio by the N 193. At the **Col de Stiletto**, take the turning on the right leading to a vineyard (fig.48).

(1) The vineyard is planted on gently sloping hillsides, on granitic monzonite with a high sand content. The rock here is coarse grained, with pink potassium feldspar, white plagioclase, biotite and traces of hornblende.

(2) Return towards **Mezzavia**. Continue along the N 193 as far as the new airport road which leads northeast. Notice the contrast between the lower Gravona valley, hollowed out of the weathered granites, and the sharp relief of the uplands of Gozzi and Aragnasco, composed of alkaline granites. The flat hills overlooking the river are old quaternary terraces.

(3) Take the new road and turn right onto the N 196 towards **Cauro**. Between the intersections with the D 55 to Porticcio and the D 302 to Pila-Canale samples of monzonite can be found.

A kilometre beyond the cork factory, proceed to a vineyard planted on weathered granitic monzonite and alluvials, between two streams known as the Morgone and the Mutulaja.

(4) Take the N 196 from Cauro as far as **Olmeto**. The road winds over Col Saint-Georges among generally deeply-weathered porphyritic monzonites.

(5) In the area of the **Abra bridge**, the presence of black ferromagnesian minerals such as black mica and hornblende, as well as plagioclases, are the classic signs of a granodiorite.

(6) After **Petreto-Bicchisano** the road runs for a while through an area with many escarpments, showing that it has entered a different kind of granite (in this case, alkaline granite).

The Baracci valley:

Leaving Olmeto, turn left onto the D 257 which leads down to the Baracci. Cross the river and take the road which runs parallel with it until you reach Propriano.

(7) Stop when you see vines growing by the road. There is diorite in the bank on the left. The vines are on weathered granite. Notice the panorama: to the north is Monte San Petro with its leucocratic granite; to the northwest is a view over the village of Olmeto; to the southwest, beyond a group of vine-clad hills, is an aspect of Propriano and the gulf.

(8) South of the intersection between the D 257 and the N 196 is a marine deposit of Pliocene sand and sandy marl.

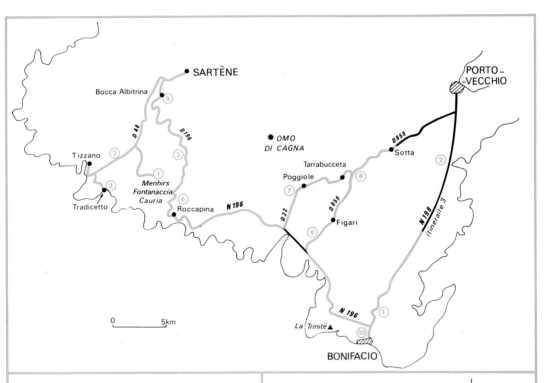

Fig. 49. — Tour 2, Sartène to Bonifacio, and beginning of tour 3, Bonifacio to Porto-Vecchio

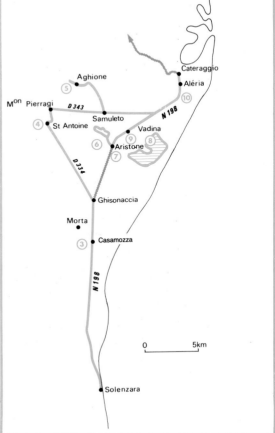

Fig. 50. — Tour 3, Solenzara to Aléria.

The lower Rizzanese valley:

⑨ Go through **Propriano** and take the N 196 to Sartène. In many places south of the Rizzanese, leucocratic granite stands out against the horizon. The banks beside the road, five hundred metres before the intersection with the D 258, give an idea of the intense weathering of the granodiorite on which the vineyard stands.

⑩ Take the D 268 as far as the Genoese bridge known as Spina at Cavallu, and cross the Rizzanese. The vineyards stand on level areas which are ancient terraces from which all pebbles have been removed. Outcrops of weathered granodiorite may be seen at many points in the fields. Notice how many diorites and gabbros can be seen in the heaps of stones. Return by the same route and take either the D 69 or the N 196 to **Sartène.**

Sartène to Bonifacio

Sartène is built entirely of local granite. Leave by the Bonifacio road, which overlooks the valley and vineyards of the lower Rizzanese (see tour 1).

The Navarra valley:

At Bocca Albitrina take the D 48 towards Tizzano. In this area there are some particularly fine outcrops of gabbrodioritic basic rocks. This valley also has many ancient megaliths which may be seen close to the vines. Stay on the D 48 for 10 km and bear left. In another 4.5 km you will reach the Cauria Plateau (fig.49).

① Visit the alignment of menhirs at **Stantari**, alongside a vineyard standing on weathered granite. Make the most of the occasion by taking a close look at the dolmen of Fontanaccia, the finest in Corsica.

② Return to the D 48. Two km further on towards Tizzano, take the sandy road off to the right, signposted "Alignement de Palaggiu". To the west the menhir alignment overlooks the granite slopes with their diorite veins and covering of vineyards.

③ Return to the D 48 and 2 km before **Tizzano** turn left onto a track to Tradicetto beach. The track skirts the side of the Punta di a Petra Nera (gabbro). On the western shore are fine specimens of gabbros and diorites. The vineyard to the north of Tradicetto stands on terraces along the edge of the Navara and on the granite slopes and basic rocks.

④ Return to **Bocca Albitrina** along the D 48. On the N 196, between 3 and 5 km after the col, notice the outcrops of diorite and gabbro as well as the onion-skin weathering in the basic rocks.

The Ortolo valley:

Pass through the hamlet of Orasi. Down below are the middle reaches of the Ortolo valley. Notice how the Ranfone ridge comes right down to the left bank. Five hundred metres before the Ortolo bridge, turn left onto the dirt road for Leva mill and continue for 1 or 2 km.

⑤ Vines cover the gently sloping hills. The constituent granite is very sandy and the scars of fluvial erosion are clearly visible between the rows. On the left bank, slabs of leucocratic granite in the Ranfone ridge carry some fine grooves. On the right bank close to the bridge, vines are planted on an ancient terrace (a gap in the talus). After the Col de Carali, the N 196 crosses a ridge of leucocratic granite.

⑥ There are many eroded notches and cavities (tafoni), and the rocks close to the Roccapina inn are like a bestiary frozen for all eternity into the shape of lions, elephants, etc. Looking to the left during the descent to Piannotoli you can see the bulk of the Uomo di Cagna. On the right by the sea is a dune formation.

The Sotta-Figari lowlands:

Pass Piannotoli-Caldarello and the Uomo di Cagna cooperative cellars, then turn left onto the D 22 towards **Poggiale**.

⑦ Just before the village, notice the vines on the left. They stand on alluvial deposits from the Canella and on colluvial sands. The panorama includes a fine view of the leucocratic granite massif of the Uomo di Cagna and the boulder field at its peak from which it gets its name. Stay on the D 22 towards Tarrabucceta. Join the D 859 towards Sotta.

⑧ The bank on the right of the junction between the D 859 and D 59 contains diorite with many acid veins. Another kilometre brings us to the Sotta lowlands. The red hills on the left are composed of alkaline granite. The uplands in the distance have peaks of leucocratic granite and their lower slopes are granodiorites and coarse-grained monzonites. As you approach Sotta from the west there is an old diorite quarry.

⑨ Return via the D 859 and continue for about 2 km beyond Figari. On the right there are large numbers of vines on the coarse-grained, mainly weathered monzonite. The view includes an outlook over the Figari lowlands with their recent alluvial deposits.

Take the N 196 towards **Bonifacio.** After the mere at Ventilegne the road climbs up through leucocratic granite to the Col d'Arbia. Mont de la Trinité with its castellated outline dominates the skyline to the left.

⑩ The **port of Bonifacio** is a ria, an ancient drowned valley known locally as a calanque. Its outlines continue inland as two dry valleys, one of which is used by the N 198. The cliffs are composed of several tens of metres of cross-bedded white limestone showing signs of the currents prevailing when the formation was deposited. The limestone dips gently towards the southeast, and the base of the formation can be seen in the north and east (see tour 3).

Bonifacio to Aleria

(fig.50)

Bonifacio - Porto-Vecchio:

① The base of the Miocene marine transgression can clearly be seen at kilometre post 5 on the N 198 towards Porto-Vecchio. It consists of a denudation

Fig. 51. — Tour 4, Cap Corse, the Saint-Florent and Patrimonio region.

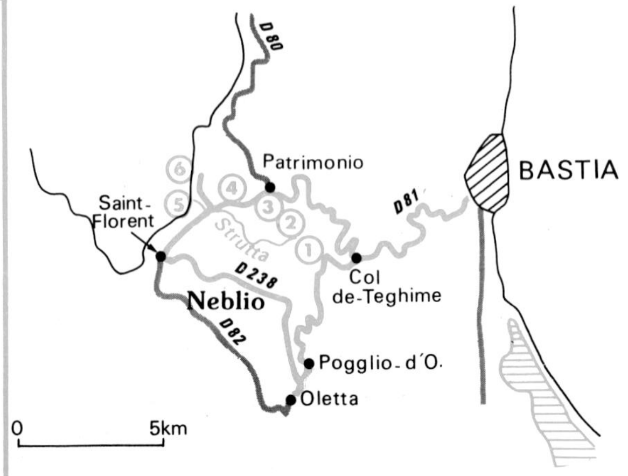

Fig. 52. — Tour 5, Saint-Florent to Calvi.

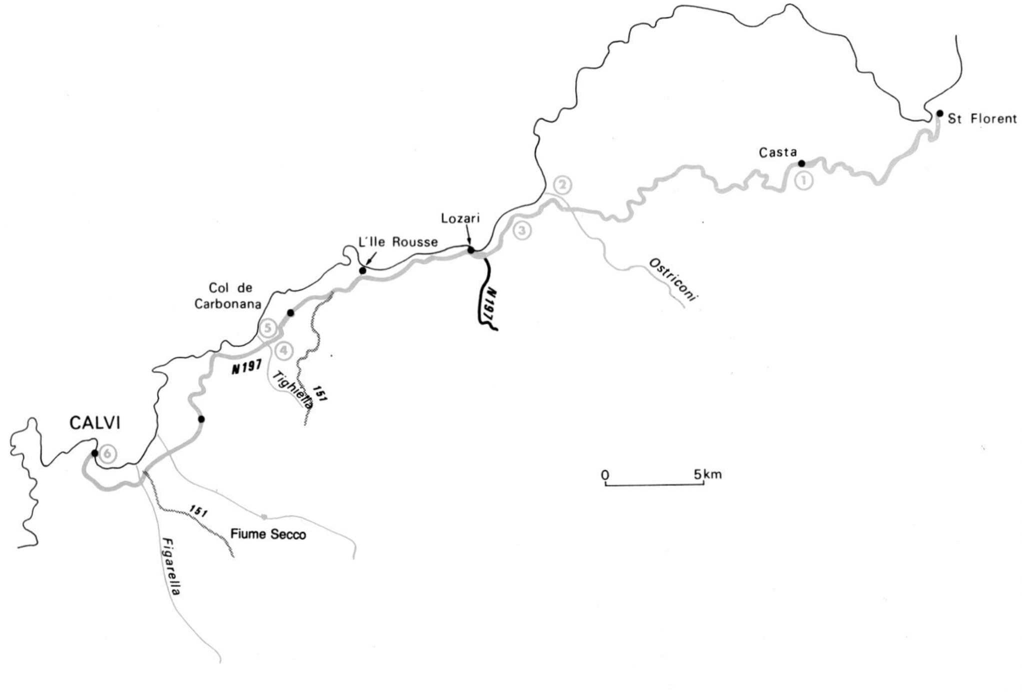

level on the underlying granite, and shows a littoral facies with a classic shoreline fauna (*pecten,* oysters, sea urchins).

② In another 15 km, opposite the Santa Giulia cooperative cellars, are vines on sandy granitic monzonite and recent alluvial deposits.

The town of **Porto-Vecchio** is built on a granodiorite with numerous veins of microgranite. The N 198 continues across the same rock to just beyond Sainte-Lucie de Porto-Vecchio. It runs through gneiss as far as Solenzara, then through the Eocene flysch of Solaro.

Solenzara - Ghisonaccia - Aléria:

Beyond Solenzara, as far as Ghisonaccia, the N 198 is built on alluvials.

③ In the Casamozza-Morta area the vineyards are on red terrace soils.

At Ghisonaccia take the D 334 to the hamlet of Saint-Antoine. As far as the outskirts of the village the road is built on more recent alluvial deposits than those underlying the township. Take the dirt road to the right of the bar "La Treille" and go down towards Fium'Orbo.

④ Recent brown terrace soils may be seen. The conglomeratic formation on the right bank opposite is the base of the Miocene, which has been strongly upthrust by faulting near the contact with Alpine Corsica.

Go to Maison Pierragi via the D 343A and turn right onto the D 343. At Samuleto wine-cellars turn left towards Aghione.

⑤ The sandy marl formation at Aghione (lower Langhian) outcrops on the left bank near the Tagnone bridge. It is locally rich in remains of plants and lamellibranchs. Beneath Aghione cemetery the sandy marls contain many sea urchins (*Schizaster*).

Return by the D 343 heading east. Then turn south onto the N 198 for 5 km as far as the Aristone sawmills. Turn right onto the road for the Alzitone dyke, then return on the N 198 as far as Aléria after doubling back on the minor road to Urbino.

⑥ In the area of Alzitone, fossil soils represent a period of land formation signifying the retreat of the Miocene sea after the Aghione formation was laid down.

⑦ At the junction of the N 198 and the Urbino road, arenaceous and calcareous sandstone formations together with coral reefs testify to a second marine transgression.

⑧ There are Quaternary deposits on the **Urbino peninsula** containing the remains of a lagoonal fauna such as Cardium and Cerithium shells. They can be seen at the top of a slope in a vineyard on the left of the road.

⑨ The Vadina region has fossil-rich deposits of grey shale of Late Tortonian age. They are the final marine formations of the Miocene.

⑩ At the southern end of a sharp bend in the N 198, between the Casabianda estate and Aléria, some generally arenaceous marls can be seen. Their marine microfauna places them in the Early Pliocene.

Below the fort of Aléria, where the D 43 crosses the N 198, is a deltaic conglomerate formation of Messinian age.

Between Aléria and Bastia, in the area around Marana and La Casinca, is a large vineyard standing mainly on the Bravona valley alluvials.

Cape Corse — Saint-Florent region — Patrimonio

Cape Corse:

The vineyards of Cape Corse have long been the pride of the island's vine-growing reputation. Their produce was even exported far and wide. At the present time they represent only a very small fraction of the total production (muscats and white wines). The time-honoured practice of withering the grape naturally or artificially to increase its sugar content still continues.

Take the D 80 from Bastia, continuing for about a kilometre beyond **Santa Severa**. The road passes first through gabbros and then through the mica schists of Santo Pietro di Tenda, where there is a small vineyard.

Stay on this road as far as **Macinaggio**. At the cemetery, take the small road connecting the D 80 to the D 53. The vineyard is mainly located on the alluvial terraces either side of a stream known as the Gioelli.

Saint-Florent region — Patrimonio

This tour takes in the Nebbio, lying between the Tenda and Cape Corse, and its main structural units can be seen: the calcareous Miocene of Saint Florent, allochthonous sedimentary formations from the Palaeozoic to the Eocene, mica schists and the original substratum. The renowned Patrimonio vineyard is located on the first two of the four units just mentioned.

Take the D 81 from Bastia as far as the Col de Teghime. The road winds among mica schists, pillow lavas (basalt which was extruded in submarine eruptions and cooled into pillow-like masses) or the old basement. As the road climbs, notice the splendid view to the southeast across the Biguglia mere and the plains of Mariana and La Casinca. In clear weather it is possible to see the Italian islands of Elba and Capraia. Leaving the Col, drive for about a kilometre along the D 38 towards Oletta and then stop (fig.51).

① From here we have a commanding view of the **Saint-Florent Basin.** Its western edge is formed by the Tenda uplands, and four limestone hills mark the boundary of the plain. In the middle distance we can see two lower ranges of hills which, like the hills just mentioned, belong to the sedimentary formations of the Nebbio.

② Return to the Col and take the D 81 to **Patrimonio,** stopping by the Post Office. A track leads away from the left-hand side of the road and makes its way between the vines planted on the alluvials of a stream called the Vaccareccia. A walk of about fifteen minutes brings us to the foot of Mount Pinzute and Mount Pughiali. The southeastern slope of Mount Pughiali is composed of detrital formations of the Permo-Trias and grey dolomites of the Triassic, and its summit is Jurassic limestone.

③ Return to Patrimonio and make for the intersection of the D 80 and the D 8. Dark basic lavas can be seen in the bank beside the road. They are of the basaltic type, with a brown patina. Pillow lavas can be recognised without too much difficulty.

④ Continue along the D 81 and stop by a small vineyard just before the **Strutta gorge.** Cross to where a fig tree marks the observation point and notice the cliff, formed of sloping limestone strata of the Middle Miocene. One of the levels is composed mainly of the remains of bryozoa, lamellibranchs and echinoderms, indicating ancient shore deposits and coastal barriers.

Take the cross valley of the Strutta, past a transformer, and follow the track on the right towards the sea. Ford the stream. Some 200 metres to the north is a marine Quaternary deposit.

⑤ The rocks in this area are dune sandstones on Miocene limestones. Their highest points are flattened and planted with vines. These sandstones date from 35 000 years (± 3 000 years) B.P.

⑥ Continue northwards along the track. Beside the stream is a superb outcrop of rhyolitic pudding-stone. This undated conglomerate marks the top of the Neogene. Return to Saint-Florent by road.

Saint-Florent — Lozari — Calvi

The main topics of interest on this trip are the granites and sediments of the Balagne district. At the end of the 18th century, vines were the third most important crop after cereals and olives. At that time they were to be found on hillsides and sloping ground close to villages. They are now the main crop, with as many as 1 100 hectares under cultivation, and have spread to the alluvial plains and low-lying granitic areas (fig.52).

① On either side of the village of **Costa** is an unmetamorphosed and deeply weathered granodiorite. It is planted with crops including vines.

② Where the Ostriconi joins the main stream, note the panorama over the Quaternary dunes on the red-brown granite of the Cima alle Forchie upland.

③ Between Ostriconi and Lozari the road has been cut "en corniche" along a cliff composed of the Eocene sandy flysch of Balagne.

The Aregno depression — Algaiola

Make for the **Ile Rousse** and then the **Col de Carbonaia** via the N 199. We can look down over the Aregno depression, hollowed out of a generally weathered pseudo-porphyritic granite with no truly fluviatile deposits.

④ At the end of the descent from the Col de Carbonaia there is a bend. Take the track on the left towards the chapel of San Cipriano. The road gradually dips down into a very weathered granite where crystals of potassium feldspar stand out in relief.

⑤ Take the track leading north 500 metres before the bridge over the Tighiella. It takes us to a quarry where a stone column of imposing proportions lies abandoned. It is composed of a lovely rock with phenocrysts of pink potassium feldspar, low amounts of quartz, a high ferromagnesian content (dark mica and amphibole) and an abundance of sphene.

Return to **Calvi** via the N 197.

⑥ At the port, below the citadel, is a lovely light-coloured granite with large crystals of potassium feldspar and crystals of honey-brown sphene. In the distance, the mountainous barrier formed by the Permian cauldron of the Cinto stands above the somewhat lower granitic uplands.

If you return to Bastia or Ajaccio along the N 197, take the opportunity to visit the little vineyard of Ponte-Leccia. It stands partly on the alluvials of the Asco and partly on very weathered serpentinite and schist.

Wines and gastronomy

Corsica produces such a wide range of wines that it is never hard to find a good accompaniment for any dish[1].

The white wines go well with seafood. Choose a very young one to drink with aziminu (Corsican bouillabaisse) and with fatty-textured fish. For other salt-water fish, as well as the small but tasty Corsican trout, choose a slightly older wine.

The same wines may be served with 'charcuterie' to start the meal, and are essential drinking with the goat cheeses to round off.

Some would rather have a rosé, provided it is young, in preference to a white. A slightly older rosé will go happily with white meats.

The red wines may be drunk with all kinds of meat and game. Choose the supple and fruity wines of the south for grills and roasts. The more robust northern wines are ideal with meats cooked in sauce and with game. It is as well to stay with the same wine when rounding off the meal with sheep cheese.

Finally there are the sweet wines. Muscat from Cape Corse or Patrimonio will accompany the dessert or the traditional toast of "a saluta" (good health) and make an excellent aperitif. Another aperitif to be tasted is rappu. This is obtained by adding an eau-de-vie or a wine-based aperitif called Cap (Corse, naturally) to the unfermented juice of the red grape.

FOR FURTHER
INFORMATION

Geology

Guide géologique Corse (1978) (Guide to the Geology of Corsica), by M.Durand-Delga et al., Masson, Paris. See especially tours 1, 5, 7, 8, 11, 13, 14, 15 and 18.

Gauthier A. (1983). — Roches et paysages de la Corse (The Rocks and Scenery of Corsica), published by Parc naturel régional de la Corse, 144 p. with many photographs and maps.

Simi P. (1981). — Précis de géographie physique, humaine, économique et régionale de la Corse (An Outline of the Physical, Human, Economic and Regional Geography of Corsica), from the Collection 'Corse d'hier et de demain', No 11, 608 p., 37 fig.

---

[1] This section is based on an article by A.Vedel.

Oenology

Vine selection: pamphlet published by Uvacorse edited by F.Mercury.

Gastronomy: pamphlet published by Uvacorse edited by A.Vedel.

The 'Société de mise en valeur de la Corse' (SOMIVAC — the Corsica Development Society) publishes a quarterly journal including numerous articles on vine growing.

Above: The Navarra valley. Vineyards and menhirs at Stantari (Photo. Gauthier).

Below: Vines in the Ortolo valley (Photo. Gauthier).

Facing page: A vineyard in the eastern plain of Corsica, Propriano region (Photo. Gauthier).

SEDIMENTARY ROCKS

a^2	Recent Quaternary
a^1	Older Quarternary
a^{ls}	Les Landes Sands
p	Pliocene
	Miocene
	Oligocene
g-e	Sidérolithique
e^2 e	Upper and Middle Eocene Undifferentiated Eocene

c^2 c	Upper Cretaceous Undifferentiated Cretaceous
J^3	Upper Jurassic (Malm)
J^2 J	Middle Jurassic (Dogger) Undifferentiated Jurassic
J^1	Lower Jurassic (Lias)
t^2 t	Middle Triassic (Muschelkalk) Undifferentiated Triassic
r	Permian
h^4	Stephanian
b	Cambrian

METAMORPHIC AND PLUTONIC ROCKS

ζ	Mica schist Sericite schist Chlorite schist, phyllite, hornfels
ζ $\zeta\zeta$	Gneiss Undifferentiated crystalline schist
δ	Amphibolite
M	Migmatite

γ γ^b	Granite Biotite granite
γ^m γ^l	Muscovite & biotite granite Riebeckite granite
η	Diorite, quartz diorite, granodiorite

DEMARCATIONS

	Bergeracois
	Côtes de Duras and Marmandais
	Côtes de Buzet
	Cahors
	Gaillac

	Côtes du Brulhois
	Coteaux du Frontonnais

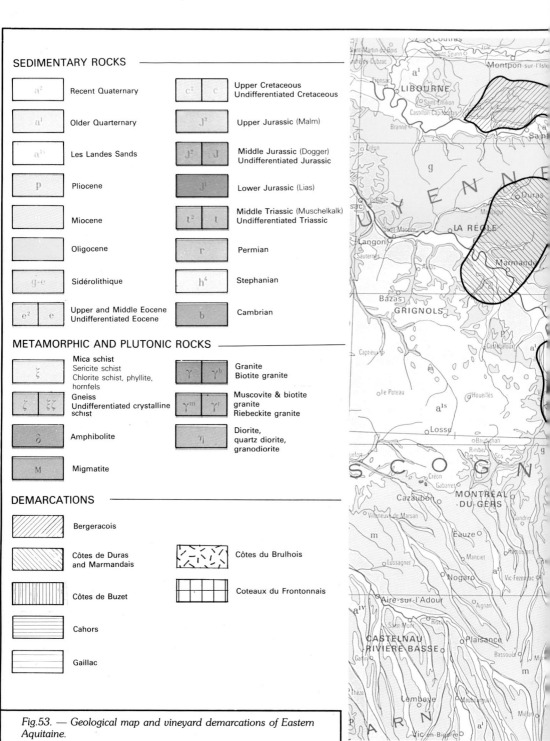

Fig.53. — Geological map and vineyard demarcations of Eastern Aquitaine.

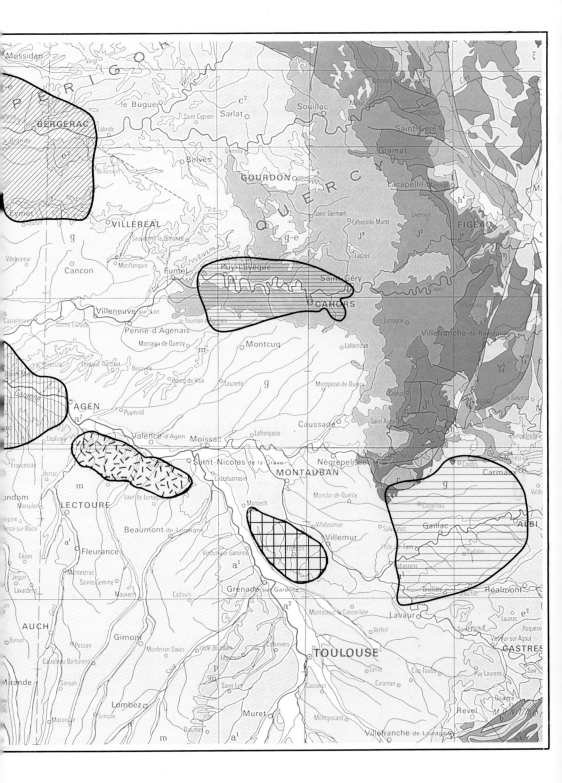

FROM THE DORDOGNE
TO THE GARONNE

The vineyards of the Bordeaux region have had a great influence on the development of closely neighbouring vineyards, from the Dordogne to the Garonne. The Gallo-Roman origins of the vineyard are as much in evidence here as elsewhere, but the reputation of their wines owes much to the proximity of Bordeaux, the centre of the wine market, which has been exporting its wines throughout the world ever since the Middle Ages, and continues to do so to the present day.

For some considerable time Bordeaux had been assured a favoured position by protectionist measures. From the 16th century onwards, however, the Bergerac region took benefit from a number of privileges, in particular that bestowed on the Burghers of Bergerac with a town residence, who were granted a charter by decree of the Parlement of Guyenne in 1511, guaranteeing their wines access to the sea by boat. In the 18th century, with increasing demand from the Dutch for sweet, heavy wines, the vineyard of Monbazillac was able to expand its production of sweet wine.

The soils are often different from those in the Bordeaux region (fig.53), but the climatic conditions in this part of the Aquitaine Basin, generally open to the influence of the Atlantic Ocean, are very comparable. Temperatures tend to be higher during the growth period of the vine (17.5°C at Bergerac, compared with 16.5°C at Saint-Emilion), humidity is lower, though still fairly high, and extremes of climate are more marked. The weather changes more abruptly, for example with rises in air temperature followed by rain showers, under the influence of the autan, a wind which blows from the direction of Toulouse, though it has largely spent its force by the time it reaches the region.

The vineyards of the Bergerac region

To the east of the Bordeaux vine-growing region, and doubtless feeling overshadowed by such illustrious estates, the Bergerac wine region has gradually improved in quality by concentrating on vineyards with a long-established reputation. The number of appellations bears witness to the diversity of wines produced.

We shall first consider the "crus" of longest standing, in white wines. Of these, Monbazillac is produced on five estates south of Bergerac. It is a sweet, rich wine produced from grapes withered by a condition known as "pourriture noble" ("noble rot") on vines of the sémillon, sauvignon and muscatel varieties. The soft and rich **Côtes de Bergerac** is produced mainly from the sémillon and has a high alcohol content (12° to 15°).

Côtes de Bergerac — Côtes de Saussignac, on the southern side of the valley, is also high in alcohol, and plumper than the latter, but not so rich and sweet as the former. We should also mention **Bergerac Sec,** produced in the traditional way from white varieties gathered throughout the district. **Montravel** is a dry wine from the right bank of the Dordogne, on the edge of the **Côtes de Castillon,** as distinct from Côtes de Montravel (12° to 15°) and **Haut-Montravel,** which are produced in very small quantities. Similarly, the curve of sloping ground forming the northern border of the Bergerac plain produces Rosette, now largely forgotten.

Among the red wines, **Bergerac** (not less than 10°) is a light, supple wine, to be drunk young and chilled. By contrast, wines for ageing are the **Côtes de Bergerac** red (at least 11°) and the **Pécharmant,** production of which is limited to four estates on the upper face of the slope, to the northeast of the plain of Bergerac. It used to be considered a good wine for laying down, full-bodied and stocky with a high colour, but lately its personality has been declining.

The soils of the Bergerac region are nonetheless generally uniform, and have little to do with the diversity of the wines produced. The Dordogne valley, emerging from the meanders it has cut through the Cretaceous limestone over 4 to 5 kilometres, divides the region into two soil types. The vine soils on the northern side are composed chiefly of Périgord Sands. The vineyards to the south are planted mainly on Oligocene continental molasse deposits, marl and limestone. These deposits generally vary in detail to suit different kinds of vine, but no precise relationship is discernible between soil and vine selection.

Itinerary

The Pécharmant district: The vineyards closest to the outskirts of Bergerac are on a terrace of the Dordogne. The soil is relatively gravel-free and leached, though fairly dark in colour with a pebbly subsoil (fig.54).

The road which climbs up to the estate at Pécharmant (D 32) is built on the Périgord Sands, which are quite pebbly in places. Along the way we find generally argillaceous soil-flows on the gentle south-facing slopes, whilst shoulders and hill-tops have a leached and even podzolic soil which is acid, light and often extremely loose.

Beyond the crossroads at Saint-Sauveur, the road to Lembras cuts through the Cretaceous limestone on which the Périgord Sands were deposited. Gravel is much in evidence and the point of contact is red. A splendid vineyard stands on this formation, occupying a south-facing position above the road, just before Lembras.

 Wines may be bought at the Pécharmant estate, or from the displays and specialist shops in Bergerac old town (the Maison du Vin is on the Place du Docteur-Cayla). Take the N 21 back to Bergerac.

Through Monbazillac: Leave Bergerac by the D 933 (the Marmande road). Beyond the Maison des Vins at Saint-Laurent-des-Vignes, turn left onto the D 14 at the bottom of a hill. Climb the hill via the D 13, which goes past the entrance to the Château de Monbazillac, returning to the D 933 by the D 14E (fig.54).

The first of the vines (sémillon and sauvignon) are on a terrace of leached brown soil, where the relatively fertile silty soil is balanced by the deep, sweet and gravelly subsoil. From here the visitor can climb up to the château by the various layers of molasse, though it is not possible to trace the facies of successive stages (which range from the Priabonian to the Upper Rupelian). It is a limy, brown soil, overlying a generally crumbly and extremely loose subsoil. This soil type is fairly common in southwest France, producing sweet, aromatic wines. The leached terrace soils of Saint-Laurent, though highly productive, grow vines with balanced, well-knit grapes of the kind which ripen soonest. They yield wines with the highest alcohol content and the grape-must is considered the best for sweet, heavy wine.

 There are numerous places to buy wine at the château and at the mill of Malfourat, with many viewing points across the plain and the vineyard.

Bergerac moelleux (soft and rich), Bergerac sec (dry), Bergerac rouge (red): Beyond the mill of Malfourat, follow the D 933 for about 6 km as far as the crossroads where the D 5 comes in from Sigoulès. From this point follow the sign-posted "Route des Vins" (Wine Route) by taking the D 15 as far as Cunèges, the D 16 via La Bastide, an ordinary local road via Gageac, Rouillac and then through

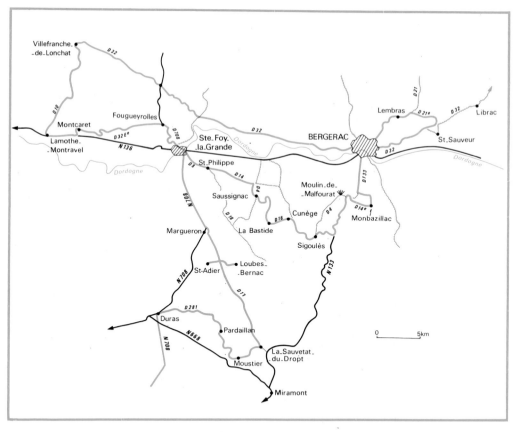

Fig.54. — Tour in the Bergerac region (Bergeracois).

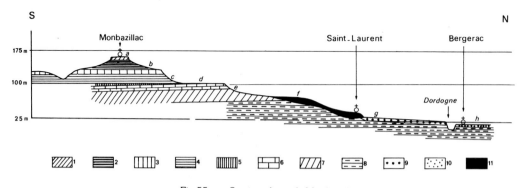

Fig.55. — Section through Monbazillac.

Geology

Aquitanian: 1. Agenais White Limestone. Stampian: 2 & 4. Agenais Molasse; 3. Monbazillac Limestone. Sannoisian: 5. Upper part of the Castillon Limestone, with millstones; 6. Lower part of the Castillon Limestone; 7. Fronsadais Molasse. Ludian: 8. Marl and clay. Holocene - present: 9. Lower terrace; 10. Low plain; 11. Colluvium and soil creep.

Pedology

a. Rendzine; b. Brown, leached soil (dialect: 'bouvaine' or 'bouvée'); c. White, calcareous soil (lithosols, or 'aubue'); d. Red, stony soil (red boulder loam); e. Brown, calcitic soil (duricrust); f. Coarse- structured, clayey soil ('terre de Brie'); g. Loam, brown and heavy leached soil ('boulbènes') and gravel; h. Silty alluvial, brown soil.

Saussignac. Take the D 4 from there to the point where it joins the D 14 at the foot of a hill and continue to Sainte-Foy-la-Grande.

The journey to Sigoulès and Cunèges takes us through red wine country (Bergerac and Côtes de Bergerac rouge). The limestone banks, which can be seen in cross-section where the road cuts through them, have formed a considerable number of structural platforms. This is true not only of the Monbazillac Limestone (Upper Rupelian), but also of the Castillon Limestone (Lower Rupelian), the upper part of which has formed into a type of millstone, with many lumpy, siliceous nodules. The soil on these shelves is of a clay type, often red, and overlies limestone which has been profoundly disturbed, shattered and split by the action of frost in periglacial areas. All these characteristics combine to give good soil for vines (boulder clay and rendzinas) and although not very fertile, they are deep enough to ensure a regular supply of water. The hillsides have brown soil on molasse, with good drainage due to the slope of the land. A good cross-section of the Castillon Limestone can be seen in a quarry below Saussignac.

Beyond Saussignac the D 14 follows the base of the hill overlooking the plain, where scree has fallen from the uppermost limestone banks to form the lower slopes, even spreading out onto the Dordogne plain. The plain itself is wetter from there on, and has no quality vineyards. The highly calcareous scree slope, however, despite its northerly aspect, is the main site for the appellation Côtes de Bergerac-Côtes de Saussignac in those places where the Priabonian clay beds are well covered with scree.

Tour of Montravel: This follows the signs for the "Route des vins" along the D 708 from Port-Sainte-Foy, changing to the D 32E at Fougueyrolles as far as Montcaret.

Beyond Montcaret alluvial fans and scree slopes have formed a flat area of clay earth which has turned into a brown soil showing few signs of leaching.

The whole of the talus and the low fringing area are well planted with vineyards in these good south-facing conditions.

There is a splendid vineyard on a clay-limestone mixture (limy brown soil) around Saint-Michel-de-Montaigne. Beyond this village the journey continues for the most part on the Périgord Sands, which in this area are mainly composed of fine particles. The vineyard is generally spread out, but flourishing and well maintained on its acid soils. Return to Bergerac across the plain, where orchards and tobacco have replaced the vineyards.

Côtes de Duras

The appellation **"Côtes de Duras"** was founded in 1937 in the canton of Duras for wines derived from grape varieties associated with Bordeaux, in particular sauvignon, muscatel and mauzac for white wines, cabernet sauvignon, malbec and merlot for the reds. The white wines are either soft and rich or dry. It is customary for wines to be produced from a single grape variety (merlot and cabernet sauvignon in particular). It is noticeable here, as everywhere, that whilst the production of red wine is increasing, that of white wine is levelling off.

The soil of Duras canton is formed from calcareous and molassic Oligocene continental deposits with a marine horizon of echinoid limestone. The topography of the area is very varied, with deep, branching valleys, and is especially noted for its limestone-capped outliers. The structural platforms on the banks of Monbazillac limestone or echinoid limestone are undergoing karstification, forming sink holes of various depths which are vulnerable to frost.

The upper terrace of the Dropt is sound, covered in a leached, sometimes niggardly soil which can support a quality vineyard. There has also been soil development on the platforms and gentle slopes which are in many cases covered with clay-silica deposits derived from the molassic beds by solifluction. All of these soils are therefore either acid or neutral with a deep-lying structure, so that nourishment of the vines is a balance between such fertility as the soil possesses and the deep-stored reserves of water.

Itinerary

To reach the Côtes de Duras growing district leave **Sainte-Foy-la-Grande** via the D 708, then take the D 13 at Margueron (which is in the Gironde) as far as La Sauvetat-du-Dropt, with brief visits on either side of the route along the way, at Loubès-Bernac and Saint-Astier, in the château region (Théobon, Puychagut).

In the region of the **Château de Puychagut,** the white limestone outlier from the Agen region is covered in splendid vines planted on a shallow, red soil formed by decalcification, capping the limestone bank which is in general deeply frost-cracked. At its foot, especially alongside the road, the vineyard covers the flat and gently sloping areas of molasse, where the leached brown soil seems to have just the right qualities for white varieties of grape-vine.

Saint-Astier stands on the edge of a limestone shelf overlooking slopes of argillaceous Fronsac-type molasse. During the drive to the village, we can see a handsome vineyard growing red and white grapes on soil formed from echinoid limestone. This rock is often soft, breaking down into lumps which tend to form a thick, porous soil in which sandy clay is rapidly decalcified. This ensures that the vines receive a regular supply of nutritious elements and water, nicely balanced to bring out all the qualities of the fruit: its high sugar content, the good balance of tannins and acid, its aromatic potential and so on. Such qualities also favour satisfactory yield levels.

The scenery of the vine-growing district between **La Sauvetat-du-Dropt** and **Moustier** is somewhat different. At Moustier the road marks the edge of an area of vineyards, now fewer in number than formerly, which have been planted on the relatively steep talus overlooking the valley of the Dropt as well as on the high river terrace with its added accumulation of soil creep from the talus and the alluvial fans emerging from side valleys. Since these soil formations are generally argillaceous they have undergone little pedological development. It is these soils which have been planted with vines, rather than those formed directly from the host-rocks. At the foot of the talus are Priabonian clays and shales, whilst to the south is Fronsac-type molasse, protected by the Castillon Limestone which caps the very summit.

By the time we reach **Duras** and the area round its cooperative wine cellars, we are back to extensive vineyards on a surface formation of Castillon Limestone. Here we can judge for ourselves the pick of the appellation. A whole range of wines is on sale at the cellars and at various wine-stores in the town. Notice, by the way, the attractive château and how pleasantly the town is laid out.

Côtes du Marmandais

The appellation VDQS Côtes du Marmandais was first recognised in 1956 for red, rosé and dry white wines. The area of production is fairly extensive, and is divided in two by the wide valley of the Garonne. In the north is a region of molassic slopes, and to the south a series of plateaux covered with Garonne pebbles stretches to the beginnings of the sands of Les Landes. Once the main grape-vines made a lengthy list of time-honoured local varieties: abouriou, fer-servadou, cot, bouchalès, mérille, with small amounts of some newly introduced varieties: gamay, syrah, cabernets and merlot. The classics for white wines were sémillon and white ugni with a low proportion of sauvignon and muscatel. Nowadays the proportions are being reversed. The cabernets and merlot are being favoured at the expense of the others in red, and sauvignon predominates among whites. The amount of white wine produced is low compared to red.

The geological substratum throughout the region is composed of molasse formations (soft sandstone with a calcareous cement) with shaly levels and limestone banks of the Tertiary. These comprise echinoid limestone (marine) and Agen-type molasse from the Rupelian, with white limestone (lacustrine), shale (with marine strata) and grey limestone from the Aquitanian. These formations crop out on the right bank, whilst those on the left bank are covered with three terraces of stones and coarse sand laid down during the Quaternary Period, and aeolian sandy silt which was deposited in the middle Quaternary on the uppermost levels of the Garonne deposits (Cocumont district) (fig.56).

As usual in a molassic topography, the soils derive from surface formations, colluvia and decalcification clays which have evolved into generally leached brown soils and relatively pure rendzinas. On the alluvials of the left bank, the soils are of the leached, podzolic type, and their state of development is directly related to the length of time since the alluvial formation was laid down.

The right bank

The best way to get to know the vineyards is to drive through the two regions concerned. Drive from the direction of Bordeaux on the N 113 until just before the boundary of the départements. Take the D 129, which is just inside Gironde, and then the D 259 in Lot-et-Garonne. Travel via Saint-Martin-Petit and Lagupie to the D 708 south of Castelnau. From there to Beaupuy, with a stop at the wine-cellars. Beyond the village continue by the hilltop route (D 139) to the D 132 and drive down to Marmande (fig.57).

This journey gives an idea of how vine-growing is organised in this district. The talus faces south, and where the slope is not too severe the vines grow in tiers on the generally eroded or slumped, calcic brown soils. At the foot of the slope, soil-flows and soil additions from surface runoff form a spreading, gently sloping rise of brown soils above the plain of Marmande. The appellation area excludes the plain itself. The plateau on the talus rim is either an erosion feature of the old Quaternary (Piazencian) or a structural platform caused by a bank of harder molasse. At all events, the leached brown type of soil is the 'top notch' of this wine district. Further away, the terrain takes on a more varied relief, where clay-limestone soils predominate and quality vineyards are found in scattered pockets, mainly determined by the way the land faces.

The left bank

Cross the luxuriant plain of the Garonne by the D 933 towards Mont-de-Marsan. Turn left onto the D 116 as far as the Marcellus crossroads on the left, one km beyond Gaujac, where a series of ordinary local roads leads to Cocumont (Cooperative). From there the D 289 goes to Samazan and the motorway which leads to Agen or the remainder of the Garonne vineyards on the Côtes de Buzet.

Côtes de Buzet

Since 1973 this appellation has replaced the highly-prized VDQS created on the basis of the Cooperative Wine-Store of Buzet-sur-Baïse. The red wine is produced mainly from merlot, a Bordeaux grape variety. The white and rosé are produced in insignificant amounts. About 900 hectares of classified vineyards yielded 45 000 hectolitres in 1981. About 93 per cent of the production is marketed through the Cooperative Wine-Store (tastings and sales), but some producers are advertised in several villages and market their own produce.

The production area extends along the left bank of the Garonne, from below Agen to right of Tonneins, including both banks of the Baïse. The Garonne valley has widened in the continental strata of the Tertiary. These dip slightly from northeast to southwest and include, from top to bottom of the 200-metre thickness concerned, the following:

— *Agen Molasse,* a rock formed of fine components, argillo-calcareous shale or soft, fine-grained sandstone bound by a crystalline carbonate of low consistency;

— *White Agen Limestone,* attributed to the Upper Chattian (Upper Rupelian final), a generally soft limestone with denser banks of brecciated or crystalline limestone reaching a thickness of 15 metres in all;

— *Middle Marls,* generally continental in origin, here occasionally interlayered with thin marine beds of oysters (Ostrea aginensis) reaching a thickness of 15 to 20 metres;

— *Grey Agen Limestone,* a more calcareous but also more variable formation than the preceding one, with levels of soft, white, sometimes sandy shale and levels of crumbly limestone or cellular dolomite, with a number of marine oyster beds. This sequence is attributed to the Aquitanian;

— *Armagnac Molasse,* which is frequently argillaceous with occasional sandier seams, representing the base of the Burdigalian which outcrops more generally to the south.

In the process of carving its wide valley the Garonne has deeply eroded these soft sediments, at the same time depositing large pebbles with a covering of silt at various levels.

The overall result is a wide variety of soils, from those which are quite thick, well-drained, deep and crumbly, providing good balance for plant growth, to silts from recent flooding, which are very fertile and close to the water table.

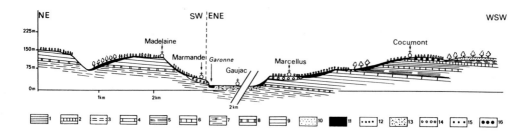

Fig.56. — Section through the Marmandais vineyard area.

Burdigalian: 1. Molasse; 2. Herret (?) Limestone; 3. Molasse. Aquitanian: 4. Agenais White Limestone; 5. Marl; 6. Grey limestone. Sannoisian: 7. Fronsadais Molasse; 8. Nodulous limestone. Stampian: 9. Agenais Molasse. Pleistocene and Holocene: 10. Les Landes Sands; 11. Colluvium and soil creep; 12. Lower terrace (Würm); 13. Low plain; 14. Middle terrace (Riss); 15. High terrace; 16. Upper levels of Garonne pebbles and boulders.

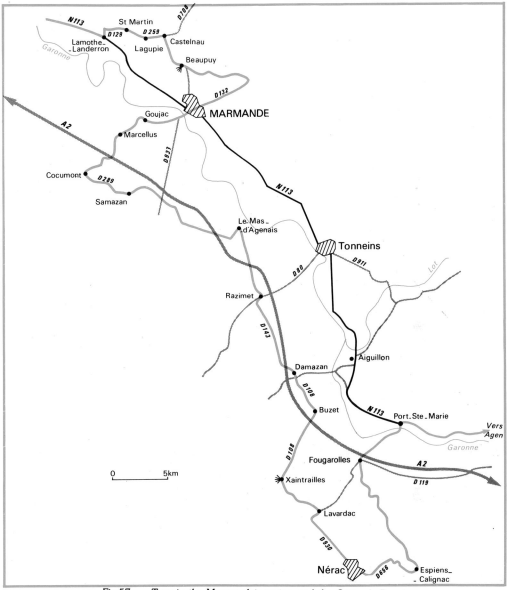

Fig.57. — Tour in the Marmandais region and the Côtes de Buzet.

Itinerary

Leaving the Marmande district behind, take the D 120 from Mas-d'Agenais to Razimet or start from Tonneins on the N 113, taking the D 120 to the southwestern edge of the plain of the Garonne. South of Razimet proceed to Damazan by the D 143 via Puch-d'Agenais. The D 108 runs from Damazan to Buzet-sur-Baïse, passing under the motorway and continuing to Xaintrailles and Lavardac. It will then be as well to take the D 930 to Nérac, even though in some places there are very few vineyards, then the D 656 to Calignac. From there proceed to Feugarolles by the ordinary local roads along the hilltops, via Espiens. From Feugarolles the D 930 and the N 113 lead to Agen.

The vineyards at Buzet have long since been incorporated into the mixed crop system. Over the last twenty or thirty years, many firms have given up the traditional family vine. Others, by contrast, have specialised in growing vines. This has caused the vineyards to be scattered in pockets of various sizes, planted on the soils most suited to producing quality. During the recommended tour, notice particularly the vineyard between Damazan and Buzet, which stands on leached brown soil of a type known locally as "boulbène" from the middle terrace of the Garonne. The many ravines in its neighbourhood keep it well drained and have even cleared it of its layer of stones.

From Buzet to Xaintrailles vines cover the stony soil-flows on the valley sides, with their long, well-drained slopes. Note the three quarries displaying their soil types: 1.5 km beyond Damazan there is a cross-section of the middle terrace in a gravel-pit; 2.5 km beyond Buzet is a quarry working the sands of Les Landes which have become podzolic at the surface; 3 km beyond Buzet is an ashlar quarry for white limestone which is frost-cracked at the surface and has rendzinoid soil.

During the drive down to Lavardac, note the vineyard standing on clay formed by decalcification of the white limestone. It is also possible to trace the topography of the landscape, soil and vines along a line from Calignac to Feugarolles, by taking the very picturesque hilltop road between the valleys of two tributaries of the Garonne.

Côtes du Brulhois

The appellation was granted VDQS status in 1982. Its vineyards are scattered along the left bank of the Garonne, occupying buttes formed from the upper terraces of the Garonne as they existed at the time of the Riss glaciation and earlier.

These alluvials originally consisted of pebble beds (6-7 metres thick) underlying sandy silt (80 cm to 1 metre thick on average) constituting a sequence of level areas separated by gentle slopes (polygenic terraces). Traces of them can still be seen on the ridges between the many valleys which dissect the substratum. The latter originated from the same layers as those found in the Buzet area: Agenais Molasse at the base, overlain in turn by White Agenais Limestone (Stampian s.s), Agenais White Marl and Agenais Grey Limestone (Aquitanian).

The various layers are not easy to see. They are in fact covered on every slope by layers of scree and solifluction flows from the beds of Garonne pebbles crowning the ridges. Vineyards are largely present on all of these gravelly formations, which have deep, well-drained, leached soils in a red clay matrix.

Red and rosé wines are produced from grape varieties typical of the southwest (malbec, fer-savadou, tannat) and of the Bordeaux region (merlot and cabernet). The wines are fruity, perfumed and light, and reasonably good for keeping. They can be obtained from the cooperative wine-cellars at either Dunes-Donzac or Goulens.

Itinerary

To visit the "Cave Coopérative" at Goulens take the N 21 from Agen. Goulens lies between Layrac and Astaffort. From Goulens take the D 204 to Dunes. This journey cuts across three ridges separated by valleys with asymmetric slopes which show the following sequence of features:

— a west-facing slope with woods in many places, up which the road climbs in a series of hairpin bends, revealing two beds of lacustrine limestone in the road banks;

— the ridge with its butte of pebbles which are reddened in situ;

— an east-facing slope on which the more or less pebbly solifluctions are widely scattered, having been undermined at their base by Post-Würmian deepening of the valley.

From Dunes take the D 30 towards Donzac, then the D 12, to rejoin the 113 at Lamagistère (bridge over the Garonne and Golfech nuclear power station). The vineyards here are accommodated on small, pebbly, undulating portions of the Garonne alluvial terrace dating from the final deposition during the last phases of the Riss glaciation. You may wish to stop at the 'Cave Coopérative', halfway between Dunes and Donzac.

Wines and gastronomy

Monbazillac is a rich, sweet white wine which becomes amber-golden when two years old. It is produced from sémillon, muscatel (which is being grown in ever fewer places) and sauvignon. It is tricky to produce, and its quality depends very much on the end-of-season climatic conditions, when the daily alternation of morning mists and hot sunshine encourages the "pourriture noble". It is a fine dessert wine, but the connoisseur drinks it with foie gras or potted meats.

Bergerac Rouge, from several varieties (cabernet sauvignon, cabernet franc, merlot, malbec, fer-savadou, mérille) is a limpid, medium-dark wine with good aroma and fine presence. The very aromatic Bergerac Sec is a dry white wine for drinking young.

Côtes de Montravel and Haut-Montravel (between 12° and 15°, 11° of which are acquired, and 8 to 54 grams of sugar per litre) are fine and well-knit white wines to be tried out in the wine-stores advertised along the road on the right bank of the Dordogne, just outside the département of the Gironde. We are coming much closer to the wines of Bordeaux!

A visit to the Château de Monbazillac is an opportunity to get to know all the wines of the appellation at the cooperative wine-store which owns all buildings on the site.

AOC Côtes de Duras is a fine, aromatic wine which is assured graceful ageing due to its well-balanced tannins.

The VDQS Côtes du Marmandais appellation includes reds, whites and rosés. The red is the mainstay of production, and has quickly made a reputation. Originally the red wines were produced from grape varieties which were mainly from the Aquitaine region (cot, abouriou) or from well outside the area (gamay, syrah) but now they are obtained mainly from Bordeaux varieties such as cabernet, cabernet sauvignon and merlot (sauvignon is the main grape variety for the white wines).

Marvellous produce can be obtained from the cooperative wineries at Beaupuy and Cocumont, where customers are assured the warmest reception in the well-kept cellars. They produce almost all of this high quality wine. It is fruity, well-structured and will keep well, and it would be a mistake to think of it as unassuming.

The appellation controlée "Côtes de Buzet" was granted by decree to the produce of this vineyard in 1973, replacing a VDQS appellation dating back to 1953, for wines which have steadily grown in reputation during the last quarter of a century (Cave coopérative du Buzet). The grape varieties (merlot, cabernet sauvignon, cabernet franc, cot) the harvesting, vatting, maturing in oak and bottling have all become traditional. Buzet is today a dependable, balanced wine, gaining finesse and aroma with age, so that its fame has now spread far beyond its region. It is an exceedingly good accompaniment to all regional fare, from poultry pâté and ragout of pigeon to cheeses and prunes!

FROM THE LOT TO THE TARN

Wines and soils of Cahors

Cahors wine has been known since the Middle Ages from contacts between the bishops of that city and their eminences of cities in other parts of Gaul. The marriage of Eleanor of Aquitaine to Henry II of England was the beginning of exports of wine from Cahors via Bordeaux. Forty thousand barrels of Agenais-Quercy passed through that town around 1310. Pope John XXII of Avignon brought in vine-growers from Cahors to cultivate vines at Châteauneuf. Francis I and Henry IV praised Cahors highly.

Trade in wine from the area relied on transport by boat along the Lot and Garonne rivers, but the town of Bordeaux had powerful privileges from the kings of England and France, and by regulating this form of transport opposed the through movement of wines from upstream. On the advice of Turgot, who was devoted to freedom of trade, these constraints were finally lifted in 1776 by edict of Louis XVI.

Nevertheless, the international reputation of Cahors wines was firmly established from the Americas to Russia. There is even a wine of present-day Azerbaidzhan which bears the name Caorskoye Vino.

Soils

The Cahors wine-growing area covers 45 districts in the département of the Lot, on both sides of the river mainly to the west of Cahors. This activity is mainly centred on the Quaternary alluvials between Luzech and Puy-l'Evêque as well as on the causse in the south of that area.

This is a very lively wine district at the present time, with production on the increase by some 10 to 15 per cent per annum. It is remarkably unified, not only because of its virtually exclusive grape selections, the cot or malbec, locally called the auxerrois, with additional small amounts of tannat and merlot, but also because of its vine-growing and wine-making techniques, especially the uniform quality of its final product.

In general terms its relief, climate and human environment give the Cahors wine district a character of its own. However, due to the history of its geomorphology there are four soil types in the region.

On limestone. The regional bedrock is Kimmeridgian limestone. Its surface was sub-aerial until the Miocene, following the peneplanation of the siderolite, and has often been so from the Miocene to the present day, particularly in Quaternary times. During the whole of this time the surface of the peneplain has been subjected to various surface processes which have broken it up for a depth of several metres, dissolving the limestone and leaving a clay residue which itself has undergone soil development. The end result is a causse soil of red clay with a granular texture, containing large amounts of weathered calcareous debris, over a bed of loose rock which has been frost-shattered to a depth of three or four metres. The hilltops and plateaux have thus acquired a highly original soil which is ideal for growing high-quality vines (fig.58).

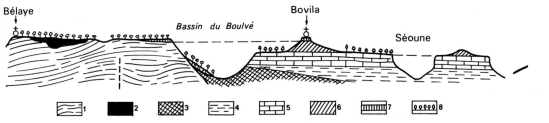

Fig.58. — *Section through the southern edge of the Causse.*

1. Jurassic; 2. Plateau Sidérolithique; 3. 'Shallow lake' Sidérolithique; 4. Molasse; 5. White limestone; 6. White marl; 7. Grey limestone; 8. Vineyard.

On the alluvials of the Lot. Having gone through the classic stages during the Quaternary, the river valley is being widened further by the development of meanders, as can be easily observed today.

On the southern edge of the area. Two types of Tertiary lacustrine deposits occur at the edge of the limestone plateau. One is a dense, brecciated limestone, weathered and frost-shattered at the surface, and the other is a compact, white shale.

Siderolithic sands and clays. These are red with occasional ferruginous crusts, filling depressions on the plateaux or forming peaks, especially towards the northeast of the area. They form a soil which is generally leached at the surface, and acid. The rather porous structure of the deep subsoil provides good balance for growth of the vine-plant.

The diversity of soils within the appellation seems at odds with the uniformity of the product, and yet there are no significant quality differences in the wines obtained.

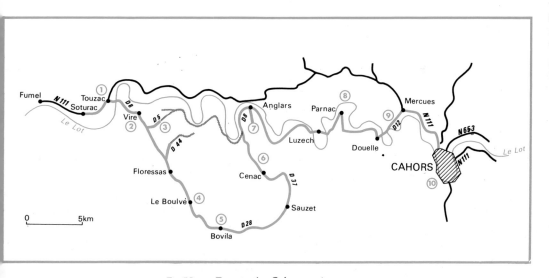

Fig.59. — *Tour in the Cahors region.*

Itinerary

The recommended tour takes in these different soils. The wine-growing area is broken into separate vineyards with fallow, wooded or rocky areas of extremely uneven ground in between. For a fuller understanding of their geology see the

'Guide géologigue d'Aquitaine orientale' (Geological Guide to Eastern Aquitaine). Our route does not always follow the circular tour signposted "Circuit de Cahors", but it does pass through localities and alongside vineyards where there are wine-cellars for tasting and buying Cahors wines (fig.59).

Approaching from Agen, Villeneuve-sur-Lot or Fumel, the first vineyards are encountered at Soturac by taking the D 911 up the valley.

From **Soturac to Touzac** we follow the line of the vineyard which stands on the Rissian terrace ("red earth") to the left of the road, and on the Würmian to the right ①.

From **Touzac to Vire** ②we skirt the foot of a cévenne, a cliff-like concave meander bank carved into the Kimmeridgian limestone, with vegetation characteristic of north-facing slopes (which are locally known as "ubac", or in this case "hiversenc").

Beyond **Vire** we can make a return journey along the D 5 and follow the line of an ancient meander of the Lot which was abandoned during the Würmian. It now supports a magnificent vineyard on the limestone scree below the slopes and on Rissian scree brought down by solifluction ③.

Passing through **Le Boulvé,** we come to a hollow in the red siderolithic deposits girdled by hills which are capped with Tertiary lacustrine limestone. Its low-lying position makes it unsuitable for vines. It is described in the *'Guide géologique'*.

The stretch of D 656 gives a chance to see the vineyard on the Tertiary lacustrine limestones and shales, particularly on and around the **Butte de Bovila** ⑤.

Beyond Sauzat we encounter the Causse vineyard, with some especially typical examples around the hamlet of Cénac, reached by crossing a siderolithic outcrop with grey sandstone and red sands, wooded with silicicole vegetation ⑥.

The journey along the valley bottom skirts the **meander of Anglars,** at the junction of two levels of the lower (Würmian) terrace. This is thickly planted with vigorous vines producing good quality Cahors ⑦. From Anglars we can take an ordinary local road on the right, to the top of the meander alluvials, where we can see vines of a more typical kind on the upper screes.

From Castelfranc to Luzech we skirt around the base of two cévennes, with vegetation characteristic of south-facing slopes (known locally as "adret", or in this case "soulelhon").

The journey through **Parnac** ⑧brings us into the very centre of the traditional vineyard area, on the Rissian terrace which can be seen in good cross-section in the bank alongside the road. Cahors wines are on sale in signposted wine-cellars.

Beyond the Douelle bridge, through Cessac as far as **Mercuès,** another vineyard cstands on the deposits of an old meander of the Lot. This, too, is Rissian with quartz scree on the slopes and "red earth" on the plain ⑨.

The wine-cellars **at Cahors** ⑩ and alongside the N 20 on the approaches to the town give the visitor an opportunity to try the wine, which is especially agreeable with a meal in one of the many restaurants serving the famed local cuisine.

Wines of Cahors and gastronomy

Cahors is a red wine with a high colour, forthcoming and full-bodied, with a pleasantly fruity, clear and delicate aroma. The same year may show some slight differences depending on the location of the vineyard, but its general features are always identical. The wine of Cahors so clearly affirms its characteristics that it is natural to associate it with the other produce of the region, substantial dishes like foie gras, red meats and potted meats stuffed with truffles.

As the valley of the Lot crosses the Aveyron département, it is also home to other vineyards of repute:

— *Marcillac* (VDQS), which is highly aromatic, is produced in the valley of the Marcillac, a peripheral depression in the shale, sandstone and psammitic rocks of the Permian, between the Decazeville Basin and the Rodez Causse;

— the white wines of the AOC estates *Entraygues and Estaing* come from the vines cultivated on the lithosols formed from granite in the case of the former and mica schist for the latter (light, acid and aromatic wines);

— *Côtes de Glanes*, VDQS, northeast of the département of the Lot, is light, slightly acid and aromatic, produced on decalcification clay of the lower Lias.

Wines and vineyards of Gaillac

Gaillac has a very long-established reputation. It is said to go back to Gallo-Roman days, when the amphorae and other earthenware pots in which it was transported were manufactured in the neighbourhood where Gaillac stands today (Montans). It has since become known for both its red and its white. In the latter form it was a great favourite with the clergy, who so to speak promoted it (in addition, naturally, to communion wine).

The wines of Gaillac found their way via the Tarn and the Garonne to Bordeaux, from where they were exported all over Europe and America, despite hostility from the wine-merchants of Bordeaux, which continued to be effective until the end of the 18th century. The proximity of the Massif central, where vines were rare and prey to many climatic hazards, meant that there was a large market close at hand. The reputation of the white wine, moreover, became firmly established in Paris during the 19th century.

Soils

The wine-growing area of Gaillac is large, covering a territory of 73 districts, from the confines of the Central Plateau in the north to the slopes of the "Albigensian Gulf" in the south. As the market for Gaillac wines kept shrinking, this large area has shrunk over recent decades to its traditional central core, covering a score of districts. Although the recommended tour keeps to the central area, it nevertheless takes in four different types of soil on the way (fig.60).

● In the north, between Cérou and La Vère, is a platform of Cordes Limestone (Middle Rupelian), dissected by deep valleys, fringed with cliffs and dominated by monadnocks of the upper marls and limestone.

● Between La Vère and the plain of the Tarn, the whole sequence of lacustrine deposits gradually gives way to Agen Molasse, which covered the Aquitaine Basin after the uplift of the Pyrenees.

● The valley of the Tarn, widened by meander cutoff in the soft Tertiary sediments, where the bed of the river has now cut a deep channel.

● In the south there are alluvial terraces on the left bank of the Tarn, where the four classic levels of the Garonne Basin can be seen.

Each of these little regions therefore has very different soil. This, combined with the large number of grape varieties in use, leads to the production of a large number of different wines with, in each one, widely differing qualities. Even so, it is noticeable that white wines have almost exclusive possession of the limestones in the north, reds are exclusive on the Tarn alluvials in the south, and mixed production is obtained on the plain of the Tarn from the colluvia brought down from the molassic slopes. This intermediate zone was classed 'Premières Côtes' when the limits of the appellation were first defined.

Itinerary

The recommended tour runs broadly speaking from north to south through the four soil types of the Gaillac wine-growing area, from the Grésigne to Albi via

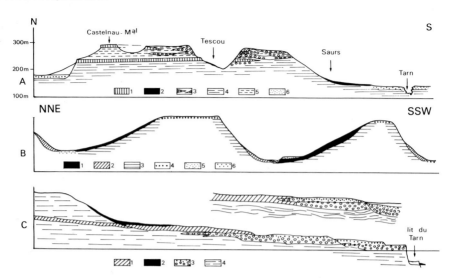

Fig. 60. — *Sequence of soils in the Gaillac region.*

A) *Edge of the Cordes causse: 1. Cordes Limestone; 2. Terrace with soil creep deposits; 3. Molasse and conglomerates; 4. Molasse; 5. White marl; 6. Tarn alluvials.*

B) *On the molasse: 1. Würmian soil creep; 2. Present-day scree; 3. Eroded soils (lithosols); 4. Leached plateau soils; 5. Würmian brown soil terrace; 6. Present-day alluvials.*

C) *Right bank of the Tarn valley: 1. Red soil terrace, with alluvial fans from the valley bottom, graduating laterally to Tarn alluvials; 3. Lower plain, with gravel banks; 4. Molasse.*

Gaillac, in a zone densely packed with vineyards. Many sales points and stands are available to the tourist everywhere on the trip. The route coincides in places with some parts of the itineraries shown in the *'Guide géologique d'Aquitaine orientale'* (Guide to the Geology of Eastern Aquitaine) (fig.61).

From the Grésigne to Cahuzac-sur-Vère

Leave the Grésigne Massif at Saint-Salvy, to the southeast of Vaour, by the D 15 which crosses the vineyard of **Campagnac** ①. This is standing on the Grésigne Conglomerates, deposited at the end of the Eocene all around the massif during the period of uplifting. The deposit is formed of rounded or worn rubble stone with geological origins as varied as the hard layers of the various stages involved in the folding, from the Permian to the Middle Jurassic. Their surface decomposition, largely attributable to frost-shattering, gives a porous, sometimes clayey soil cluttered with pebbles of all sizes. This and the sunward orientation make a splendid site for vineyards.

During the drive down, note the viewpoint across the **Causse de Cordes,** a platform of the main lacustrine limestone level, beyond the north-south valley marking the limit of the Campagnac vineyard. One kilometre beyond the village climb back up this valley by the D 8 to the plateau. The road runs along a dry valley towards Cordes and has a bank of Middle Rupelian white limestone alongside, very weathered and infiltrated with red clay.

Three kilometres beyond Campagnac turn right onto the D 33 for six kilometres as far as the intersection with the D 122 (Gaillac-Cordes). Follow the D 122 for three kilometres to the Souel crossroads. There is a busy, well-kept vineyard here, standing on the rendzinoid soil of the Cordes Limestone platform. This soil is red, pebbly and well-drained. Note the view over the village of **Souel** and its vineyard of Mauzac ②. Notice the numerous places selling *Pétillant de Raisin*. This is not a wine but a slightly fermented natural grape juice, which generally has a pleasant, fruity taste.

At the Souel Crossroads double back and take the D 122 as far as **Cahuzac-**

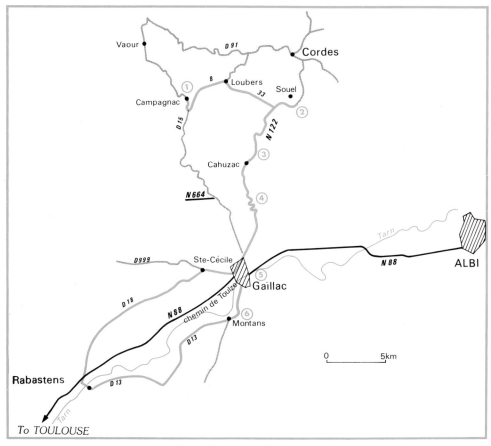

Fig.61. — Tour in the Gaillac region.

sur-Vère ③. The drive down, from 298 metres to 100 metres, takes place on a series of structural platforms over various levels of Rupelian limestone. The lowest level, where the road descends to the valley of the Vère, is incised by the road, and easily observed.

From Cahuzac-sur-Vère to Gaillac ④

After crossing the valley of the Vère, with its flat alluvial floor and no vines other than a few parcels of vineyard for family consumption, stop at Cahuzac-sur-Vère, a small vine-growing village where wines are displayed for sale, built on the previous limestone level. Then follow the D 24 to Gaillac.

The landscape changes over this section. The banks of limestone give way on the southern side to molasse consisting of clay and sandstone banks with varying amounts of limestone. The soils formed from the surface decomposition of this molasse are leached on the peaks with a clay-limestone mix on the slopes, occasionally formed from solifluction of red clay, in particular on the north-facing slopes. They are then wooded (for example near the bends three kilometres from Cahuzac). The vineyards, once planted with mauzac and recently replanted with duras, braucol, gamay or syrah for making red wine, cover every site. This area has in fact been classified the "Premières Côtes" in Gaillac since 1950. The road down to the valley of the Tarn cuts through the Cahuzac limestone bank, overlooked by the Château of Tauziès, 800 metres to the left of the road (wine displays and sales).

A few kilometres before **Gaillac,** the bases of the slopes have a clay soil, brought down by solifluction during the Würmian and spreading as far as the alluvial plain. This soil, too, supports an active vineyard with red grape varieties, also classed as "Premières Côtes". Visit Gaillac and the exhibition stand in the main square ⑤.

213

From Gaillac to Rabastens

Leave Gaillac heading west on the D 999 towards Montauban. On reaching the church of Sainte-Cécile after 3.5 km, turn left onto the **Chemin de Toulze** (D 18), the famous spine road of a long renowned vineyard area. The road runs along the base of the molassic talus which overlooks the plain of the Tarn and is crowned with little churches, their bell-towers standing solitary amid the vineyards. The soils which cover this talus are argillo-calcareous, occasionally leached, colluvial or the result of solifluction. They are generally derived from a very gravelly molassic formation beyond the talus which also supports a few vineyards and is generally wooded on its north-facing slopes.

On the left of the Chemin de Toulze, towards the Tarn, an attractive vineyard stands on a terrace of uniform red soil several metres deep. Despite the nutrient characteristics of the soil it produces quality wine given adequate drainage.

Rabastens to Gaillac along the left bank of the Tarn

Cross the Tarn at Coufouleux and turn left onto the D 13 towards Loupiac, Saint-Martin and Montans ⑥. The soils, though poor, are of traditional wine-growing type, but the vineyards are nowadays planted in the areas of best drainage on the edges of the little tributary valleys.

Beyond **Montans** we can see how renewed erosion in one of these streams, due to recent widening in a meander of the Tarn to the southeast, has carved a gully in the molasse. This can be observed for 25 to 30 metres alongside the road embankment. Take the D 87 to **Gaillac,** crossing a bridge over the Tarn near the Abbey of Saint-Michel. This lovely, brick building has played a part in the story of Gaillac wines since the turn of the century, but today it is in disuse, not unlike the vintage itself which, with a little effort, could regain its former reputation.

Wines of Gaillac and gastronomy

The white wine was traditionally either dry, pale and fruity or sparkling and somewhat sweeter, produced with breaks in fermentation by filtering, fining or copper sulphate dressing. This is still the method with mauzac and some other white grape varieties such as muscatel. It is slightly heavy for a white, and not very refreshing if the tannins have not mellowed, but it is fruity with good body. A lightly sparkling wine developed at Labastide-Lévis retains the fruit and makes a light, refreshing drink.

The red wine, produced mainly on both banks of the Tarn, has a bright, vermilion colour and a clean, round, fruity taste. It is at its best between one and three years old, after which it may oxidize or be slow to acquire the aromatics of ageing.

The pleasant, fruity rosé is produced from juice drawn off from the must. Like the red, it comes from a mixture of grape varieties. The main one tends to be the traditional duras with the addition of syrah, gamay, fer-savadou and others.

Other wines from the district include "Moustillant", which is a sparkling wine, relatively low in alcohol, the "Pétillant de Raisin" which is a sweetened grape juice with very little alcohol, "Gaillac Nouveau" made from the gamay variety, and "Vin Clairet" from Técou, made from the portugais bleu variety. Here and there you will encounter "Cabernet" and "Merlot", both excellent and characteristic of the grape.

There is thus a whole range of good wines to explore in this district. They go with any dish, but particularly well with potted poultry and red meats (choose a two-year old red), with stews, cassoulet or offal (a red or a rosé), with fish (the slightly sparkling white) or with desserts (a sparkling white).

Coteaux du Frontonnais

The wines of the "Coteaux du Frontonnais" gained VDQS status in 1945 and were designated AOC in 1975. The supple, fruity red keeps its qualities well for a number of years, but is not for prolonged keeping. There are over 1 000 hectares under vine, producing around 55 000 hectolitres of wine for the appellation.

The main vine variety is the négrette. This local grape is more or less confined to local soil, to which it is well suited. It is grafted onto stocks which encourage just the right growth rate, thus ensuring the fineness of the wine. Gamay, cabernet sauvignon, malbec and syrah also feature among the vine-stock selection.

The wine-growing area is accommodated on the upper terraces of the Tarn, which at this point are only partially dissected by very short lateral tributary valleys. The terraces rise in tiers, and the lowest of them are quite easily distinguished. All are covered by their original layer of silt, which has evolved, since it was first laid down, into a type of soil known locally as "boulbènes". This name is applied to a silty soil originating from particularly efficient podzolic development which took place during the Würmian periglacial period. In profile we find first a discoloured horizon, then a subsoil of accumulated, more or less reddened clay, and finally, at a depth varying between 80 and 150 cm, a layer of reddened pebbles for the vine roots to explore. The whole sequence combines low fertility and a good, well-drained depth of soil which ensures a well-balanced supply of water.

The climate provides the vineyards with a further advantage in the form of a warm, dry southeast wind (autan), with September and October being generally fine.

Itinerary

From Montauban, take the N 20 heading south as far as the Campsas crossroads. The D 50 goes to Campsas and then Fabas, from where you can continue to Fronton, or turn off before there and take the D 29 to Villaudric. There are cooperative wine-cellars in both these places. Fronton also has sales outlets for wines from particular estates.

Along the way, notice the attractive vineyards on the middle terrace (Riss) and on the low, rounded hills covered in gravelly soil creep originating from the upper terraces. The landscape is open. Where the itinerary crosses a shallow valley, the west-facing slope sometimes reveals a cross-section of the alluvial material. It should also be noted that some of the pebbly outcrops standing slightly proud of the silt plain are not only favoured sites for vines. They have also yielded rich prehistoric surface deposits of large quartzite and quartz carved stone tools (Late Acheulean) as well as smaller tools carved in quartz pebbles from the Cévennes region (Early Mousterian). These are on display in museums at Montauban and Toulouse.

The way to Toulouse from Villaudric is via the D 63 and D 4 as far as Bouloc. Beyond there, the journey continues through a flat landscape in which a brown, unleached soil overlies Stampian molasse. None of this is very suitable for quality vines.

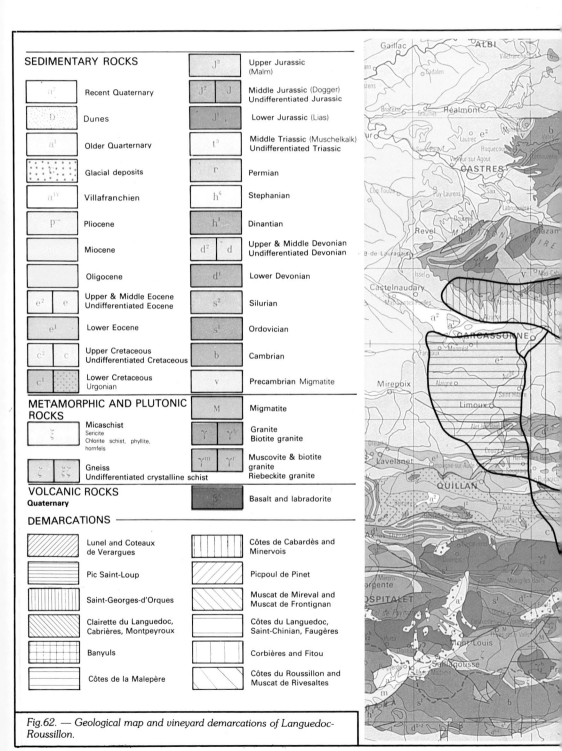

SEDIMENTARY ROCKS

a^2	Recent Quaternary	J^3	Upper Jurassic (Malm)
D	Dunes	J^2 / J	Middle Jurassic (Dogger) / Undifferentiated Jurassic
a^1	Older Quaternary	J^1	Lower Jurassic (Lias)
	Glacial deposits	t^3	Middle Triassic (Muschelkalk) Undifferentiated Triassic
a^{IV}	Villafranchien	r	Permian
p^-	Pliocene	h^4	Stephanian
	Miocene	h^1	Dinantian
	Oligocene	d^2 / d	Upper & Middle Devonian Undifferentiated Devonian
e^2 / e	Upper & Middle Eocene Undifferentiated Eocene	d^1	Lower Devonian
e^1	Lower Eocene	s^2	Silurian
c^2 / c	Upper Cretaceous Undifferentiated Cretaceous	s^1	Ordovician
c^1	Lower Cretaceous Urgonian	b	Cambrian
		v	Precambrian Migmatite

METAMORPHIC AND PLUTONIC ROCKS

	Micaschist Sericite Chlorite schist, phyllite, hornfels	M	Migmatite
	Gneiss Undifferentiated crystalline schist	γ / γ^b	Granite Biotite granite
		γ^m / γ^r	Muscovite & biotite granite Riebeckite granite

VOLCANIC ROCKS
Quaternary

β	Basalt and labradorite

DEMARCATIONS

	Lunel and Coteaux de Verargues
	Pic Saint-Loup
	Saint-Georges-d'Orques
	Clairette du Languedoc, Cabrières, Montpeyroux
	Banyuls
	Côtes de la Malepère
	Côtes de Cabardès and Minervois
	Picpoul de Pinet
	Muscat de Mireval and Muscat de Frontignan
	Côtes du Languedoc, Saint-Chinian, Faugères
	Corbières and Fitou
	Côtes du Roussillon and Muscat de Rivesaltes

Fig.62. — Geological map and vineyard demarcations of Languedoc-Roussillon.

Languedoc-Roussillon

Languedoc-Roussillon has been a wine-growing area since early antiquity. Vineyards have shaped the landscape, the soil, the villages, the habitat itself. The Romans were instrumental in developing vine cultivation. There was an active trade in wine using the Via Domitiana, the port of Narbonne and the Rhône Valley to reach countries where the climate was less favourable for wine production. Vineyards became very widespread and it was necessary to call a halt to further planting (fig.62).

The fall of the Roman Empire threw the market into disarray, but the vineyards became greater still with the appearance of the chasselas, muscat and carignan grape varieties. Saracen invasions and feudal disputes checked this expansion, but the abbeys gave it new impetus in the 12th and 13th centuries with the introduction of new varieties brought from the East by returning crusaders. New markets opened up at that time in Flanders and Britain. There was another round of expansion after the Hundred Years War, with royalty expressing their concern for an improvement in quality even then!

Under the old régime, population growth made self-sufficient land management essential. The slopes remained the habitat of the vine whilst the plains became a vast granary. The authorities in fact often had to intervene to maintain this balance, and, during several periods, all new planting was forbidden. Such crises are as old as vine-growing itself.

Yet, wine production continued to increase. By the beginning of the 19th century Languedoc's 200 000 hectares of vineyards were producing 3.5 million hectolitres of wine.

But soon after, a series of catastrophes upset the stability of vine-growing in the area: 1837 witnessed an outbreak of mealy-moth. In 1850 there was widespread attack by vine-mildew. Sulphur quickly brought it under control, but production was cut by two-thirds. Between 1870 and 1880 vines were decimated by phylloxera, bringing Languedoc to the brink of starvation.

The main grape varieties in the mid-19th century were grenache, cinsaut, aspiran, clairette and muscat. Production centred around good quality wines of distinctive personality. The highest volume, from carignan and aramon, was distilled into Languedoc brandy and exported throughout the world. The coming of the railways, the birth of an industrial society and urban growth led to a demand for low-priced wine. Flying in the face of its traditions, much of the Midi began mass-producing low quality, "industrial" wines.

After the phylloxera outbreak, the use of grafting helped vine-growing to recover quite quickly. Output substantially exceeded its 1900 level, but was now coming to a market which had new sources of supply, notably Algeria. In 1906, with 450 000 hectares under vine, there were more than 35 million hectolitres of wine in the Midi, and market prices collapsed. The first grumblings of discontent had been heard as early as 1904, when vine-workers went on strike over poor pay. Trade unions began to form, and by the end of 1905 the strike was solid. The most resolute group of vine-workers was led by Marcellin Albert, "le grand boulegaïre". There were meetings and marches. In April and May 1907, hundreds of thousands of demonstrators thronged the cities of the Midi. A crowd of 600 000 met in Montpellier on 9th June. Elected officials sided with the people and organised an administrative strike. The Mayor of Narbonne was arrested and imprisoned on 19th June. The government sent the troops into the towns, inflicting casualties. One regiment refused to fire on the crowd. Marcellin Albert went to Paris to plead Languedoc's cause, but gave in to Clémenceau. The movement faded out at the end of June when new laws seemed to offer hope. The vines were waiting. Work resumed and the harvest was brought in.

The years following this crisis saw the development of the cooperative (there were 217 such cellars in 1914, twice as many as today). Vineyards continued to expand, but output of "ordinary wine" kept rising, despite a slump in sales exacerbated by imports of Algerian wines. There was a return to the old Gallo-Roman methods. Vines were uprooted, new planting was banned, excess production was distilled and attempts were made to convert vineyards to other use, along with irrigation (the lower Rhône canal). The problem has still not been resolved, and Algerian wines have given way to Italian wines imported from within the Common Market. There is one crisis after another, some as acute as in 1907, with casks being wrecked, roads and railways blocked, "ghost town" campaigns, tractor processions and the occasional ugly incident.

Post-industrial lifestyles have led to reduced consumption of ordinary wine and increased demand for fine wines.

The vineyards of the Midi have been slow to change over to quality wine production, and then only recently, but craftsmanship is gradually being superimposed on the vast vine-growing industry. Starting in several areas of mountainous foothills, vine-growers are gradually giving way to wine-makers.

Vines are in their natural habitat here, as they are around the whole of the Mediterranean Basin. Winter temperatures are mild enough to protect their resting stage (except for a catastrophe like 1956). The heat and sunshine of summer prolong and intensify the growing cycle, though there is a risk of spring frosts on the mountainous fringes and total rainfall is sometimes too low for certain soils.

The sea is close enough to give the right level of atmospheric humidity for fertilization of the raceme and good ripening of the grape, whilst the frequent north wind (the mistral or tramontane) clears the air and stops outbreaks of cryptogamic diseases which would otherwise spread easily in the overcrowded vineyards.

The shape of the landscape creates microclimates. These, together with the great diversity of soils and morphology, lead to unique regional differences between the remarkable foothills of the Pyrenees, the Corbières, the Montagne noire and the Cévennes, forming a huge, sun-drenched arc protected from continental and Atlantic influences. Vines may therefore be found at altitudes of up to 650 metres in the Eastern Pyrenees and 500 metres in the Hérault region. The produce of such localities can acquire unrivalled quality and personality.

The vineyards of Hérault

The département of Hérault, which holds the record for the highest output of wine in France, is of course known for what we nowadays call its "table wine". However, a few small estates specialising in choice red or rosé wines led the way, and gradually one or two wines of VDQS standard emerged, some achieving full AOC status. In 1963 these VDQS reds banded together for marketing purposes as a single appellation, **Coteaux de Languedoc**. Its wine-growing area includes all the Hérault districts which were producing VDQS at the time of the formation except the Minervois districts, but including La Clape (Aude), a number of new districts in Hérault and the district of Langlade (Gard).

A tour from southwest to northeast, taking in the upland foothills of the Massif Central, shows the wide range of soils supporting the estates from which these characteristic wines come (fig.63).

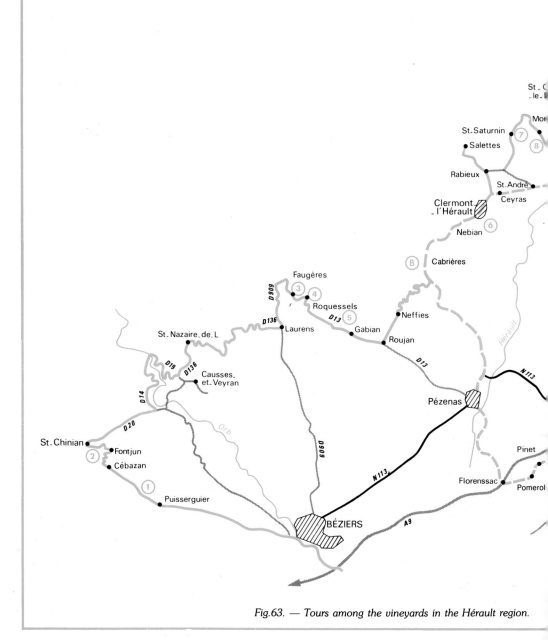

Fig.63. — Tours among the vineyards in the Hérault region.

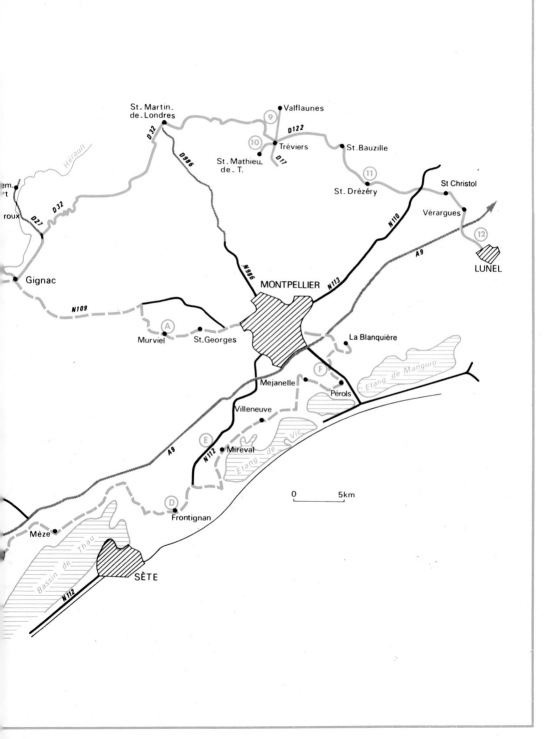

Béziers to Clermont-l'Hérault

Leave Béziers by the N 112 and drive to **Saint-Chinian,** using the *'Guide géologigue'* along the way (page 61). Note the wide range of soils which support the vineyards of AOC Saint-Chinian. From **Puisserguier** onward the vines are on a coarse, blocky Miocene conglomerate ①which filled gullies in the substratum during the Serravallian and Langhian. We then meet some lovely vineyards planted on light, deep, very red soils of the Paleocene. Before reaching the Col de Fonjun, we can see that where the Hettangian dolomitic limestone, the Rhaetian arenaceous limestone or the variegated shale of the Norian and Carnian come to the surface, they all give deep, lithic soils which are deep enough to support vines. The same is true of the Senonian covering the bauxite pockets. The viewpoint from beyond the Col gives a view over the attractive Saint-Chinian vineyards. They are thriving and being actively renewed (Pierreru site) ②.

Once we have passed Saint-Nazaire-de-Laderez, but still within the Saint-Chinian district, we enter the region of AOC **Faugères** and its underlying Carboniferous schist.

Take the D 136 as far as Laurens. It winds through an interesting vineyard on level stretches of schist. These surfaces are generally ancient, with a mixture of acid, red, clay-silica soils and quartz gravel ideally suited to raising some beautiful vines yielding a fine, well-structured wine which ages well.

The soil is more uniform at **Faugères** ③ and along the road to Roujan. From there we can visit **Roquessels,** a little hamlet perched on a ridge of marble from the Cambrian ④. Just before **Gabian** we can also visit a lovely vineyard on a very blocky Villafranchian scree ⑤.

From Neffiès, on the D 15, our journey again coincides with tour No 6 in the *'Guide géologigue'* as far as **Clermont-l'Hérault**. At Cabrières in particular, with its extremely complex geology, notice the thriving vineyards which produce several nicely typical wines.

Clermont-l'Hérault to Saint-Saturnin and Montpeyroux

From Clermont-l'Hérault the journey takes us up the valley of the Lergue on the N 9 as far as the crossroads for **Salelles,** a wine-growing hamlet a kilometere from the main road. Return through Rabieux, take two left turns to the N 109, then proceed to Saint-Saturnin, ⑦**Arboras and Montpeyroux** via the D 130. The D 9 leads via Lagamas to Gignac.

This section of the tour through the estates of Hérault shows vineyards standing prettily on Permian psammite and schist of a brilliant, brick-red colour. The wines from here (known locally as "ruffes") are tannic, full-bodied and aromatic. Nowadays they are part of the **Coteaux de Languedoc** appellation (*'Guide géologigue'*, page 101).

Saint-Saturnin has a solid reputation for quality wines, which its locality lives up to. The same goes for neighbouring **Montpeyroux,** which has kept its separate identity even though by and large its soil is similar ⑧.

Montpeyroux to Lunel

Between Montpeyroux and the peak of Saint-Loup there is quite a long break in the belt of foothill vineyards. The D 32 takes the traveller across from beyond Gignac to Saint-Martin-de-Londres, then the D 122 and the D 1 continue on to Tréviers (fig.64).

The first part of the journey takes place on the Jurassic causse of Viols-le-Fort to the pass between the peak of Saint-Loup and Hortus (*'Guide géologigue'*, page 122).

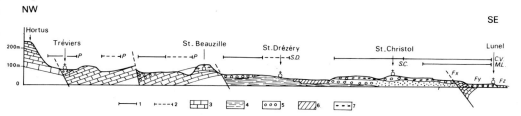

Fig.64. — Section through the formations between Pic Saint-Loup and Lunel.

1. Closely-spaced vineyards; 2. Scattered vineyards (vineyards: P, Pic Saint-Loup; SD, Saint-Drézery; SC, Saint-Christol; CV, Côteau de Vérargues; ML, Muscat de Lunel); 3. Valanginian; 4. Eocene (marl and red sandstone); 5. Oligocene and Miocene (conglomerates and molasse); 6. Miocene (soft limestone; Castries Stone); 7. Villafranchian (scree); Fx, Fy, Fz, Quaternary terraces.

The Pic **Saint-Loup** vineyard (VDQS since 1953) begins this side of the Saint-Mathieu-de-Tréviers crossroads.

A round trip northwards to **Valflaunès** gives a good idea of the soils in this wine-growing area. They were formed on marly limestone and shale of the Valanginian, and on the Oligocene conglomerates preserved at the bottom of the N-S synclines affecting the whole of this region ⑨. Few of the soils on the Valanginian are suitable for vines, which adapt poorly to the compaction of the source rock and the clay-limestone soil-flows which have accumulated in the depressions. Even so, some splendid vines are to be found on slopes where the scree has become coated with a coarsely-structured clay, as well as on the shoulders of the valley bottoms and depressions. By contrast, on the Oligocene conglomerates, where the lateritic soil is very pebbly and red, vines find favourable conditions for balanced growth. They yield a good quality wine (Cave de Saint-Mathieu) which is supple, aromatic and still fruity after two years ⑩ .

On the other side of Saint-Bauzille-de-Montmel, the tops and gentle slopes of the same conglomerate formation grow good quality grapes yielding wines of a similar type, at **Saint-Drézery** (VDQS from the Cooperative cellars), **Saint-Christol** and **Vérague**s ⑪ .

In the direction of **Lunel,** these remnants of the Villafranchian alternate with alluvial terraces of gravelly soil ⑫ . These circumstances produce AOC **Muscat de Lunel,** a natural sweet wine distinguished from the other Hérault sweet wines by its delicacy and lighter aroma. These characteristics are due perhaps to the low acidity of the leached soils on their generally siliceous base.

The old appellations of the Hérault region

For a long time now a number of special vintages have stood out from the great mass of Hérault wines due to the appreciation they have earned as the coast has been opened up more and more to tourism. A tour of the area around Montpellier shows that their attractiveness is related directly to the special geological features of their soils.

The tour starts from the town and crosses a number of estates: Saint-Georges-d'Orques, Cabrières, Pinet, Frontignan, Mireval and Méjanelle, in this order.

Saint-Georges-d'Orques Ⓐ

The vineyard became well-known by being close to the town. In 1957 it gained VDQS status, becoming part of Coteaux de Languedoc in 1972. Reds and rosés are produced from three grape varieties, carignan, grenache and cinsaut. The vineyard stretches over the Villafranchian alluvials of the Saint-Georges plateau as well as the slopes and combes of Murviel's Liassic formations.

Leave Montpellier by the N 109 towards Lodève. Cross the village of Saint-Georges (where wines are on sale and display) and head towards **Murviel-lès-Montpellier** Ⓐ. Beyond the village the road cuts through a succession of features. First there is a brecciated Rupelian limestone yielding a calcimorphic soil full of jagged pebbles. Then as we head towards a stream we find flinty pebbles which may be Villafranchian, originally coming from the Aalenian cherty marl, giving very red and acid soils.

Take the D 27 back to the N 109 and continue as far as Gignac. Take the the D 908 to Clermont-l'Hérault and proceed via the D 608 and the D 15 to Cabrières.

Clairette du Languedoc Ⓑ

Clermont-l'Hérault is famous for its dessert grapes (chasselas). **Cabrières** is the birthplace of AOC Clairette du Languedoc, a white wine produced from that very grape variety but nowadays thought little of by the wine trade. The red vine-varieties give a red, and a highly prized rosé which was accepted into the VDQS Coteaux du Languedoc in 1963.

We can get to know the soils of Cabrières from the 'Guide géologigue', tour No 6, which can be followed exactly to discover the vineyard where the dark green of the grenache mingles with the soft, vegetable green of the clairette, growing on shaly soils which are ideal for vines.

Le Picpoul de Pinet Ⓒ

From Cabrières take the D 124 to Lézignan-la-Cèbe and rejoin the N 9 to Pézénas. From there take the D 32 as far as Florensac. To see the vineyard area take the D 18, D 51 and N 113 via **Pomerols** and **Pinet** to **Mèze**.

This appellation is given to a white wine with a hint of sea green, limpid and fruity, to be drunk within a year of harvesting. It is especially good with seafood and fish from the neighbouring Lake Thau. The grape grows on scree from the Montpellier fold of Cretaceous limestone and the soft, sometimes pebbly limestone of the Miocene.

Le Muscat de Frontignan Ⓓ

At Mèze, stay on the N 113 to the Sète crossroads, then take the D 2 as far as Balaruc-les-Usines and the D 129 towards Frontignan ('Guide géologigue', page 21).

The road negotiates the complex foothill slope below La Gardiole covered in vines of the small-seeded muscat grape which is the basis of the natural sweet wine at the centre of the famous appellation. The visitor can take a tarmac track through the vineyard on either side of the main road and see an entire cross-section of the soil types. The main one is limestone scree mixed with red clay, as is often the case with white wine or muscat vineyards in the Midi.

Le Muscat de Mireval Ⓔ

Follow the D 908 for three kilometres, then turn right onto the 114 E towards Les Aresquiers via Vic-la-Gardiole to Mireval (tasting and sales of Muscat).

The Muscat de Mireval vineyard follows on the one just mentioned, below the D 908 at the foot of **La Gardiole,** where there is an entire low-lying area just 10 metres above sea-level. This area is interesting to observe, especially near Les Aresquiers, which is an "island" of hard Jurassic limestone in the process of being joined to the mainland by the silting-up of the intervening strait.

La Méjanelle Ⓕ

The journey from Mireval to La Méjanelle can be made along coastal roads. Take the D 116 as far as Villeneuve-lès-Montpellier, the D 185 and the D 996 to Lattes, and then the D 132 to **Pérols.** Leave Pérols on the D 21 heading towards Montpellier as far as Boisarques, then take the D 189 to the estate of La Blaquière. This stands on the slope below a plateau and can be reached from a little road skirting the eastern edge of the estate.

By following the recommended tour, the visitor reaches the vineyard at La Méjanelle from the south via the village of Pérols. The vines, standing on this plain at about 10 metres above sea-level, are planted on a soil containing small pebbles of quartz and quartzite in a very red, clay-sand matrix. The water table is three or four metres down and the vines are very vigorous and productive.

Further on it is possible to observe soil on Villafranchian in situ: larger pebbles, surface discoloration, with a level of very red clay sub-soil over seven or eight metres of loosely bonded scree. The vines have excellent conditions for balanced growth and show average vigour. Several signposted estates display La Méjanelle, a vigorous, full-bodied wine full of the character of the Midi. Take the D 24 back to Montpellier, but stop on the way for an interesting visit to the Flaujergues estate.

The vineyards of Aude

A wide expanse of the département of Aude faces the Mediterranean. It is also open westwards towards the Atlantic through the wide Naurouze Ridge. This gives rise to a quick succession of different climates between the coast and the hinterland, and the rugged landscape of the Corbières has a determining influence on certain typical features.

These features help the produce of certain estates to acquire a good reputation despite the fact that wine-growing is organised locally for volume production. The vineyards of different wines are often quite far apart, and though there are no vines of great value on the road between, there is often much of interest from the geological point of view. We have attempted to combine the discovery of these vineyards with the tours suggested in the *'Guide géologique Pyrénées orientales - Corbières'* (Geological guide to the Eastern Pyrenees and the Corbières'). Its reader will discover some fascinating geological facts.

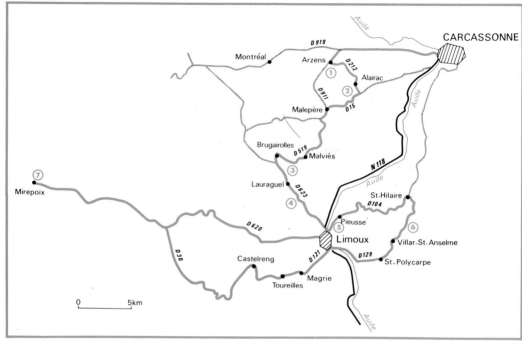

Fig.65. — Tour among the vineyards in the Aude region.

Côtes de La Malepère

This rapidly expanding VDQS is a recent appellation. The vine-growing area is the closest to the Atlantic of all those in the Midi, and is aware of its unique situation in these southern parts. With the introduction of grape varieties from Bordeaux in addition to varieties from the Midi, it produces a full-bodied, well-structured wine which is also fruity and capable of acquiring a pleasant bouquet.

Situated to the Northwest of the Corbières uplands, which isolate it from Mediterranean influences, the district includes the massif of La Malepère (bad stone). This culminates in a crag some 414 metres high to the southwest of Carcassonne, with a radius of some ten kilometres, and consists of a more or less cemented conglomerate block with effective resistance to erosion. It stands between the valleys of the Aude and its tributary the Sou on one hand, and the Fresquel and its tributary the Rébenty on the other. These conglomerates were laid down during the Upper Eocene (Bartonian) at the base of the subsiding depression between the chain of the Pyrenees and the Montagne noire. On the western side the molasse formations, a soft sandstone with calcareous cement, are separated by conglomerate beds tilted in a northerly direction. This has formed a landscape of hill-slopes oriented east-west called the Razès, many districts of which are included in the vine-growing area of La Malepère (fig.65).

The northern slope: On both sides of the D 919, the road is built on a pebble terrace from the lowland between the Corbières and the Montagne noire, where today the Fresquel flows. A kilometre beyond **Arzens** is the site of grenache vineyards on the same terrace ①.

Beyond the village of **Alairac** ②there are many gullies in the deeply weathered arenaceous molasse where the soil is turning brown, but in locations which are too lowlying for quality vineyards. Clay colluvial deposits have obliterated the very blocky molasse in places, elsewhere giving way to a very weathered and broken conglomerate (the typical soil of this vineyard).

226

The southern slope: The journey down from La Malepère illustrates the contrast between the growing pattern on the slopes of this range of pebbly hills and the concentration of vineyards around the villages huddled close to their châteaux.

Malviès to **Brugairolles:** ③After crossing the Sou, which seems such a small stream for such a wide valley, we climb up to the terrace with its covering of vines. As we reach the D 623 we can look to the right and see the Cave des Routiers, with its enormous wine-making machinery.

Beyond **Lauraguel** the terrace is interrupted by a small valley. The road then enters a deep cutting where the visitor can observe molasse deposits interlayered with beds and lenses of conglomerate ④. This is the edge of La Malepère growing district. We are about to enter the Blanquette de Limoux district.

Blanquette de Limoux

The basic grape-variety is mauzac. It gives a well-structured white wine with full body and fruit which can be made suppler and finer by adding a small proportion of chardonnay. Blanquette is produced by the "méthode champenoise" and has acquired a great reputation among sparkling wines.

Keeping pace with the Blanquette, wine-producers have recently improved their red wines. At Limoux, now that there is renewed interest in the local cuisine, the range is worth tasting in such places as restaurants, exhibitions and wine shops.

The wine-growing area extends into the valley of the Aude, where it runs north-south at each end of the narrow passage caused by the western edge of the Mouthoumet uplands. Vineyards are also especially abundant in the lateral valleys to the east and west, beyond the Alet narrows.

The area contains Cretaceous and Lower Eocene formations of limestone strata interlayered with shale beds. There are also continental deposits of the Middle and Upper Lutetian and Bartonian where conglomerate alternates with marl or soft molasse. These formations have given rise to a landscape of hillslopes aligned east-west with their brows facing generally south. The recommended tour goes to the east of the Aude, with a loop to the west, before going off south along the valley.

East of the Aude

Leave Limoux on the D 104. Two Kilometres beyond the bridge over the Aude is a Würmian terrace of pebbly, leached soil which can be seen in cross-section in a quarry on the left of the road ⑤. Beyond Pieusse the D 104 winds along the hillside, overlooking the valley. On the left the hill is sheer, with beds of conglomerate.

Glance back at the outlines of successive cuestas to the west. You may also wish to visit the Fourn estate.

At **Villar-Saint-Anselme,** a lovely vineyard of mauzac and chardonnay stands on the lower slopes ⑥. Looking south from **Saint-Polycarpe** you can see a high, wooded hill silhouetted against the horizon. This is the faulted backslope of the Mouthoumet uplands, with an altitude of 700 to 800 metres (see 'Guide géologique Pyrénées orientales — Corbières', pages 68 and 69).

West of the Aude

Take the D 626 towards Mirepoix ⑦. Make your way up to the Cave Coopérative and back, then take the D 30 to Castelreng. Turn left in the village, cross the Cougain, and two kilometres later, on reaching the Col de La Plaine, turn left onto the D 321 via Toureilles to Magrie. The D 121 brings you back to Limoux.

The D 30 follows the asymmetrical subsequent valley of the Cougain. The lower right-hand slope (brow of hill) shows a series of beds which are interlayered with the main conglomerates over a thickness of some 100 metres. Metre-thick calcaro-siliceous beds of occasionally indurated clay and marl alternate with seams of variegated, dark or ochrous sandstone from the Upper Lutetian. The residual soil is an atypical argillo-calcareous lithosol which is very suitable for the mauzac, traditionally the main variety here. The pebbly terrace of the Cougain is part of the wine-growing district and planted with "vin de pays" varieties.

Le Corbières

In 1951, when VDQS Corbières was created in this region of 94 village districts, a VDQS Corbières supérieures was also granted. It applies to 39 of the districts concerned, which are required to produce a wine of 12° minimum for the red and 12.5° for the white, with a lower yield per hectare than is the case with the Corbières.

AOC **Fitou** was created in 1948. Its area covers five village districts on the seaward hillslopes towards the southwest, and a further four such districts inland. All these districts, with the addition of Cascatel, are also part of the wine-growing area of the AOC "vins doux naturel" (the VDN fortified wines) called Rivesaltes and Muscat de Rivesaltes.

The Corbières region is mountainous. Its southwestern half is nowhere below 300 metres, with peaks of 800, 900 and 1200 metres (Bugarach). The landscape is often rugged. Streams have carved deep, erratic gorges, but there are many basins, separated by spurs, which have been planted with isolated vineyards.

In the region of the Aquitaine Basin nearest the Mediterranean, the western side is subject to oceanic influences. It is generally open to a drying wind known as the tramontane (or cers), and the marin, a moist, southeast wind blowing from the Mediterranean in spring and autumn.

Rainfall is low and very irregular in some years. Good conditions for balanced growth require porous soils with a layer of deep, loose subsoil which can act as a reservoir in dry years.

It would take a very long tour to get to know the Corbières vineyards properly, especially if the aim is to understand the structure of the territory, with its very varied geological history. In this respect the 'Guide géologique Pyrénées orientales — Corbières' will be very useful to the visitor on foot. The recommended route, from Narbonne to Carcassonne via the seaward edge and inland via the Corbières, will give a good idea of the range of soils. For the Tuchan Basin, please refer to the section dealing with the vineyards of the Eastern Pyrenees.

From Narbonne, take the N 9 to Cabannes-de-Fitou (fig.66). On the way out of Narbonne heading south, notice the plateau of Villafranchian scree on the northern edge of Lake Bages. The soil here is pebbly, leached, and reddened to a great depth. It stands some 30 metres above sea-level, and supports a small vineyard of a reputed VDQS known as *Quatourze* ①

Vineyards of the Corbières Maritimes

These vineyards are situated on yellow or light-coloured marly soils of the Miocene, and are generally open to the influence of the sea.

Along the D 50 as far as **Treilles** ② are outcrops of marly limestone and shale deposits from the Liassic and Triassic. In some low lying areas these yield soils which are unsuitable for quality output, but on the tops and slopes their physical qualities

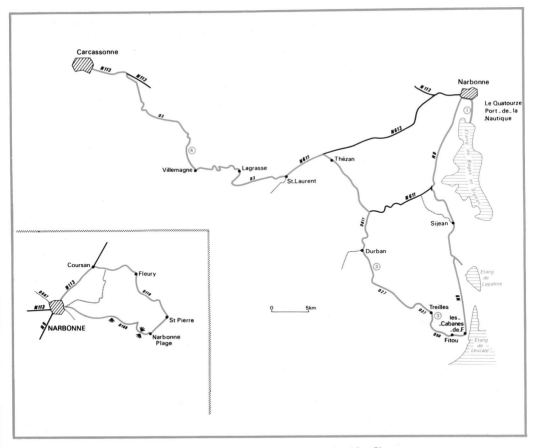

Fig.66. — Tour among the Corbières and the vineyards of La Clape.

have been improved by scree from the Urgonian massif. We leave the old Villafranchian peneplanation and enter an area of hard, barren limestone before arriving at Feuilla. On the floor of this shallow depression are a few ridges of Silurian schist and Triassic sandstone beneath layers of Urgo-Aptian debris (see *'Guide géologique Pyrénées orientales — Corbières'*, page 153).

The central Corbières

Beyond the Col de Feuilla, which crosses the last spur of Urgonian limestone, the route passes through Saint-Jean-de-Barrou and enters the **Durban Basin** ③. This shallow Triassic depression is composed mainly of red shales, with deep clay-sand soils on the tops (surface weathering) and on the valley floors (colluvial deposition), covered here and there with scree from the various limestone ridges. They are soils of average fertility, warm and light, with good water reserves. Such soils are the archetype for this vine-growing area, from which the fertile low-lying areas are excluded.

The Val d'Agne ④

This vineyard area is a well-defined basin. It lies southwest of the Alaric and its plateaux of Thanetian limestone, to the east of the Lower Lutetian conglomerate hills, and to the north of the edge of the Mouthoumet uplands. The subsoil is formed of dark and grey marls interlayered with limestone banks of the Lower Eocene. The basin is bordered to the north and east by an escarpment of sandstone, conglomerate and limestone giving rise here and there to barren crests and hillsides, rising above the vineyards on the gravelly colluvial deposits of the lower slopes.

From the D 3 there is a view of the Chapitre quarry (*'Guide géologique Pyrénées orientales — Corbières',* page 80) then the route follows the Alaric peripheral depression in the shales of the Lower Lutetian, planted with the same type of vineyard as the Tournissan depression.

The vineyards of La Clape

In Languedoc the Pre-Pyrenean system is subdivided by wide depressions leaving isolated blocks. Running from the west to the northeast, these are: the Corbières, the Narbonne-Bages Basin, La Clape, the Aude Basin and the Saint-Chinian Range. The fold tectonics of each massif are the same, but only the Cretaceous crops out at La Clape, in a faulted anticline with sides which are tightly folded in places (Armissan Syncline).

The landscape is predominantly limestone, especially on the lower slopes where the Urgonian limestone base is over 100 metres thick. Typical shapes of a Jurassic landscape abound, with anticlinal valleys, crests and vast structural platforms. Every superficial or deep-lying feature of karst scenery can also be found here (karren, dolines, poljes, shaft caves and surface reappearances).

The layer of Albian limestone outcrops less regularly. It is massive, sandstone-like and reddish in colour, appearing on the northern backslope of the anticline (fig.67).

Detrital formations accumulated around this massif in the Tertiary: quartz pebbles and limestones of the middle Rupelian, capped with pebbly limestone, conglomerates and marine sands of the Helvetian. Finally, in the older Quaternary, large pebbles were distributed widely around the whole of the massif, while frost action covered the lower slopes with scree and terra rossa accumulated in the karst basins and dry valleys.

The vine-growing area is therefore very fragmented. A diversity of vineyards is separated by barren, hard limestone plateaux of "garrigue" (wasteland). Vine-growing is currently thriving on the basis of the classic varieties of the Midi (carignan and grenache with the recent addition of cinsaut, syrah and mourvèdre). The wines are forthcoming, full-bodied, fruity in their second year, and keep well. They include red, rosé and white.

Take the D 168 from Narbonne to Narbonne-Plage. Go to Saint-Pierre, then return to the starting point on the D 118 to Fleury and an unclassified road to Narbonne and Coursan. Look out for the following on the way:

— calcimorphic clay-sand soils on the approaches to the vineyard at Maujan;

— vineyard on rendzinoid soils on the Albian calcareous limestone slopes below the Urgonian cliff (L'Hospitalet);

— decalcification clay soils, generally the result of solifluction, on the sides of the anticlinal valleys (as the road descends towards Narbonne-Plage) or on their floors (as the D 118 climbs back to the plateau, beyond Saint-Pierre);

— vineyard on an elevated plain, formerly the bed of a karst basin (polje), one kilometre this side of **Fleury,** with leached red soils, whilst the basin floor is coated with fine, quite fertile silt which is excluded from the appellation (Lake Taraillan);

— beyond Fleury the vineyard is on undeveloped calcimorphic soils from the Helvetian molasse. Beyond the autoroute crossing it stands on pebbly soils of the Villafranchian (Château du Pech and Château de Céleyran).

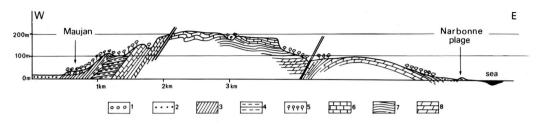

Fig.67. — *The uplands of La Clape.*

1. Recent alluvials; 2. Older alluvials; 3. Tertiary formations; 4. Albian arenaceous limestone (Lower Cretaceous); 5. Vineyards; 6, 7, 8. Lower Cretaceous horizons (Aptian).

Le Minervois

The Minervois region gets its name from the ancient city of Minerva, a Roman stronghold in the region of Narbonne and the celtic lands of the Montagne noire. The Minervois vintage has long been identified, having received legal status in 1909 in Aude and gradually extended to 61 village districts (16 of which are in the département of Hérault). Its geographical delimitation was established by decree in 1979 (VDQS).

It is a red wine, produced from traditional Midi varieties with a predominance of carignan, and gradually improved with successive additions of grenache, cinsaut, syrah and mourvèdre.

Protected from cold northerly winds by the Montagne noire and its eastern extensions (Monts du Minervois and Monts du Pardailhan), with peaks rising to 1200 metres, the region comprises a series of hills which vary between 100 and 300 metres in height. The climate is noted for frequent winds in the Carcassonne corridor, particularly from the west; the sudden onset of precipitation from the southeast or northwest with very variable annual extremes; and Atlantic influences towards the western edge of the zone, sometimes to the detriment of the ripening process for the carignan grown on that side.

Geologically, the Minervois constitutes the northern edge of the vast Carcassonne syncline, comprising an assortment of soils from various sources, some being marine (Thanetian limestone, cavernous limestone from the Ilerdian), some lacustrine (limestones of Ventenac and Montaulieu) and some continental (shales, clays and sandstones from the middle Eocene to the Bartonian) (fig.68). This diverse succession of strata, dipping generally to the south, has resulted in an undulating landscape with south-facing backslopes which are very suitable for vineyards. Incision during the Quaternary created deep gorges which segmented the whole area into sloping plateaux, whilst at the foot of the hills, on the plain of the Aude, the rivers flowing down from the Palaeozoic massif deposited three or four series of pebbly alluvial terraces.

The tour starts from Carcassonne and crosses the Minervois region to Saint-Chinian, linking up with one of the Hérault tours.

Leave Carcassonne by the D 918. At the Bezons crossroads take the D 620 via Villegly to Caunes.

Between Villegly and Caunes we enter the Minervois wine-growing area. About two kilometres before the village of **Villegly** ①, after a bend in the road, we come across a ruined windmill surrounded with vineyards planted on a Riss terrace of pebbly, leached soils from the Clamous. Beyond the village the road skirts a vineyard on the left of the road, standing on residual, unleached brown soils over red Ventenac clays of the middle Lutetian, interrupted by ridges of conglomerate with

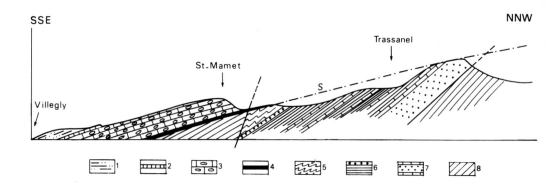

Fig.68. — N-S section through the centre of the Minervois region.

1. Upper Lutetian (marl and sandstone); 2. Middle Lutetian (Ventenac Limestone); 3. Ypresian-Ilerdian (Alveolina limestone); 4. Sparnacian- Ilerdian (Alveolina limestone); 5. Lower Ordovician (schist); 6. Acadian (sandstone and shale); 7. Georgian (limestone and sandstone); 8. Devonian (limestone and shale); S. Palaeogene surface.

pebbly, well-drained colluvial deposits on their slopes. Further away to the north, "garrigue" covers the surface of the cavernous limestone (Ilerdian), broken only by a few vines planted in the dry valleys.

At **Caunes** ②it is interesting to look at the marble quarries. For details see page 53 of the 'Guide géologique Languedoc méditerranéen - Montagne Noire' (Guide to the Geology of Mediterranean Languedoc and the Montagne Noire). Also visit the former quarry of Saint-Roch chapel and see a complete cross-section of the Ilerdian ('Guide géologique Pyrénées orientales — Corbières', page 119).

As far as Azillanet in the heart of the Minervois vine district, the vineyards occupy the upper terraces. There are wine cellars at **Pépieux** and **Azillanet** where wine may be purchased. Beyond there the road cuts through an excellent cross-section of the Middle and Upper Eocene ('Guide géologique Languedoc', page 59). See the outstanding site at Minerva ③.

Between Minerva and Bize the vineyards are much more fragmentary in nature, standing mainly on clay-limestone colluvial deposits which are quite deep in places. From the D 10 there is a lovely view over the gorges of the Cesse, carved into of Alveolina limestone. The road is built on lignitic marl and the higher ground is Ventenac limestone from the Middle Lutetian, a rock of lacustrine origin containing fossils.

Between Aigues-Vives and Agel the vineyard to the north of the D 20 stands on the Limestones and Marls of Agel (Upper Lutetian) ④.

The little muscat vineyard of **Saint-Jean-de-Minervois** is classed AOC ⑤. The soil is an extraordinary mass of pebbles resulting from spalling of the Middle Lutetian Ventenac Limestone and the Ilerdian Alveolina Limestone. It overlies a Pre-Tertiary surface of Ordovician sandy shale which has thoroughly broken down into a layer of arenaceous, variegated clay.

The Minervois tour may be combined with the tours of Saint-Chinian and of Faugères (Hérault) via Assignan.

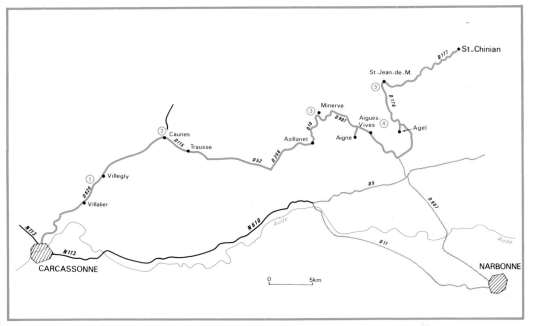

Fig.69. — Tour in the Minervois region.

The vineyards of the eastern Pyrénées

The northern area of the département of Pyrénées-Orientales (Eastern Pyrenees) spills over into the true Roussillon and is therefore Catalan. The whole region is as individual in its wine-growing as it is in other respects. Climate and landscape together create vineyards with settings, methods and produce which are characteristic of the area. In fact the département produces most of the French VDN ("Vingdoux naturels") sweet wines. These are based on musts with at least 14° alcohol from four varieties: grenache, macabeo, malvoisie and muscat. Together they are the famous generic "crus" of **Banyuls, Maury, Rivesaltes and Muscat de Rivesaltes.**

Besides its VDN sweet wines, the region produces other kinds of wine from the same grape varieties in combination with others from the Midi, the carignan in particular. The resulting AOC wines are becoming more and more popular for their highly typical and often individual style. The district lies entirely within the département boundaries but is generally bigger than the area producing sweet wines. AOC **Côtes du Roussillon** is derived from 120 village districts. AOC **Côtes du Roussillon-Villages** comes from 28 districts on the southern backslopes of the Corbières, with two 'terroirs' (Caramany and Latour-de-France) allowed specific appellation. AOC Collioure is produced in the same area as Banyuls.

The effect of climate on wine quality is naturally quite strong, and in some respects even more important than the sun. The growing area for sweet wine is bounded by the 13° C isotherm and the 700 mm rain contour whilst keeping to the lower slopes. Roussillon is a singularly uniform orographic and climatic entity and could, by the way, make better use of its potential for quality.

Muscat de Rivesaltes and Côtes du Roussillon

Head north out of Perpignan on the N 9. After seven kilometres turn left towards **Rivesaltes** (fig.70).

233

Between the N 9 and Rivesaltes a vineyard covers the **Crest,** a complex stony plain between 25 and 30 metres above sea-level, where torrential alluvials have been deposited since the Quaternary.

Several hundred hectares of this elevated plain are covered with a layer between four and six metres deep of very rounded limestone pebbles. Those on the surface have a patina, whilst at 30 and 50 cm below the surface some are encrusted with crystalline limestone (calcsinter or "taparas"). The waters of the Roboul have scoured a narrow ravine through these alluvial deposits, and some lovely cross-sections can be seen from the road.

As far as **Vingrau** the D 12 makes its way across Lower Cretaceous beds ①. The infrequent vineyards are planted in marly soil on the floors of depressions and on lower slopes in the accumulations of frost-cracked limestone scree.

Its extensive development makes the Vingrau Syncline a typical schistose basin of the Corbières region in its broadest sense. The vines around the basin are on limestone scree brought down from the slopes, which gives way further on to eroded soils on schist, with the remains of calcareous alluvial fans rising in steps.

From Vingrau to the **Paziols Basin,** the Urgonian ridges of the western rise of the syncline have only a few dry valleys dedicated to vines ②. On one of these limestone peaks stand the ruins of the Catharist Château d'Aguilar.

The vineyards of Tuchan-Paziols (département of Aude): AOC Fitou, Corbières Supérieures and VDN (Sweet Wines) ③

The low-lying part of the vine-growing area is bounded on the west by the Cenomanian limestone basement of Mont Tauch. This has a cap of Urgonian limestone at 900 metres which is older than the pedestal rock supporting it, proof that there is an overthrust. Its base is the Middle Triassic limestone to the west of Tuchan. This is covered by Upper Cretaceous shale (Santonian — Coniacian) in the southern part of the basin.

Basin formation was completed during the Villafranchian, no doubt by karst erosion, which would explain the steep sides and the rocky stumps which stud its floor (hums from an ancient polje).

We leave the vineyards of Tuchan by travelling up the valley of the Verdouble, overshadowed by the Château de Padern. The road overlooks the gorges of the Verdouble, carved in the Cenomanian limestone, then beyond the village the D 14 continues to Cucugnan in formations of the Upper Cretaceous (limestone and sandstone) which are synclinal outside the vine-growing area. The D 123 climbs to Grau du Maury ④ with its commanding view of the Fenouillèdes basin.

The Maury vineyards: AOC Côtes du Rousillon-Villages, Maury Sweet Wines ⑤

The Fenouillèdes Complex Syncline outcrops seemingly as a wide band of Albian schist which in reality is interbedded marl and sandstone.

The Agly vineyard (AOC Côtes du Rousillon-Villages)

The geology from beyond the Maury Syncline to Ille-sur-Têt will be examined in the light of the 'Guide géologique Pyrénées orientales - Corbières' (pages 95 to 99) which describes the various outcrops. Each of these has a different soil type:

Beyond the Col de Maury, which cuts through the southern ridge of the Albian syncline (observe the tilting of the limestone towards the north) vineyards cover the Saint-Arnac Granite. This largely underlies a Neogene surface, showing onion-skin weathering of the granite. The sandy soil is deep and highly evolved, and

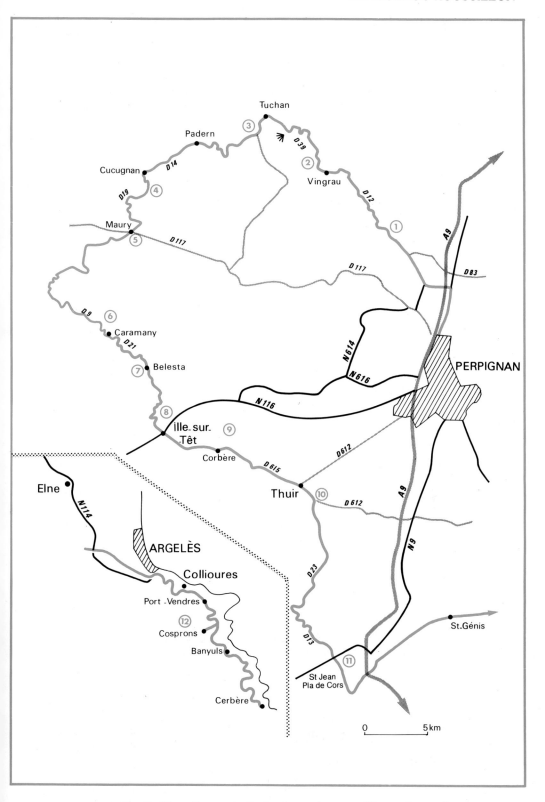

Fig.70. — Tour in the Pyrénes orientales region (Eastern Pyrenees).

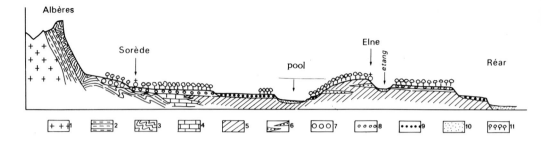

Fig.71. — The vineyards in the south of the Roussillon district.

1. *Granite; 2. Gneiss; 3. Schist; 4. Overburden rocks in the axial zone of the Pyrenees; 5. Molasse; 6. Sands and gravels of Pliocene age; 7. Early alluvial fans; 8. & 9. Quaternary terrace; 10. Recent alluvials; 11. Vineyards.*

clay has accumulated between 1 and 1.5 metres below the surface, leaving an arenaceous matrix. These factors combined with the altitude are not very conducive to quality vineyards.

Around Caramany ⑥on the south bank of the Agly valley a lovely vineyard stands on the Pre-Cambrian gneiss of the Agly massif. The soils which develop from it are very suitable for high-quality vines. They produce AOC Côtes du Rousillon-Villages, Caramany.

Around Bélesta ⑦the soil overlies migmatic gneiss and does not encourage quality vines, except on slopes devoid of a covering of sand (lithosols).

The road down to **Ille-sur-Têt** ⑧runs through "maquis", which is the typical form of vegetation in this acid environment. Near the lowest point in the journey there is a good view of earth pyramids caused by present-day erosion of an outcrop of white Pliocene molasse which is very gravelly in places.

The Aspres vineyards: AOC Côtes du Rousillon, and AOC Sweet Wines Rivesaltes and Muscat de Rivesaltes

The schistose terrace of La Têt

Beyond Ille-sur-Têt we cross the lower valley of the Têt. For four to six kilometres either side of Corbères-les-Cabanes the D 615 is built on the middle terrace of the Têt, about 100 metres above sea-level ⑨. This is formed of a considerable thickness of pebbles with angular fragments of grey schist, gneiss and quartzite from the Canigou massif.

Les Aspres

Between Thuir (the Byrrh cellars) and Llupia, the road climbs the succession of terraces formed by the Adou ⑩ . The lowest terrace has rounded quartzite pebbles and leached soils. Here Llupia is built. On the middle terrace, with its schistose pebbles, stands Terrats. The terrace outside the village is being eroded by the Canterrane, and there is a meander face with a splendid cross-section showing eight or ten metres of the Pliocene molasse capped by three metres of schistose gravel where the pedologic horizons are quite clearly defined.

The terraces of the Tech

The terraces of the left bank of the Tech (fig.71) are formed of a considerable thickness of large, well-rounded pebbles and sand. Excellent cross-sections may be observed below **Saint-Jean-Pla-de-Corts** ⑪ . They extend as far as Maureillas, and their vineyards are being refurbished.

The vineyards of Banyuls (AOC Sweet Wines) and AOC Collioure

Where the Pyrenees meet the sea they halt abruptly as a rugged slope with a hinterland of jagged relief. There is only one road to follow on the round trip from Argelès to Banyuls. Sadly the vineyards along the way are adversely affected by urban development and the effects of tourism on the physical and human environment. It is still possible to find good vineyard on the way by turning off halfway between Port-Vendres and Banyuls onto the **Cosprons** road, looping via the hamlet from one side of the valley to the other ⑫

The vineyard stands on schist, mica schist and chloritic gneiss from the axial zone of the Pyrenees. These Cambrian schists have undergone little metamorphosis but strong folding. The soil is generally eroded lithosol on jointed and fractured rock. The surface is loose and consists of an accumulation of highly fragmented debris. Below 0.20 to 0.50 metres it gradually gives way to firmer rock. The fragments often occur coated in the sandy clay currently being produced by their decay process.

Such soils retain moisture but are light and permeable. The vine roots grow deep and enable the plants to withstand long summer droughts.

There are traditional measures against soil erosion, such as miniature walls supporting narrow terracing, and channels constructed of schist slabs placed obliquely or "peu de gall" (chicken-foot fashion) at the slightest sign of a gully. The soil is thicker on the lower slopes, where there are the beginnings of small alluvial fans.

Displays and wine-cellars in the three townships of **Collioure, Port-Vendres and Banyuls** help the visitor to appreciate Banyuls and the various wines mainly derived from grenache. The red variety, with few secondary varieties, produces the best wines.

During the journey back to Perpignan observe the vineyards on the plain, for the most part on pebbly terraces, generally of older Quaternary age, with well-rounded stones and red soil. They stand alongside the road between Le Canet and Perpignan as it dips gently down towards the sea (Lesparrou).

Wines of Languedoc-Roussillon and gastronomy

The wines of Languedoc-Roussillon have long been an essential part of the gastronomic scene. The good table wines can be appreciated in their own right. The whites, rosés and reds, as well as the VDN sweet wines, can be served with any dish, from light hors-d'oeuvre through filling entrée to roast main course and fresh dessert without palling. In this range more than any other, it is said, sweet wines are to be served well chilled (not iced), whites chilled, rosés at mid-range and reds at room temperature — but remember just how warm rooms can be in this part of the world ... No wine should be drunk if it is below 3° or 4°C, or above 17° to 18°C.

The white goes naturally with raw vegetable salad, pizza, shellfish and seafood, fish however cooked, bouillabaisse, bourride (fish soup), "catigot" of eel or cod "Minervoise".

A subtly fruity rosé goes well with "aïoli" (garlic mayonnaise) as well as dishes with less body. It is also good with vegetable ragout, white meats and charcuterie. It is used in recipes for poultry, lamb or vegetable ragouts, and artichokes with pork liver.

The red makes excellent marinades and stews of beef or wild boar, in such local dishes as daubes, salmis and carbonades. It is required drinking with even very strong cheeses such as Chèvre (goat), Roquefort or an aged Pyrenees. Red also goes on picnics and with sandwiches. There is nothing like a Fitou with the "cargolade", a country feast beneath the trees, with roast snails alternating with hot sausages and cutlets roast on the spit.

Whilst discussing food and wines we should not forget that the Midi is famous for aromatic wines such as hazelnut, peach, chervil or rosemary, obtained by macerating the leaves of these plants in a fortified wine which is then sweetened. These are recipes which the manufacturers of vermouth and 'cooked wines' have made popular as apéritifs.

Then there are the special, Madeira-type wines, which our modern tastes seem to appreciate less than hitherto but which make full-bodied sauces for tender meats or lobsters and prawns, aromatic dishes which can be washed down with a two-year old rosé. Established custom says that sweet wines like Banyuls, whether made from grenache or muscat, are drunk as an apéritif or with dessert, but may also be blended with melon or fruit salad (why should it always have to be Port?) and indeed with a few fatty dishes such as poultry liver, canard aux fruits or very mild cheeses.

FOR FURTHER
INFORMATION

Geology

Eastern Aquitaine:

Geological guides (Masson, Paris): *Aquitaine occidentale* (Western Aquitaine) (1975), by M.Vigneaux et al. (see especially tours 4, 5 and 6). *Aquitaine orientale* (Eastern Aquitaine) (1977), by B.Gèze and A.Cavaillé (see especially tours 1, 7, 8 and 10).

Languedoc-Roussillon:

Geological guides (Masson, Paris): *Languedoc méditerranéen-Montagne Noire* (Mediterranean Languedoc-Montagne Noire) (1979), by B.Gèze (see especially tours 2, 3, 4, 8, 9 and 10). *Pyrénées orientale-Corbières* (Eastern Pyrenees-Corbières) (1977), by M.Jaffrezo et al. (see especially tours 4, 5, 8 11 and 12).

Bousquet J.-C. and Vignard G., (1980). — Découverte géologique du Languedoc Méditerranéen (Discovering the Geology of Mediterranean Languedoc) BRGM, Paris.

Oenology

Eastern Aquitaine:

Baudel J. (1977). — Le vin de Cahors (The Wine of Cahors) Cave Coop. de Parnac Luzech, 2nd edition.

Beauroy J. (1965). — Aspects de l'ancien vignoble et du commerce du vin de Bergerac du XIVe au XVIIIe siècles (Aspects of the Old Vineyards and Wine Trade of Bergerac from the 14th to the 18th Century) University of Toronto.

Cavaillé A. and Leclair P. (1981). — Rapport de délimitation de l'AOC Cahors (Report on the Boundaries of AOC Cahors) INAO publication.

Got A. (1949). — Monbazillac. Edit. Aquitaine, Bordeaux.

Jouanel A. (1951). — Bergerac et la Hollande (Bergerac and Holland) Imprimerie Trillant et Compagnie, Bergerac.

Paloc J. (1980). — Le Bergeracois et ses vins (The Bergerac Region and its Wines) INAO Bulletin.

Languedoc-Roussillon:

Astruc H. (since 1980). — Publications écologiques et oenologiques de la Chambre d'Agriculture, Carcassonne.

Marcellin H. and Torrès P. (1980). — Vignobles et vins du Roussillon (Roussillon Wines and Vineyards) *Bulletin technique Pyrénées-Orientales.*

Sanchez G. (1978). — L'Hérault, ses sites, ses vins (The Sites and Wines of Hérault) APV Béziers.

Above: The Monbazillac vineyards. In the foreground, on boulder clay from white limestone; further away, on leached brown soils from the Agenais Molasse (Photo. Cavaillé).

Below: The Corbières vineyards and Cucugnan village (Photo. Petzold).

Above: Saint-Chinian. Vineyards in the Pierrerue lowlands of the Trias and Lias; the village directly ahead is on red sandstone of Lower Eocene age (Photo. Cavaillé).

Below: The Maury vineyard from the south. The vineyard and cooperative wine-cellars stand on Albian schist. On the horizon, a range of hills of Urgonian age, on the northern side of the Fenouillèdes syncline (Photo. Cavaillé).

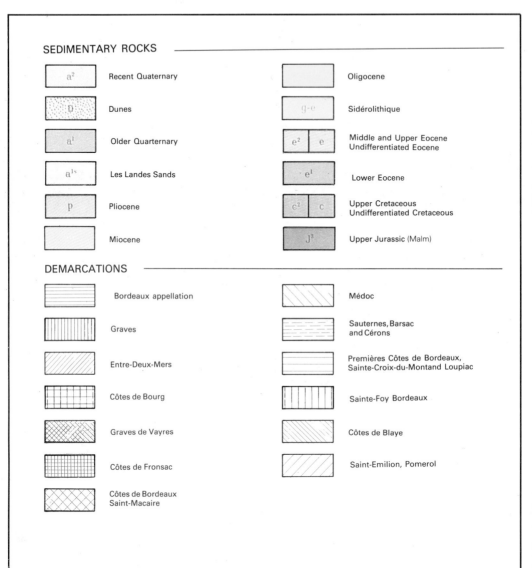

SEDIMENTARY ROCKS

a²	Recent Quaternary			Oligocene
D	Dunes		g-e	Sidérolithique
a¹	Older Quarternary	e²	e	Middle and Upper Eocene Undifferentiated Eocene
a¹ˢ	Les Landes Sands		e¹	Lower Eocene
p	Pliocene	e²	c	Upper Cretaceous Undifferentiated Cretaceous
	Miocene		J³	Upper Jurassic (Malm)

DEMARCATIONS

	Bordeaux appellation		Médoc
	Graves		Sauternes, Barsac and Cérons
	Entre-Deux-Mers		Premières Côtes de Bordeaux, Sainte-Croix-du-Montand Loupiac
	Côtes de Bourg		Sainte-Foy Bordeaux
	Graves de Vayres		Côtes de Blaye
	Côtes de Fronsac		Saint-Emilion, Pomerol
	Côtes de Bordeaux Saint-Macaire		

Fig.72. — Geological map and vineyard demarcations of the Bordelais region.

Bordelais

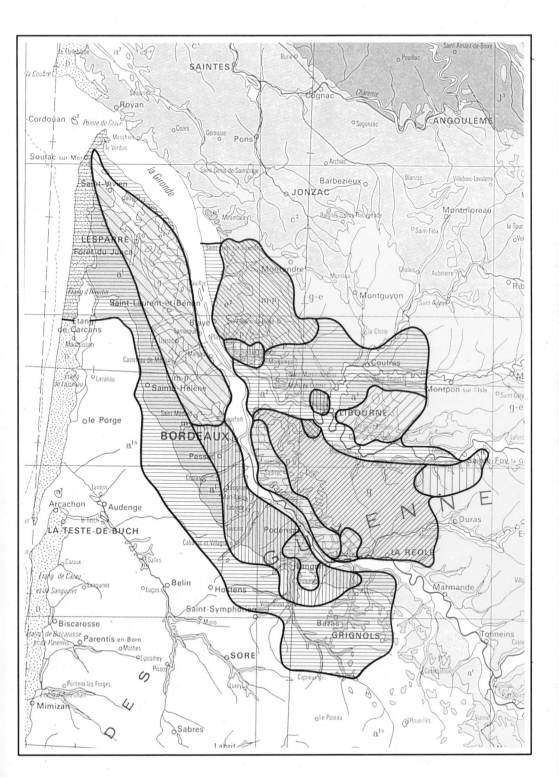

The Romans much appreciated the wine of Bordeaux, yet it seems to have fallen into disfavour in the 12th century, early on in the period of English rule. It is not mentioned in an edict of King John Lackland (1199) which quotes Poitou as first rate. Its fame returned in the 13th century, with the support of Henry Plantagenet (Henry III of England), reaching its apogee in the 14th century, when a thousand ships sailed to England laden with nine-tenths of the country's total wine imports. This was a reason why Aquitaine remained loyal to the Kings of England for two centuries, long after the other English possessions on French soil had been lost.

Bordeaux wine had special protection in two ways. First there was a ban on the transit of wines from the hinterland, with the exception of the Dordogne (Bergerac), which lasted until the 17th century. Then there was a prohibition on cultivating certain regions, such as Médoc, even though the soil was suitable for vines. It was in the 18th and 19th centuries that the wines of Bordeaux finally achieved their worldwide reputation.[1]

Vines and soils

Geology

The vineyards of Bordeaux occupy a surface area in excess of 100 000 hectares in the northwest of the Aquitaine Basin. They produce about five million hectolitres of wine a year. Although this wine-growing area is mainly famous for its red wines, they come from only about 60 of its surface area.

The best vineyards are on the hillsides and alluvial terraces along the Gironde estuary and the lower reaches of the Garonne and the Dordogne, roughly between 15 and 120 metres above sea-level.

Vineyards of a lesser quality stand on the lower valley slopes, at an altitude of 5 to 10 metres.

The geological formations of the Bordeaux vineyards are not particularly varied and belong exclusively to the Tertiary and Quaternary. In the north these formations lie on Jurassic and Cretaceous beds of the Charente region bounding the Aquitaine Basin. The main features are marl, molasse and limestone of the Eocene and Oligocene, together with gravelly and arenaceous Plio-Quaternary alluvial formations, often hidden beneath a layer of silt.

From north to south and from east to west, the main wine-growing regions (fig.72) may be characterised schematically by the following geological substrates:

— the region of **Premières Côtes de Blaye** produces a good quality red wine and is located on the right bank of the Gironde estuary, about fifty kilometres northeast of Bordeaux. The underlying formations are Eocene, mainly marl and limestone of marine, though occasionally of brackish-lagoon and lacustrine origin, and belong to the eastern part of the Blaye-Listrac anticline which is at right-angles to the estuary;

---

1. This chapter is condensed from 'Bordelais', travel guide 210 C, 'Géologie et vins de France' (The Geology and Wines of France) from the 26th International Geological Congress (Paris, 1980). Bull. Inst. géol. Bassin d'Aquitaine, Bordeaux, 1980, No 27, pages 171-199.

— to the south of the area just mentioned, the region of **Côtes de Bourg** also produces some very pleasing red wines which earned great fame when England ruled Aquitaine. The vine slopes of Rupelian echinoid limestone are generally covered by a formation of gravel in an argillaceous matrix believed to be Pliocene, itself covered in a layer of Quaternary silt.

— the **Saint-Emilion** region, on the right bank of the Dordogne to the east of Libourne, produces red wines rivalling Médoc in prestige. The region has no truly uniform characteristics, but the very widespread nature of the calcareous or molassic Oligocene substratum may be thought of as a common feature of the various soils in the region. Weathering and surface overlap contribute to wide variations in soil type;

— adjoining the Saint-Emilion region, the **Pomerol** region also produces a very famous red wine. Here the Oligocene deposits are covered by Quaternary gravelly alluvial formations. These are rather thin in places and come from the Dordogne or its right-bank tributary, the Isle;

— the **Entre-Deux-Mers** region, which derives its slightly misleading name from the fact that it lies between the Dordogne to the north and the Garonne to the south, is one of the great producers of dry white wines. The geology is fairly varied, consisting mainly of continental or lagoonal facies of the Oligocene and Miocene, such as lacustrine limestone, molasse and sandstone. Surface formations of the gravelly clays of Entre-Deux-Mers are common to all parts of the region and may be several metres thick;

— to the south of Entre-Deux-Mers is the region of **Sainte-Croix-du-Mont** and **Loupiac,** producing a famous sweet and rich white wine. The vineyard slopes are of pebbly clay on Miocene limestone, sandstone, molasse and marl. Together they form the right bank of the Garonne, rising as much as a hundred metres above the river in places;

— the left bank of the Garonne, between Langon and Bordeaux, accommodates several large wine-growing regions. Upstream, the plateau of **Sauternes** is the home of famous rich, sweet white wines; the pebbly soil is from the ancient terrace of the Garonne which, locally, overlies Miocene oyster-rich marls. About ten kilometres downstream, **Barsac** also produces excellent sweet, rich white wines; the highly karstic Oligocene limestone substratum is covered with argillaceous, slightly pebbly red sands. Still further downstream the **Graves** region stretches to the very gates of Bordeaux. It, too, yields high quality red and white wines, several of which are classed among the great Bordeaux "crus"; the soils have a generally high content of pebbles from the Quaternary terraces of the Garonne and the substratum is Oligocene (echinoid limestone) or Miocene (Falun — the shelly sand of the Bordelais region);

— the **Médoc** region is a strip some ten kilometres wide along the left bank of the Gironde, and its famous red wines have made a significant contribution to the reputation of Bordeaux wines. There can be no doubt that the dominant geological feature of Médoc wine-growing soils is the very good development on the Quaternary gravel terraces, which frequently exceeds ten metres in depth. These formations cover Eocene marl and limestone, where the Blaye-Listrac anticline brings them close to the surface, or Oligocene (reef or near-reef echinoid limestone). Westward, the vine-growing area is bounded by the sand formations of the Landes, a Quaternary eolian sand supporting extensive coniferous forest in a northern continuation of the forest-clad Landes massif.

Soil and climate

In general, the nature of the underlying geology does not seem to have a decisive influence on the quality of wines in the Bordeaux region. Thus vineyards producing the best red wines may grow their vines on source rocks as diverse as Quaternary alluvials of gravel and sand, echinoid limestone, or even certain very argillaceous outcrops. Conversely, the same source rock may give rise to wines which vary markedly in quality between wine-growing regions.

The soils are generally fairly low in humus and soluble cations, but the low cation exchange capacity means that the adsorbing complex is easily saturated, so that highly acid soils are rarely found. Even though roots may grow to considerable depths, conditions for mineral take-up are poor because at least one of a number of limiting factors is generally present. There may be a deficiency of nitrogen or magnesium, the latter possibly aggravated by potassium antagonism (over-manuring). Nevertheless, these chemical properties actually have little effect on wine quality, provided that the soil is not fertilised to excess causing a big increase in production.

In fact, average temperatures and sunshine hours in the Bordeaux region are not adequate for producing quality wine in large quantities. It is as though climatic conditions were just sufficient for producing limited amounts of colouring, aromatic and flavouring substances which are diluted and corrupted if yields increase to any great extent.

For a better idea of what determines quality we need to examine the physical properties of the soils, such as the way they are built, their structure, porosity, permeability, and the effect of all these on the vines' root growth and water take-up rate.

It seems likely that the rate at which the vines take up water has the greatest influence on wine quality, since it is governed by most of the factors affecting production and quality. These include geological and pedological factors (the nature and structure of formations and soils); edaphic factors (topography, water tables, usable reserves of water, permeability, structure, root growth, etc.); climatic factors (rainfall and the effect of sunshine, temperature and relative humidity on the transpiration potential, that is the "climatic demand"); biological factors (grape varieties and vine-stocks); and human factors (soil pattern, drainage and in particular the methods of vine cultivation, such as plant density and size, training, pruning, soil maintenance techniques, etc.).

Whilst there must be good conditions for water take-up during the early stages of the growing cycle, it has been shown that a reduction in the supply of water to the vine during the grape-ripening stage has an important bearing on the quality of red wines, controlling yield and resulting in grapes with a finer bouquet, superior colour and lower acid content.

Most of the major estates have means of compensating for the effects of prolonged drought or excessive rainfall, including depth of root growth, soil permeability and natural or artificial drainage. In this way it is possible to produce good quality wine, even in summers when climatic conditions are extreme.

Vine varieties

Of equal importance to quality is the vine-stock selection, and this aspect is strictly controlled.

Production is centred on a small number of varieties. In reds, the main ones are cabernet franc, cabernet sauvignon and merlot with the addition of cot and petit verdot. White varieties are sémillon in particular, with sauvignon, muscatel and some ugni blanc. These varieties are outstanding not only for their suitability in wine-making, but also for their growth characteristics (strength, fertility, yield, ripening season, resistance to grey mildew, etc.).

Red varieties:

There are certain morphological and organoleptic similarities between the cabernet franc, cabernet sauvignon and merlot varieties. They are combined in varying proportions in different districts to produce wines where individual features complement one another to create a distinctive harmony.

Cabernet franc is widespread throughout the western vine-growing regions from the Loire to the Pyrenees. In this particular region it produces wines which are somewhat full-bodied but supple and with good bouquet. It occurs principally in the Libourne district.

Cabernet sauvignon gives full-bodied, deeply coloured wines with a characteristic aroma. They are rich in tannin but this mellows with age, developing a remarkable bouquet. This is the main variety of Médoc.

Merlot has a less reliable yield than the others because it is relatively sensitive to pollen wash-out in the spring rains. It gives a wine which is strong in alcohol but supple, and gains from being used in combination with the cabernets. It is the variety most commonly cultivated throughout the Bordeaux region.

Petit verdot has a lower and later yield than the previous three, giving a deeply coloured wine which is rich in tannins. It is not widely grown, particularly in Médoc.

Cot is the earliest of the red varieties. Its yield is unpredictable, because it, too, is sensitive to pollen loss. Its wine is supple with a high colour, but not very aromatic. It forms only a small part of the full range of varieties.

White varieties:

Sémillon is the basic choice of grape for white wine vineyards. It yields highly alcoholic wines which are low in acid and lacking aroma. It has the special distinction, in certain conditions, of benefiting from a process of 'pourriture noble' (noble rot), allowing the wine producer to make richly sweet ("liquoreux") wines such as Sauternes. By contrast it is not well suited to the production of dry white wines.

Sauvignon is low yielding and when combined with other white varieties gives full-bodied and aromatic high class wines of the dry or liquoreux type.

Muscatel gives a slightly aromatic wine, though less fine than wine from the sauvignon. It is combined in only low proportions.

Ugni blanc is virtually the only variety in Charentes, where it produces wine for distillation into cognac. It is used in the Gironde for making dry white wine in combination with sauvignon, which adds its aroma to the blend.

Colombard is an old variety now in decline, still frequently found in the white vineyards on the right bank of the Gironde (the Blaye and Bourges districts).

Taking the distribution of varieties over the Bordeaux wine region as a whole, we find that three types of grape produce over three-quarters of the red wine, and a single grape variety produces more than half the white. Yet it should be emphasised that most Bordeaux wines, especially the reds, are made by combining several varieties in proportions which vary widely between growing areas. This means that no matter how small the quantity involved, a variety thought of as marginal can make a significant contribution to the quality of the final product.

It is only quite recently that the vine-stock selection which we see today has become so relatively uniform. There were far more varieties before French vineyards were attacked by phylloxera at the end of last century. In the interests of rebuilding, the varieties which gave the greatest growing problems were eliminated, even though some were better for wine-making.

Many other factors contribute directly or indirectly to the eventual quality of the grape by their effect on the vine. These include the soil, the microclimate, the root-stock and the vine cultivation methods. The actions expected of the vine-grower in these matters have gradually become established by tradition, and science cannot always explain the processes taking place.

Since it is also true that the relationship between grape quality and wine quality is only imperfectly understood, the oenological know-how of the vine-grower continues to play an important role in the making and subsequent development of the wine.

Itineraries

Saint-Emilion — Pomerol — Entre-Deux-Mers

The main purpose of this tour is to study the substrata beneath the Saint-Emilion and Pomerol vineyards. We return to Bordeaux across the northwest part of Entre-Deux-Mers.

The oldest formations we shall encounter belong to the Oligocene base (Lower Rupelian), but we shall also see Rupelian, lower Miocene and Pliocene (?), the latter covered with Quaternary silt.

The Saint-Emilion and Pomerol region derives its individuality from the *extraordinary variety of the formations to be found*. This diversity is reflected not so much in nutrient elements as in physical properties such as texture, structure, capacity for water retention, etc. These differences, which are apparent from vineyard to vineyard, are related to topography and the nature of the source-rocks. Just within a limited area of the Saint-Emilion and Pomerol districts it is possible to identify at least five distinct soil types:

— argillo-arenaceous soil of a generally calcareous nature, formed on the Fronsac molasse (Lower Rupelian);

— shallow soil on echinoid limestone (Rupelian), derived from rendzina, where root development goes no deeper than a few tens of centimetres. There is abundant calcium to encourage growth structures giving excellent stability;

— soils on rounded hills, formed by the gravel and sand alluvials of the Isle, where the vines can put down deeper roots;

— sandy soil of the same geological provenance, but with no stones or pebbles, where root extension is sometimes held in check by a relatively high water table;

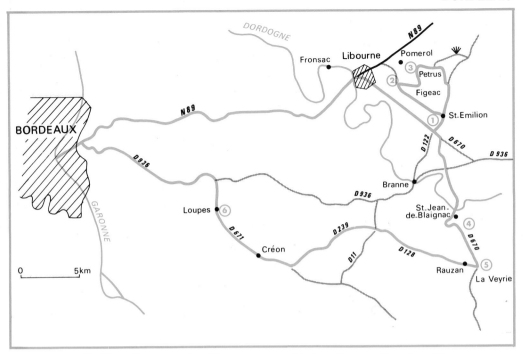

Fig.73. — Tour in the Bordelais region: Saint-Emilion, Pomerol, Entre-Deux-Mers.

— soil with a very argillaceous texture, at Pomerol in particular, where the proportion of particles below 2 micrometres in size is so great that at first glance there would be some doubt about including them in the appellation area but for the fact that they are currently producing wines of exceptional quality.

The most famous vineyards from this region are therefore situated on a great variety of soils, derived from very varied geological formations. They produce wines of good, very good, and, indeed, exceptional quality.

Climatic measurements made in a number of localities in these districts have failed to reveal any favoured mesoclimates which might explain the ranking of the wines. We have however been able to demonstrate the existence of a mechanism which regulates water supply to the vines on the molasses and Tertiary limestones (Château Ausone) and in the Quaternary alluvial formations: sandy gravels and underlying clays (Château Cheval Blanc, Château Pétrus). This hydrological approach to microclimate is nevertheless not enough to explain the differences in the types of wines which result (G. Seguin).

To reach **Saint-Emilion** (fig.73), leave Bordeaux going northeast on the N 89 towards Libourne. The road climbs the hillside or cliff of Cenon. The overhang to the north of the town is related to a substantial fault with vertical displacement. This cliff exists due to the limestone which forms most of the escarpments overlooking the Garonne as far as Réole in the east, as well as the banks of the Dordogne, one of the main right-bank tributaries, well to the east. The cliff consists of echinoid limestone which marks the Rupelian transgression. On the plateau, which has an elevation of some 60 to 80 metres and forms the western part of the Entre-Deux-Mers plateau, no further outcrops of this limestone bed are visible. It is in fact concealed under a deposit of about 30 metres of "Entre-Deux-Mers pebbly clay and sand". A cross-section of this will be observed at the end of the tour. A few kilometres beyond Beychac and Caillau we reach the old terrace of the Dordogne, which produces a wine of the **Graves de Vayres** appellation.

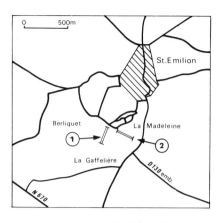

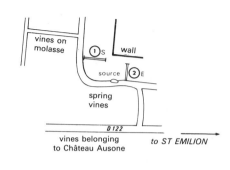

Fig.74. — *Diagrams showing the location of the two cross-sections in the area of Saint-Emilion.*

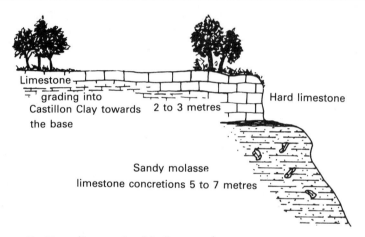

Limestone grading into Castillon Clay towards the base

Hard limestone

2 to 3 metres

Sandy molasse limestone concretions 5 to 7 metres

Fig.75. — *Cross-section 1 in the area of Saint-Emilion (southern aspect).*

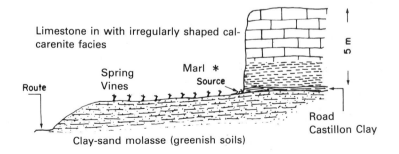

Limestone in with irregularly shaped calcarenite facies

5 m

Route

Spring Vines

Marl *
Source

Road
Castillon Clay

Clay-sand molasse (greenish soils)

Fig.76. — *Cross-section 2 in the area of Saint-Emilion (eastern aspect).*

250

Where the land becomes markedly lower, on the approach to Libourne, we enter the recent alluvials of the Dordogne. This flood plain is given over to grass. There are no vineyards except for the occasional plot situated on the levees where drainage is somewhat better. These low, frost-riven areas produce wines for everyday drinking purposes which have not been awarded an appellation.

Go through **Libourne,** the capital of the region's wine trade, and take the D 670A towards the east, leading to the foot of the Saint-Emilion slopes.

The tour runs through vineyards. Those on the left of the road can claim the Saint-Emilion appellation by virtue of obvious colluvial deposition processes from the upper formations which provide soil of the same type as those found at Saint-Emilion itself.

Beyond Grand-Bigaroux, the thalweg along which the D 122 runs gives an idea of the thickness of the Oligocene formation, chiefly composed of echinoid limestone. The town of Saint-Emilion stands on this formation. The interfluves are sandy and suitable for vines, since the topography gives the good drainage so essential for good quality vineyards.

① Near the Châteaux of **La Gaffelière** and **La Magdelaine,** southwest of Saint-Emilion (fig.74), note the cuesta below the top of the divide. It gives two cross-sections. The way up to these cross-sections passes through the vineyard of La Magdelaine which stands on molasse with a clay-sand-limestone structure or its colluvial deposits. This is known as Fronsac Molasse, named after the Fronsac district some ten kilometres to the west. It is a continental formation composed of molasse sandstone or a thick band of generally arenaceous clay, depending on locality. At Saillans, some kilometres to the west of Saint-Emilion, the clay is 30 metres thick.

The slope at the highest point of the vineyard exactly marks the upper part of this formation, which outcrops here for five to seven metres (south-facing cross-section, fig.75). The transition from this molasse to the echinoid limestone is not easy to see, but will be more evident in the east-facing cross-section we shall look at next. Here a layer of greenish clay or marl of early Oligocene age, roughly 0.80 to 1 metre thick, seems to mark the transition to the overlying three metres of echinoid limestone. This bed of green clay-marl can clearly be seen in the east-facing cross-section (fig.76), and its presence is further underlined by the many springs which perfectly mark the base of the echinoid limestone throughout the whole region. This level occurs even in the town of Saint-Emilion itself, at the Source de la Médaille and the Puits des Jacobins. The echinoid limestone actually corresponds to the maximum extent of the Oligocene transgression. It is found at an elevation of 60 to 80 metres and is 25 metres thick.

The monolithic church (9th to 12th century) and the Saint-Emilion catacombs are hollowed entirely out in this formation. This rather exceptional instance of a church hewn in the living rock is worth visiting, and gives an idea how thick this limestone is. The monolithic church, which actually has three naves, is 32 metres long, 15 metres wide and 16 metres high.

Naturally this limestone formation has been exploited for building. The subterranean quarries are nowadays used in part as a store for wine in casks because there are no noticeable temperature changes throughout the entire year.

The tour crosses Saint-Emilion heading north and takes the D 17 as far as a place called Le Cros. It then heads for Pomerol and comes to Château Figeac.

② **Château Figeac.** These famous vineyards are located midway between Pomerol and Saint-Emilion, on a substrate composed of gravelly soil from an arm of the lower terrace of the old Isle alluvials. These alluvials are the home of all the **famous vineyards of Pomerol.** Bearing in mind the topography of this location, it is quite probable that the site is also a receptacle for colluvials from the Saint-Emilion plateau. Continuing northwards for about two kilometres brings us to the vineyards of the best Pomerol cru, Château Petrus.

③ **Château Petrus.** The vineyard is planted on a level of the old Isle terrace. The soil is therefore gravelly, but this layer is only about 0.30 metres thick with a clay-type subsoil which checks depth of rooting. This limits the yield, a fact which is often synonymous with quality. The underlying blue and chocolat clays probably come from partial reshaping of the terrace and underlying Fronsac Molasse.

Saint-Emilion. An opportunity to visit the town. Admire the panorama over the valley of the Dordogne and the view of its left bank. The tour continues that way. Leave Saint-Emilion by the D 122, then the N 670.

④ **Saint-Jean-de-Blaignac.** The town is on the edge of the Dordogne. Note the asymmetric valley. The cross-section again shows the formation previously observed and gives an idea of the thickness of the Fronsac Molasse. It shows the overlying echinoid limestone (level 53) together with the covering layer of soil which is used for vineyards. The soils here are probably clay from decalcification of the echinoid limestone mixed with Pliocene deposits seen in a cross-section further on.

⑤ **La Veyrie.** Continue along the D 670 as far as Villesèque. From there the D 127E towards Blasimon leads to a place called La Veyrie. There is a little knoll on which it is possible to observe, starting at the base and working upwards:
— clays with concentrations of limestone;
— molasse similar to the Fronsac type, a lateral equivalent of echinoid limestone;
— grey lacustrine limestone in association with clays in which planorbids have been found.
These are the final levels of the Upper Oligocene.

⑥ **Commune de Loupes.** This cross-section (fig.77) gives an idea of how the overburden of the Pliocene sands and gravels is composed, and of its thickness. Notice on the sketch that there is a Quaternary covering of silt, probably eolian, in a layer 0.10 to 0.50 metres thick. This latter type of deposit generally occurs in Entre-Deux-Mers beneath much thicker layers.

The vineyards of **Canon Fronsac** and **Fronsac** lie to the west of Libourne near the confluence of the Dordogne and the Isle, the second of which separates them from Pomerol and Saint-Emilion. These vineyards stand partly on echinoid limestone but mainly on Oligocene Fronsac Molasse. They produce high quality red wines, some of which have many points in common with those of Saint-Emilion.

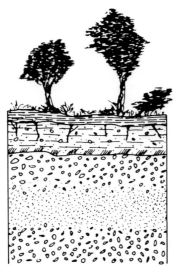

Loam (10 to 50 cm) Root runs (reduction of iron) Clay is sandy, gravelly beige brown, reddened

Gravel

Sand

Gravel

Fig.77. — District of Loupes

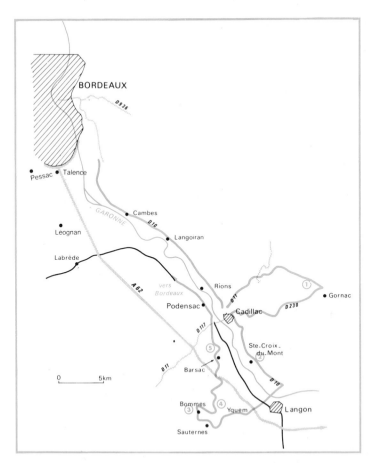

Fig. 78. — Tour in the Bordelais region: Graves and Sauternais districts.

To the south of the region, but on the old terrace on the right bank of the Dordogne, stands the appellation **Graves de Vayres,** with distinct characteristics of the vineyards of Entre-Deux-Mers.

The Graves and Sauternes region

The next itinerary concerns the wine-growing regions each side of the Garonne valley between Langon and Bordeaux. On the right bank this includes Entre-Deux-Mers, Premières Côtes de Bordeaux and Sainte-Croix-du-Mont; on the left bank, Sauternes, Barsac and Graves.

The route (fig. 78) first crosses the Saint-Jean bridge to the right bank of the river. The D 10 runs along the valley skirting the lower slopes of Entre-Deux-Mers. A significant difference in levels is immediately apparent in the topography of both banks of the Garonne. Although the road winds along an alluvial plain similar to the one on the left bank of the river, it also skirts an escarpment which forms the underlying structure of the Entre-Deux-Mers plateau. This difference in elevation is due to the presence of a strike fault with an Armorican trend (NW-SE) known as the Bordeaux Fault.

The first part of this tour is on the hinge zone between the Podensac Syncline in the west and the anticlinal fold of Entre-Deux-Mers in the east. In the region between

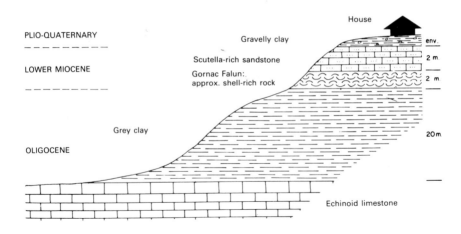

PLIO-QUATERNARY

Gravelly clay

House

env.

2 m

Scutella-rich sandstone

Gornac Falun:
approx. shell-rich rock

2 m

LOWER MIOCENE

Grey clay

20 m

OLIGOCENE

Echinoid limestone

Fig.79. — Cross-section at Gornac.

Bordeaux and Paillet the limestone cliff, rendered less sheer by accumulations of scree, is composed of Rupelian echinoid limestone. This limestone abruptly reappears at the surface beneath the villages of Langoiran (at the base of the château), Lestiac and Paillet.

At Rions and beyond, the edge of the Entre-Deux-Mers hillslopes softens and then turns eastward. We are entering the eastern periclinal zone of the Podensac Syncline.

The echinoid limestone plunges almost in the shape of a ship's hull. The only surface outcrop is a clay with inclusions of limestone nodules overlying the Rupelian limestone. There are also scree slopes derived for the most part from the gravel clays of Entre-Deux-Mers. The lowest part of the topographic basin is occupied by the town of Cadillac.

From Cadillac the tour turns eastward into Entre-Deux-Mers as far as Mourens and Gornac. There we can observe the transition between the Oligocene and Miocene formations. After leaving the valley of the Garonne, the D 11E climbs up to the gravelly hills formed by the gravel clays of Entre-Deux-Mers.

① **Gornac.** At Gornac and Laurès (fig.78), one can observe the formations of the uppermost Oligocene underlying the transgressive formations of the Lower Miocene.

Driving from the direction of Saint-Pierre-de-Bat, we can see alongside the D 19, starting from the bottom and working upwards:

— a whitish marly-sandy limestone with a fairly sparse microfauna of foraminifera in association with ostracods, characteristic of a coastal marine environment (Oligocene);

— a grey argillaceous bed devoid of foraminifera with an upper horizon containing Chara oogoniums (lacustrine formation);

— an arenaceous, poorly consolidated limestone which covers the clay just mentioned;

— a yellowish brown shelly sand (Gornac "falun") rich in coastal or brackish-water foraminifera, along with a number of ostracods, all dating from the Early Miocene;

— an unconsolidated, sandstone-like limestone containing forms with stronger marine affinities;

— and finally, gravelly and sandy limestone at the summit, with foraminifera, gastropods, lamellibranchs, echinoderms, crustacea and melobaesiae, corresponding to a littoral environment swept by strong coastal currents. This is a similar limestone to the one comprising the capping of the Sainte-Croix-du-Mont plateau.

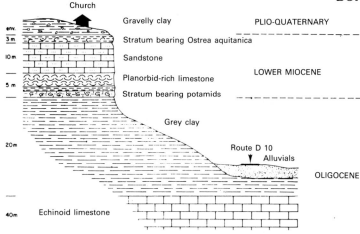

Fig.80. — Cross-section at Sainte-Croix-du-Mont.

The geological cross-section which the Gornac outcrops provide shows two successive sedimentary phases: a regressive episode marking the end of the Oligocene followed by a transgressive movement dating from the Early Miocene.

② **Sainte-Croix-du-Mont.** At Sainte-Croix-du-Mont (fig.80) successive hill-slopes make it possible to observe Neogene formations in detail.

At the foot, the echinoid limestone (Oligocene) is hidden by scree. This is followed by shale with inclusions of limestone nodules, planted with vines; lacustrine limestone; argillaceous faluns containing potamids and oysters. Calcareous sandstone some fifteen metres thick, with Scutella bonali and Amphiope ovalifera, forms a sizeable bar. A bed with rich deposits of Ostrea aquitanica caps the summit. It is this which forms the highly developed oyster reef beneath the château and church of Sainte-Croix-du-Mont.

The tour continues next on the left bank of the Garonne, first crossing the **Sauternes** region, which produces a richly sweet white wine (15° alcohol plus 5° to 6° sugar) with a great reputation.

The classed growths ("grands crus") of Sauternes, Bommes, Fargues and Haut-Preignac are located on low gravelly hills (maximum elevation 70 metres) formed when the Quaternary terraces of the Garonne became dissected by water and wind. The deep, gravelly and sandy soils are rather similar to those found in Médoc. In general the alluvial layers are more argillaceous here, probably because they are so close to the Lower Miocene oyster marls which locally underlie the terraces of the Garonne.

③ **Bommes quarry.** The cross-section in this quarry reveals the gravelly alluvial formations of the old Garonne terrace to a depth of six or seven metres. The deposits contain a high proportion of generally average-sized gravel (3 to 4 cm) showing alternately coarse and fine banding. Cross-bedding occurs frequently. Near the top of the quarry a concretionary formation marks a depositional discontinuity. The ferruginous cement is associated with pedogenesis. Below this concretionary level are various signs of glacial shaping, such as wedge-shaped fissures filled with finer sand, and tilted stones. Lastly, the cross-section clearly shows the great depth to which vine roots will grow.

④ **Château Yquem.** We stop here to visit the most famous "cru" in the Sauternes region.

The vineyard stands on a dome of clay and shale at the transition between the Oligocene and the Miocene, clad in a thin layer of gritty sand. The clay is impervious, encouraging the formation of areas of perched groundwater. These would cause asphyxiation and threaten root development were not the entire property drained.

At Yquem the harvesting and vinification of the grapes are still carried out by the traditional methods which have given the wines of Sauternes their character and reputation. Richly sweet wines (about 15° of alcohol plus 5 to 6° of sugar) are obtained from grapes in which the juices have been highly concentrated by a microscopic fungus (Botrytis cinerea) which breaks out in the form of a rot described as "noble", as opposed to common rot. Quality vintages (toasted or macerated grapes, carefully sorted and selected after picking) can only be obtained if Botrytis cinerea develops on ripe, unburst berries. On the other hand, if the grapes burst after a heavy fall of summer rain, this encourages attack by the common rot.

In fact, natural permeability and depth of root growth, together with artificial methods such as drainage, control sudden surges of water to the grapes and as often as not prevent them from bursting after a summer downpour.

⑤ **Barsac.** La Hourcade-Videau quarry. In contrast to the Sauternes region, with its succession of rounded hills and thalwegs, Barsac, which also produces sweet and rich white wines, is notable for the flatness of its landscape.

The vineyards are planted on a thin bed of sandy colluvial deposits from the old lower terrace of the Garonne, generally 0.40 to 0.50 metres in depth, which itself covers a highly karstic platform of Rupelian echinoid limestone. Root growth therefore remains close to the surface and is mainly confined to these generally reddened siliceous sands.

The quarry of La Hourcade-Videau shows the contact between the karstic limestone substratum and the superficial alluvial formations. These are composed of a red, slightly argillaceous sand sparsely mingled with small gravel of about 1 cm in diameter. These formations contain no discernible horizon which would be likely to indicate possible pedogenesis.

Return to Bordeaux across the **Graves** region. It occupies the left bank of the Garonne from southeast of Langon to north of Bordeaux, omitting the Sauternes and Barsac districts (fig.81). As the name of the appellation suggests, the vineyards are usually accommodated on the gravelly-sandy terraces of the Garonne (Quaternary), which have to a large extent been carved into sections by wind and runoff water. These are coarse-textured and somewhat heterogeneous siliceous alluvials of variable thickness. They overlie Tertiary formations: echinoid limestone (Rupelian), clay, marl and 'faluns' (Aquitanian and Burdigalian). These formations crop out if they have been uncovered or incised by the minor tributary valleys of the Garonne.

This diversity of soils and subsoils can often be found within a single property, and almost certainly accounts for the individuality which is so typical of the wines from many of the "crus" in this region.

In the southern portion the "graves" (gravels) are often covered in a thin blanket of sand or silt. Here, production of dry white wines and, less commonly, rich and mellow whites takes priority over production of red (predominance of merlot). In the north, around the **Léognan** and **Pessac** districts, we find the Grands Crus Classés of the Graves appellation. The wine from here is mainly red (predominance of cabernet sauvignon, as in Médoc), but there are also some dry whites which are among the best in the whole of the Bordelais region.

During the Middle Ages, at a time when the Médoc region was virtually deserted and just about devoid of vines, the best-known Bordeaux wines were being produced very close to, and even within, the area where the modern town now stands. These estates, with their potential for high quality, have all but disappeared, and are still retreating before the onslaught of urban development and road-building. The only ones to be spared, and then only in part, are some of the **Talence** and **Pessac** Grands Crus, which strangely enough still manage to survive as islands of green in the very heart of Bordeaux. This is the case with some very famous wines, such as Mission Haut-Brion and Pape Clément, as well as the illustrious **Château Haut-Brion,** known to 17th century London as "Ho-Bryan". As far as anyone can prove, this was the first wine to be sold under the name of the estate where it was produced rather than, as with every other wine at the time, the name of its parish of origin, or at any rate the owner of the estate.

During the winter months, Château Haut-Brion enjoys an average urban climate which hastens the growing cycle and protects it from spring frosts. Its harvests are early, and though they are generally finished by the time the heavy autumnal rains arrive, the quality of the grapes can be affected in some years. Being the oldest, and the one which most regularly reaches a very high standard of quality, it is often considered to be the foremost Grand Cru Classé for red wines. It also produces small quantities of a remarkable dry white wine, though without the Grand Cru classification.

At **Léognan,** in years with a dry summer, Château Haut-Bailly produces supple, round red wines of extraordinary fineness and amazingly complex aroma and taste. These are at their best after three or four years, when the bouquet has developed with age but the original grape aromas have not yet disappeared. Among other years, the 1981, when tasted in 1984 (it is now no longer quite what it was) represented for F.Coste "the finest expression of the heights to which the wine of a very great Bordeaux cru can aspire". The Domaine du Chevalier, also at Léognan, produces one of the finest Graves reds, but unlike Haut-Bailly, it matures very slowly. From the sauvignon and sémillon varieties, it also produces a dry white wine of rare quality, fermented and raised in oaken casks, which should be kept for drinking ten or twenty years after bottling. Still at Léognan, Château Olivier (which is expanding) produces its red wines from a strip of sand-gravel terrace, whilst its white wines come from clay-limestone soils (Miocene) located opposite and below, beside a little stream (G.Seguin).

Côtes de Bourg — Premières Côtes de Blaye — Médoc

This tour studies the vineyards on the slopes alongside the Gironde estuary (fig.81). On the right bank are the vineyards of Côtes de Bourg and Premières Côtes de Blaye, whilst on the left bank are those of Médoc.

The right bank of the Gironde estuary: Bordeaux to Blaye

Leave Bordeaux crossing the Garonne by the Aquitaine bridge and head north. A viewpoint overlooks the town, the river and the Lormont cliffs (echinoid limestone). These cliffs are a northern extension of the Cenon cliffs seen on the first tour. Between Lormont and Saint-Vincent-de-Paul the journey takes us across the western edge of Entre-Deux-Mers by the A 62 autoroute heading towards Paris. The Oligocene substratum in this area (echinoid limestone and Fronsac Molasse) is covered by the clays, sands and gravels of Entre-Deux-Mers and by the old terraces of the Dordogne. Cross the Dordogne at Cubzac. Opposite and below is a marshy area on recent alluvials of the Dordogne (marshes with vineyards). At Cubzac are outcrops of Fronsac Molasse and echinoid limestone.

Beyond Saint-André-de-Cubzac (45th parallel) take the N 37 towards Saintes, then the D 13 towards Saint-Laurent-d'Arce and Marcamps, in the southern part of the Côtes de Bourg region.

① **Marcamps quarry.** Many quarries have been dug on both sides of the road in the Rupelian echinoid limestone. This was extracted over many years for building material, often from gallery workings of gigantic size. These workings have since been used as cellars for mushroom cultivation, but this has now been partly discontinued. Various types of materials are once more being extracted (chippings, building stone) for use in road building.

There are many cross-sections showing that the echinoid limestone is tens of metres thick. It occurs all over the Bordeaux region, though outcrops are rare.

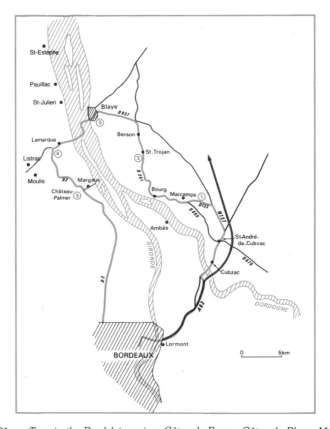

Fig.81. — Tour in the Bordelais region: Côtes de Bourg, Côtes de Blaye, Médoc.

The near-reef facies is biodetritic and generally friable, so that many fossils may be gathered (molluscs, echinoderms, sea-urchins, algae, bryozoa). It also occurs as massive, compact banks, and these too are fossil-bearing. Cross-bedded deposits, representing tidal deltas, are common.

The tops of these quarries show the soil to be shallow and mainly composed of clay formed from decalcification of the limestone.

Beyond Marcamps, on the right-hand side of the road in a coomb adjacent to the valley of the river Moron, the Pair-Non-Pair limestone cave was found, which yielded a rich fauna of vertebrates and tools of the Mousterian Palaeolithic. Various rock-carvings can still be seen on the cave walls.

Return on the N 669 towards **Bourg-sur-Gironde.** This little town with a population of some 3 000 now stands by the Dordogne, not the Gironde, since the alluvials brought down by the Garonne and the Dordogne have extended the Ambès spit which marks their confluence.

Beyond Bourg the tour takes the D 9E towards Berson. The route crosses the Côtes de Bourg vineyards, which stand on Oligocene limestone slopes (elevation 70 to 90 metres) The slopes are covered in gravels which are presumed to be Pliocene, and silty Quaternary formations of hydro-eolian provenance. The diversity of the soils in this region is explained by the varied source rocks and the topography of low, rounded hills which encourage erosion and colluvial deposition. These soils nevertheless all share the following characteristics:

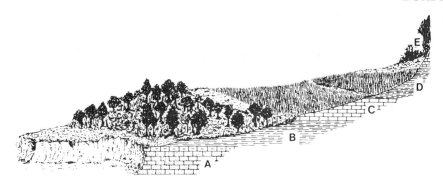

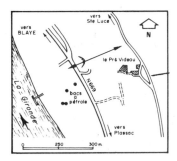

Fig.82a. — Cross-section from the Octroi to Pré Videau.

— from the point of view of texture, fine fractions predominate and there is a high percentage of clay;

— they are lacking in humus;

— their cation exchange capacity is low, but still among the highest in relation to the other vine-growing soils of the Bordeaux region;

— reserves of usable water and trace elements increase at and below the topmost metre of soil, and account for the significant root growth observed in most soil cross-sections.

The rate of vine growth and grape ripening varies significantly from place to place. This is mainly due to differences in the growth and depth of the root system, which affect the efficiency with which vines take up minerals and, especially, water.

② **Saint-Trojan.** The purpose of this stop is to observe the complex of cross- and obliquely-bedded sands and gravels. It is very well developed in the Côtes de Bourg region, where it crowns the echinoid limestone buttes. It has a characteristic red colour and is the remnant of a sizeable deltaic structure (10 to 15 metres thick), indicating an east-west transport direction. The exact age of these deposits is undetermined (Post-Oligocene, presumably Pliocene).

The deposits consist of argillaceous red sand with small quartzose gravel. Pebbles of white kaolin measuring tens of centimetres across are plentiful throughout. They are derived from the reworking of Lower Eocene kaolin lenses which occur frequently in the north and northwest (the Charentes siderolites). The only fossils found are silicified Cretaceous oysters. The observed current direction indicates that this deltaic system drained towards the west.

At certain points in the quarry the very plentiful kaolin pebbles are tilted in the region of a discontinuity marking cessation of the deposition. This phenomenon may perhaps be caused by cryoturbation processes akin to those which tilt quartzose pebbles.

Beyond Saint-Trojan the D 9E leaves the Côtes de Bourg region and enters the vineyards of the Premières Côtes de Blaye at Berson. From the geological point of view, we shall be coming into contact with increasingly ancient formations, since the tour will be following the southern flank of the dome known as the Blaye-Listrac Anticline. Although this is a low-amplitude anticline, from the regional standpoint it constitutes a major ground feature with a Variscan orientation (NE-SW). It lies across the Gironde estuary giving Premières Côtes de Blaye and certain parts of Médoc their highly individual geological character.

Between Berson and Blaye the route runs through an area of vineyards planted on chiefly argillo-calcareous Eocene formations. The most ancient components of these (Middle Eocene) will be observed on the Blaye outcrop at the centre of the anticlinal bulge.

The "sous-préfecture" of **Blaye** has a deep-water port on the estuary and is famous for its imposing citadel, constructed in the 17th century by Vauban during the reign of Louis XIV. This citadel, the Fort Paté on an island in mid-estuary, and the Fort Médoc on the left bank, were the forward defences of the town of Bordeaux.

③ **Blaye.** *Section from Octroi to Pré-Videau.*

The following features can be observed on this section (fig.82):

A — The lowest point is the quarry, composed of light, yellow bioclastic limestone (top of the Middle Eocene). There are many traces of molluscs, echinoderms (especially Echinolampas burdigalensis) and foraminifera including large, flat Orbitolites.

Above is a shell bank containing pecten (0.80 metres thick). The top of this is channeled by limestone and marl containing miliolids (1.5 metres thick).

B — Among the bushes at the top of the quarry, grey dolomitic marl can be seen for a distance of 3 or 4 metres. It contains Ostrea cucullaris, which are small, finger-nail sized Upper Eocene oysters.

C — Continuing towards the top of the butte we cross a layer of whitish lacustrine limestone some 5 to 10 metres thick, containing Limnaea. This bed (Plassac Limestone) gives way to white, azoic marl at its very top.

D — The next part of the climb shows a layer some twenty metres thick of green shale containing Ostrea bersonensis, then just below the top of the hill are marls bearing echinoderms (particularly Sismondia).

E — The butte itself is about three metres thick and has two components, a slightly quartzose limestone (Saint-Estèphe Limestone), containing miliolids, oysters and anomiae, capped with a shell bank.

Formations B, C, D and E all date from the Late Eocene.

The Blaye section closes the first part of the tour, which is devoted to the vineyards on the right bank of the Gironde. To reach Médoc on the left bank we take the ferry across the Gironde, on the way noticing the upstream characteristics of the estuary: several channels, many islands, including the isle of Fort Paté, and a number of shoals.

The left bank of the estuary: the Médoc region from Lamarque to Bordeaux

Most of the "crus" which built the reputation of Bordeaux red wines in the 18th century, and are keeping their prestige high today, are situated in **Haut Médoc.**

The "Grands Crus Classés" (of which there are over 61) are found among the appellations **Haut-Médoc, Margaux, Saint-Julien, Pauillac** and **Saint-Estèphe.** They are planted on the Quaternary alluvials on the left bank of the Gironde. Here, too, the terrain has been dissected into rounded hummocks by water and wind erosion, but the gravelly, arenaceous formations are more uniformly textured than in the Graves or Sauternes regions.

There are some very good but lesser-known vineyards (Crus Bourgeois supérieurs, Crus Bourgeois), particularly at **Moulis** and **Listrac,** and generally throughout **Médoc** (formerly known as "Bas Médoc" — Lower Médoc). Some of the vines in these "crus" have been planted on various more or less carbonaceous Eocene and Oligocene outcrops.

The siliceous soils of the "Grands Crus Classés" were once very acid, but this is rarely still the case since their adsorbent complex, with its low exchange capacity, has been largely saturated by applications of manure and soil improvers. The soil remains low in usable water and available elements, but root growth goes very deep here (as much as five metres), and it is easy to see how vines can thrive in soils which are apparently so impoverished and dry.

All the soils of the "Grands Crus Classés" are more or less similar, varying mainly in the depth available for root development. This is limited by the closeness of the water table, where conditions will effectively drown the roots. The best vineyards are therefore located on the tops and sides of the mounds, where the roots have sufficient usable depth of soil. On the other hand, vines of any quality are not found in the wet and marshy hollows between hillocks, since the water table lies so close to the surface, and any that do occur are certainly not of AOC class.

When conditions are good, the old, deep-rooted vines continue to receive water until the end of the growing season, which is generally when the grapes begin to ripen. During the first part of the growing cycle, when the vine is growing vigorously, rootlets develop in the zone left behind by the falling water table, from main roots which survive the anaerobic conditions of winter. As the rootlets absorb water from micropores in the soil it is more or less replenished by rainfall. Rootlets can also absorb water easily from the upper limit of the capillary fringe, where aeration is sufficient for them to breathe properly since water content is in balance with water retention capacity (only the micropores hold water, whereas the macropores are full of air). In many soils this additional supply of water is vital if periods of low rainfall occur during spring and early summer.

From August onwards, however, vine growth stops. The continued lowering of the water table is no longer counter-balanced by rootlet growth. In these sandy-gravelly textured soils, where water rises to only a limited extent under capillary action, the water table begins to have less and less effect. The vine is then dependent on rainfall for its water supply during the ripening season, as well as on the amount of water stored in the soil during the period close to the moment of ripening.

In view of all the above, and especially the depth of soil to which the roots penetrate, old, deep-rooted vines are highly resistant to drought, even during the ripening season when the water table ceases to play any part in their water supply. By contrast, shallow-rooting vines, especially when very young, suffer from water shortage during the worst periods of drought.

Conversely, when rainfall is particularly high, vines are unaffected by excessive moisture since the soils are remarkably permeable. This is partly due to the coarse texture of the country-rock, and partly to the topography of the "grands crus", which are situated on rounded hills alongside the Gironde and its minor tributaries. Both circumstances encourage good drainage. After heavy rain, hydrological profiles (which relate soil water content to soil depth) show that rainwater percolates very rapidly. When measured 24 hours after heavy rainfall, water content rarely or only temporarily exceeds the water retention capacity of the soil, whereas in impervious and ill-drained soils, roots are found to be water-logged.

It should also be noted that when rainwater from a *summer shower* falls on partially dried out soil it stays largely within the surface layers, where rootlets are few if root growth is deep. It has been shown in these circumstances that water is absorbed at a much lower rate by deep-rooted vines than by shallow-rooted plants, which have almost all of their root-spread within the rain-soaked layer. The soil-plant system thus checks but does not totally eliminate the harmful effects of a surge of water to the grapes during ripening (burst grapes, invasion by common rot, pigment loss, sugar dilution, high acidity, etc). There is a greater chance of harvesting ripe, sound grapes than is the case with other soil types. This also means that in years when the weather has given problems, the superiority of the best "crus" is even more marked.

These *gravel-sand soils with old, deep-rooted vines* therefore have ways of regulating and limiting the undesirable effects of excessive rainfall and severe drought alike, so that watering levels can be kept reasonably consistent from year to year. Thus the "Grands Crus" still produce wine of satisfactory quality, even when the weather in August and September turns out to be poor. It can also be understood why the best wines come from vines of the right age (at least ten years old in Médoc), since when they have had time to develop their root systems to sufficient depth they can take advantage of these regulatory mechanisms (G.Seguin).

From the ferry landing-stage in the port of **Lamarque,** the route follows the D 5 to observe the succession of vegetation and cultivation governed by the topography and the nature of the subsoil. The D 5 first crosses a low-lying, marshy area on recent alluvials of the Gironde (elevation 0 to 5 metres). These peaty, clay-silt sediments were deposited during the Holocene, and give hydromorphic soils suitable only for impoverished grassland.

Just before Lamarque the road rises as it crosses the lower Quaternary terrace of the Gironde (elevation 6 to 15 metres). Abruptly the soil is seen to contain many sizeable pebbles (0.05 to 0.10 metres) and meadow gives way to vineyard.

④ **Malescas quarries.** These gravel workings give a clear idea of the type of formation on which many of the best Médoc vineyards are planted.

The deposits lie on calcareous Eocene formations from the Blaye-Listrac anticline, although these are not visible here. The working face is between 4 and 5 metres high, and reveals a characteristic facies of the Gironde Quaternary deposits. The material is a light-hued mixture of sand, gravel and pebbles, with very few signs of clay except in a few thin bands. The pebbles are generally quite large, and mainly of quartz and quartzite.

A number of cryoturbation features can be seen at the top of the section, particularly in the form of wedge-shaped cracks filled with a clay-humus crust. This testifies to podzolic pedogenesis on the formation known as the Landes Sands (Sables des Landes), which are Quaternary aeolian sands supporting the Landes forest area and forming the western boundary to the Médoc vineyards.

The route then takes the D 2 towards Margaux. It follows the hillslope overlooking the "palus", which are low-lying alluvial plains alongside the estuary.

⑤ **Château Palmer.** Until a few years ago, this famous **Margaux** vineyard had the distinction of continuing to make wines by traditional methods. Wood was used exclusively in processing and storing the grapes and the resulting wine. The grapes were destemmed by hand on wooden hurdles and fermentation took place in wooden vats, after which the wine was stored for two years in oaken casks. All of this equipment is still on view in the winery at the château.

It is worth spending at least a day in Haut-Médoc. The geologist will not get a great deal out of it, since there is not much more to see than gravel and pebbles, especially when the rain washes them into an almost unbroken layer on top of the ground. All the Grands Crus Classés (red wines only) are planted on thick, hilly formations of gravel and sand close to natural drains (the Gironde or "jalles"). These dry, warm soils help the cabernet sauvignon grapes to ripen slowly but thoroughly, and to develop their potential to the full. On the other hand, the variety is hardly grown at all in the cooler, moister and more clayey soils of Saint-Emilion, where the oceanic climate of the Bordeaux region makes it difficult for the grapes to ripen fully. Cabernet sauvignon accounts for over 50 per cent of the vines grown in the Médoc area, and can be as high as 70 to 80 per cent in the best Haut-Médoc "crus". Cabernet franc (10%) contributes its fine bouquet and merlot noir (averaging 34%) is a vital foil to cabernet sauvignon, giving the wine its supple roundness and alcoholic strength and, though the locals pretend to be scornful of it, the delicacy of its aromas.

The most famous "crus" are enormous estates of 50 to 100 hectares. This means that in the light of climatic conditions during the year, it is possible to adjust the relative proportions of the different varieties which go towards making up the "great wine". It is all in the blending! Wines produced from young vines, and any found to be of insufficiently high quality, are sold (too dearly) under a brand name which is specific to each "cru".

Architecture lovers will be delighted with the individuality and variety of the châteaux. In Médoc perhaps more than anywhere, these buildings deserve this typically "Bordelais" description for a wine-growing firm. An exhibition about the Châteaux of Bordeaux was held at the Centre Georges Pompidou in Paris in 1988 — together with a bibliography, since the best looking châteaux do not always produce the best wines. Some of them are very old, but many were built in the 18th and 19th centuries. A few (but not many) are actually on the site of an ancient feudal seat. The closing years of the 20th century have also made their architectural mark. As prosperity has increased, wineries of unprecedented luxury have been erected or refurbished in recent years, like temples to the greater glory of wine!

Itinerary

It is impossible to recommend a selection of the 61 Grands Crus Classés and the 300 or so Exceptional and Superior "Crus Bourgeois", let alone the ordinary "Crus Bourgeois", some of which deserve to be ranked more highly among the "crus" of Médoc.

Leave Bordeaux by the Barrière du Médoc, naturally. Cross the Bouscat and turn right onto the D 2E heading for Blanquefort. Then take the D 2 for **Margaux** and **Pauillac**. All "crus" are well signposted on this great vineyard route. The first of the châteaux you meet are not very easy to see from the road. La Lagune (Ludon) is on the right, then Cantemerle (Macau) and Giscours (Labarde) are on the left. Go through Cantenac village. On the left-hand side of the road one catches a glimpse of Château Brane-Cantenac. It stands back from the Gironde, on the edge of a "jalle". Palmer, with its elegant and graceful château, has already been mentioned. It is over to the right beside the river. Château Margaux, standing slightly apart from the village which bears its name, is not to be missed. The building is at the end of a drive lined with plane-trees. The portico is in the form of a Grecian temple and its magnificent wine-store has been renovated. Lascombes is another of the Margaux "crus classés" worth visiting.

Leaving the Margaux hilly formations behind, the route rises and falls among vineyards and occasionally marshy lower-lying areas. After crossing the "Grande Jalle du Nord" it climbs steeply to Saint-Julien. Immediately on the right, the sumptuous architecture of Château Beychevelle (18th century) comes into view. Go round to the back and look at what is in fact the front elevation of the building, pausing to admire the terrace, the formal gardens and the vista overlooking the Gironde.

The **Saint-Julien** appellation has the greatest number of Grands Crus Classés, including Ducru-Beaucaillou, Gruaud-Larose and the three Léoville "crus" (Barton, Poyferré and Las-Cases).

A small low-lying area separates Léoville-las-Cases from the vineyards of Château-Latour (Saint-Lambert-Pauillac). These too are on the banks of the Gironde. There is an old tower which can just be seen from the road, but other than this only the immense prestige of the "cru" is likely to attract the traveller. Adjoining Latour is the attractive Château Pichon-Longueville — Comtesse de Lalande (now known as Pichon- Lalande) with its new winery, and the neighbouring Pichon-Longueville-Baron.

Drive through Pauillac and along the quays, from where you can get a good idea of the width of the Gironde (3 km). Then drive up towards Le Pouyalet. At Mouton-Rothschild visit the immense first-year store, full of staid and traditional casks, and the remarkable museum exhibiting some elegant and extremely rare works of art on the theme of wine. The morphology at the nearby Château Lafite-Rothschild is absolutely typical of the Médoc grands crus: a thick hilly formation of gravels, dissected by erosion, overlooking the Jalle du Breuil (which drains surface water into the Gironde). Part of the château is very old. Do not fail to visit the new winery designed by Catalan architect Ricardo Bofill: a Grecian temple shaped like a Roman arena!

After crossing the Jalle du Breuil, fringed with meadows and poplars, the road climbs steeply again towards Château Cos d'Estournel (Saint- Estèphe) with its extravagant Oriental architecture. Stop to admire the sculpted wooden gate from Zanzibar. The château itself is simply a wine-store, with a façade and walls concealing a courtyard for storing agricultural machinery. The Château-de-Marbuzet (Bourgeois Supérieur) is a little architectural jewel surrounded by gardens of the Romantic school. At **Saint-Estèphe** are two very famed châteaux, Calon-Ségur (its good years are very smooth) and Montrose (one of the highest tannin contents of Médoc).

A brief trip into Bas-Médoc beyond Saint-Seurin-de-Cadourne will give the geologist a chance to study various outcrops of Tertiary limestone and marl (they can also be seen to the west of Saint-Julien, Pauillac and Saint-Estèphe).

Return to Bordeaux along the D 1. About 10 km from the Gironde, the road skirts the western edge of the vineyard before passing through several more vineyards and some oak and sea-pine forests growing on the Quaternary formation of Les Landes Sands.

The route goes into the village of Listrac and close to Moulis, where the vineyards are standing partly on marl outcrops of Eocene age. They are home to some "crus" of very high quality Bourgeois. You must stop at the Listrac cooperative cellars. They have long been famous as one of the main suppliers to the Compagnie des Wagons-Lits.

It is customary to contrast the delicate and elegant breeding of the Margaux to the full body, power and fullness of the Pauillac. Between the two, the Saint-Julien is said to combine the qualities of its neighbours, whilst the Saint-Estèphe is supposed to be stronger in alcohol, more robust and higher in tannin content. It is true that the gravel is deeper and practically devoid of clay at Margaux, whereas the texture of the sub-soil is a little finer around Pauillac and even more so at Saint-Estèphe. Yet these subtle differences are not of a general nature.

Latour and Mouton-Rothschild produce powerful, tannic wines which are somewhat hard to approach when young (they are obtained from a high proportion of cabernet sauvignon and spend a long time in vat). They reach their finest and fullest development only some 15 to 20 years after bottling. Lafite is also located at Pauillac, and produces supple, elegant wines which are more like those from Château Margaux and Haut- Brion (in the Graves district). Just a touch more merlot during blending seems to make all the difference.

Taking a lead from Château Margaux and its traditional Pavillon Blanc, produced from heavier soils, some Médoc "crus" have for some time been trying their hand at producing dry white wines. Though the result is not without quality, these wines are no match for the best "crus" from the Graves district (G.Seguin).

Wines of Bordeaux and gastronomy

Just as the wines of Bordeaux are among the best in the world, so French cuisine is one of the great achievements of our age. Regional cuisine is meanwhile going from strength to strength in Bordeaux with every day that passes, and is poised at any moment to become France's leading culinary region. Others may shout or whisper in protest. Let those who are still unconvinced spend some time in Guyenne just looking, savouring the cooking aromas, and tasting the food and wine![1]

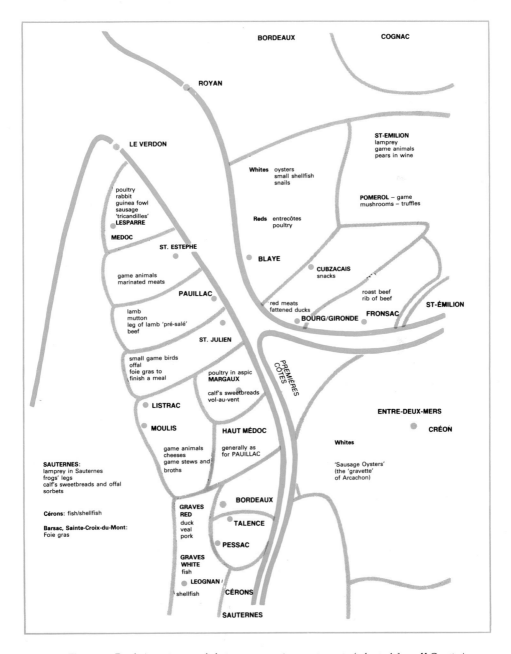

Fig.82b. — *The main Bordeaux wines and their gastronomic counterparts (adapted from K.Gautier).*

It was probably the aristocratic stance of the Bordelais vineyards which browbeat the region's cuisine into a humble supporting role. Certainly Bordeaux wines have every reason to be proud of their great and noble lineage. The quality and breadth of their range makes them the greatest wines in the world. Yet even they have evolved with time, and this process of development is still going on. It is no different with the cuisine! There are some cooking methods, or rather, misplaced feats of daring, which can insult, injure or incapacitate even the finest of wines. Surely we have all at some time met a wine which has made even the most perfect example of culinary art seem ridiculous. Essentially, there should be an ideal partnership between the two.

As for cooking in wine, what could be better? There is so much variety! Lamprey "à la Bordelaise", coq au vin, Bordelaise sauces made with red or (mellow) white wine. If you like fish, there is shad with sorrel in Entre-deux-Mers, or mackerel "aux Côtes de Blaye". Then there are the "daubes", or regional stews cooked with wine and shallots.

When we hear the name "Bordeaux" we should not think of red wines alone.

The excellent white wines in the sweet and rich category have all but been forgotten except by the most discerning palates. You really should try something like frogs legs in ginger and Sauternes. And have you never tried putting the world to rights with a good 6° Sauternes?

Bordeaux dry white wines have been making a comeback for some years now. There are some excellent ones from Graves and Sauternes which are marvellous with shellfish!

As a general rule, a wine can go with several dishes, but a dish can go with several wines. We can only make a few suggestions in this area.

Look, then, how the Garonne and the Dordogne meet at the Gironde, like the tail of some mythical bird, imprinting the soil of Aquitaine, land of rivers, with the outlines of the loveliest, most varied, subtlest, most vigorous and most amazing vineyard in the world!

You may recall those maps tucked away in the corners of our school atlases, showing the areas where such and such a crop was produced or grown. Follow our recommendations and draw a map of your own, showing the département of the Gironde, and spilling over into the Dordogne region: but this one showing wines and dishes only

---

[1] This chapter is by Mme K.Gautier, Le Rouzle, Bordeaux.

FOR FURTHER
INFORMATION

Geology

Guide géologique Aquitaine occidentale (1975) (Guide to the Geology of Western Aquitaine), by M.Vigneaux et al., Masson, Paris. See especially tours 1, 3, 7, 8 and 10.

Pratviel L. (1972). — Essai de cartographie structural et faciologique du bassin sédimentaire ouest-aquitain pendant l'Oligocène (Proposed Structural and Faciological Cartography of the Western Aquitaine Sedimentary Basin during the Oligocene), Doct. Thes. Nat. Sci., Bordeaux, 2 vols, 632 p., 35 pl.

Pedology and Oenology

Duteau J. (1976). — Le vignoble des Côtes de Bourg. Les sols et le climat. Influence sur la croissance des sarments at sur la maturation du raisin (The Côtes de Bourg Vineyards. Soils and Climate. Their Effects on Vine-Shoot Growth and Grape Ripening), Speciality Doct. Thes., Bordeaux II, 135 p., 15 fig.

Guilloux M., Duteau J. and Seguin G. (1978). — Les grands types de sols viticoles de Pomerol et Saint-Emilion (The Major Types of Vine-Growing Soil in Pomerol and Saint-Emilion), Connaissance de la vigne et du vin, 3, pp. 141-165, 7 fig.

Pijasson R. (1980). — Un grand vignoble de qualité, le medoc. 2 vol. Paris.

Pucheu-Planté B. (1977). — Les sols viticoles du Sauternais. Etude physique, chimique et microbiologique. Alimentation en eau de la vigne pendant la maturation et la surmaturation du raisin (The Physics, Chemistry and Micro-Biology of the Vine-Growing Soils in the Sauternes Region. Watering of the Vine during the Grape Ripening and Over-Ripening Season), Speciality Doct. Thes., Bordeaux II, No 27, 165 p.

Seguin G. (1970). — Les sols de vignobles du haut Médoc. Influence sur l'alimentation en eau de la vigne et sur la maturation du raisin (Vineyard Soils in Haut Médoc. Their Influence on Vine Watering and Grape Ripening), Doct. Thes. Nat. Sci., Bordeaux, 141 p.

Above: The old Château Certan (Pomerol): gravel on clay (Photo. Duteau & Seguin). ət

Below: The town of Saint-Emilion is built on an echinoid limestone escarpment (outcrop on the right). The vineyard stands on Fronsadais Molasse (Photo. Duteau & Seguin).

The 'Côtes de Bourg' vineyard stands on formations of Pliocene age (Photo. Duteau & Seguin).

SEDIMENTARY ROCKS

a²	Recent Quaternary	
a¹	Older Quarternary	
t	Glacial deposits	
a^ls	Les Landes Sands	
a^lv	Villafranchian	
p	Pliocene	
	Miocene	
	Oligocene	
	Sidérolithique	

e² e	Middle and Upper Eocene / Undifferentiated Eocene	
e¹	Lower Eocene	
c² c	Upper Cretaceous / Undifferentiated Cretaceous	
c¹	Lower Cretaceous / Urgonian	
J² J	Middle Jurassic (Dogger) / Undifferentiated Jurassic	
J¹	Lower Jurassic (Lias)	
t³	Upper Triassic (Keuper)	
d¹	Lower Devonian	

METAMORPHIC AND PLUTONIC ROCKS

ζ ζζ	Gneiss / Undifferentiated crystalline schist
γ γ^b	Granite / Biotite granite
σ	Periodite and Serpentinite / (Pyrenean Lherzolite)

OPHIOLITIC ROCKS

Mesozoic

	Alpine ophiolites / Pyrenean ophiolites

DEMARCATIONS

	Tenarèze
	Haut-Armagnac
	Bas-Armagnac

Fig.83. — Geological map and vineyard demarcations of Armagnac.

Armagnac

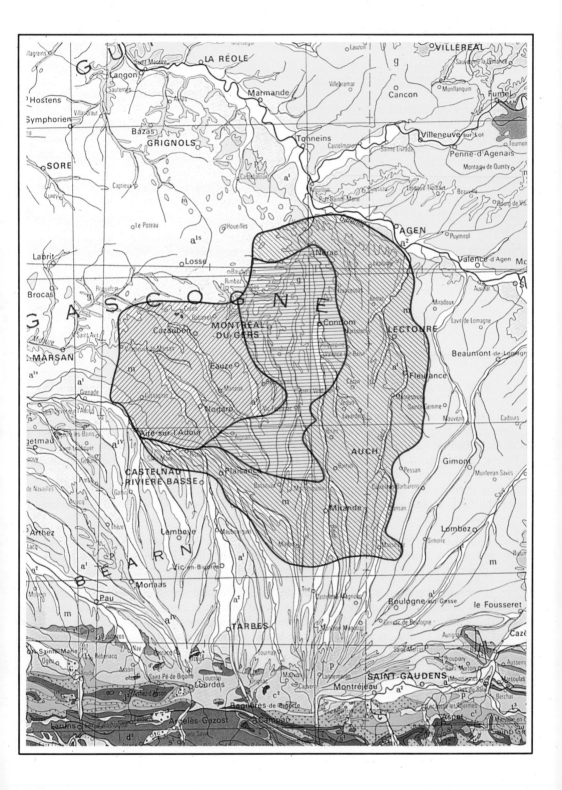

The Armagnac wine-growing region covers a vast triangular area in the southwest of France between Agen, Masseube and Mont-de-Marsan. It includes a large part of the département of Gers as well as some cantons of the Landes, in the west, and of Lot-et-Garonne, in the north.

Some 50 000 hectares are under cultivation, of which only half are suitable for producing wines for distillation.

Three regions are entitled to an appellation (fig.83):

1) **Bas Armagnac** (Lower Armagnac), or **"Armagnac noir"**, with its dense forests of abundant oak, has some 10 000 to 11 000 hectares of vineyard, planted on buff-coloured sand, producing high quality brandy spirits known widely for their fineness. The *'Bureau national interprofessionnel de l'Armagnac'* (National Inter-trade Office of Armagnac) has its head office in the regional capital, Eauze.

2) **La Ténarèze**[1] is an asymmetric anticlinal dome with a rather pronounced structure. The region is calcareous and occasionally arenaceous. Some 8 000 to 9 000 hectares of vineyard produce brandies which are somewhat harder and fuller in body.

3) **Haut Armagnac** (Upper Armagnac), or **'Armagnac blanc'**, with Auch, the capital of Gascogne (Gascony), is a limestone region "par excellence". However, it is not a big producer of spirits, with just 500 hectares under vine.

Vines and soils

Formations

The vineyards stand on Oligo-Miocene formations which are the underlying skeleton for the entire region. They were formed in a geological epoch dominated by deposition from piedmont areas, great lakes and rivers. The history of these formations began at the end of the Oligocene, with the sea retreating westwards after the deposition of echinoid limestone in Aquitaine, whilst continental deposits were being laid down in Armagnac. At about the same period, detritus from the denudation of the Pyrenees, which was a basic material for the molasse formations, were transported to the eastern part of the basin, where a lacustrine environment became established. A range of lacustrine and fluviatile deposits (White Agen Limestone, molasse, etc.), marks this "continental transition zone".

The Lower Miocene shows an early marine phase marked by intermittent transgressions, a middle lacustrine phase during which the Grey Agen Limestone was laid down, and a late marine phase during which the sea advanced eastwards.

During this period the sea repeatedly advanced and retreated across Armagnac, building sizeable accumulations of fluviatile and lacustrine continental deposits (quartz sand, lacustrine limestone, marl) and forming littoral marine deposits such as oyster and cerithium shales on the site of successive ancient shorelines.

During the Upper Miocene the sea had a general tendency to retreat from Haut Armagnac. Although the continental deposits were not laid down to the same extent as in the previous period, the fossil beds are famous (Sansan).

---

[1] 'Ténarèze' means a 'hilltop path'.

A brief transgressive episode occurred in Bas Armagnac. The sea surged eastwards into a narrow gulf (the Gulf of Lectoure) where it laid down buff-coloured sand which is mainly littoral but occasionally estuarine.

Soils

Each of the three appellation regions has different soil types.

Most of the hillslopes in Lower Armagnac are covered with fine quartz sand. This generally contains ferruginous elements which impart a characteristic buff colour. These argillo-siliceous formations are not suitable for cereal cultivation, and have therefore been planted with thriving vines which give some of the most reputed brandies.

The quality of the brandies from Lower Armagnac is closely connected with the underlying formations. Connoisseurs unanimously agree that the best brandies come from the westernmost part of Lower Armagnac, between the Landes and Gers. This little region was called "Grand bas Armagnac" (Great Lower Armagnac), as opposed to 'Fins bas Armagnac' which covered Panjas, Estag, Campagne and Eauze, and as distinct from "Petits bas Armagnac" which included Aire, Nogaro and Manciet. Although no longer used as designations, these names do reflect the individuality of the various formations.

Some soils have undergone podzolic development and an iron-rich horizon has formed, known locally as "terrebouc". The depth at which this occurs differs from one place to another. The best vines are always found where the "terrebouc" lies deepest.

At Ténarèze, on the western edge of the Miocene molasse and limestone, the residual formations are generally in an early stage of development and result from mechanical and chemical breakdown of these deposits.

Vines for brandy production are planted for preference on formations covering limestone structural platforms. These calcimorphic soils (rendzinas) are variable in depth and generally eroded at the surface, sometimes right down to the source-rock. They are known locally as "peyrusquet". In some places vines are also grown on argillo-calcareous formations ("terreforts") resulting from surface breakdown of marl and molasse. These shallow, superficial deposits are equally suitable for low-yield mixed cultivation.

Upper Armagnac consists essentially of marl and molasse deposits which alternate with banks of limestone to form long "corniches", adding variety to the landscape. Vines generally occupy the middle slopes and are planted on terreforts or, in places, on "boulbène". These acid soils usually occur on slopes but may be found even on valley floors. They tend to be water-logged in winter and very dry in summer.

Vine varieties

Vine-stock selection is another factor which has a considerable bearing on quality in Armagnac, and is subject to very strict regulations. White wines for distillation must be produced from white varieties, including among others folle blanche, saint-émilion, colombard and bacco 22 A.

The vineyards of Armagnac have very ancient origins. According to those who have investigated the subject, these vineyards go back at least a thousand years, and possibly even two thousand.

For centuries one particular variety dominated the region, that is the folle blanche, known locally as picquepoul ("tingle-lips") because it produces a very dry wine with a touch of acidity which can take the uninitiated by surprise!

In the closing years of the last century phylloxera destroyed most of the vineyards in the region, but not the well-established tradition, thank Heavens! The new varieties which are now appearing are catching on quickly, and include saint-émilion, colombard and bacco 22 A, which is a hybrid from noah and picquepoul.

Wine and distillation

A number of factors, including temperature, the moist Atlantic air-flow prevalent in the southwest, and periods of sunshine which could not be described as excessive, combine to produce a white wine which is low on alcohol (generally below 10°) and ideal for distillation.

The still traditionally used in the Armagnac region is wood-burning, producing the basic, immature brandies by a single-pass distillation process. When the wine has finished fermenting, usually in December, two specialists called "burners", or "brûleurs", take turns operating the still in a process which has to continue round the clock. This activity critically affects brandy quality in several respects (hardness, aroma, bouquet). Particular attention is paid to the following points:

— heating must be applied steadily to avoid producing a brandy which is hard and harsh (heat too fierce) or lacking in consistency (heat too low). This difficulty is overcome nowadays by fitting stills with gas-burners;

— various aromas are produced (plum, violet, lime-blossom, etc.). They reflect not only the distillation process, but also the vineyard soil, the ripeness of the grape and the quality of the wine.

At the present time, Armagnac is distilled to an alcohol content of 58-63°, and therefore has to be "reduced" before sale. "It is blended and then reduced to 40-42° with small quantities of water. Here we have an Armagnac reduced to 15° of alcohol by dilution with distilled water, and which has been "settled" in oaken casks before use" (Vigneau, 1976). This is a delicate process, intended to produce brandies which are lighter and pleasing to the customer.

On leaving the still, the brandies are put into casks of local oak which have an odour of their own (oak from the Monlezun forest provides the best quality wood).

The ageing process

The Armagnac will be aged for many years in darkened store-rooms at a constantly reasonable temperature. Early in the ageing process, six per cent of the brandy is lost by evaporation each year (this is called "the angels' share"). This proportion becomes less with the passage of time. Meanwhile the degree of alcohol gradually reduces as the brandy acquires its individuality (a brandy changes from 52° to 45-47° in about twenty years).

Armagnac so produced is drinkable in about two or three years, but has to "settle, mellow, knit together within itself and take on hue". With constant tending and frequent checking, it will take about thirty years to reach its peak, and sometimes very much longer.

Itinerary

The proposed tour through Upper Armagnac, Ténarèze and Lower Armagnac is quite long, and may be spread out over two or three days for greater convenience (fig.84). The time will be spent studying the formations underlying the vineyards (source-rocks and soils), observing the grape varieties and visiting cellars.

The tour through **Upper Armagnac** starts from Agen, heading first towards Le Castéra to study some of the limestone banks and molasse formations of the Lower Miocene.

To reach Le Castéra, take the N 121 out of Agen towards Auch. On reaching Lectoure turn onto the D 7 towards Condom, then immediately right onto the D 36 towards Nérac. Travel a further five kilometres beyond that intersection and take the D 219 as far as Le Castéra railway station.

Le Castéra ①. A track climbs the slope. From the foot of this track to its top the following features can be observed along the way:

— an equivalent of the White Agen Limestone (Lower Aquitanian, elevation 85);
— a white equivalent of the Grey Agen Limestone (elevations 110, 115);
— ash-grey limestone equivalent to Pellecahus Limestone (elevation 165);
— Lower Lectoure Limestone (elevation 177) forming the upper face of the slope, from where there is a splendid view of the Gers Valley.

Take the same road as far as Lectoure, then go towards Fleurance along the Gers Valley noticing the lacustrine limestone which caps the hills on either side.

Fleurance ②. Here it is possible to visit cellars used for ageing the brandy. Then take the N 654 towards Condom. The road climbs the hillside before winding across argillo-calcareous soils and "peyrusquets" with a sparse covering of vines (La Sauvetat).

Ténarèze is located roughly half-way between the valleys of the Gers and the Baïse, in a mainly molassic landscape. Formations of lacustrine limestone and molasse from the Lower Miocene are locally incised by the marine formation of Tortonian age (Upper Miocene), marking the final marine transgression into the Gulf of Lectoure.

An old quarry at Caussens has a fine example of this formation. To get there, turn right onto the D 232, go through Saint-Orens and head north on the D 204.

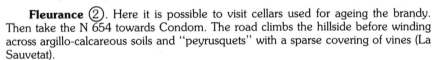

Caussens ③. On the right, about 2.5 km from the village, is a cross-section of the very fine sand bearing lamellibranchs (Ostrea crassissima, Cardita jouanneti, Scutella rotundata, Flabellipecten larteti). This site is one of the most remarkable in the region.

Return to **Condom** via Caussens and the D 7, go through the town and drive towards Agen via the N 131. After about 8 km turn left onto the Peyrusca road. A small town called Estrepouy stands a few hundred metres from the crossroads.

Estrepouy ④. The small valley shows a cross-section in which, working from base to top, it is possible to observe the following:

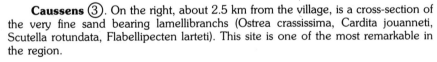

— white limestone in the floor of the valley;
— oyster-bearing marls and shales (Ostrea aginensis);
— Grey Agen Limestone (elevation 110);
— marls bearing Ostrea aginensis;
— crumbly marl;
— fossil-bearing sands (elevation 125) with mammal remains.

Leave Estrepouy and head for Sos via Ligardes and Mézin northwards on the N 131, then westwards on the D 112, D 149 and N 656. About 2.5 km from Sos turn left onto a dirt road to Matilon quarry.

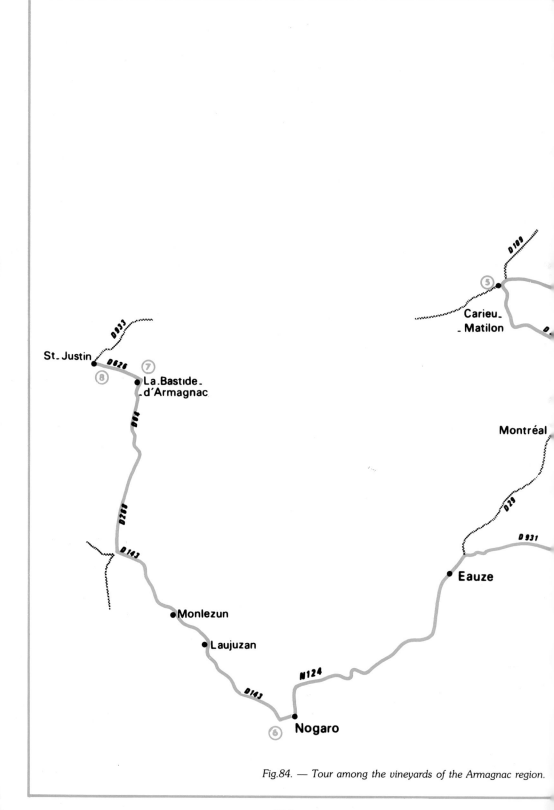

Fig.84. — *Tour among the vineyards of the Armagnac region.*

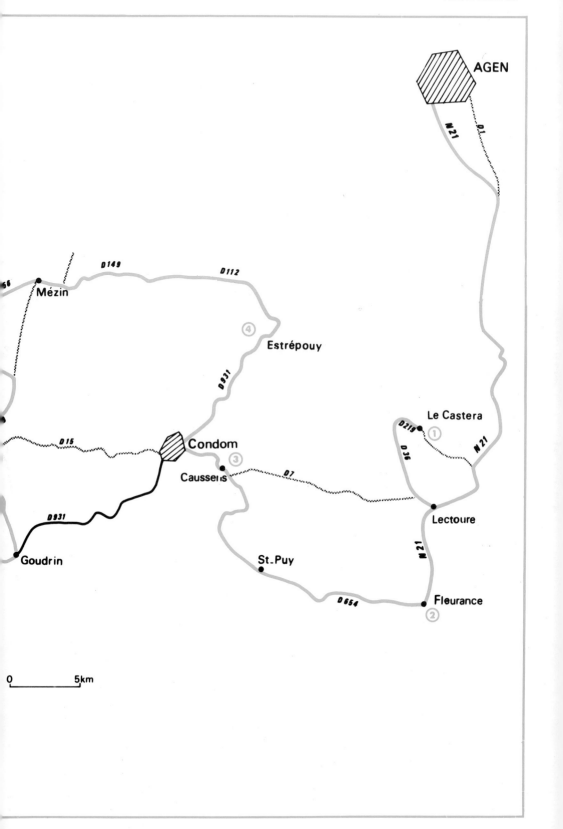

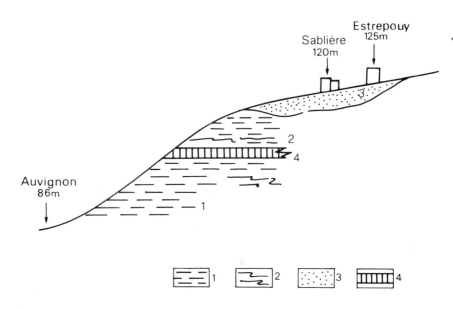

Fig.85. — Cross-section in the area of Estrepouy.

1. Marl bearing Ostrea aginensis; 2. Crumbly marl; 3. Fossil-bearing sand; 4. Agenais Grey Limestone.

Matilon quarry ⑤. A buff-coloured sandy marine limestone (Helvetian) rises to a height of 20 metres. It includes many lamellibranchs, gastropods, bryozoa and crustacea. It is overlain with sands of probably Pliocene age. The whole formation overlies a grey limestone horizon which can be seen in places.

Next we go through the town on the N 656. On the right as we leave is an outcrop of Grey Agen Limestone. Travel via Saint-Maure on the D 109, Fourcès on the D 114, Montréal on the C 29 and Gondrin (D 113) to Nogaro. This journey takes us through a landscape of molasse and lacustrine limestone which outcrop due to the presence of the valleys. Along the way, notice the argillo-calcareous soils and 'peyrusquets' which form the main environment for the Ténarèze vineyards.

Nogaro ⑥. Miocene formations outcrop in a quarry south of the town. An examination from base to top reveals the following:

— some three metres of bluish marl, of Burdigalian age, giving way to a further three metres of greenish marl which is slightly arenaceous;

— white sands with localised gravel and peaty formations, giving way to buff-coloured sands of Tortonian age;

— reddish, argillo-arenaceous Quaternary colluvial deposits with oxidation-reduction stains, beginning with a solifluction flow (gravel, pebbles and some ferruginous fragments).

The tour takes us to the boundaries of **Lower Armagnac** (Labastide, Saint-Justin) passing through the valley of the Midour, where it is possible to observe some excellent cross-sections of the buff-coloured sands at Caupenne (D 147), Laujuzan and Monlezun (D 143).

On reaching Montégut, proceed via Lannemaignan on the D 268 and the D 64, then via Saint-Justin on the N 626, to Labastide-d'Armagnac. The route takes us through some famous vineyards. At **Labastide** ⑦ and **Saint-Justin** ⑧ it is possible to visit vineyards planted on sands. The varieties of vine are varied: bacco 22 A, colombard and saint-émilion stand alongside folle blanche, now recovering since the phylloxera outbreak. At appropriate times of the year the visitor can form an appreciation of the respective qualities of each variety through their vines, their grapes and their wines. Lastly, in the shade of the spirit stores, there is a chance to sample the famous qualities of the brandies.

FOR FURTHER
INFORMATION

Geology

Geological guides (Masson, Paris): *Aquitaine occidentale* (Western Aquitaine) (1975), by M.Vigneaux et al.; *Aquitaine orientale* (Eastern Aquitaine) (1977), by B. Gèze and A. Cavaillé.

Alvinerie J. (1969). — Contribution sédimentologique à la connaissance du Miocène aquitain. Interprétation stratigraphique et paléographique (The Contribution of Sedimentology to a Study of the Aquitanian Miocene. A Stratigraphic and Palaeographic Interpretation), *Thès. Nat. Sci., Bordeaux, 462 p., 31 maps, 16 pl., 60 fig.*

Durand-Delga M., et al. (1980). — Itinéraires géologiques. Aquitaine, Languedoc, Pyrénées (Geological Tours. Aquitaine, Languedoc, Pyrenees), *Bull.Research Centre Explor.Prod. Elf-Aquitaine*, Pau, Mem.3, 438 p., fig., tabl.

Oenology

Dufor H. (1982). — Armagnac. Eaux-de-vie et terroir (Armagnac. The Brandy and the Vineyard), Privat, Toulouse, 316 p., 279 fig.

Vigneau J. (1976). — L'Armagnac. Techniques de production et éléments de qualités (Armagnac. Production Techniques and Aspects of Quality), Dithane et Bnia, 4 p.

SEDIMENTARY ROCKS

a² — Recent Quaternary

a¹ — Older Quarternary

t — Glacial deposits

a^{IV} — Villafranchian

p — Pliocene

Miocene

Oligocene

e² e — Middle and Upper Eocene
Undifferentiated Eocene

e¹ — Lower Eocene

c² c — Upper Cretaceous
Undifferentiated Cretaceous

c¹ — Lower Cretaceous
Urgonian

J³ — Upper Jurassic (Malm)

J² J — Middle Jurassic (Dogger)
Undifferentiated Jurassic

J¹ — Lower Jurassic (Lias)

t³ — Upper Triassic (Keuper)

t² t — Middle Triassic (Muschelkalk)
Undifferentiated Triassic

t¹ — Lower Triassic

h⁴ — Stephanian

s¹ — Ordovician

METAMORPHIC AND PLUTONIC ROCKS

ζ ζζ — Gneiss
Undifferentiated crystalline schist

γ γ^b — Granite
Biotite granite

OPHIOLITIC ROCKS

Mesozoic

Alpine ophiolites
Pyrenean ophiolites

DEMARCATIONS

Irouléguy

Tursan

Béarn

Jurançon

Vic-Bilh and Madiran

Fig.86. — Geological map and vineyard demarcations of Southwestern France: Chalosse, Béarn, Pays Basque.

Béarn, Pays basque

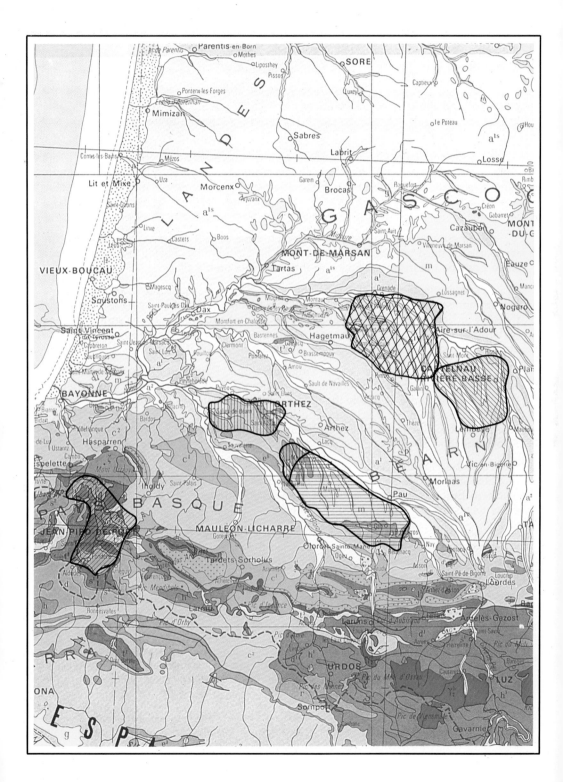

CHALOSSE, BÉARN, PAYS BASQUE

The regions of Southwestern France from the Atlantic to the Pyrenees, especially the Pays Basque and Béarn, enjoy an exceptionally fine climate which has long been known for its gentleness. Long periods of sunshine combine with the seasonal rainfall to encourage the growth of crops and vegetation alike. Autumn in the Béarn region, generally noted for warm, dry winds from the south, is gentle and provides good ripening conditions for the grapes. They are generally harvested late, sometimes into the second half of November (Jurançon). The soils have developed on siliceous clastic rocks (alluvials, flysch, etc.). They form easily and are suitable for vines (fig.86).

The main features of the Pyrenean landscape, which are determined by the structures and lithology of the Pyrenees themselves, add up to a complex foothill area, in part consisting of detrital fans overlying generally folded and fractured Tertiary and Mesozoic formations.

This combination of factors gives rise to micro-climates, some of which are characterised by an almost total absence of spring frost and by a low rainfall pattern. Where in addition the foothills of the Pyrenees provide some measure of shelter (Irouléguy), or on slopes with a southerly exposure, we find the best conditions for vineyards.

For these reasons, unlike other French vineyards (Bordeaux, Bourgogne), the vineyards of the Pyrenean region seem to lack continuity, having been established since perhaps before the Romans in the most favourable places.

According to tradition, the vineyards of the Pays Basque and Béarn go back to Roman timess, if not earlier. It is certainly true that here and there, remains such as the mosaics of Lescar (the ancient capital *Benehamum*) showing Bacchus surrounded by garlands of vine-shoots and branches, and the mosaics at the Roman site on which the abbey of Sorde was built, may prove the point.

Following the calamities of the Great Invasions, Pyrenean vineyards re-emerged with the rise of the abbeys. The abbey of Madiran (1030) and the monastery of Sainte-Foy (1079) were very probably the origins of the vineyards in the Madiran district and Vic-Bilh. The abbey of Sorde and the fortified abbey of Montgiscard originated the vineyards of Bellocq and Salies-de-Béarn; and the vines of the abbeys of Aire-sur-Adour and Mas developed into the vineyards of Tursan.

After the Hundred Years War, trading links with Bayonne — and thus the means of distributing Pyrenean wines — decreased sharply along with ties to England and Northern Europe. But several causes were to contribute to the subsequent revival of these wines in the 17th and 18th centuries.

A geological problem, namely the tendency for the mouth of the Adour to shift between Capbreton and Bayonne — hence the rivalry between these two towns — was resolved by stabilising the mouth at Boucau. Trade with southern Aquitaine thus fell to Bayonne.

Whilst fine wines from the regions of Bayonne, the Pays Basque and Chalosse could be shipped easily and rapidly down to Bayonne via the lower reaches of the Adour, the same was not true for Béarn wines.

In the 17th century, Isaac de Lom d'Arve, Baron of Lahontan, near Bellocq, opened the first direct river link between Bayonne and Saint-Pé-de-Bigorre, west of Lourdes. It took this determined Béarnese from 1630 to 1658 to open up this waterway. He did so at his own expense and often at great risk to his life.

The baptism in 1553 of the future King Henry IV ("lou nouste Henric" - "our own Henry"), during which his lips were rubbed with garlic and Jurançon, gave Pyrenean wines their royal charter of nobility.

Following the Revocation of the Edict of Nantes (1685), Pyrenean wines reminded Protestant exiles of what Edmond Rostand called "an old song from the land of sweet, beguiling rhythm". Protestants from Béarn fled to England and Holland along with others from Aunis, Saintonge and the south of France, creating a demand for wines from the Pyrenees in their host countries.

The vineyards of the Pyrenean region have re-emerged brilliantly since the Second World War. This has been largely due to the quality of the various "crus": rosé and red from Irouléguy; rich and dry white from Jurançon, Pacherenc and Vic-Bilh; red from Madiran; white, rosé and red from Béarn.

Each of these wines, in its own way, is a hymn to the Pyrenees, blending harmoniously with the gastronomic traditions of these lands of ocean and mountain.

Vines and soils

There are two contrasting varieties of vineyard in the Adour : those of the Midi type (Pau is further south than Nice) and those of the mountain foothills kind. The pedology reflects this duality, to which is added a third consideration: the influence of the Atlantic Ocean, by way of the Gulf of Gascony.

Soil components

As with all French soils, those on the sweep of the Adour form a mosaic which reflects many interacting factors.

The basic factor is climate, which in this case is complex and has the following characteristics:

a rainfall gradient which decreases from west to east, that is from the Atlantic coast towards the Gers, and gives rise to soils of the podzolic type in the west;

high summertime temperatures which in some years last well into the autumn (very good for producing sweet wine), but can cause significant dewatering of the soil;

slight coolness on higher ground, which has undeveloped, skeletal soil with unincorporated organic matter.

There is also a considerable diversity of source-rocks. They fall into four main categories:

• undeveloped alluvials with an insignificant clay phase. These also include thin coverings of Landes Sands, a siliceous, aeolian formation lacking a fine matrix;

• old alluvials which have undergone lengthy pedogenesis. The granites are weathered and there are sizeable neo-formations of clay. They are heavy, impervious soils giving rise to seasonal hydromorphic processes. There is also advanced ferrous development associated with the successive periods of rubefaction which occurred during the Quaternary interglacials;

• hard siliceous substrata are the most common, whether of Palaeozoic quartzite, Triassic sandstone, Cretaceous flysch or Cenozoic molasse. Naturally these soils are predominantly acid;

• calcareous substrata are uncommon beyond the mountains themselves. There are just a few minor outcrops of Jurassic dolomite or Urgonian limestone and some banks of lacustrine limestone occurring in the vicinity of Gers.

Morphology is another dominant factor: fairly well-drained, cultivated plateaux; unstable, gullied hillsides planted with trees to check erosion; wet, poorly drained low ground used only for grassland. The soils match this arrangement: well-balanced on the plateaux, leached and even eroded on the slopes, hydromorphic in the low-lying areas with seasonal gleying.

Soils and vineyards in the Adour region

The six vine-growing areas which occupy the sweep of the Adour can be categorised broadly as follows:

- **the Irouléguy vineyard,** in the Pays Basque, to the west of the region, stands on soils with obvious Atlantic characteristics;

- **the Salies-de-Béarn vineyard** is planted on richer, less leached soil similar to the brown soils;

- **the vineyards of Chalosse** (Mugron, Montfort) and Tursan (Geaune) have similar characteristics (sound earth and sweet earth);

- **the vineyards of Jurançon-Monein** grow on heavier soils which vary according to the proximity of the calcareous substratum (conglomerates) or the depth of the siliceous alluvial nappe. These hillside vineyards are planted in sweet earth enriched in places with iron;

- lastly, **the Vic-Bilh vineyards,** from which **Madiran** is produced, are on soils representing the first occurrence of the Gers type (''terrefort'', ''boulbène''). By tradition the vines were planted in darkened terreforts on hillslopes. Recent expansion has extended their range to boulbènes in the valleys, which have characteristics of their own (high iron content).

Even so there are many local variations. On the sand-gravel of the Adour the vines produce a light wine, whilst on the limestone slab of Viella-Saint-Mont the wine resembles that produced on the terreforts of Gers. It is worth recalling at this point that the best Armagnac is produced in Lower Armagnac from the argillo-siliceous soils, with their low limestone content, covering the littoral formations of buff-coloured sands from the gulf of Marsan.

Itineraries

The Irouléguy vineyard

The Irouléguy wine-growing area extends northwards from Ursuya and the Aldudes, the Palaeozoic uplands of the Basque country, and east of Saint-Etienne-de-Baïgorry. The pretty village of Irouléguy is at its centre.

The Irouléguy appellation was conferred in 1952. The cooperative wine-cellars of Irouléguy and the wines of the Pays Basque were founded in 1954. The AOC wines of Irouléguy are found in an area covering nine administrative districts: seven in Saint-Etienne-de-Baïgorry canton (Ascarat, Anhaux, Irouléguy, Bidarray, Osses, Saint-Martin-d'Arossa and Saint-Etienne-de-Baïgorry); and two in Saint-Jean-Pied-de-Port canton, known in Basque as Donibane-Garazi (Ispoure and Jaxu).

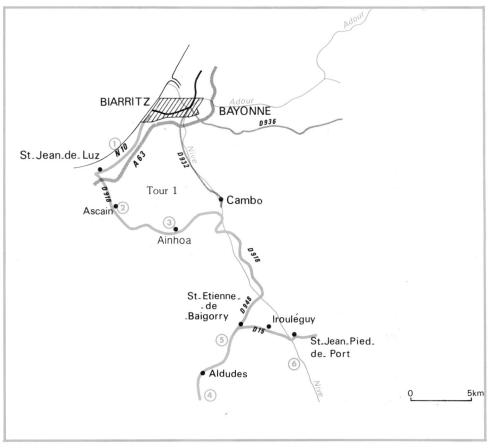

Fig. 87a. — Tours among the vineyards of Southwestern France.
(Tours 2, 3, 4, p. 286)

The vines have the benefit of long periods of sunshine. They are sheltered from the spring frosts by being trained espalier fashion, and also enjoy protection afforded by the low mountain barrier which tempers the cold winds. In autumn the warm south wind ensures an even ripening of the grapes.

The vineyards are scattered unevenly among small plots of land because of their situation in the mountains. They stand on slopes at elevations between 200 and 400 metres. In addition to traditional growing methods, terrace cultivation is now being used.

The AOC zone extends over a geologically complex region, consisting mainly of Permian sandstone, argillaceous Triassic sandstone, and limestone of Jurassic and Tertiary age. Alluvials are developing around Saint-Etienne-de-Baïgorry.

The once large numbers of grape varieties have been reduced since 1970. Cabernet and tannat are used in making red wine. The varieties for white are courbu and menseng. The Fox of the famous Fable had a preference for certain grapes. He would no doubt have approved of those from a variety of cabernet known by its Basque name of acheria (meaning fox).

The varieties used are happy on clay formations, and even on pebbly or gravelly slopes of Permian and, particularly, Triassic age (cabernet franc). Tannat understocks Nos 3309 and S04 can even withstand 10 per cent and 20 per cent respectively of active lime. Cabernet franc grows well on shaly, acid formations and is well suited to the pebbly and gravelly slopes of the Trias. Although a white AOC has been granted, production is divided evenly between rosé and red.

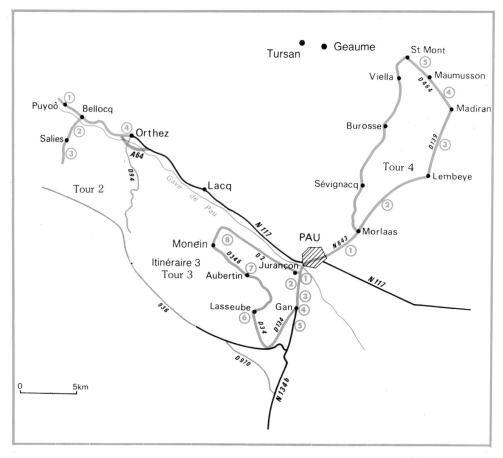

Fig. 87b. — Tours among the vineyards of Southwestern France (see also p. 285)

The Pays Basque is enchanting. White houses and pretty villages make a happy scene, showing off their roofs against a backdrop of hillsides, streams and mountains. There is something new to see at every turn. The tour suggested below is a combination of geology, scenery and vineyards (fig.87, tour 1).

① Entering **Saint-Jean-de-Luz** on the N 10 from Biarritz, take the turning on the right towards the 'Motels basques'. Follow this road for quite some distance as far as a huge layby and leave the car there. Walk along a footpath skirting the blockhouses of the Atlantic Wall. This path gives some splendid views of the Basque coast and the port of Saint-Jean-de-Luz. Note the flysch from the Upper Cretaceous. Continue walking down, to the right of the chapel, as far as Sainte-Barbe point, where the Upper Cretaceous flysch has a magnificent, northwest-tilted knee fold (see *'Guide géologique Pyrénées occidentales'* — Guide to the Geology of the Western Pyrenees, tour No 9).

② **Saint-Jean-de-Luz,** Ascain, La Rhune (Trias), Sare and Ainhoa (a very attractive Basque village with old houses).

③ Ainhoa, Espelette, Itxassou, Saint-Martin-d'Arrossa, Saint-Etienne-de-Baïgorry.

④ **Saint-Etienne-de-Baïgorry** marks the beginning of the Palaeozoic uplands of the Basque country. A cross-section of their Ordovician and Devonian formations can be taken in the very pretty Aldudes valley (quartzo-sideritic veins and copper-bearing sulphides of the Banca Ordovician). Visit Aldudes village (church with wooden barrel-vaulting and galleries).

On the way back from Aldudes take the road for the Col d'Ispéguy, where a very good cross-section shows the Ordovician formations clearly.

⑤ Return to Saint-Etienne-de-Baïgorry for a look around this very ancient Basque village (Roman bridge over the Aldudes torrent). The village is built along the valley, and its two halves with the torrent in between were once rivals. Its church is worth visiting.

Leave Saint-Etienne-de-Baïgorry heading for Saint-Jean-Pied-de-Port. The "Cave coopérative **d'Irouléguy** et des vins du Pays basue" (Cooperative wine-cellars of Irouléguy and the wines of the Pays Basque) distribute the whole of the wine production. After passing the cooperative wine-cellars, still heading towards Saint-Jean-Pied-de-Port, take the first road on the right. Soon we come to a vineyard growing on alteration zones. These date mainly from the Trias and have a high clay content.

The many flocks of sheep (called "manèches" in Basque) represent the main farming activity, with here and there the occasional "pottiok" (small Basque horse). Return by the same road and head towards Saint-Jean-Pied-de-Port. Notice the vines at widely-spaced intervals along the way.

⑥ Saint-Jean-Pied-de-Port (known as "Donibane-Garazi" in Basque) and its citadel of Vauban are built on Triassic rocks, which have been used as building material for the town.

The Trias can be observed particularly well in a quarry alongside the road at Ascarat. Triassic formations include the Pic de Jarra (795 metres) northwest of Saint-Jean, and the Arradoy (661 metres) to the north. It lies unconformably upon the Aldudes, of Palaeozoic age, seen earlier in the tour.

The Béarn vineyard

Based around the districts of Bellocq and Salies-de-Béarn, the Béarn vineyard has acquired an excellent reputation, and the appellation now includes not only the original vineyard, but also those of Jurançon and Madiran (sixty-three administrative districts in Pyrénées-Atlantiques) taking in a little portion of Gers and Hautes-Pyrénées (six districts).

This is a very ancient wine-growing area, connected with the Bayonne wine trade. The best route from which to see it is certainly between Bellocq and Salies-de-Béarn.

Vines are grown mainly on south-facing and east-facing hillslopes, on soils consisting of Cretaceous and Palaeocene flysch. They are also planted on Tertiary detrital formations (molasse and conglomerate) as well as on old torrential alluvials around Bellocq and Lahontan.

There are whites, rosés and reds of AOC status.

The grape varieties cultivated for rosés and reds are tannat, cabernet franc (bouchy), cabernet sauvignon, fer (pinenc), black manseng and black courbu. Red wines use no more than 60 per cent tannat.

Whites wines use petit manseng, gros manseng, courbu, lauzet, camarelet, raffiat de moncade and sauvignon. The wines must have an alcohol content of at least 10.5° and the yield must be 50 hectolitres per hectare.

① The tour starts from Puyoo, via the D 30 to **Bellocq.** On the left bank of the torrent, below the Château de Bellocq, notice the outcrops of "Nay Marl", of Maastrichtian age, alongside the limestone from the Cretaceous-Tertiary transition which forms the bedrock of the château (fig.87, tour No 2).

② **Bellocq.** The château was built between 1250 and 1280 and the first fortress in Béarn was established in 1281. The château has seven towers, one of which has collapsed into the torrent. The edifice was razed in 1621 on the orders of Richelieu to prevent it being used as a Protestant stronghold. In fact, in the tradition of Jeanne d'Albret, a Protestant community flourishes to this very day in the little Béarnese town of Bellocq. On the outskirts, the cooperative cellars handle the wine from these vineyards.

③ Drive through Bellocq. At the roundabout turn right onto the Salies road. Some 300 metres further on, at the wayside Calvary on the left-hand side, take the village road on the left.

This road comes to a fork, with a nursery on the left-hand road which raises many of the grafts and root-stocks for the varieties used in Pyrenean vineyards. At this fork take the right-hand road, then turn left onto the road to Cabé which climbs towards Castéra (Roman camp). This road crosses an area of espalier-trained vines spaced at intervals of 2 metres (for old vineyards) to 3 metres. These vines are growing on argillaceous soils partly originating from flysch.

There are crossroads at the top of the slope. Turn left onto the hilltop road known as the "Chemin royal" (Royal Road). Hilltop roads of this type, such as the Chemin des Ossalois (or "cami oussalès" in the local dialect) are ancient indeed, probably megalithic in origin. This was a defensive road, flanked with sacred trees (oaks), leading to Castéra. Follow it as far as the second crossroads, then turn right onto the D 30 towards Salies-de-Béarn.

Salies-de-Béarn owes its name, as does the river Saleys, to the salts of the Trias. The Trias of Salies extends westwards to the neighbourhood of Sorde, with large outcrops. Salies-de-Béarn is a pretty town. It stands by the river Saleys, which is bridged by the Pont-de-la-Lune and flanked by galleried, 17th-century Béarnese houses. It is also a spa town.

④ From Salies go to **Orthez** (worth a visit; the former capital of Béarn; the fortified bridge over the stream and the Moncade tower). From there proceed to Pau, stopping on the way at **Lacq** (gas field, petrochemical complex). On the N 117, opposite the factory entrance, is a visitors' centre and exhibition about the Lacq field.

The Jurançon vineyards

To the west of Pau, between Jurançon and Monein, stand these hillside vineyards, made famous by the baptism of the future King Henry IV of France. In fact they have enough individual qualities to ensure that their solid reputation travels far beyond the borders of southwestern France.

The growing conditions are individualistic: a hillside terrain; small, scattered vineyards enclosed (and therefore hidden) behind trees and shrubs; and a moist, warm Atlantic climate. From the geological point of view, the subsoil consists of Cenozoic formations which are either marine (laid down before the raising of the Pyrenees) or continental (sequences of conglomerate and gravelly sandstone). These all overlie the deep structure enclosing riches of another sort: the Meillon-Rousse gas field. Drilling towers amid the vineyards show that both activities can co-exist.

The vineyards are family-run, on little farms with no more than two to five hectares under vine. This is a long-established vine-growing area which developed due to investment by the nobility and bourgeoise of Pau (it is worth mentioning that in the days of the Ancien Régime, Pau had a Parliament). By tradition, these vineyards produce red wine from tannat and white wine from petit manseng, gros manseng and courbu. At the turn of the century, fashion dictated a sweet, rich white wine produced from over-ripened grapes (by "pourriture noble" — noble rot). This wine has a characteristically sweet yet acid taste (the flavour of acid drops or guava) which stops it being mawkish and has made it famous. The reds and whites are currently undergoing a revival of fortune.

① Leave Pau heading south (fig.87, tour No 3). After the tunnel of the Pont-d'Espagne, driven in Jurançon Conglomerates, we come to the village of **Jurançon,** an old suburb of the capital of Béarn standing on a terrace. It is situated at the foot of a range of hills formed by detrital continental formation, the Jurançon Conglomerate of Miocene age. Its mainly limestone pebbles were wrested from Mesozoic matrices in the Pyrenean chain.

② These formations can be studied on the way up to **Clos Joliette** on the narrow VO 5 local road overlooking Jurançon. The summit is capped with clay containing siliceous gravel and pebbles of Ponto-Pliocene age (the Joliette Gravels formation). The famous Clos Joliette vineyard stands in a warm, humid little valley which encourages ripening. The presence of ironstone caps of Pliocene age complicates agriculture but gives this very typical wine a special cachet.

③ **The Jurançon-Gan ridge** (follow the D 321) was once a drovers' road for the transhumance of local flocks making their way to the plain of Pont-Long. The landscape is typical of a hillslope district: low-lying ground is wet and given over to husbandry; sloping ground is steep and covered in large trees which stabilise the shifting clay soils of the hillsides; high ground is flat and under cultivation. This triple system of farming (agriculture-forest-animals) is dictated by the nature of the formations (surface horizons of Pliocene clay-sandstone and siliceous pebbles, which creep on sloping ground). Some of the best vineyards of Jurançon are found here, scattered in the vicinity of the little chapel of Rousse: Cru du Lamouroux, Château Les Astous, Clos de Gaye. From here we drive down to the town of Gan.

④ **The Gan Basin:** The cooperative wine-cellars are located in a basin of marine marl which contains some good fossils of Ypresian age. This marl can be seen in the old brick fields (see 'Guide géologique Pyrénées occidentales' — Guide to the Geology of the Western Pyrenees, page 60). The area is dominated by a wooded conglomerate cuesta and is situated on the Pyrenean unconformity.

⑤ **The Pont-Labaud Cuesta:** Take the N 134 south, and then the road which follows the east bank of the Hies. We cross the thick formation of Ypresian marl and then the Palaeocene flysch (which does not crop out). We eventually reach the calcareous cuesta of Danian age with remains of marine fauna. This is planted with vines by M.Mondinat (proud owner of fine fossil specimens; Clos Labau). Return via the N 134 which passes the gates of the excellent Clos Husté.

⑥ **Lasseube:** To reach this lovely Béarnese village, follow the D 24 to the Bel-Air viewpoint (note the fine view over the northern Pyrenees). Then take the D 34. West of Lasseube are some quarries which show Eocene marls and some Triassic horizons. Ridges of Danian limestone, called Lasseube Limestone, are common. Vineyards on these formations have a character all their own (the wine is sweeter, less acid).

⑦ **The Aubertin Ridges** (D 346): Take the D 24 from Lasseube towards Gan. At Bouix take the D 346 northwards. We then cross the Aubertin - Saint-Faust winegrowing area, which is very typical of hilltop vineyards. From a geological point of view these are complex clay-sand formations with siliceous pebbles, of early Plio-Quaternary age, overlying Jurançon Conglomerate with limestone pebbles. There are many "crus", among which we should mention: the Herrua vineyard, Clos Burgué, the J.Burgué vines (a taste of violets), Clos Clamen and the very good Clos Reyan, located on a rounded hill overlooking the valley.

⑧ **Monein:** The route takes us to Monein, an old strong point with a fortified church dating from the 14th century. It is at the centre of an area of rich soils. Here the hills are not so steep, and vines are found on the slopes. The wines are varied (reds and dry whites) and quite distinctive, though less typical than the true Jurançon. The wines with the best body come from the gravelly plateaux where ironstone caps are common.

Return to Pau along the torrent of Pau (left bank), overlooking the Saligue, or flood-plain, planted with root-stocks and disturbed by intensive gravel workings.

The Vic-Bilh vineyards

The region of the "Vic-Bilh", or old country, was annexed to Béarn at a very early date (around 950 AD). For the transhumant herdsmen it was a vital adjunct to the Ger plateau and the Pyrenean valleys of Lavedan. In fact this region of hills, so reminiscent of Gascogne, is entirely within the foothills of the Pyrenees.

In geological terms it consists of complex continental alluvial blankets distinguished by their terracing and the extent of their weathering. The oldest now hold only corroded and weathered quartzites and quartz, but the youngest still retain 50 per cent of their granitic components.

The region also has a distinctive pattern of agriculture: the climate is drier than elsewhere in Béarn, agriculture is more varied, despite the recent advent of single-cropping maize, and vine-growing is developing. It is an ancient tradition, possibly introduced by the Romans but known for certain to the monks in the Middle Ages, and comprising two equally distinctive vine selections: for the red, tannat, which is combined with cabernet to produce **Madiran;** and **ruffiac** for the white. The latter gives **Pacherenc,** which the authors prefer in its original form of a slightly harsh, dry white wine, rather than in its modern style as a sweet wine imitating Jurançon.

This vineyard is expanding vigorously. Starting from the ridges, it is now coming down into the valleys and colonising the Adour valley. To appreciate all its subtleties we recommend a tour from south to north, from Pau to Saint-Mont, returning to Pau via Garlin, where the sub-soil conceals recently discovered petroleum deposits (fig.87 tour No 4).

(1) **Pau-Morlaas.** Follow the Pont-Long plain to the foot of the Morlaas hills where the very dilapidated Romanesque church serves as a good introduction to the Romanesque architecture of Vic-Bilh and its richly carved decorations. Morlaas is the headquarters of the merchants who deal in some of the wines from Vic-Bilh.

(2) **Morlaas-Lembeye.** This part of the route crosses three terraced alluvial blankets: as we leave Morlaas we find the lowest, called the Morlaas blanket, with quartzites and vague traces of granite; named after Saint-James in Brittany: the great Saint-James nappe, with large pebbles of quartzite and argillitic granite; on the high ground (Monassut, Simacourbe, Lembeye), the uppermost blanket, with reddened quartzite pebbles, known as the Maucor blanket (Pliocene).

Visit the Romanesque church at Simacourbe and the medieval fortress at Lembeye. The estate of Château Peyros, at Corbère, north of Lembeye, is considered to produce one of the finest examples of the Madiran "cru".

(3) **Lembeye to Madiran.** Here we cut through a system of large rounded hills lying north-south. Their base consists of Miocene molasse and their top is the Pliocene blanket. On the slopes are colluvial deposits showing signs of soil-creep. We are at the heart of Madiran wine country, centred on Crouseilles cooperative cellars. Several of the "crus" from here are distinguished by their heavy reliance on tannat.

(4) **Madiran to Maumusson.** Follow the Bergeron valley via the D 48 and the D 164. Here we see the classic asymmetry of the valleys: the gently sloping western flank with colluvial deposits; the steep eastern slope with erosion of the hard Tertiary formations. The vineyards stand on the western side. Around Maumusson we find some good estates for red wine: Bouscasse, Talleurguet, Teston, Barrejat and a newcomer Lou Parsa. There are some good white Pacherencs, too, such as Bouscasse.

(5) **The Saint-Mont sector.** This point is the outer limit of the Madiran district. A village stands on lacustrine limestone overlooking the terraces of the Adour, which at this spot runs East-West, following the line of recent faulting.

Visit the very picturesque village of Saint-Mont, with its Romanesque church and its bustling cooperative wine-cellars, which markets wines from hillslopes and the plain of the Adour alike.

The "**Côtes de St-Mont**" appellation includes the districts of St-Mont, Aignan and Plaisance in the area between Madiran and Bas Armagnac. The wines from the area include tanic reds from the clayey sandy slopes, light reds from the terraces of the Adour, and whites from west-facing slopes. One of the whites to note is the Colombard. It has a distinctive bouquet and goes very well with fish and seafood. When distilled it yields a good Armagnac.

The **Tursan** vineyard (VDQS) lies east of the Chalosse, in a bend of the Adour (fig. 87, page 268). It stands on molasse and light brown sand of Miocene age overlying piercement folds (Audignon Anticline). The Geaune cooperative sells most of the wines from the district. These include light rosés produced from the bouchy variety (another name for the cabernet), pleasingly structured reds based on tannat (75%) and cabernet sauvignon, and highly individual whites with good body from a local variety known as the barroque.

Wines and gastronomy

The Pays Basque and Béarn are best at bringing out that joy of living which comes from a climate which is sunny in winter and sparkling in autumn.

One of the loveliest panoramas of the Pyrenees is that from the terrace of the Château de Pau and from the Boulevard des Pyrénées. Above a succession of ever more distant views, where colours and hues gradually fade and blend, rises the east-west sweep of the mighty range of the Pyrenees, often with a covering of snow.

Not only in the large towns of the Pays Basque and Béarn, but in the villages too, we find inns serving regional specialities which go splendidly with the wines of the Pyrenees.

The white and rosé wines of Béarn and the rosé of Irouléguy, all of them light and fruity, make good companions for the local dried ham, the Béarnese stew (garbure), the pâtés "en croûte", the eels fried in garlic and the mushroom omelettes.

The white wines of Béarn, the dry Jurançon and the Pacherenc blanc with its subtle bouquet, are all perfect with seafood, salmon, trout from the mountain streams, eels in parsley, etc.

The red wines (Béarn and Irouléguy) blend well with entrées, light poultry recipes, grilled or roast meats and mild mountain cheeses.

The deep red Madiran is usually full-bodied and forthcoming. It ages superbly and is excellent with jugged game such as hare, pigeon and Pyrenean goat (isard), or with small game birds on canapé and so on. It is also good with potted goose or duck and with steaks (entrecôte béarnaise, naturally) as well as with cheeses from the mountains and even the stronger varieties.

The Jurançon is soft and rich with a velvety texture and a unique bouquet which often differs from one property to another. This wine goes well with "foie gras" of goose or duck, prepared the simple way or with, say, grapes or wild mushrooms. It is also a dessert wine and, of course, has also been used for baptism.

FOR FURTHER
DETAILS

Geology

Geological guides (Masson, Paris): *Aquitaine occidentale* (Western Aquitaine) (1975), by M.Vigneaux et al., (see especially tours 3 and 12); *Pyrénées occidentales, Béarn, Pays basque* (Western Pyrenees, Béarn, Pays Basque) 1976 by A.Debourle and R.Deloffre (see especially tours 3, 6, 8 and 9).

Oenology

Doleris J.-A. (1920). — Le vignoble et les vins du Béarn et de la région basque (Vineyards and Wines of Béarn and the Basque Region), 55 p., at M.Massignac, bookseller in Pau, rue Henri IV.

Durquety M. (1960). — Le vignoble et la viticulture pyrénéens (Vineyards and Vine-Growing in the Pyrenean Region), *Le progrès agricole et viticole*, 77th Year, 153 and 154, Nos 9 to 15, 63 p.

Hillau J. (1975). — Un vignoble au Pays basque: l'appellation Irouléguy contrôlée (A Vineyard in the Pays Basque: the Appellation Contrôlée of Irouléguy), Cave coop. d'Irouléguy and Ec.sup.Ing. et Techn.Agric., Paris, Mémoire de fins d'études (End of course year book), 35 p.

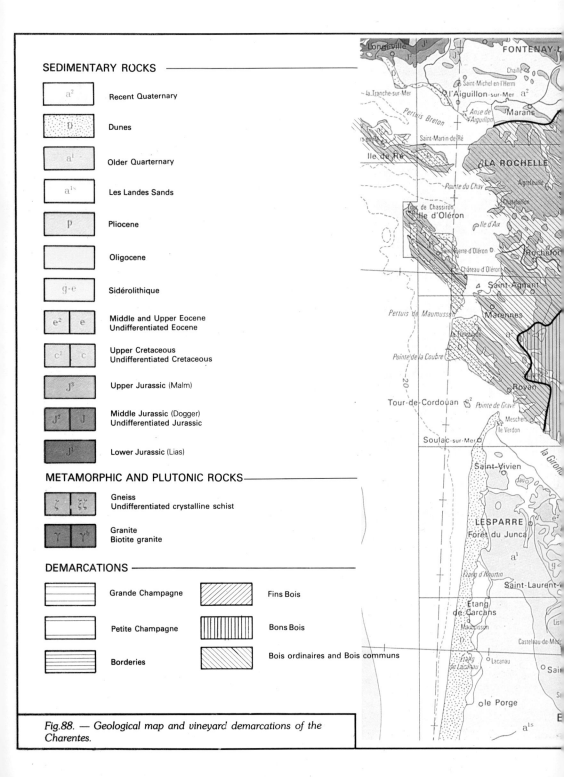

SEDIMENTARY ROCKS

a^2 — Recent Quaternary

D — Dunes

a^1 — Older Quarternary

a^{1s} — Les Landes Sands

p — Pliocene

— Oligocene

g-e — Sidérolithique

e^2 e — Middle and Upper Eocene / Undifferentiated Eocene

c^2 c — Upper Cretaceous / Undifferentiated Cretaceous

J^3 — Upper Jurassic (Malm)

J^2 J — Middle Jurassic (Dogger) / Undifferentiated Jurassic

J^1 — Lower Jurassic (Lias)

METAMORPHIC AND PLUTONIC ROCKS

ζ $\zeta\zeta$ — Gneiss / Undifferentiated crystalline schist

γ γ^b — Granite / Biotite granite

DEMARCATIONS

Grande Champagne

Petite Champagne

Borderies

Fins Bois

Bons Bois

Bois ordinaires and Bois communs

Fig.88. — *Geological map and vineyard demarcations of the Charentes.*

Vignobles des Charentes
Cognac et Pineau

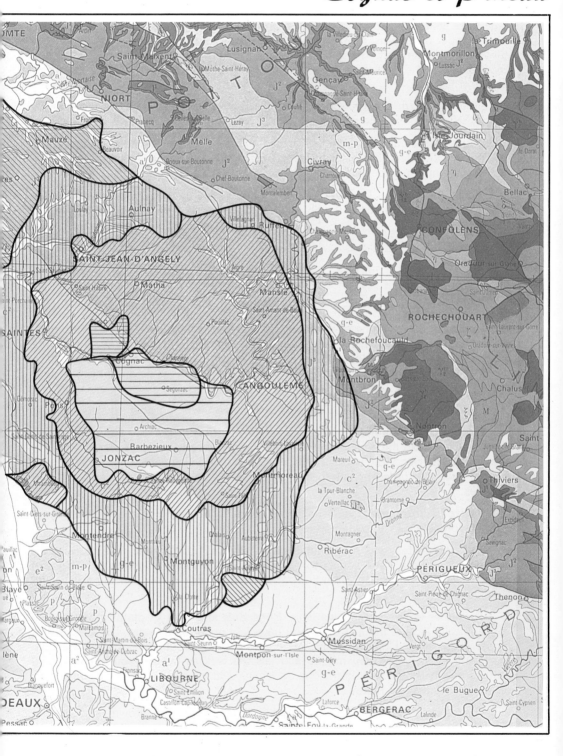

The vineyards of Charentes owe their fame to Cognac and Pineau. They are the natural outcome of bringing geology and human expertise together, representing the fruits of four centuries of experience combined with a full and profound understanding of vines and wines.

It was during the 16th century, in a climate of economic constraint and a slump in wine sales, that distillation was tried out for the first time. Charentes wine was in crisis for a number of reasons: problems with keeping because of its acidity, a low alcohol content, excess production and taxes on transportation. The situation was such that in 1636 a number of peasants took part in the "révolte des Croquants" (Peasants' Revolt).

From the 17th century onwards distillation developed, and trade in brandy supplanted the wine trade with Nordic and English-speaking countries.

In the 19th century, ageing techniques made it possible to improve quality and return to well-ordered harvesting. The market opened up in America and nowadays new market opportunities are arising in the Middle East and Southeast Asia.

More recently than Cognac, Charentes Pineau has seen the light of day in the area known as the Borderies (fig.88), by blending the juice of white grapes with old Cognac.

Vines and soils

Vineyards

Cognac is the outcome of three natural influences which have a combined effect on the vineyards: relatively moderate rainfall, temperatures which encourage the grapes to ripen without loss of aroma, and a soft, friable, calcareous soil which provides the vines with an even supply of water and develops a varied microflora of natural yeasts.

The exact limits of the six Cognac "crus" have been laid down by decree.

Grande Champagne consists mainly of the chalky facies of Campanian and Santonian age with the addition of limited outcrops of Conacian and Mesocretaceous age. This is the Segonzac region, between Cognac and Châteauneuf-sur-Charente. It has the lowest recorded rainfall in the Charente département and produces the best brandies.

Petite Champagne is very similar to Grande Champagne in geology, but enjoys a less favourable rainfall pattern.

The Borderies cover a limited area northwest of Cognac, with formations ranging in age from Cenomanian to Santonian. In the southeast these show signs of Tertiary decalcification. The brandy from these vineyards is mild on the palate and ages quickly.

The other three "crus", Fins Bois, Bons Bois and Bois Communs, are located concentrically around the first three and have less uniform sub-soils. These consist of Upper Cretaceous, Upper Jurassic, Middle Jurassic and Tertiary continental formations, and even Quaternary marine alluvials. As well as the sub-soils, climate also reduces quality. In the west this is due to oceanic factors, and in the east to influences of a more continental nature.

The main grape variety is the saint-émilion. Others are grown, such as the colombard, but in lower proportions.

Soils

There are various soil-types on the vineyards of Cognac.

- The *"terres de Champagne"* (Champagne clays) come from decalcification of the Campanian and Santonian argillaceous limestone, producing white and grey clays.

- The *"terres de groie"* (boulder clays) are red decalcification clays mixed with many calcareous fragments. These soils have developed on the Coniacian, the Middle and Upper Turonian, the Middle Cenomanian and the Middle Portlandian.

- The Borderies region is characterised by soils known locally as *"varennes"* ("wastes") and *"varennes-cailloux"* or *"griffées"* ("stony wastes" or "scratchies"). The Cretaceous horizons underwent incomplete decalcification during the Tertiary. The "varennes" are shallow soils, very differentiated and low in clay. They are loose, being sandy on the Lower Cenomanian and calcareous on the Turonian. The "griffées" are deep and fine sandy-clay soils containing flint fragments (the "stones" in the local name). They grow woods and silicicolous plants, and may be found mingled with a ferruginous clay called "brizard".

- A deep covering of *strong and undeveloped soils* overlies the Purbeckian clays in the Low Country north of Charente. This is the only region where the vineyards resisted the outbreak of phylloxera at the end of last century. Moisture and gypsum in the soil have been put forward as possible explanations.

Climate

The prevailing winds in Cognac and the surrounding region are moist, oceanic westerlies and northwesterlies. Wind speeds are below 21 km/h for more than half of the year, and exceed 36 km/h for 20 days a year or thereabouts. Temperature records for 1946-1980 show an annual average of 12.4°C. Monthly average temperatures for the same period show that September is as warm as June and October is nearly as warm as May. Records show that it rains for an average of 785 hours per annum, spread over 159 days of the year, with only 23 days of heavy rain and 116 days of average rainfall. Even in this respect the months of September and October appear to be especially favoured, with a very similar rainfall pattern to that of August.

Average sunshine was 2 234 hours per annum for 1956-1980, with 32 days of continuous sunshine and 46 sunless days. Finally, storms are observed on an average of 23 days a year.

These weather records emphasise the fact that the fine-weather season extends beyond the end of summer into early autumn (September-October). Such regional climatic trends obviously provide optimum ripening conditions for the grapes.

Distillation and ageing

The grapes are first crushed and then pressed once or even twice. The resulting must is put to ferment in casks or vessels holding as much as 200 hectolitres. The rapid vinification process yields a product which is quite high in acidity, but this is necessary for further fermentation and helps the liquor to keep until distillation.

The wine and its lees are then put through the first distillation, which produces the "brouillis", or "rough", with an alcohol concentration of 20° to 30°. A second pass, called the "bonne chauffe" (proper heating), raises the concentration to 72° and earns the Cognac appellation.

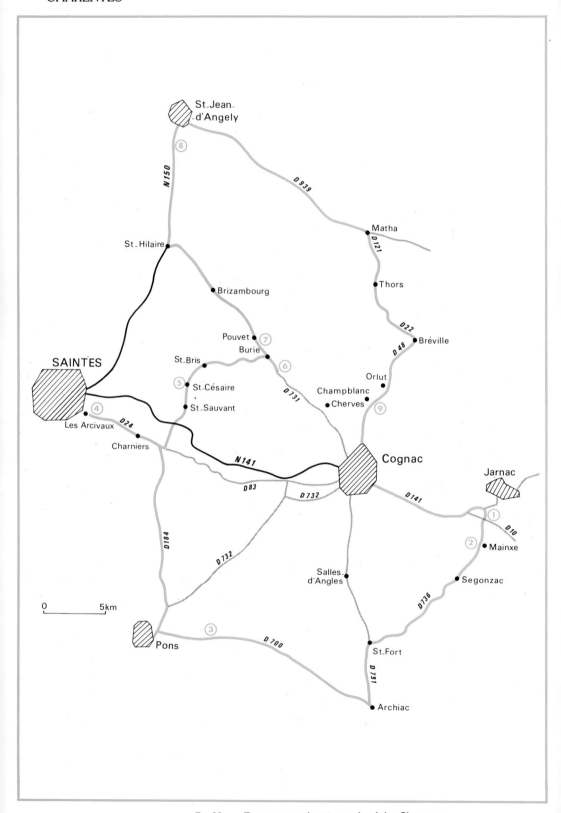

Fig.89. — Tour among the vineyards of the Charentes.

The still is required to have a boiler which may vary in shape but must be made of beaten copper, called a "cucurbit", a head and a cooling system surrounding a coil.

It produces a "White" (or rather, colourless) spirit which is somewhat bitter at this stage. It will become Cognac through ageing. This takes place in casks of Limousin oak. Exchanges take place between the brandy and the atmosphere through the wood, and between the wood and the brandy, which takes up some of its tannin. It is the tannin which gives the Cognac its golden yellow colour and its aroma.

The raw Cognacs are diluted by blending "crus" of different ages and vineyards, producing varieties and qualities of Cognac which are officially approved and certified (alcohol concentration: 45°).

The Fine Champagne quality is obtained by blending equal parts of both Grande and Petite Champagne.

Pineau is a blend of the best white grape musts and old Cognac from the Borderies vineyards. Pineau is aged, like Cognac, in casks of Limousin oak.

Itinerary

The route is deliberately kept to a short tour around Cognac. To gain a deeper insight into the Cognac region requires other elements to be taken into account, such as history, human geography, economic geography and so on. Such knowledge could be gained from a more thorough visit of the area. There are two essential tours: **Cognac,** naturally, the capital of the Charente vineyards, followed immediately by Cognac's second capital, **Jarnac.** These two towns are the production and marketing centres of the brandy trade, and the home of most of the famous labels. Along with these, the towns of Segonzac, Châteauneuf-sur-Charente and Barbezieux in the south and southwest, Rouillac in the northeast and Burie in the northwest represent the best producing regions, and give the best impression of the vineyards and soils (fig.89).

The morphology of the Cognac region

Leave Cognac by the D 141 towards Angoulême. The Coniacian limestone is hard and gravelly, forming large slabs which dip Southwestwards. The greater part of the formation is under vine, but it is still possible to see remaining traces of the original "chaume", or thin coppices of oak and holm-oak. The surface of this substratum consists of red, shallow till mixed with decalcification clays and large numbers of limestone fragments broken out of the 'banche', the slabby, weathered top of the Coniacian formation.

Stop beyond Le Veillard, at the junction with the N 736 ①, and observe the natural NE-SW sub-divisions. Working from north to south, we find the following succession of features (fig.90):

• A *Jurassic zone* with few undulations, in the north of Charente.

The Upper Portlandian is formed into wide, rounded monadnocks. These are plentifully covered in fine calcareous platelets or rhombic fragments, giving an arid impression.

The Low Country Purbeckian is a mixture of loose, marl and clay deposits containing gypsum, with thin interbeds of very fine crystalline or argillaceous limestone, known locally as 'platins' (flats). This formation makes its mark on the landscape as a moist depression occupied by the wide alluvial valley of the Charente.

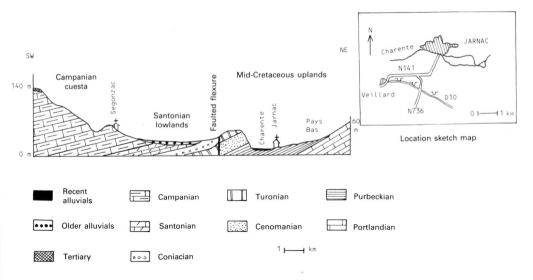

Fig.90. — The morphology of Jarnac in the Charentes region.

- A *Middle Cretaceous upland,* first appearing as a steep slope above the river. The N 736 first cuts into marly limestone, then into coarse bioclastic limestone of Lower Cenomanian age. It then cuts through fine Middle Cenomanian rudistid-bearing limestone and lastly through layers of Late Cenomanian age, bearing pycnodonti. The route then intersects the D 10. There are several quarries by the road here (Brandard, Abbaye, Grand Fief) showing gravelly and recrystallised limestones of Late Turonian age underlying sandstone of the basal Coniacian, with a dip of 45 to 50°. The latter is the result of a faulted flexure which is a major element in the Upper Cretaceous regional structure.

- A *varied Cenonian morphology* comprising: a gentle Coniacian slope immediately south of the D 10, resulting from tailing out of the flexure; a Santonian depression, or Petite Champagne; a series of Campanian cuestas, or Grande Champagne, consisting of a succession of gentle hills cleanly dissected by the valleys.

The Champagne Campanian

Driving towards **Segonzac** on the D 736, the route first takes us through Mainxe across a significant alluvial cap of the Charente middle terrace. This may be seen in the old gravel-pits of Chez Prévost and Semeronne ②. On the surface is a white loessic silt which has yielded carved flints. It covers quartz and limestone gravel, sand and pebbles of quartz and eruptive rocks. These alluvials have yielded carved flints and the remains of large mammalian fauna.

Between Segonzac and **Saint-Fort-sur-le-Né** the tour runs through strata of Campanian age, which alternates monotonously between greyish white limestone with a soft, chalky, frost-shattered consistency, and, in the middle part of the formation, small faults with black siliceous matter.

From Saint-Fort, follow the D 731 as far as the outskirts of Archiac and take the right fork, onto the D 700 towards Pons. We are very soon in the upper part of the Campanian, consisting of clay-chalk limestone and gravelly, bioclastic facies, which may be seen near Echebrune ③.

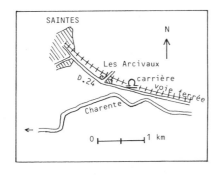

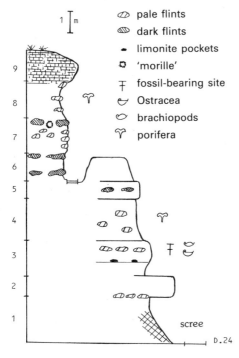

Fig.91. — Cross-section at Les Arcivaux.

1. Friable, off-white limestone with a clear band of flints in the upper section (at the entrance to the underground quarry; 2. Identical facies forming the roof of the underground quarry; 3. Highly frost-weathered argillaceous limestone with a bed of flints in the upper section and small, limonite-bearing rocks at about mid-section (the upper section is fossil-bearing: Rhynchonella vespertilio vespertilio, Rh. difformis, Pycnodonta vesicularis, Arcostrea zeilleri, Exogyra plicifera, plentiful bryozoa; ammonites have also been reported); 4. Horizons of isolated flints and generally silicified sponges; 5. Limestone bank with an unbroken bed of dark flints; 6. White argillaceous limestone, then limestone itself, with an unbroken bed of large dark flints in its upper section; 7. Highly frost-weathered white limestone with isolated rounded flints (in its upper section is a bed of pale flints, above which is an unbroken bed of large dark flints and 'morilles' in the form of geodes; 'morilles' are small, pale, corrugated flinty inclusions — chalcedony - generally smaller than a fist, and better known in their redistributed state in alluvials and soils); 8. Yellowish-white, frost-weathered limestone with rounded flints and sponges; 9. Layered, jointed white limestone.

The Saintes Santonian

Just before Pons, take the N 732 towards Cognac as far as Bougneau. Then take the D 134 towards Saintes. The road rejoins the D 24 just before Chaniers and we reach Saintes via Les Arcivaux. Stop on the edge of the town ④ to examine the Santonian cliff skirting the hill (fig.91; see also *'Guide géologiqe Poitou, Vendée, Charentes'* — Guide to the Geology of Poitou, Vendée and Charentes, page 51).

The Saint-Césaire Upper Turonian and Coniacian

Return towards Cognac on the D 24, as far as the crossroads to the east of Chaniers, and turn left towards Saint-Bris-des-Bois Saint-Césaire on the D 134, following the course of the Coran valley. The **Saint-Césaire** quarries provide a composite cross-cut through the valley ⑤. The most complete cross-section is to be found on the left bank. The site can be visited by permission. Apply at the office on the opposite side of the road (see *'Guide géologiqe Poitou, Vendée, Charentes'* — Guide to the Geology of Poitou, Vendée and Charentes, page 49 and fig.34).

Four sequences of lithology and fauna are in evidence:

• The lowest part of the quarry contains Upper Turonian horizons of soft and gravelly white limestone, in banks many metres thick which are quite massive in places. Thin beds or platy layers are interbedded in several parts of the formation.

• A formation of Early Coniacian age overlies the Turonian, separated from it by a banding of oxidized glauconitic clay some centimetres or decimetres thick, marking the discontinuity. The formation is arenaceous and massive (8 metres), varying from a greenish to a yellowish hue depending on the degree of oxidation, with cross-bedded zones, indurated nodules and localised concretions, especially at the top. The sand is an excellent raw material for glass.

• The Middle Coniacian forms a limestone cliff some dozen metres thick, with banks varying from thick to massive, and zones containing nodules. Karstification has developed fissures and washouts, filled with flinty clay originating from decalcification during the Santonian.

• The Upper Coniacian is represented by 5 metres of soft, frost-cracked limestone, somewhat argillaceous and glauconitic, with platy inclusions. There are remains of sea urchins, bryozoa and in particular a horizon of oyster-bearing shelly limestone.

The Middle and Lower Cenomanian can be seen between Burie and Brizambourg. It consists of sand, together with limestone bearing rudists and prealveolinae. Return to **Burie** on the N 131 as far as the N 731 crossroads. Turn right towards Cognac for 500 metres as far as the former Burie railway station. At a place called Malakoff, a quarry for road-building materials cuts into the Middle Cenomanian layers bearing rudists and prealveolinae ⑥.

The quarry reveals a series of chalky, medium-thick calcareous banks, broken by large numbers of uneven and erratic internal joints locally forming deep clefts. The hard outer layer is uniform and crystallised into fine sparite, although some lower levels in the formation exhibit slightly coarser-grained horizons. The featured elements are bioclastic remains, small gravel fragments (pelletoids) and foraminifera (see 'Guide géologiqe Poitou, Vendée, Charentes' — Guide to the Geology of Poitou, Vendée and Charentes, page 47).

Continue on the N 731 towards Burie. Stay on that road to the outskirts of Pouvet village, then turn right towards Peu Deis butte ⑦. Temporary sand-workings have uncovered detrital horizons of Lower Cenomanian age which can be seen here, working from bottom to top, as the following layers: yellow sand; lamellar clay; marl with calcareous nodules; and at the very top, platy limestone with exogyrae and orbitolinae.

The Upper Jurassic.
Saint-Jean-d'Angély to Rouillac and Cognac

To reach Saint-Jean-d'Angély take the D 371 as far as the crossroads for Saint-Hilaire-de-Villefranche and turn right onto the N 150. Between Saint-Jean-d'Angély and Rouillac, the Cognac vineyards are generally planted on the most carbonaceous of the terminal Jurassic formations.

Here the Kimmeridgian formations are about 300 metres thick and consist of two distinct units:

• The *Lower Kimmeridgian* is represented by a thick carbonate bar locally terminated by biogenic deposits.

• The *Upper Kimmeridgian* consists of marl facies composed of bioclastic and argillaceous limestones in association with grey marl.

About fifteen kilometres northwest of Saint-Jean-d'Angély, at a place called Les Chênaies (district of Bernay), these formations are exposed in a roadcut of the N 139. The terminal Kimmeridgian alternates between compact banks of bioclastic limestone, then argillaceous limestone, and lastly marls with lamellibranchs and ammonites. The most typical outcrops of this formation are to be found on the site of the old railway track, south of Saint-Jean-d'Angély, in the Fossemagne, Petite-Clie and Château-Gaillard cuttings ⑧.

The *Portlandian* formations comprise four main units, exhibiting lateral facies variations. The base of the stage, between Angoulême and Rouillac, is taken up by about twenty metres of oolitic and bioclastic limestones bearing nerineae. This formation is capped by a limestone bar containing gravesiae (cephalopods) about thirty metres thick, within which fine-grain limestone alternates with argillaceous limestone, with numerous bioclastic horizons. The fauna consists essentially of lamellibranchs (*corbula, cardium, mytilus, arca, cyrena,* etc.) and cephalopods (*gravesia*), concentrated mainly at the base of the formation. The best outcrops of gravesia-bearing limestone are to be found to the south of Saint-Jean-d'Angély, in the railway cuttings of La Renardière and Roumagnolle.

Above, a pre-evaporitic facies characterised by abundant corbulae, consisting of white, platy limestone with a chalky, fine-grained, slightly argillaceous consistency, alternates with banks of foliated, lamellar limestone with burrows.

Lastly, the terminal Jurassic regression is marked by deposits of green and black argillites with evaporitic interlayering (Purbeckian facies).

From Saint-Jean-d'Angély, take the D 939 to Matha and turn back towards Cherves-de-Cognac on the D 121 as far as Thors. Then take the D 121e from Thors to Bréville, and finally the D 48 (signposted Cognac) as far as Orlut. South of the village is the Champblanc gypsum quarry ⑨. Ask at the Garandeau premises for permission to visit.

Details of the formations appear in the '*Guide géologiqe Poitou, Vendée, Charentes*' (Guide to the Geology of Poitou, Vendée and Charentes). The reader is recommended to refer to tour No 2 on pages 45 and 46. In summary, the Purbeckian formation exhibits at this point two masses of granular gypsum associated with the fibrous variety, interbedded with layers of marl, including a bank of grey to black marls which quarrymen call 'soapstone'.

The lithological diversity of the Kimmeridgian and Portlandian formations moulds the morphology of the region into a gently contoured series of depressions, cuestas and plateaux. The gravesia-bearing and platy limestones of the Cognac region give rise to a gently undulating, tabular and dry landscape which slopes gradually towards the southwest, whereas the gypsum marls make their presence felt in the form of the wet Low Country depression (Pays-Bas).

Cognac and gastronomy

Cognac can be drunk at any stage of a meal, depending on the tastes of the diner, even with specialities from outside the region. It is used as a flavouring in many different kinds of sauce.

Before going to your table, you can rely on a red or white Pineau to give your appetite an edge.

Many entrées are all the better for the taste of Cognac, especially pâtés and pies: pâtés such as grouse, small game birds (perhaps served "en croûte à la rabelaisienne"), woodcock with foie gras (maybe "à la Fine Champagne"), hare with truffles, duck epicure, terrine of hare, game pies "à la vosgienne", etc.

In seafood you have a choice of prawns in a Cognac sauce; lobster soufflé, broth or timbale "Moitrier"; coquilles Saint-Jacques "à l'armoricaine"; crayfish "à la crême", in "Hippocampe" (sea-horse) pastry boats or on toast with sauce cardinal;

'obster "à la crême", gratiné "de Dunkerque" or "en Demoiselles de Cherbourg à la ~age".

Cognac also helps to bring out the flavour of certain types of fish, such as fillet of sole "Syda", bream "à la batelière" or supreme of pike "à la dijonnaise".

Cognac really comes into its own, however, in the company of poultry, meat and game, when it is in the highest traditions of French culinary art and at the pinnacle of gastronomic appreciation.

We can then recommend: braised duckling with Poitou turnips or new peas; chicken "flambé au Cognac"; gamy or stuffed guinea-fowl; Bresse chicken braised or served with rice; stuffed chicken in a traditional stew (daube); chicken "Archiduc" (Archduke) or "Belle Meunière"; "coq au blanc" (chicken in white wine) "gratiné à la Charentaise". You might try: beef "à la mode" or "à la bourguignonne"; braised rump steak; tournedos Marie; calves' kidneys "bourbonnais" or "flambé à la forestière"; sauté of young goat "chasseur"; leg of mutton; braised calves' liver "à la Briade" or "à la Vénitienne". Lastly, there is also: ragout of woodcock or pheasant; quails on the spit or with grapes "Fine Champagne"; larks "Du Guesclin"; stuffed capercaillie with foie gras; pheasant "Bellevue", "Charbonnière" or stuffed; small game birds on canapé; saddle of rabbit in tarragon or "Braconnière"; saddle of hare "à la crême" or with mulberries; rabbit "à la Duchambey" or "Mère Marie"; jugged hare in prunes; or partridge sausage "à la forestière".

Among vegetables, certain ways with mushrooms in Cognac have earned richly-deserved fame: truffles in Madeira; truffles surprise "à l'impériale"; and the delicious wild mushrooms in Cognac.

A number of desserts go well with Cognac: walnut slab, prune biscuit, gâteau "des rois de Bordeaux", cabinet pudding, pancakes, jam omelette, coffee cream, apple and rice meringue, fruit flambé.

After the meal, keep the Cognac bouquet on your palate by enjoying a Fine Champagne which you have warmed for a moment or two in a balloon glass cradled in the hollow of your hand. A most necessary precaution.

FOR FURTHER
INFORMATION

Geology

Guide géologiqe Poitou, Vendée, Charentes' (Guide to the Geology of Poitou, Vendée and Charentes) (1978), by J. Gabilly et al., Masson, Paris (see especially tour 2 by P. Moreau).

Coquand H. (1857). — Sur l'influence du sol dans la production des diverses qualités d'eau-de-vie (The Influence of the Soil on the Various Qualities of Brandy), *Bull. Soc. géol.* Fr., 14, p. 885.

Oenology

Coquillaud H. (1964). — Le Cognac, chef d'oeuvre du sol de France (Cognac, a Masterpiece of the French Soil), *Rev.géogr.industr.Fr.*, La Charente, No 69, pp. 78-82.

Lafond J., Couillaud P. and Gay-Belile F. — Le Cognac sa distillation (The Distillation of Cognac), Baillère, Paris.

Above: A cask some 500 years old (Photographs by courtesy of the Courvoisier, De Polignac and Hennessy companies).

Below: Modern copper still.

Above: Bending with the aid of heat. The cask is kept wet with a damp cloth called a 'vadrouille' (swab), and heated from within. The heat softens the wood and prevents the 'douelles' (staves) from splitting. The winch cable gradually draws the staves together, shaping the barrel in readiness for the hoops to be fitted. The hoops are positioned using a hammer and a 'chasse' (punch).

Below: A stack of casks in a traditional ageing store.

Facing page: A cross-section of plant growth at Château-Carnel (Côtes- de-Bourg) showing the root system of a vine in thick plateau loam (Photo. Duteau & Seguin).

SEDIMENTARY ROCKS

a^2 — Recent Quaternary	j^1 — Lower Jurassic (Lias)
a^1 — Older Quarternary	t^3 — Upper Triassic (Keuper)
v — Glacial deposits	t^1 — LowerTriassic
p — Pliocene	r — Permian
Miocene	h^4 — Stephanian
Oligocene	h^1 — Dinantian
e^2 e — Middle and Upper Eocene / Undifferentiated Eocene	d^2 d — Upper & Middle Devonian / Undifferentiated Devonian
J^2 J — Middle Jurassic (Dogger) / Undifferentiated Jurassic	

METAMORPHIC AND PLUTONIC ROCKS

Micaschist / Sericite schist / Chlorite schist, phyllite, hornfels	M — Migmatite
Gneiss / Undifferentiated crystalline schist	γ — Anatectic granite
Amphibolite	γ γ^b — Granite / Biotite granite

VOLCANIC ROCKS

Quaternary

ρ^4 τ^4 α^4 — Rhyolite, trachy-andesite, andesite	Andesiteejecta
Basalt and labradorite	Basalt and labradorite
Basaltic ejecta	Phonolite

Tertiary

ρ τ α — Rhyolite, trachy-andesite, andesite

Palaeozoic and Precambrian

Devonian and Carboniferous tuff

Saint-Pourçain

Appelations from north to south:
Côtes d'Auvergne
1 Châteaugay   3 Corent
2 Chanturgue   4 Boudes

Châteaumeillant (see Loire Valley)

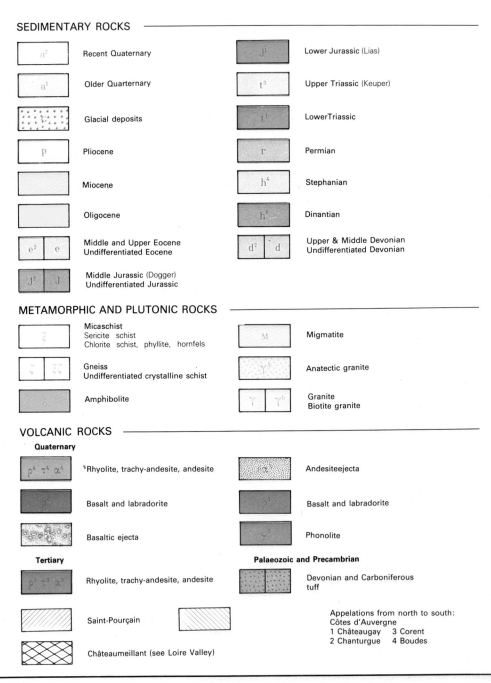

Fig.92. — Geological map and vineyard demarcations of Bourbonnais and Auvergne.

Bourbonnais et Auvergne

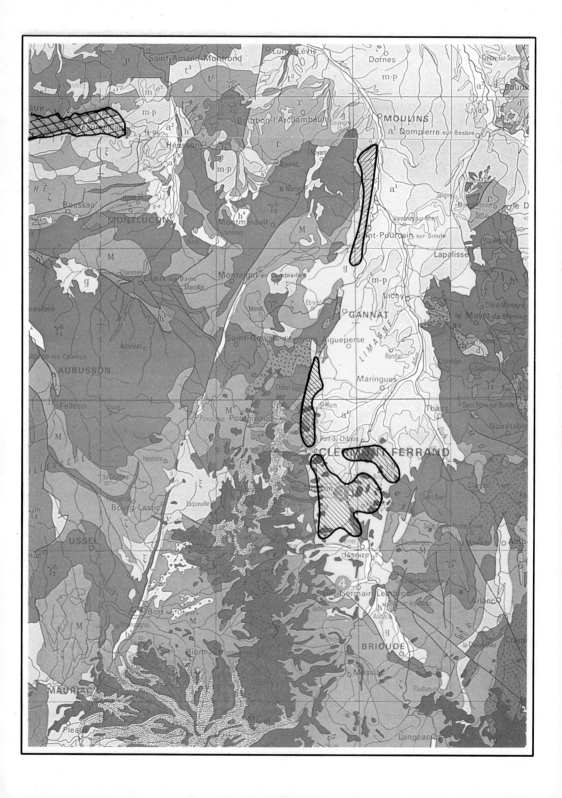

As long ago as the Middle Ages, the link between the extremely diverse vineyards of the Bourbonnais, the Auvergne and the Pays de Loire was the waterway using the river Sioule, the Allier and the Loire.

The Auvergne and Bourbonnais regions are known as the Limagne, and wines from here were already highly thought of by the Romans. Saint-Pourçain is the best-known wine from the area. Its popularity reached a peak in the 13th and 14th centuries. It was supplied to the royal household, enjoyed great prestige with the aristocracy and, like spices, even had value as a currency. In addition to these red wines verging on brown, the Saint-Pourçain vineyard produced "delicate white wines which were mainly harvested, in the 16th century, near the confluence of the Sioule and the Allier, around the river port of La Chaise, from where they were brought to Paris" (Dion).

Vines and soils

The wines of the Auvergne and Bourbonnais regions (VDQS) are produced in the Limagne, a rift valley some 140 km long, drained by the Allier, between Brioude and Moulins (fig.92). Like the Rhine gorge or the Rhône-Saône corridor, the hillsides along its edges carry vineyards. These tend to be on the western side, sheltered from the west winds by the crystalline plateaux and volcanic uplands which rise above the area, keeping rainfall relatively low. The Saint-Pourçain vineyards are here, and further south are those of the Côtes d'Auvergne (Châteaugay, Chanturgue, Corent and Boudes).

A visit to the vineyards of the Auvergne and Bourbonnais regions will help us find out about the main sequence of Tertiary formations in the Limagne. A brief insight into how the geology of the region evolved during that period would therefore be a useful forerunner to the tour.

Towards the end of the Eocene the region was at the stage of a flattened crystalline massif. The climate was tropical, and the area was covered in lateritic clays, the "red earths", or palaeosols, of the regional Sidérolithique phase. These soils occasionally occurred in situ, but were more often somewhat reworked. The Oligocene sediments were laid down later, after the formation of the Limagne fault trench.

During the early Miocene (Aquitanian) the Bourbonnais part of the Limagne (the region around Moulins and Saint-Pourçain) still contained lakes in which travertine and limestone with phryganeae (the caddis-fly, similar to the dragon-fly; its larvae surround themselves with a limestone tube) were deposited and reefs of biohermal limestone were being built among the more marly or arenaceous sediments. Also in the Bourbonnais region, towards the end of the Miocene and during the Pliocene, a vast expansion of fluvio-lacustrine formations deposited the Bourbonnais Sands and Clays which cap the hillslopes in the Moulins area.

Further south, in Auvergne, the geology of the area was subject to volcanic influences. In the Limagne it gave rise to numerous flows of alkaline basalt, with ages ranging from 20 to 12 million years. These have now been exposed as plateaux by recent erosion, which has largely cleared the softer Tertiary sediments from the surrounding areas. Also of Miocene age is peperino, composed of lava mixed with sedimentary material, described in greater detail in connection with the Châteaugay vineyard.

Although there was less volcanic activity in the Limagne during the Pliocene, it still gave rise to the Corent plateau, known today for its wines (see *'Guide géologique Massif central'* — Guide to the Geology of the Massif Central).

Lastly, the Quaternary volcanoes of the Puys Range arose along a zone of fractures running parallel to and west of the Limagne. They were first active about 30 000 years ago, their main period of activity occurring between 13 000 and 7 500 years ago (established from carbon-14 dating of charred wood).

Itineraries

The Saint-Pourçain vineyards

Travelling southward up the valley of the Allier, on the N 9 from Moulins, we find the terraces and alluvial plain flanked on the west by hills and plateaux of Oligo-Miocene sediments. A few kilometres further westward still, these overlie the Tréban Granite, marking the edge of the crystalline plateaux. The first of the vineyards are planted on these sedimentary hillslopes in the neighbourhood of Chemilly, extending in a broken line southwards towards Montord, 2.5 km west-southwest of Saint-Pourçain. The total area under vine is 1 000 to 1 200 hectares. The first wines produced here were rosés and the dry, supple, brilliantly clear whites, recently improved by the addition of sauvignon. More recently there has been a trend towards producing a light and fruity red from a combination of the gamay and pinot varieties. This, like the other wines of the Limagne, is a worthy companion to "coq au vin", which is claimed to have originated in the Auvergne (Clos Jouve).

Some of the vines, around Chemilly and Besson, are planted on the cover of the Bourbonnais Sands and Clays, especially on the pebbly sands which occur near the base of this formation and overlie the calcareous formations of Oligo-Miocene age.

Around Saint-Pourçain the vineyards are on the upper, wholly lacustrine levels of the Rupelian and Aquitanian formations. Here we find marly and arenaceous detrital layers, but the most spectacular and specific facies are the reefs of travertine containing phryganeae and concretions of algae. These hard bodies of rock crown the peaks of the landscapes in which they occur, and the hillsides are cultivated with vine. Underlying and surrounding formations are more akin to marl. These crop out quite rarely, and contain detrital intercalations as well as banks of limestone with concretions.

The vines grow, in fact, on hillside colluvial deposits containing the remains of reef formations from the edge of the plateau, whilst the more marly sub-soil in situ comprises the matrix. Reef limestone used to be extracted for commercial purposes, but the quarries are now falling into disuse. One of these (run by the firm of SICHO) is still operating about a kilometre southwest of Gannat.

Châteaugay and Chanturgue

Continuing south on the N 9 we pass Riom and enter the volcanic region of the Auvergne. About twelve kilometres to the west, the recent Puys range forms the skyline. Closer to hand, on the right, looms the Châteaugay plateau, then the Côtes de Clermont, the Puy de Var and the Puy de Chanturgue. All of these uplands are capped with ancient basalt and planted with well-known vineyards.

The village of **Châteaugay** is easily recognised from far away by its castle tower. It is built on the edge of the plateau, where the wind-swept surface of the terminal Miocene basalt carries very few vines. These tend to be on the southeastern slopes, with their relatively complex geological structure. The substratum actually consists of marls underlying lacustrine marly limestone of Rupelian age. Between the latter and the lava flow, however, are intercalations of red feldspar sands (spread out during the Miocene) topped by green clays. Elsewhere, in and below the village, this formation is crossed by a sizeable mass of "peperino".

Peperinos in general are composed of granules of vitreous basalt (which look like grains of pepper, whence the name) and larger fragments of the same, in a matrix of sedimentary material. In the Limagne generally, this matrix is usually marl, but at Châteaugay it is a sandy marl with many grains of quartz and white feldspar measuring a few millimetres across.

The peperino formation at Châteaugay is partly covered by the terminal lava flow. An outcrop of peperino may conveniently be observed on the road from Cébazat, 200 metres before the junction with the Pompignat road (D 15E). Peperino may also be seen under the lava flow, between the castle keep and the northern part of the village. Cellars have been hewn into this formation, which is not too hard but long-lasting. Outcrops can also be seen along a rocky ridge in the vineyard 500 metres east of the outcrop first mentioned.

The soil on which the vines stand is of a fairly composite nature. It is a gravity deposit of mixed components which vary in proportion depending on the weathering rate of the rocks and the downhill creep rate of the debris. The mixture contains a marl-limestone cement; grains of sand and feldspar from the feldspar sands or the peperinos; granules and fragments of lava from the latter; and small pieces of basalt which have fallen from the terminal flow. The result is a brown, fairly loose soil with not too much clay.

Urban development is continually nibbling away at the territory of the **Chanturgue** vines, on the very outskirts of Clermont-Ferrand. They are still there, though, above the brand-new houses, on the eastern slopes of the Puy de Var in the north and the Puy de Chanturgue in the south, separated by a local fault. Their situation is similar to that of Châteaugay (without the peperinos), since they too are standing on marl-limestone slopes beneath Miocene basalt, with intercalations of feldspar sands which reach 25 metres in thickness at Chanturgue. At the Puy de Var there is another alkaline basalt flow, separated from the first by about twenty metres of flint sand (chert) of Late Miocene age. The soil in which the vines are planted is also a colluvial mixture of fragments including marl-limestone and especially basalt in a mainly marly matrix.

Corent

The Corent Plateau is famous for, amongst other things, its rosé wine. The plateau dominates the Allier valley, 15 kilometres to the southwest of Clermont-Ferrand. It is capped by a basalt flow. This carries on its southwestern part a cinder cone which has been very eroded and stunted with time, its rim slightly breeched in the northeast, and incised in the south by a large quarry. The elevation of the flow above the Allier and radiometric potassium-argon dating of an amphibole in the cinder cone (3 million years) assign these formations to the Pliocene.

The formations on which the vine slopes stand are of Rupelian age, and relatively shallow. The basic arkose crops out on the banks of the Allier, upstream of the bridge across the river, north of Longues.

This arkose can be observed, along with a spring of sparkling mineral waters, at the fountain of Saint-Jean on the north bank of the Allier. It stands 125 metres upstream of the railway bridge, almost below the power lines as it crosses the river (access is via a narrow track which goes left from the route des Martres-de-Veyre, 250 metres northeast of the Longues bridge). See also the *'Guide géologique Massif central'* - Guide to the Geology of the Massif Central — 2nd edition, page 99.

Overlying the arkose are about a hundred centimetres of yellow, somewhat sandstone-like marl-limestone, interbedded with lamellar marl containing Cypris and some gypsum horizons. This lagoonal facies of Rupelian age has marine affinities. The formation above the lagoonal facies consists of lacustrine marl and limestone containing lymnaea, of Late Rupelian age. Fragments of it are sometimes turned up by the plough, especially on the eastern slope, but outcrops are rare.

On the flanks of the Corent Plateau, the steep gradients and the marly nature of the substratum have enabled slabs of basalt to slide down the slopes from the uppermost table. Some small and disjointed ones may be seen on the northern slope, but the largest (one of them is over 100 metres long) are to be found on the lower eastern slope. There is an old quarry at this point which can be reached from a track leading southwest from the hairpin-bend on the D 8 between Corent and Longues.

The soil in the vineyards around the plateau is yet another colluvial mixture of marl-limestone material, with variable proportions of limestone fragments and basalt derived from the scree of the upper table or the breakdown of the sliding slabs. These processes have formed a loose, calcareous and argillaceous soil which is saved from being too compact by the admixture of pebbly fragments.

Boudes

No rapid review of the Auvergne vineyards would be complete without the vineyard of Boudes. Once famous and flourishing, it was badly affected by the phylloxera outbreak but is now regaining its rightful place thanks to concentrating on quality. It now covers about fifty hectares, producing rosé wines, as well as reds based on the gamay variety with occasional additions of pinot. This vineyard deserves a return to its former importance.

Boudes is situated four kilometres west of Saint-Germain-Lembron and some 36 km south of Clermont-Ferrand as the crow flies. The little district of Lembron is known, in the geology of the region, for its development of red clays (Sidérolithique).

A short walk in the valley of the Saints is rewarded by the sight of some spectacular outcrops of this material, a kilometre west-southwest of Boudes. They have been eroded into pointed pinnacles which, with imagination, look like gigantic statues (giving the valley its name). To reach the spot, make your way through the narrow, mediaeval village streets, cross the bridge, take the track on the left 100 metres beyond the cemetery, stay on it for 500 metres and then take a pathway off to the left which goes down towards the valley floor.

The greater part of the vineyard is on the slope north of Boudes, with an excellent south-facing position. The sub-soil consists of distinctly banded red and green clays with some sandy horizons and some banks of pink crystalline limestone a few tens of centimeters thick. At this point we are near the base of the Rupelian formation, where lateritic siderolitic clays are being reworked whilst their variegated colours are retained. It outcrops in recent cuttings and trenches.

The slope is capped with a basalt flow forming an elongated plateau (inversion of the topography). This originally flowed from the Leiranoux volcano (sometimes called the "volcan des Ranoux") about ten kilometres to the west. The vine slopes are covered with one or two metres of colluvial deposits with a fairly loose marl-limestone matrix, containing blocks of harder limestone and fragments of basalt from the upper slopes. This mixed formation overlies variegated clays but is well drained on account of the gradient, giving a soil which suits vines perfectly.

The cliff of Turonian micaceous and yellow tufas at Rochecorbon with its crowning lantern tower (Photo. Macaire).

SEDIMENTARY ROCKS

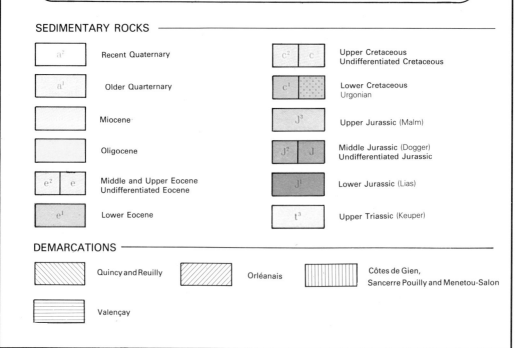

a²	Recent Quaternary
a¹	Older Quarternary
	Miocene
	Oligocene
e² e	Middle and Upper Eocene Undifferentiated Eocene
e¹	Lower Eocene

c² c	Upper Cretaceous Undifferentiated Cretaceous
c¹	Lower Cretaceous Urgonian
J³	Upper Jurassic (Malm)
J² J	Middle Jurassic (Dogger) Undifferentiated Jurassic
J¹	Lower Jurassic (Lias)
t³	Upper Triassic (Keuper)

DEMARCATIONS

Quincy and Reuilly	Orléanais	Côtes de Gien, Sancerre Pouilly and Menetou-Salon
Valençay		

Fig.93. — Geological map and vineyard demarcations of the Pouilly, Sancerre, Quincy and Orléans districts.

Val de Loire
Berry et Orléanais

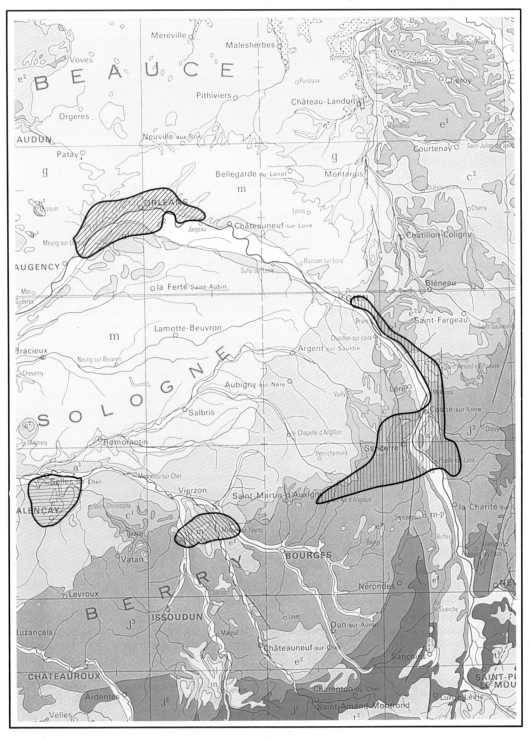

The vineyards of the Loire Valley cover about 42 000 hectares, producing around 1 500 000 hectolitres of wine a year. Some 90 per cent of this is from a named appellation (AOC and VDQS). The vineyards are located in the south and southwest of the Paris Basin and the southern central section of the Armorican Massif, lying on either side of the Loire and along the lower reaches of some of its tributaries, such as the Loir, the Cher, the Vienne, the Layon or the Sèvres-Nantaise (fig.93 and 96).

After the intense cold of the final Quaternary glaciation, the wild vine reappeared in the pollen diagrams about 5 500 years ago, during the Atlantic phase of the Holocene (Planchais, 1972).

The earliest indications of viticulture in the Loire Valley date back to Gallo-Roman times. In the 5th and 6th centuries, vine growing developed around the abbeys, for example the abbey of Saint Mesmin in the Orléans region or Saint Martin's at Tours. The monks produced wine for religious and medicinal use. Gregory of Tours (6th century), in his 'History of the Franks', tells of the natural and human calamities which befell the vineyards of Anjou and Nantes.

The expansion and destiny of the vineyards then became subject to the whims of commerce (Dion). The Loire, which was navigable until the turn of the century, played a key role in encouraging the introduction of new vine varieties and transporting wines for the export trade.

The very ancient vineyards of Sancerre and Orléans were truly famous. Wines made from the auvernat variety (pinot noir), with echoes among the wines of Bourgogne, were transported by cart to Paris and Flandres. Wines of Anjou, made from chenin or cabernet, went mainly to Brittany, Normandy and by sea to England. Its position on the map did not favour exports from Touraine, which had difficulty selling its production.

Writers and poets of the 16th century Renaissance, such as Rabelais, Ronsard and du Bellay, came from the region, and were inspired by the delicate, subtle but also fortifying qualities of the wines to write in praise of their many virtues.

In the 17th and 18th centuries, the consumption of wine amongst the people in France increased. Foreign trade was principally with the Dutch. The latter purchased not only quality white wines, but also wines for everyday drinking and eaux-de-vie. Wine growing adapted to demand and evolved differently depending on the situation of the vineyard.

In the districts of Orléans and Blois, quality wines gave ground to ordinary wines for the Parisian market, and had ceased to find favour with royalty from the time of King Henry IV onwards. The districts of Touraine (Vouvray) and Anjou (Coteaux du Layon), situated upstream of the Ingrandes-de-Bretagne customs barrier, supplied the Dutch with some celebrated wines. Down river in the Nantes region, a variety known as the "melon de Bourgogne" or muscadet was introduced, whilst the local variety, gros plant, was mainly used for making brandy.

In the 19th century, phylloxera dealt the coup de grâce to the vineyards of Orléans. The other wine-growing provinces were also attacked, but have recovered strongly in the 20th century. In the valley of the Cher, at Vouvray and Saumur, vinification has partially yielded to the fashion for fully sparkling wines which arose in the 17th century in Champagne. Muscadet, from the Nantes region, has grown in popularity.

In conclusion, it will be noticed that the vineyards of Touraine, and to a lesser extent Anjou, have made gradual progress, whereas those around Orléans and Nantes have, mainly for economic reasons, declined badly.

Vines and soils

Appellations

For close on 500 km between Sancerre and Nantes, the Loire generally runs through wine-growing districts where the landscape is dotted with châteaux. The three largest wine-growing areas, downstream of Blois, are Touraine, the Anjou-Saumurois region, and the Pays nantais (district of Nantes). They lie on either side of the river, and also along the lower reaches of its tributaries close to their confluence with the main stream (Cher, Vienne, Layon, Sèvre). Wines of AOC and VDQS status are produced here (fig.96). The vineyards of Orléanais, Giennois, Sancerre and Pouilly, in the immediate vicinity of the Loire, are its fourth great wine-growing region: Centre (Central Area) (fig.93). Though the vineyards are less extensive than in the other regions of the Loire, some of them produce very famous wines.

There are other accredited vineyards some distance from the Loire Valley proper, but associated with it because of the great similarity in their soils. In the Centre these include the appellations Châteaumeillant (VDQS) and Quincy (AOC); in Touraine the vineyards of Côteaux du Loir (AOC) and Coteaux du Vendômois (VDQS); and in Anjou, the VDQS estates of Haut-Poitou.

Because the vineyards are widely scattered, there is a great deal of variety in the wine produced in the Pays de la Loire. The wines of the Loire owe their reputation to certain high quality village appellations produced in a relatively restricted area (Sancerre, Vouvray, Bourgueil, etc), but the wines of the whole region have the common characteristic of being fresh, light and fruity with a good bouquet. There are many time-honoured appellations hereabouts, such as the "Noble Joué" from near Tours. Wine-growers are doing their utmost to ensure that such appellations continue to have their own separate identity.

The region produces mainly white and rosé wines. They range from the driest (Quincy, Sancerre, Muscadet du Pays nantais) to the sweetest and richest (Coteaux du Layon), with every level in between, such as the wines of Vouvray, Montlouis and Saumur. But Touraine and Saumur, too, have their great red wines, Chinon, Bourgueil, Saumur-Champigny. They represent about a fifth of the total production from the Loire Valley. Foaming or sparkling wines are also found in great number and variety, such as at Vouvray and Saumur.

To sum up, the Pays de la Loire produce not only wines for every stage of the meal from apéritif to dessert, but also thirst-quenching wines for drinking at any time.

Geology and soils

The wine-growing districts through which the Loire runs are flat or sometimes slightly undulating, at an average elevation of 100 metres. The most marked undulations occur in the hills around Sancerre, which can reach 350 metres. There are two very important factors giving rise to the diversity of wines, however. These are the geology of the formations on which the vineyards are planted, and the quality of the soils derived from them. Figure 96 shows that the formations divide into two quite distinct geological areas: the Armorican Massif in the west, and the Paris Basin in the east.

The Armorican Massif

Some of the vineyards of Anjou and the district of Nantes are located on eruptive, metamorphic and sedimentary rocks of Precambrian and Palaeozoic age. Their major

315

folds are attributed to the Cadomian and Hercynian Orogenies. The vineyard soils in this region are mainly leached brown, acid brown, leached or undeveloped (drift or erosion soils). The pebbles contained in the soil are in many cases dark, so that they store heat efficiently and encourage the grapes to ripen.

The Paris Basin

The vineyards of the Centre, Touraine, Saumur and Anjou are partly on Mesozoic and Cenozoic sedimentary formations of detrital or calcareous origins, overlying the basement which is several hundred metres or even over 1 000 metres below. The soils on these sedimentary formations are varied. In addition to the shallow erosion soils on the steep slopes where vineyards commonly occur, the prevailing types on calcareous source-rocks are rendzinas, brown calcareous soils and brown soils. Leached and podzolic soil types are frequent on siliceous rocks. Vineyards cover most of the formations and soils in the southern Paris Basin, except for the the Miocene formation in Sologne, where there is too much clay and moisture for growing quality wines.

Climate

The main features of wines from the Pays de Loire are due in large measure to the climate, which is temperate and moist overall. At Tours, the average annual temperature is 11 °C, ranging between 0 °C in winter and 25 °C in summer. Average annual rainfall is 650 mm, spread fairly evenly throughout the year, though early autumn is generally sunny. This favours late varieties such as the chenin blanc.

The climate changes subtly from west to east. It is oceanic, milder and moist during the autumn around Nantes, but has continental trends, with early frosts, around Sancerre. The micro-climates associated with the orientation of the hillsides also play a key role. This combination of factors explains the longitudinal zoning observed in the distribution of vine varieties.

Vines

Many grape varieties are grown in the Loire Valley. Some are specific to the region, and were developed from selecting the best of the vines which once grew wild near the river. Others were introduced at various times in the past from different regions of France (Guyenne, Bourgogne).

Chenin blanc or "pineau de Loire"

This is the Loire variety "par excellence". It is unknown elsewhere. It is especially widespread throughout Anjou and Touraine, where it gives some very well-known white wines (Coteaux du Layon, Vouvray, Jasnière). These are dry or mellow depending on the micro-climate, the harvesting method and the vinification technique. Chenin blanc is a late variety and relatively undemanding with regard to the soil. It is especially well suited to steeply sloping pebbly-clay soils formed from Senonian "clay with flints" (called locally "perruches") or to Palaeozoic shale-sandstone formations.

Sauvignon

This variety, too, may well have originated in the Loire Valley. It is an early variety, preferring climates with continental affinities. It is found above all in Centre vineyards where it yields the famous Sancerre white wines. Westwards it is scarcely found beyond the Touraine region. It prefers porous soils which warm up quickly, overlying either Jurassic limestone or Quaternary alluvials.

Muscadet or "melon de Bourgogne"

This was introduced to the Pays nantais from Bourgogne in the 17th century, and is now the chief variety of the district. It is virtually unknown in any other part of the Loire region. It is well suited to the oceanic climate. After an early harvest from a variety of soils it produces an abundance of light, white wine.

Gros plant or "folle blanche"

This long-established native of the Pays nantais prefers gravelly formations, giving low yields of a very pale, dry white wine.

Chasselas

Not a widely grown variety, though it occurs just about everywhere along the Loire, especially at Pouilly-sur-Loire where the continental trend in the climate suits it best. It produces white wine for early drinking.

Chardonnay

A quality white grape, originally from Bourgogne. It was once well known from the Loire Valley to Touraine, but has now all but disappeared from modern wine growing, and is found in appreciable quantities only around Orléans.

Cabernet franc

Because cabernet franc was introduced from the vineyards of Bordeaux via the ports of Lower Brittany, it is known locally as "breton". It occurs in many places all along the river, which forms the northern boundary of its range. It is found as far afield as Orléanais, but is at its best in Anjou and Touraine, where the late season is often sunny with low rainfall, giving ideal conditions for its late-ripening tendencies. Quaternary formations of gravelly, carbonaceous alluvial sand overlying Turonian tufa are its favourite domain. Cabernet franc produces some great, tannin-rich red wines noted for their fine bouquet (Chinon, Bourgueil, Champigny). It is also sometimes made into rosé.

Cabernet sauvignon

A relative of the previously mentioned variety, and often found in the same areas. It is used mainly in rosé wines.

Gamay

An early variety, this undisputed king of Beaujolais also occurs widely in the Pays de la Loire (Touraine, Giennois, Châteaumeillant), being at home in clayey soils with poor exposure which would be unsuitable for producing the best qualities. It makes red wines for early drinking.

Groslot

Planted mainly in Anjou and Touraine. It prefers sandy-gravelly formations and produces rosé wines (Rosé d'Anjou).

Côt

This excellent variety is better known as the malbec of the Bordeaux region. It is grown in Touraine to enhance certain red wines, or vinified as a rosé in conjunction with the groslot (Azay-le-Rideau).

Pineau d'Aunis or "chenin rouge"

Related to the chenin blanc, the pineau d'aunis is another typical variety of the Loire. Its range is virtually restricted to calcareous and argillo-siliceous slopes along the valley of the Loir, where it produces reds and rosés of a highly individual character.

Pinot noir

The Pays de la Loire have few remaining examples of the noble varieties from Bourgogne, though these were once grown in the Centre vineyards, especially in the Orléanais region. Sancerre red wines are the best exponents.

Gris meunier

This pinot variant has taken over from the pinot noir in Orléanais and at Châteaumeillant, where it is happy with various kinds of formations and is reasonably productive. It gives a light rosé known as "gris".

Pinot gris

Known in the Loire region as "malvoisie" (malmsey), this variety is also the tokay of Alsace. It is found in certain villages all along the Loire Valley and appears to have been ancestral to wine growing in the region. On its own, it produces a pinkish white wine. In association with gris meunier and pinot noir it makes a highly individual rosé, such as the "Noble Joué".

In addition to the large number of grape varieties, there is also a wide divergence of vinification methods in this region where wine-growers are noted for their individuality, and traditions are rooted in centuries of colourful history. This explains not only the many great "crus" but also the multitude of pleasing wines available under local labels.

It can be seen that the geological, pedological, climatic, biological and human factors involved in wine production in the Loire Valley are many and varied. For close on 2 000 years in some cases, these factors have been observed, filtered through experience, subtly combined, and adapted to economic necessities. This is why the resulting wines are of such value. They are part of a heritage rooted in history, combining the hard-working pragmatism of the peasant classes with the pomp of royalty.

Itineraries

There is no greater pleasure than to taste these wines on the spot where they were born. Five excursions are recommended below, taking the visitor to the main vineyards in the Loire Valley and examining their geological setting.

The sauvignon in Nivernais and Berry; the vineyards of Pouilly-sur-Loire, Sancerre and Quincy

The vineyards of Pouilly, Sancerre and Quincy are the best known in the Central France wine-growing region, which also includes the appellations Vins de l'Orléanais and Coteaux du Giennois of VDQS status, and the AOC Menetou-Salon and Reuilly.

The characteristic grape variety in the Berry and Nivernais districts is the sauvignon. It gives a vigorous and fragrant dry white wine which can be served not only with seafood and fish, but also with delicatessen sausage and certain other kinds of meat. For drinking 'in situ' it is usually accompanied by goat-cheese. The bouquet and flavour of wine made from the sauvignon differs from vineyard to vineyard. This is because the grape variety is quite sensitive to the way it faces the sun, and particularly responsive to the nature of the soil.

The climate of the region is temperate tending towards the continental, with greater seasonal contrast than in the western Loire Valley. The average temperature ranges between 26 °C in summer and -1 °C in winter. Rainfall varies between 600 and 800 mm depending on elevation, and the prevailing wind is from the northeast. Micro-climates dependent on the orientation of the hillslopes are extremely numerous.

The vineyards of Pouilly and Sancerre lie on each side of the Loire in the Nivernais district, in a region of picturesque hills around 350 metres high. This is the aureole contact zone between the Jurassic formations outcropping in the south and the Cretaceous beds situated in the north. The geology of the region is complicated by the presence of north-south faults which have caused a graben through which the Loire now flows.

The best soils are on the Kimmeridgian formations. They are calcareous, generally shallow and pebbly. There are also rendzinas or brown soils, depending on the steepness of the hillsides. Slopes which face east or southeast are not suitable because of the risk of early frost. The wines of Pouilly and Sancerre are outstanding for their distinctive fragrance and finesse.

The vineyards of Quincy are in the valley of the Cher, about 15 km upstream from Vierzon. The landscape is relatively free from undulations, its Jurassic beds concealed by the Berry lacustrine limestone of Eocene and Oligocene age. The wine-growing area covers mainly the Quaternary sands and alluvial pebble beds overlying the lacustrine formation. This means that the soils, which are siliceous and generally leached, differ greatly in nature from those around Sancerre. The sauvignon variety here gives a fresh, very dry wine with a more discreet bouquet than is the case with the Sancerre and the Pouilly.

The vineyards of Pouilly-sur-Loire

Pouilly-Fumé is derived from the sauvignon variety. Its fragrance is both "musky and spicy" (Bréjoux) and it ages well. It comprises about four-fifths of the production from Pouilly. Pouilly-sur-Loire is prepared from the chasselas variety, to which sauvignon is sometimes added. It is for drinking young, and is at its peak when grown on the Eocene argillo-siliceous soils, from which it acquires a flinty taste.

From Pouilly take the N 7 towards Cosne (fig.94). Just after leaving the town, turn left onto the D 153 in the direction of Les Loges. The road winds among vineyards standing on well-exposed slopes (facing west or southwest) consisting of marls and limestone bearing *Exogyra virgula,* of Late Kimmeridgian age. This is sauvignon country. Although the soils are pebbly on the surface, they are clayey and retain moisture fairly well. On the way down to the village of Les Loges, enjoy the magnificent view over the Loire Valley and the hills around Sancerre, consisting of Cretaceous and Eocene formations.

At Les Loges proceed under the railway bridge and continue by the D 243, which is on the right. The road follows the Loire. Beyond the level crossing, on the right, the vineyard spreads out across very fine crystalline Portlandian limestone. On the surface a fine, sandy fraction, carried on the wind from the alluvials of the Loire, mingles with the limestone fragments.

From Boisbigault follow the D 247 as far as the N 7 and head towards Pouilly. To the left of the road, notice Saint-Andelain hill, consisting of Kimmeridgian marl capped by siliceous Eocene scree. Just before Pouilly, at the intersection with the road for Les Loges, turn left onto the D 153 towards Saint-Andelain. As we climb the hill we leave behind the marly soils planted with sauvignon and come to siliceous soils more suited to the chasselas. Notice the scree (rounded flints and flinty fragments in an Eocene alluvial environment) among the vines near the cross as you reach the village ①.

From there take the turning on the right towards Le Bouchot. The vineyard is less dense on the eastern slope of the hill because of the risk of spring frost. On arriving at Le Bouchot, we leave the dark brown marly soils and come to drier, reddish-brown soils, called "caillotes" (clumps) formed by the breakdown of hard limestone of Middle Kimmeridgian age (*astarte limestone*). Then beyond Le Bouchot we meet very fine crystalline limestone of Early Kimmeridgian age (Tonnerre Limestone).

At Le Bouchot cross the D 25 and continue towards Garchy. Then return to Pouilly via the D 184.

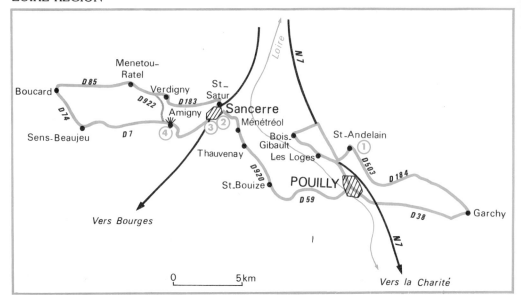

Fig.94. — Tour among the vineyards of the Pouilly and Sancerre districts.

The vineyards of Sancerre

We at once notice the attractive countryside around Sancerre, with its landscape of fairly steep hills and the Loire Valley. These features are due to the hillside (cuesta) formed by the Upper Jurassic strata to the west, and to two southerly faults (the Sancerre and Thauvenay Faults) which are the point of contact between the downthrown Cretaceous and Eocene formations in the east, and the Jurassic formations in the west (see 'Guide géologique Val de Loire' — Geological Guide to the Loire Valley — page 49).

The Sancerre region also owes its reputation to its vineyards (sauvignon and pinot noir grape varieties giving rosé and red). Then there is the town of Sancerre itself, with its medieval streets and gastronomic inns, adding to the attractions of the region.

Cross the Loire at Pouilly and follow the D 59, then take the D 920 towards Sancerre. The road follows the base of the western slope of the Loire Valley. Beyond Saint-Bouize, at Thauvenay, the route crosses the first of two faults. This one is the contact zone between the Albian sand and clay to the east and the Upper Kimmeridgian marl to the west.

On reaching the bridge over the canal at Ménétréol, turn left. Climb the eastern slope of Sancerre hill, which takes you past the church and under the viaduct, and a little further on, follow the signpost for Sancerre (D 307). In the village districts of Thauvenay and Ménétréol the marl and limestone (Upper Jurassic) which form the lower face of the slope are planted with vines, despite their relatively unfavourable exposure. The vineyards continue up to the Orme au Loup woods, standing on clayey sand formations of Lower Cretaceous age and on Cenomanian chalk and marl. The argillo-siliceous soils are better suited to pinot noir, and indeed to gamay or chasselas, here cultivated by the wine-growers for their own use, rather than sauvignon.

At the edge of the wood, on the right, is a track. Follow it to an old quarry ②, now being refitted, which has been opened up in the brown flinty clays of Upper Cretaceous age, just visible beyond the winch. Enjoy the attractive panorama over Sancerre, the Loire Valley and, towards the southeast, the Pouilly vineyards. Return to the road and keep climbing through the wood. Some 200 metres further on, take the second track on the right. Walk for 300 metres as far as another quarry being used for tipping ③. Above, in the wooded talus forming the upper face of the hill, notice the Eocene conglomerates. These show fragments of variously rounded flint in a sandstone-like, chalcedony-rich matrix. This material is very hard, and accounts for the inversion of the landscape (fig.95).

Return to the road, still heading towards **Sancerre.** On leaving the wood the road intersects the Sancerre Fault. The vines opposite and below towards the west are standing on limestone of Early Kimmeridgian age. A few hundred metres further on, turn left at the junction and then immediately right onto the road leading to the D 955.

Return towards Sancerre and after a short distance take the D 293 towards Menetou-Râtel. The road climbs the cuesta in the Jurassic formations. About a kilometre beyond the Amigny road you will see a magnificent panoramic view of the entire Sancerre wine-growing area ④. Looking from west to east we can observe the following (fig.95):

— The edge of the plateau, consisting of hard Portlandian limestone. This area is used for growing cereals. There are also meadows on limestone, with herds of goats.

— The upper face of the cuesta, formed from the same Portlandian limestone. Because they are excessively steep and lack shelter from the north and east winds, these areas are not planted with vines and are generally left fallow.

— The talus of the cuesta consists of Upper Kimmeridgian marl. When suitably exposed to the sun, the "white soils" on these slopes are the terrain which the sauvignon variety prefers. They give wines with a bouquet which keeps well.

— The shoulder opposite and below, with its collection of villages, consists of harder limestone of Middle Kimmeridgian age. There is a gentle rise in the land where the formation changes to Lower Kimmeridgian limestone. At the line of the fault the latter is in contact with the formations of Late Cretaceous or Eocene age observed earlier. The vineyards stand largely on limestone, which gives dry soils called "caillotes" (clumps). The wine from this soil must be bottled early. Its bouquet is very marked when the wine is young, but has a tendency to fade quickly (Bréjoux). From there go to Sancerre via Verdigny and Saint-Satur, examining the Jurassic formations along the way (see '*Guide géologique Val de Loire*' — Geological Guide to the Loire Valley — tour No 3), and pausing in the villages to taste the Sancerre wines.

The vineyards of Quincy and Châteaumeillant

The vineyards of Quincy may be visited if so desired. Here the sauvignon variety is cultivated on alluvials, and the soils are different from those of Pouilly and Sancerre.

The **Châteaumeillant** (VDQS) vineyard is known for its "vin gris" (grey wine), made from pinot and gamay grown on Triassic sand and clay (see map on page 289). Its clarity, fine bouquet and lively colour have earned its VDQS accolade. White and red are also produced, but in smaller quantities.

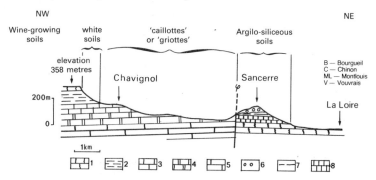

Fig.95. — Cross-section through the cuesta in the Jurassic formations and the landscape inversion caused by the Sancerre fault.

The lower block, on which the town of Sancerre stands, is east of the fault. It rises above the softer, more eroded Upper Jurassic formations to the west of the fault.

1. Portlandian (limestone); 2. Upper Kimmeridgian (marl with Exogyra virgula); 3. Middle Kimmeridgian (Astarte Limestone); 4. Lower Kimmeridgian (Tonnerre Limestone); 5. Upper Oxfordian (limestone); 6. Eocene (gravel, pebbles, very hard siliceous conglomerates); 7. Cenomanian, Turonian ? (chalk, marl, clay with flint); 8. Hauterivian (limestone), Barremian, Albian (sand and clay).

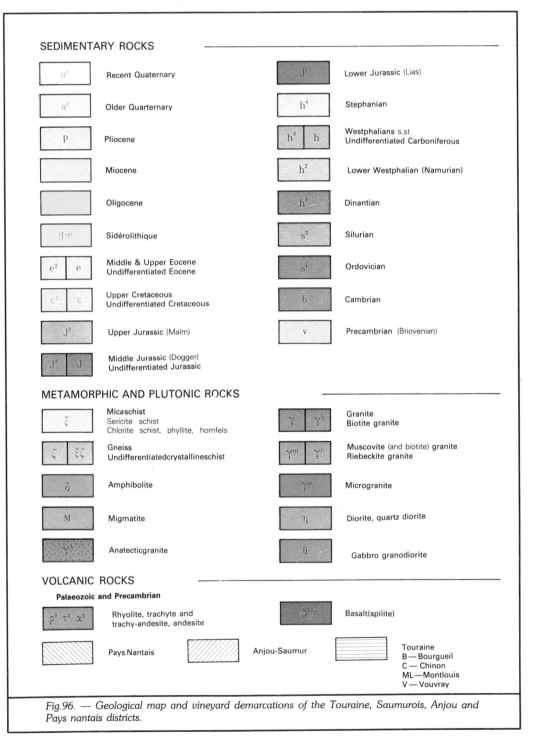

SEDIMENTARY ROCKS

a²	Recent Quaternary
a¹	Older Quarternary
p	Pliocene
m	Miocene
	Oligocene
g-e	Sidérolithique
e² / e	Middle & Upper Eocene / Undifferentiated Eocene
c² / c	Upper Cretaceous / Undifferentiated Cretaceous
J³	Upper Jurassic (Malm)
J² / J	Middle Jurassic (Dogger) / Undifferentiated Jurassic
J¹	Lower Jurassic (Lias)
h⁴	Stephanian
h³ / h	Westphalians s.st / Undifferentiated Carboniferous
h²	Lower Westphalian (Namurian)
h¹	Dinantian
s²	Silurian
s¹	Ordovician
b	Cambrian
v	Precambrian (Briovenian)

METAMORPHIC AND PLUTONIC ROCKS

ζ	Micaschist / Sericite schist / Chlorite schist, phyllite, hornfels
ζ / ξξ	Gneiss / Undifferentiated crystalline schist
δ̂	Amphibolite
M	Migmatite
γ^μ	Anatectic granite
γ / γ^b	Granite / Biotite granite
γ^m / γ^r	Muscovite (and biotite) granite / Riebeckite granite
γ^μ	Microgranite
η	Diorite, quartz diorite
θ	Gabbro granodiorite

VOLCANIC ROCKS

Palaeozoic and Precambrian

ρ¹ τ¹ α¹	Rhyolite, trachyte and trachy-andesite, andesite
β¹	Basalt (spilite)

Pays Nantais	
Anjou-Saumur	
Touraine	B — Bourgueil / C — Chinon / ML — Montlouis / V — Vouvray

Fig. 96. — *Geological map and vineyard demarcations of the Touraine, Saumurois, Anjou and Pays nantais districts.*

Val de Loire
Touraine, Anjou, Pays nantais

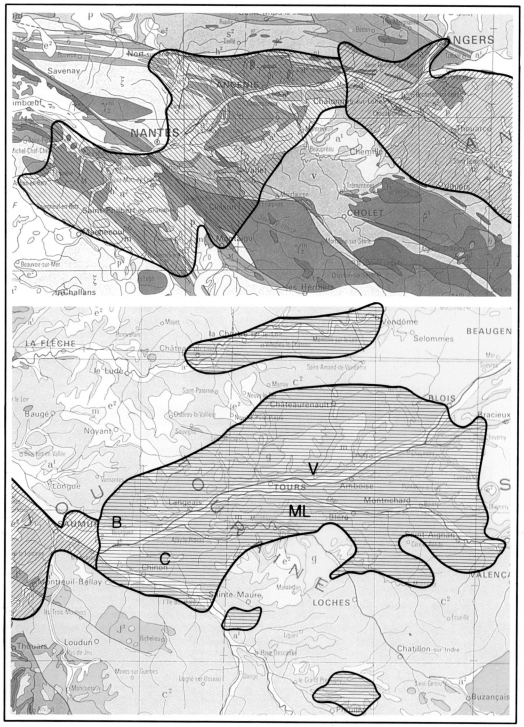

The white wines of Touraine; the vineyards of Montlouis, Touraine-Amboise and Vouvray

The appellation districts of Montlouis and Vouvray, and the sub-region of Touraine-Amboise (fig.96), are part of the vast wine-growing area of Touraine (10 000 hectares). The area produces mainly still, lightly sparkling or fully sparkling white wines. These may be dry, richly sweet or very sweet according to the year, and are derived from chenin blanc or pineau de Loire. They can be served as an apéritif, with the first course or for dessert. They are also used in the preparation of many regional specialities (fish from the Loire, potted meats, etc.).

The climate of Touraine is temperate (average temperature varies between 0°C in winter and 25°C in summer), rather moist (average rainfall is 650 mm annually), and the prevailing winds blow from west-southwest. Storms mostly affect the slopes north of the Loire and frosts are to be expected near woods.

Vineyards are mainly situated on low plateaux. These occur as a result of morphological sectioning where the Loire and Cher valleys meet. In the side valleys, which are less steep, only the slopes are occupied by vines, in those places with a good aspect to the sun. The valley floors are generally too damp for vineyards.

This region is the home of the Turonian Stage. Upper Cretaceous marine levels and continental detrital levels of Cenozoic age occur here as outcrops. The Turonian Stage is represented by argillaceous chalk at the base and tufa (detrital limestone) in the middle and upper levels. In the Loire Valley, the tufa has formed very steep, yellow-coloured slopes. Towns and villages back onto these, burrowing into the rock as if to form cave-dwellings. The Cher valley contains Villedieu Chalk, of Senonian age. Above are the Senonian argillo-siliceous formations (clay with flints) which yield the very pebbly soils of the vineyards at the edges of the plateaux.

The chenin blanc grape is not choosy about the nature of its soil (Bréjoux), and is as happy in sandy soils as in clay soils with flints (called "perruches") or calcareous soils (called "aubuis"). Only soils which are too heavy and damp ("bournais") do not suit it. Harvesting and vinification procedures differ from grower to grower and according to the way the vines are facing. For this reason the white wines of Vouvray and Montlouis, which are always delightfully fragrant and tasty, vary a great deal in actual detail.

As for the tufa, in fact it has a key influence on wine quality. Being rather soft and porous, but full of cherty slabs, it makes strong, sound cellars in which the Montlouis and Vouvray reach their peak, generally after five to ten years.

The vineyards of Montlouis

From Tours take the N 751 which skirts the south bank of the Loire and head towards Amboise and Blois. The road runs through a valley 4.5 km wide which is shared by the Loire and the Cher. The levee on which the road runs is one of a series first built in the 11th century, later becoming more widespread in the 15th century under Louis XI. On the left flows the Loire. Its flow-rate (average 380 m3/s) can vary seasonally by a factor of five.

To the right of the road are "varennes", sandy alluvial areas which were once prone to flooding and are now occupied by market gardens and cereal crops. The sparse vines are not in an AOC area, since the soil is wet on account of the shallow water level of the alluvial sheet. At kilometre post 31 ①, notice on the left, to the north of the Loire, the cliff of **Rochecorbon** consisting of Turonian micaceous and yellow tufas.

The route continues to **Montlouis** ②. On the right is a view of the spur separating the Loire and Cher valleys. The vineyards on it are planted mainly on sandy soils and gentle slopes facing south-southwest. The white wines from here are of the same type as those from Vouvray (see below), but overall less full-bodied. The

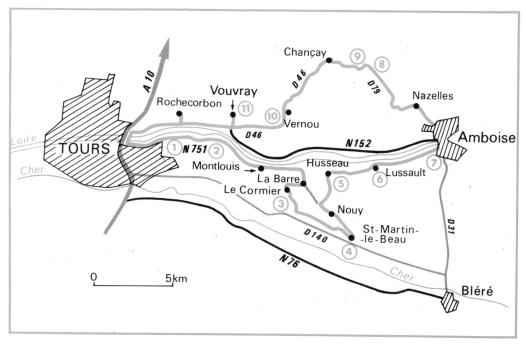

Fig.97. — Tour in the Touraine district.

town of Montlouis backs onto the yellow tufa escarpment rising gradually towards the east. On the way out of town, notice that the cellars of the wine cooperative have been tunnelled into this tufa, which is present in thick banks and contains flinty slabs (cherts).

Turn right onto the D 40 towards Saint-Martin-le-Beau, then on leaving La Barre turn right again towards Montlouis. After another kilometre bear left towards **Le Cormier** ③. We enter an area of vineyard which owes its expansion almost entirely to the sandy, clay-free covering of Quaternary age. This consists of early Quaternary alluvial sand containing quartz gravel and siliceous rocks, mixed with sand carried on westerly winds from the floor of the Loire alluvial plain during the Recent Quaternary. These sands support impoverished, well-drained soils. The vine roots generally reach down to the Senonian flint-clays or the underlying Turonian tufa. The vineyards in this area have been planted among orchards, cereals and woods.

Drive through Le Cormier and take the C 300 towards Azay-sur-Cher. The road descends into the valley of the Cher, intersecting the Senonian argillo-siliceous formations. This side of the level crossing turn left onto the C 22 towards Saint-Martin-le-Beau. We now cross an area of market gardens on a low terrace of wind-eroded alluvial from the Cher. In the woods near the **Saint-Martin-le-Beau** waterworks, go left (fig.98) onto the track leading to an old sand quarry, locally known as "des Sablons" ④. Notice the following:

— at the base, the Villedieu Chalk, of Senonian age, is soft, nodulous, glauconitic and rich in brachiopod and lamellibranch fossils;

— at the top, the old Cher alluvials are sandy with siliceous gravel and pebbles, and partly remodelled by colluvial deposition and wind-erosion. This is the preferred substratum on which to grow the chenin blanc grape in the AOC Montlouis area.

Return to the C 22 and head towards Saint-Martin-le-Beau. Just on the edge of the village, turn left onto the D 40 towards Montlouis. The route winds along the eastern slope of a former alluvial channel which has incised the interfluve and connected the Cher and Loire valleys. On leaving Nouy turn right towards **Husseau**

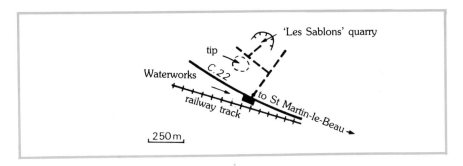

Fig.98. — Sketch map: the 'Les Sablons' quarry at Saint-Martin-le-Beau.

⑤. The route crosses a homogeneous sandy zone given over entirely to vines. Beyond Husseau join the N 751 and head along the Loire Valley towards Amboise.

On the right just before Lussault is a large quarry in the yellow tufa of Turonian age ⑥. This is a detrital limestone consisting of grains of mainly quartz sand, glauconite and organic debris in a crystallised calcitic cement. Ramifying or tabular beds of flint and cherts can be observed in the formation (see *'Guide géologique Val de Loire'* - Geological Guide to the Loire Valley — page 78).

The vineyards of Touraine-Amboise

Stay on the N 751 towards Amboise. Our route takes us into the AOC area of Touraine-Amboise. Output is varied. There are white wines produced from chenin blanc, rosés and reds from gamay, cabernet and côt, and a range of sparkling wines. Wines made from sauvignon and groslot must use only the Touraine regional appellation. A variety of soils are used for growing vines. Some are carbonate, overlying tufa on upper slopes, or more generally siliceous and fairly heavy, overlying argillaceous sands and gravels of Post-Helvetian age or even silt from the plateaux (gamay).

In the valley, close to the axis of the Amboise Anticline, argillaceous chalk from the base of the Turonian can be seen. It is not so easy to dig out for cellars as the previously mentioned variety. It can be observed in the old quarry known locally as "Four-à-Chaux" ("Lime- Kiln") ⑦. On the way into **Amboise** turn right towards La Fuye, then take the track branching left from the first bend. This leads to a large open space with a view of a 12-metre thickness of the argillaceous chalk. This is white near the top with beds of black flint nodules, and greyish towards the base with pyrite nodules (see *'Guide géologique Val de Loire'* — Geological Guide to the Loire Valley — page 79).

Before leaving Amboise take a look at its château. Then cross the Loire and follow the D 5 as far as Nazelles. Then take the D 1 towards Noizay. The road skirts the slope, which consists of micaceous and yellow tufas.

About 1.5 km beyond Nazelles bear right, via the D 79, towards **Chançay.** The road crosses the northern vineyards of Touraine-Amboise, planted on argillaceous formations of sand and gravel or of silt. These formations can be seen in the old workings ⑧ to the north of the brick works (turn right after kilometre post 4).

The vineyards of Vouvray

Return to the D 79 and turn right towards Chançay. We are now entering the AOC area of Vouvray. After five hundred metres, on the edge of the wood ⑨, notice some large blocks of conglomerate in front of the Serpot works entrance. These have siliceous components and cement, and are called locally "perrons".

The road then runs down into the valley of the Brenne, following a small valley in which cellars and homes have been hollowed out of the rock. At Chançay take the D 45 left towards Vouvray. The road first runs across a low terrace of the Brenne. Notice the contrast between the gentle western slope with its covering of colluvial deposits, where vineyards are gaining ground, and the steep, wooded eastern slope. Further on, at Vernou, the road skirts the yellow tufa hillslope before reaching the Loire Valley.

The essential elements of the Vouvray vineyards are to be found on the plateau. The geological formations and the soils (calcareous, arenaceous or argillo-siliceous) are of the same type, and just as varied, as in the vineyards of Touraine-Amboise, but here only the chenin blanc is cultivated. On the slopes with the best aspect there are several late harvests of grapes affected by noble rot, yielding rich, full-bodied wines. Even so, the chenin is also used for making dry white wine. Vouvray wine has a natural tendency to effervesce. Part of the harvest, usually from the poorest soils, is made into lightly sparkling and fully foaming wines.

Continue towards Vouvray. A very few vineyards are to be found on the slightly raised areas on the Loire Valley floor, such as the terrace across which the D 46 runs.

About 900 metres beyond kilometre post 3, turn left onto the GR 3 towards the Loire. There are no vineyards once we move from the terrace to the 'varennes' of the old flood plain. Beyond La Cisse, notice the slight rise in the ground at a sharp bend in the road (fig.99). It stands 1 to 3 metres above the floor of the alluvial plain and is known locally as a "montille" (hillock). It indicates a recent alluvial deposition level of the Loire. Vines are also cultivated on these drier sandy soils. Close by, some diggings ⑩ have exposed alluvials from subrecent flooding of the Loire.

Return to the D 46 and continue towards Vouvray following the tufa escarpments. Just before Vouvray, turn right towards La Croix-Buissee at kilometre post 1. Proceed onto the plateau for a short tour of the vineyards (fig.100), which at this point are very sensitive to bad weather, especially hail. The road also intersects a number of the small valleys so typical of Touraine ⑪ .

Return to Tours along the famous yellow tufa cliff of Rochecorbon with its crowning lantern tower. There is a wine museum worth visiting in Tours, near the church of Saint-Julien.

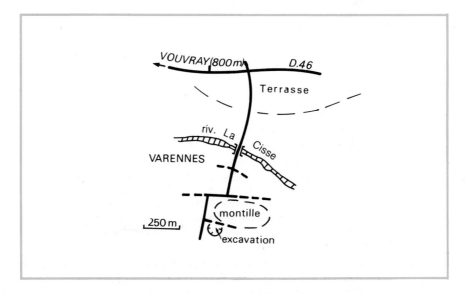

Fig.99. — Sketch map: the area east of Vouvray.

327

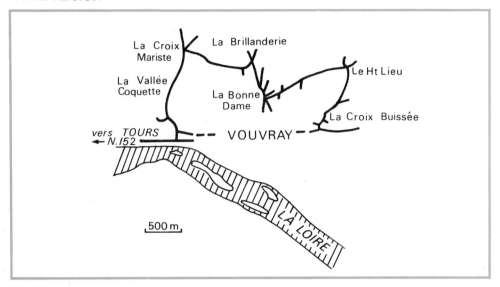

Fig.100. — *Tour of the district around Vouvray.*

The red wines of Touraine and the Saumur region; the vineyards of Bourgueil, Saumur-Champigny and Chinon

The red wines of the Loire Valley are all based on the same variety of grape, the cabernet franc, called "breton" locally, and produced from vineyards located within the wine-growing areas of Touraine and Anjou. The areas entitled to use the appellation Bourgueil, Saumur-Champigny and Chinon are around the confluence of the Vienne and the Loire.

The climate in this sector is drier than that of its neighbours. Annual rainfall is often less than 600 millimetres.

The sub-soil consists of sedimentary formations which have been folded. The Chouzé Anticline, which is peripherally faulted, is the major structural feature. Jurassic limestone crops out at its eroded centre.

There is little sign of the sand, clay or marl formations of Cenomanian age, since they have been masked by the Quaternary alluvials in the valley bottom. The lower and middle levels of Turonian age are chalky (tufa). This whitish chalk commonly occurs as a steep outcrop on valley edges, and is a fundamental feature of the landscape in this region. The upper part of the Turonian formation, which is calcaro-arenaceous, and the formation of Senonian age, which is more sandy than argillaceous, reflect the era when the Cretaceous sea was becoming shallower and its shoreline was nearby.

The plateaux are covered with continental formations of Eocene age: fragments of siliceous conglomerates bound in sand and clay ('perrons'), and lacustrine limestone at Champigny. During the Quaternary, both the Loire and the Vienne deposited alluvials in two distinct terraces above their flood plains. There are even higher structural benches, now deprived of their alluvial cover. During the periods of greatest cold, a part of the alluvial sandy silt fraction was carried onto the plateaux by the wind.

Depending on the appellation, vines are grown either on the alluvial terraces (**Bourgueil, Chinon**) or on the plateaux (**Saumur-Champigny**). The nature of the sub-soil is therefore varied, and the wine produced shows many nuances. The cabernet franc is, in fact, sensitive to soil type. Morlat *et al.* have shown that root growth is better, both on slopes and on plateaux, in the carbonate formations of Turonian age than in the sand-gravel and clay soils of Senonian or Eocene age. This means that wines produced on tufa in years with a dry autumn improve significantly with ageing. The cabernet variety is not fond of clay-rich formations, and yields wines of a delicate colour, fragrance and taste which are at their best with meat, game or cheese.

The vineyards of Bourgueil and Saint-Nicolas-de-Bourgueil

The 1 500 hectares of vines are situated on part of the vast alluvial terrace (20 km long and 2 km wide) on the right bank of the Loire, some 15 metres above the river (fig.101). They also occupy roughly the lower half of the northern valley slope. There are three types of soil: the "gravels" (Quaternary alluvials), the "tuf" (Turonian) and the "sand" (Senonian). The first two are the largest. By tradition the wine-makers prefer to vinify the grapes from each of these soils separately.

From **Bourgueil** take the D 35 towards Longué (fig.102). The route takes us along a terrace among the vineyards. On the right is the northern slope of the valley. Vines cover its gentle lower slopes, where the substratum consists of micaceous and yellow tufas of Turonian age. These are masked by aeolian sands and arenaceous colluvial deposits from the sands of Senonian age. The upper face of the slope, and the plateau with its argillaceous and siliceous sub-soil, are covered with forest.

The journey continues to **Saint-Nicolas-de-Bourgueil** (AOC), famous for the "gravels wines", which are very fruity from first youth. From Saint-Nicolas take the right-hand turning towards Vernantes, then at La Jarnoterie turn right again towards Martellière and Chevrette. The road winds along the foot of the hill. It passes through some typical little townships, their tufa buildings roofed in slate brought from Anjou along the Loire in its navigable days. Colluvial deposits can be seen here and there in the bank of the road. Cellars have been dug out in the micaceous tufa, beneath the covering of sand.

On arriving at **Chevrette,** take the "no-through road" leading to a quarry ①in sand and clay of Senonian age (Coniacian to Lower Campanian). Working from bottom to top, notice the following:

— 5 to 6 metres of fairly coarse, ochrous sand containing some gravel;
— 6 to 8 metres of fine sand and clay in beds of ochre, grey or red, with Porifera (sponges) and flints.

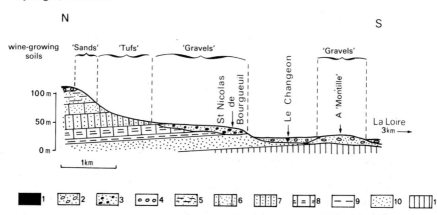

Fig.101. — *Cross-section through the Bourgueil terrace.*

Quaternary; 1. Aeolian sand; 2. Recent alluvials; 3. Older alluvials. Eocene; 4. Siliceous conglomerates. Senonian; 5. Sand and clay with porifera. Upper Turonian; 6. Yellow tufa. Middle Turonian; 7. Micaceous chalk. Lower Turonian; 8. Argillaceous chalk. Upper Cenomanian; 9. Marl with Ostracea. Middle and Lower Cenomanian; 10. Clay, sand and gravel. Oxfordian; 11. Limestone and marl.

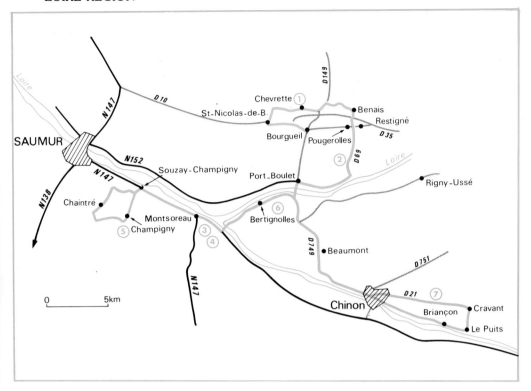

Fig.102. — Tour in the region of Saumur.

From Chevrette continue towards Benais to the Bourgueil AOC district. The route crosses the valley of the Changeon to join the D 35 (realigned). Turn towards Tours. After about a kilometre rejoin the terrace. Notice to the left the village of Benais, standing on outcrops of argillaceous and micaceous chalk of Turonian age. This is undoubtedly the best known region for "vin de tufs", which has more body than the "gravels" variety and is best kept for a few years.

In a little while, turn right onto the D 69 to La-Chapelle-sur-Loire. The road is built on alluvials, and beyond Fougerolles comes down onto the alluvial plain. Here vines are cultivated on the "montilles" only, for instance at kilometre post 2 ②. These hillocks testify to a recent alluvial depositional level 2 or 3 metres higher than the present flood plain.

From **La-Chapelle-sur-Loire** bear right on the N 152 as it skirts the Loire towards Saumur. At Port-Boulet take the N 749 towards Chinon. On crossing the Loire, notice the Chinon nuclear power station on a low terrace to the left. Immediately beyond the bridge, turn right onto the D 7 towards Candes-Saint-Martin. The road skirts the Chinon vineyard, which is on the left.

Proceed to Candes-Saint-Martin, at the confluence of the Loire and the Vienne. In the village of **Candes,** where Saint Martin died, take the signposted track behind the 12th century church to the viewpoint. On the way there, the path winds among old quarries ③and cave houses hollowed out of the micaceous tufa of Middle Turonian age. This is a grey or white detrital limestone. It is glauconitic and soft, in thick banks with ramifying layers of cherts.

From a point near spot height 87 ④, there is a view over the Véron region and the confluence of the Loire and Vienne valleys. These rivers have virtually scoured the arenaceous beds of Cenomanian age from the centre of the Chouzé Anticline.

The Vienne has been following the same course as the one we know today since the Upper Pliocene at least. It is a significant stream (370 km long, half of this in the

330

Massif central, and an average flow of 300 m³/$_s$). It has carved a wide, deep valley and deposited an abundance of alluvials with a high proportion of pebbles from eruptive and metamorphic rocks.

The Loire is 1 000 km long. Its average flow rate at Tours is 390 m³/$_s$. It was a more recent arrival in Touraine, after abandoning its northern course towards the English Channel and joining the Vienne southwest of the Paris Basin early in the Quaternary.

Away to the northeast the vineyards of Bourgueil are situated between the foreground tree margin alongside the Loire and the plateau defining the horizon. In the northwest is a plateau south of the Loire on which the Saumur-Champigny vineyards can be seen.

The vineyards of Saumur-Champigny

The vines stand on the interfluve plateau between the Loire and Thouet valleys. They grow on the carbonate soils formed from the tufa and calcareous sand of Turonian age, as well as on the slightly acid, leached and partially hydromorphic clayey sand soils developed from the detrital formations of Senonian or Eocene age. Little remains of the vineyard which once stood on the lacustrine limestone and brought fame to the village of Champigny (Bréjoux). The wine of Saumur-Champigny has a fine colour and is generally quite full-bodied.

From Candes-Saint-Martin take the N 147 towards Saumur, following the course of the Loire. The alluvials are 4 to 8 metres thick. There is a lower level of sand, gravel and pebbles (in local dialect: "jard") which is separated from the sandy clay upper level by a band of dark clay containing plant debris (dialect: "jalle").

Beyond Montsoreau, on the left, the road follows the Turonian cliff. The base is argillaceous chalk, gradually giving way to micaceous chalk in which former underground workings have been converted into cellars for wine-storage or mushroom-growing. There is only one tufa quarry still operating today, extracting building stone at **Saint-Cyr-en-Bourg.** Notice how well the villages blend with the rock, which has been hollowed out to form dwellings.

Turn left at **Souzay-Champigny** onto the D 205 towards Champigny. Just beyond Souzay turn right onto a road winding among the vineyards. The surface on which the road is built is alluvial in origin, but its deposits have been scoured. The formation is micaceous chalk and calcareous sand of Turonian age, standing some 30 to 40 metres above the present level of the Loire. Vines also occupy the hillslope (Senonian and detrital Eocene) which leads up to the plateau and its cap of lacustrine Champigny Limestone.

In another 2 km turn left onto the C 2, towards **Chaintré.** In Chaintré itself, notice the enclosure walls made of tufa, with a few blocks of "perrons", the siliceous conglomerate in a ferruginous cement, of Eocene age. These walled enclosures were intended to protect the vines from intruders and the west winds, but they also play an important role in the ripening process of the grapes, thanks to the thermal qualities of the tufa. This porous rock efficiently stores heat during the day and returns it to its surroundings at night.

Champigny brings us to the lacustrine limestone. Vines are no more to be seen. The formation can be observed in a large quarry ⑤ to the right of the D 145, some 300 metres from Champigny in the direction of Fontevrault. This limestone of Priabonian age is white or grey, hard and cavernous, with millstone nodules.

Return to Souzay-Champigny. Just before the village turn right onto the signposted "Circuit touristique du vin" (Wine Route), which leads to Montsoreau through vineyards studded with windmills. The road is built on sands of Upper Turonian and Senonian age, incising the underlying micaceous tufa at the heads of small valleys. Return to Candes-Saint-Martin.

The vineyards of Chinon

Chinon consists of 1 200 hectares of well-scattered vineyards on both sides of the Vienne valley, up to 40 km upstream from its confluence with the Loire. Its vines are mainly grown on slopes of micaceous and yellow tufa of Turonian age, as well as on the old alluvials which rise some 5 to 10 metres above the Vienne.

Unlike their counterparts in Bourgueil, the wine-growers of Chinon deliberately mix grapes from different soil types. They obtain a wine with an unusual violet fragrance, preferably for drinking while still young and fresh. Its reputation has never looked back since François Rabelais, a native of the region, sang its praises. The Chinon region also produces a small quantity of rosé from cabernet franc or cabernet sauvignon.

From Candes-Saint-Martin cross the Vienne again, taking the D 7 towards Rigny-Ussé and Tours. The road crosses the flood plain, leaving it at Bertignolles and climbing up to the vine-clad alluvial terrace (some 5 to 8 metres higher) on the right. This terrace is very extensive, and consists of imbricated deposits of different ages. Its basic shape was acquired towards the end of the last glaciation. In 45.5 km a small quarry ⑥ gives an opportunity to study the alluvials.

Staying on the D 749, the route follows the Vienne. In this area the flood plain occupies the entire width of the valley. At Chinon, notice how the cellars on the left are hollowed out of the micaceous tufa. The town backs onto the Turonian cliff on which stands the château made famous by King Charles VII of France and Joan of Arc.

Drive through Chinon and take the D 21 towards Cravant, following the steep slope of uniform micaceous tufa into which the cellars have been driven. The formation can be studied in quarries ⑦ at **Malvault**. Vines have been planted on the upper face of the hillslopes, on yellow tufa or clay with flints of Senonian age. They are also to be found on the edge of the forest of Chinon and on the higher parts of the alluvial plain.

At **Cravant**, turn right onto the D 44 and head for Le Puy. Then take the D 8 towards Briançon and Chinon. In this area the bed of the Vienne is some 8 to 10 metres incised into its alluvial plain. Extensive areas of the old alluvials are no longer part of the flood plain, and therefore suitable as vineyards. These are separated by elongated, low-lying areas of wet pasture. Downstream from Briançon this type of land-use finally predominates.

Return to Chinon. With its medieval charm it makes a good overnight stop. Among other attractions, the visitor can enjoy the interesting museum dedicated to wine and the cooper's craft.

The white and rosé wines of Anjou; the vineyards on the "coteaux" of the Layon, the Aubance and the Loire

Anjou is famous for producing virtually equal amounts of white and rosé wines, which may be dry, but just as commonly medium-dry, medium-sweet, sweet or even very sweet and rich.

To produce wines in the sweet to very sweet range, the grapes have to be harvested late (end of October to early November), so that they are very ripe. They are then repeatedly sorted and selected to find those which have been affected by noble rot. This whole process produces high concentrations of sugar, glycerine and alcohol (up to 20). The climate is similar overall to that around Chinon or Bourgueil, but the generally steep slopes give rise to greater variations between micro-climates. The exposure of the vineyard is the determining factor. The valley sides, or 'coteaux', of the Loire, the Layon or the Aubance which face south or southwest have the best known vineyards.

Most of these slopes are on formations associated with the Precambrian and Palaeozoic basement of the eastern edge of the Armorican massif. The main formations are schist, sandstone, conglomerate and limestone, with interbedded volcanic rocks.

Towards the east, vineyards can also be found where the basement is covered by transgressive, sandy-glauconitic Cenomanian strata, "faluns" dating to the Miocene, and red sands of Pliocene age. Vineyards in this zone represent a gradual transition towards the Saumur type.

The white wines are produced exclusively from the chenin blanc grape variety. It is not too choosy about the soil type, and because it is semi-late fruiting, as well as being the basis of the most prestigious wines from the region, it is given the best-exposed sites (Bréjoux). It is often planted on steep slopes where the bare, eroded soil on shale is hard, pebbly and clayey.

The rosés come from cabernet franc (AOC Cabernet d'Anjou) or groslot (AOC Rosé d'Anjou), and less commonly from pineau d'Aunis, côt or gamay. Cabernet franc and groslot give of their best on more permeable soils consisting of gravel and siliceous sand or limestone of Cenomanian or Neogene age.

These white or rosé wines are preferably served chilled, and are especially pleasant as an apéritif or with dessert. During the meal they go well with fish or white meat.

The region also produces red wines from gamay, cabernet franc or cabernet-sauvignon, but output is kept fairly low because the clayey soils of Anjou are not best suited to producing quality red wines from these varieties of grape.

The vineyards of the Coteaux du Layon

The river Layon is a right-hand tributary of the Loire. For almost its whole length both banks are covered in vineyards. The total area under vine comes to some four thousand hectares. The best known estates are in and downstream of the Thouarcé region, where the river cuts across the Precambrian and Palaeozoic formations.

Leave **Thouarcé** by the D 120 along the right bank, heading towards Faye-d'Anjou and Rochefort. On the way out of the area, notice the red to violet soils on the right (the colours are derived from the shales). The top of the steep, ideally exposed slope is the beginning of the Bonnezeaux local appellation area, where two-thirds of the production is rosé wine made from the cabernet variety, since the sands and gravels of the Pliocene extend over a very large area of the plateau (fig.103).

In another 2.5 km turn left onto the D 133 towards Valanjou, then after crossing the Layon turn right towards Rablay. After 1 km turn left and head for Le Champ-sur-Layon. The road climbs the southern slope of the Layon valley. Here the vineyards have a good position relative to the sun, because although the slopes are north-facing they are gentle. The Brioverian schists crop out on the valley sides, whereas the interfluve areas are covered in "faluns" of Miocene, or red sands and gravels of Pliocene age. The soils vary between heavy clay types (which are good for chenin blanc), siliceous types, or carbonaceous and permeable types (dedicated to the cabernet and groslot varieties). Their suitability for vine-growing therefore varies accordingly.

At Breil, some eight hundred metres further on, an old quarry ① discloses a 3-metre thickness of the Pliocene red sand and gravel.

In another two kilometres, opposite **La Grouas,** another old quarry ② has cut down into the Miocene "falun" revealing four metres of highly consolidated yellow carbonate sand with local inclusions of white quartz gravel. The formation is cross-bedded and there are many fossils and debris of Bryozoa and other fauna.

Proceed via the D 199 as far as **Le Champ-sur-Layon,** where there are

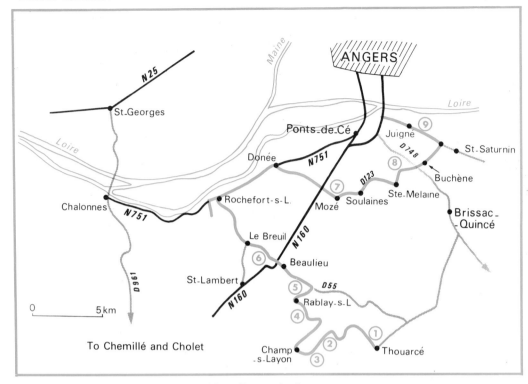

Fig.103. — Tour in the Anjou region.

buildings both of Brioverian schist and Miocene "faluns" (Grouas stone). Turn right onto the D 124 towards Fay and Mozé. After 2.5 km, in the vicinity of two places called L'Angelière and La Petite-Grouas, there is an old quarry on the left, in the bottom of a small valley ③. It reveals the Brioverian formation of light-coloured schist and sandstone varying between beige and bluish-grey, with commonly occurring white mica, and small veins of quartz. The whole formation is thoroughly jointed and there is local micro-folding.

Take the D 125 towards Rablay. In the bank of the road at the crossroads ④ about a kilometre beyond the road to Mozé, notice the red sand and gravel of Pliocene age cutting into heavily weathered red schists of probably Brioverian age.

The road goes down through a gently undulating landscape towards **Rablay.** Notice the escarpment to the north of Layon, consisting mainly of Carboniferous formations associated with the lower Loire coal belt. In the area we have just reached, the production of white wine under the Coteaux de Layon appellation is increasing at the expense of rosé. This is because there is a greater expanse of shaly soils, the well-exposed slopes are longer, and the local micro-climates are sheltered from the north winds, helping the ripening process of the chenin.

From Rablay take the D 54 towards **Beaulieu.** Cross the Layon. The Brioverian schist crops out behind the former crossing-keeper's house. Immediately beyond turn right onto the C 7, which climbs the hill and crosses the Layon Fault in the first few turns. Among the vines the Carboniferous shale gives furrowed soils varying from black to violet. Near the top of the hill is a small car park ⑤ for a viewpoint across the Layon valley. In the bank of the car park, notice the conglomerate with large pebbles of quartz, schist, limestone and eruptive rocks in a blackish to brown argillaceous matrix with slate breaks or sandstone bands. The strata dip sharply towards the northeast. Mine-shafts have been sunk to exploit veins of lean coal at Beaulieu-sur-Layon.

Drive through Beaulieu and turn left onto the N 161 towards **Chemillé.** At the foot of the hill, just this side of the Layon, a track on the right leads to an old quarry ⑥ for limestone of latest Silurian age. This is a greyish, fine or coarse grained crystalline rock containing small pyrite crystals. It occurs in banks between two and three metres thick with slaty breaks and veins of calcite. Return by the N 161. At Beaulieu turn left onto the D 54 towards Rochefort-sur-Loire. The road passes a large Silurian limestone quarry which is in exploitation.

The route crosses the northwestern vineyards of the Coteaux du Layon. These have been planted indiscriminately on all the formations of the complex Ordovician to Devonian Series of Saint-Georges-sur-Loire, whether shaly, calcareous, eruptive, acid or basic. On the left of the road, before reaching the Château du Breuil, are the 42 ideally exposed hectares of the most famous "cru" of the Layon: the "Quarts-de-Chaume" where wine-tasters are welcomed. The white, rosé and red wines from **Thouarsais** and **Haut-Poitou** in the south of Anjou are noted for their light, fresh qualities.

The vineyards of the Coteaux de la Loire

They occupy the right bank of the Loire between Angers and Ingrandes. The largest part of the wine-growing area stands on the formations of the complex Ordovician to Devonian Series of Saint-Georges-sur-Loire (see *'Guide géologique Bretagne'* — Guide to the Geology of Brittany - page 16). Towards Angers it also extends onto the Ordovician to Silurian schist of the Bouchemaine and Erigné Complex.

The mainly white wines from here, derived from the chenin, are fruity and have good body. They are generally drier than their counterparts from the Coteaux du Layon. This can be explained in the main by the fact that many of the slopes face southeast, and are therefore less able to provide a prolonged ripening period for the grapes.

The **Savennières** vineyard is the best known. It can be reached from Rochefort-sur-Loire via the D 106, which crosses the Louet and the Loire. At Savennières (10th century church) take the D 111 towards Epiré. The road side provides a good cross-section of the different facies of the Saint-Georges Complex. The route passes close to the famous estates of Coulée-de-Serrant and La Roche-au-Moine. Return to Rochefort.

The vineyards of the Coteaux de l'Aubance

The Aubance is a little river between the Loire and the Layon which everywhere runs parallel to the main structural directions, southeast to northwest. Its stream has incised the plateaux only about 30 metres. The slopes are therefore gentler than those of the Coteaux du Layon. The vines are consequently less sheltered from the north winds. In addition to this, the clayey silt derived from superficial weathering of the schist is relatively uneroded and therefore quite thick. It gives a heavier and wetter soil which dries out less quickly than is the case on the Coteaux du Layon.

The appellation district of the AOC Coteaux de l'Aubance covers the various units of the northern flank of the Saint-Georges Syncline, continued in the north by the Ponts-de-Cé Anticline. Generally fresh and light white wines are produced here. They are not so full-bodied as their cousins from the Layon and the Loire. Towards the east, the basement is covered by transgressive strata of Late Cretaceous age or by residual gravels of indeterminate age. The estates here produce rosé from the cabernet and groslot varieties.

From **Rochefort-sur-Loire** take the D 751 towards Denée and the D 123 which crosses the plateau towards Mozé. The vineyard stands on the sedimentary and volcanic formations of the Saint-Georges-sur-Loire Complex. In places these formations are masked by an extensive cover of alteration brown clayey silt.

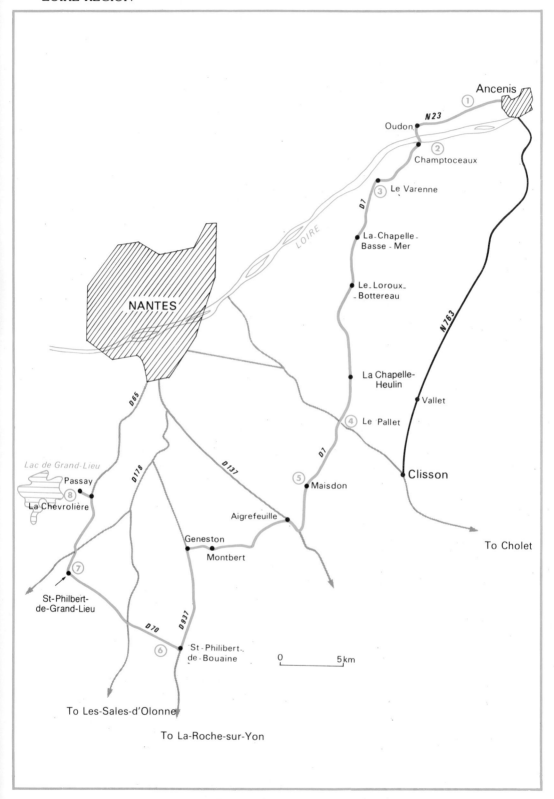

Fig.104. — Tour in the Pays nantais.

At **Mozé,** acid volcanic activity has formed a granite porphyry rock which is extracted for use in manufacturing road asphalt. It is a greyish rock with quartz crystals, alkaline feldspar, chloritized dark mica and veins of calcite. There is access to the eastern side of the quarry ⑦ from the D 123 for Soulaines-sur-Aubance.

Continue towards **Soulaines** and **Sainte-Melaine.** The route takes us onto the Bouchemaine and Erigné Schists (Ordovician to Silurian). The vineyards on this slope are fairly scattered. On leaving Sainte-Melaine turn left at the cemetery towards Buchêne and Saint-Jean-des-Mauvrets. Cross the Aubance and then immediately after, at Bas-Versillé, note the old quarry face on the left ⑧, where the schist used to be worked for rough slabs ranging in thickness from a few centimetres to several decimetres, used mainly as local building stone.

Continue towards **Saint-Jean-des-Mauvrets.** The northern slopes of the Aubance have good exposure and are under intensive vine cultivation. At **Buchêne,** the journey moves onto a glauconitic sand covering of Cenomanian age overlying Angers Schist of probably Middle Ordovician age. The area is noticeably on the axis of the Ponts-de-Cé Anticline. The schist is blue-black and easily cleaved, and has been worked by the Angers-Trélazé slate-quarries since the 19th century. The slates used to be taken down the Loire to the Orléans region by boat, and are now an integral part of the Loire Valley landscape. The schist has also been used for making vine stakes, which have been sent as far afield as the Bourgueil district, and also for making unusual enclosure walls in the form of wide sheets standing on end, which can be seen in the district around Buchêne and Saint-Jean-des-Mauvrets.

Before reaching Saint-Jean-des-Mauvrets, the village of Saint-Saturnin comes into view to the right of the D 232. It stands on a slope (cuesta) of Cretaceous age. At the base this consists of Cenomanian sand and marl, which is covered by Turonian chalk higher up, with sandstone and sand of Senonian age at the top. The cabernet variety likes the light, carbonate soils on these slopes.

At Saint-Jean-des-Mauvrets, take the N 751 towards **Juigné** ⑨. On the way into the village, note the backfilling of highly fissile schist on both sides of the road, from the old slate-quarries.

Muscadet and Gros Plant from the Pays nantais

The Pays nantais is **Muscadet** country. This light, dry white wine with the pale yellow colour has become very popular. It is produced from the grape variety of the same name, also known as "melon de Bourgogne", which was introduced into the regions of the lower Loire in the 17th century. The 10 000 hectares of muscadet are divided into three AOC areas: Muscadet, Muscadet des Coteaux de la Loire, and Muscadet de Sèvre et Maine.

Most of the vineyards are on low hills (some tens of metres high) on both sides of the Loire. The climate is oceanic and relatively wet (average annual rainfall 600 to 800 mm depending on the position). Seasonal temperature extremes are one or two degrees less than in the regions further east. Frosts also occur less frequently.

The landscape is based on the mainly metamorphic and eruptive formations of the Armorican massif, forming elongated bands lying roughly NW-SE.

In the northeast are outcrops of the Ordovician to Carboniferous formations of the Ancenis Syncline. These formations overlie the Champtoceaux Nappe, a complex structure of Precambrian metamorphic rocks. Further south are the gabbro uplands of Le Pallet.

Southwest of this vast undulation are metamorphic, Precambrian to Hercynian formations, forming the depression which contains the Lac de Grand-Lieu. There are occasional monadnocks consisting of Eocene deposits, and an extensive sheet of marine formations of Pliocene age covers this low-lying area.

Soils of various textures have developed on these formations. Arenaceous or clayey silty soils have formed from weathering of the micaceous and feldspathic rocks where the topography is flat. The slopes have shallower, stonier soils. In general the soils are of the acid or leached brown type, hydromorphic in places.

Overall, the muscadet variety seems happy on every soil type and in any orientation. For these reasons, in some sectors (the Sèvre et Maine region, for instance) the vineyards stretch as far as the eye can see, and the differences are less marked from one AOC to another. To capture their aroma, the grapes must be harvested as soon as they are ripe (September). The wine is best for drinking when it is young. It goes especially well with fish, including all forms of shellfish.

The Pays nantais has been producing another white wine for even longer than the Muscadet. It is called **Gros Plant,** and is made from the folle blanche variety of grape. Drier and paler, it too is excellent with seafood as well as fish from the Loire or the Lac de Grand-Lieu. Its VDQS demarcation overlaps perceptibly with the Muscadet appellation. The sandy gravel soils on the formations of Pliocene age around the Lac de Grand-Lieu are particularly well-suited to producing this wine.

Lastly we should mention the VDQS appellation Coteaux d'Ancenis, which produces other white wines from the chenin, pinot gris or verdelho de Madère varieties, as well as rosés and reds from gamay and cabernet.

The vineyards of the Coteaux d'Ancenis and Muscadet from the Coteaux de la Loire

These vineyards are on both sides of the Loire, upstream and downstream from Ancenis. Their estates partially overlap the Gros Plant VDQS area. They are mainly located on the Palaeozoic formations of the Ancenis Syncline, and spill over onto the very faulted northern sector of the Champtoceaux Nappe.

Take the N 23 from **Ancenis** towards Nantes. On leaving the town, the route runs between vineyards planted on sandstone and mudstone formations in the axial zone of the Ancenis Syncline, which dates from the Hercynian folding. Between Saint-Géréon and La Pommeraie the road incises the limestone and lyddite interbedded with the sandstone and mudstone (fig.104).

At **La Pommeraie** we encounter the schists and quartzites from the margin of the syncline. These crop out on the left of the road just before kilometre post 24 ①. The highest points of the landscape consist of sandstone horizons. Throughout this sector, the vineyards are somewhat scattered among cereal crops, market gardens and orchards. On slopes with good exposure the wines are generally produced by mixed-crop farmers, and tend to vary in style.

Turn left onto the D 323 towards Oudon and cross the Loire. Notice that the metamorphic substratum of the Loire has been incised some 15 to 20 metres below the present level and refilled with alluvial deposits. This deepening in comparison with sectors further upstream is due to the effects of a drop in the level of the Atlantic Ocean during the last glacial period.

Continue as far as **Champtoceaux,** from where there is a fine view over the Loire Valley. The pinnacle is composed of gneiss from the centre of the nappe. It can be observed as the road climbs up to the village ② (see *'Guide géologique Bretagne'* — Guide to the Geology of Brittany - tour No 14).

Muscadet de Sèvre et Maine

Almost nine-tenths of the Muscadet from the Pays nantais is produced under this appellation. It is noticeable that beyond La Varenne much more land is dedicated to vines, especially on the west-facing slopes.

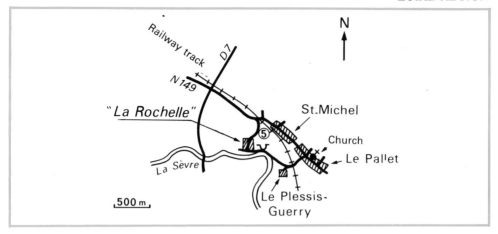

Fig.105. — *Sketch-map showing the location of 'La Rochelle' quarry in gabbro at Le Pallet.*

At **La Bréhardière,** a kilometre beyond La Varenne in the direction of Loroux-Bottereau, a large quarry can be seen on the left ③. It produces leptynite, a bluish-grey rock which splits into thick slabs.

Continue towards **La Chapelle-Basse-Mer.** In the west, the northern escarpments of the Loire Valley, consisting of Mauves-sur-Loire Mica Schist, can be seen. Here the D 7 winds its way across mica schist which occurs as chloritic and garnetiferous horizons in the bank to the left of the road on reaching La Chapelle.

In the vicinity of **Loroux-Bottereau,** vineyards stretch as far as the eye can see, regardless of the lie of the land or the soil type. Among the vines nestle little villages of red-tiled houses built of gneiss. In this district the muscadet grape leaves plenty of room for the gros plant variety.

Stay on the D 7 heading for **La Chapelle-Heulin.** After 10.6 km, at the hamlet of La Roche, the road runs onto an outlying formation of highly altered (serpentinous) gabbro ④.

La Chapelle-Heulin is in a low-lying area (elevation 10 metres) with the Goulaine Marshes in the west and a covering layer of recent, sandy clay alluvials. Beyond La Chapelle, take the D 7 and then the N 149 towards Le Pallet and its gabbro uplands.

The gabbro can be sampled in an old quarry at a place called 'La Rochelle' on the banks of the Sèvre ⑤(fig.105). From above this spot there is a fine viewpoint looking across the valley and the vineyards.

Return to the D 7 and cross the Sèvre towards Aigrefeuille-sur-Maine. At Maisdon we come to the Clisson-Mortagne Granite. The vineyards are less close together and the granite gives the wine a stony taste.

Gros Plant and Muscadet

From Aigrefeuille take the D 117 towards **Montbert.** Although we are now entering the AOC Muscadet district, this area is mainly the province of the gros plant variety, because the sand-gravel soil which it prefers is common here. These soils are formed from the detrital formations left behind by the Pliocene sea. The formations are fossil-bearing in places.

Continue from Montbert towards Geneston, then follow the N 137bis towards Saint-Philbert-de-Bouaine. The basement gneiss is covered with isolated lenses of sand and sandstone of Eocene age, forming outliers, such as at Montbert, and there are also more extensive sheets of Pliocene sands and plateau silt.

The metamorphic formations can be observed in the large quarry called "La Gerbaudière" ⑥. From Saint-Philbert-de-Bouaine follow the D 74 towards Corcoué for a kilometre. The track leading to the quarry crosses leptynite, gneiss with dark mica, and veins of pegmatite with kyanite crystals. The quarry is extracting banded eclogite (see *'Guide géologique Bretagne'* — Guide to the Geology of Brittany — tour No 14).

From **Saint-Philbert-de-Bouaine** follow the valley of the Boulogne to Saint-Philbert-de-Grand-Lieu, which has one of the oldest churches in France (9th century). The slopes, which have gravelly and siliceous soil, are still used for growing the gros plant variety. Cultivation is generally by mixed-crop farming, as can be seen from the relatively scattered vineyards.

From **Saint-Philbert-de-Grand-Lieu** take the D 65 towards La Chevrolière. Just before the village, go down to the Lac de Grand-Lieu at Passay ⑦, where the peat and ooze of Holocene age contain pollen from the Vitis (Planchais). This wild vine, or lambrusque, which has since undergone repeated cross-selection, is probably the ancestor of the chenin blanc, the characteristic native variety of the Loire Valley vineyards.

FOR FURTHER
INFORMATION

Geology

Regional geological guides, Masson, Paris: '*Massif central*', *2nd edition*, (1978), by J.-M.Peterlongo (see especially the introduction and tours No 6, 11 and 27); '*Val de Loire*' (Loire Valley) (1976), by G. Alcaydé et al. (see especially tours No 3, 5, 7, 8 and 9); '*Bretagne*' (Brittany) (2nd edition, 1985), by S. Durand, H. Lardeux *et al.* (see the introduction and tour No 14).

Macaire J.-J. (1981). — 'Contribution a 'étude géologique et paléopédologique du Quaternaire dans le sud-ouest du bassin de Paris (Touraine et ses abords)' (Some Research into the Geology and Palaeopedology of the Quaternary Era in the Touraine Region of the Southwestern Paris Basin), State Doct.Thes., University of Tours, 1, 304 p.; 2, 126 p.

Planchais N. (1972–73). — 'Apports de l'analyse pollinique à la connaissance de l'extension de la vigne au Quaternaire' (Pollen analysis and its Contribution to Knowledge about the Expansion of the Vine during the Quaternary), *Naturalia monspeliensia*, Bot ser. (23-24), pp. 211–223.

Rasplus L. (1978). — 'Contribution à l'étude géologique des formations continentales détritiques tertiaires de la Touraine, de la Brenne et de la Sologne' (Some Research into the Geology of the Detrital Continental Formations of Tertiary Age in the Touraine, Brenne and Sologne regions), *State Doct.Thes.*, University of Orléans, 454 p.

Oenology

Bisson J. and Studer R. (1971). — 'Etude des sols du Sancerrois viticole nord' (The Vineyard Soils of the Northern Sancerre District), *Bull.de l'INAO* No 111.

Blancher S. (1983). — 'Les vins du Val de Loire' (The Wines of the Loire Valley), Edit.Jemma, Saumur.

Bréjoux P. (1974). — '*Les vins de la Loire*' (The Wines of the Loire), La revue du vin de France, Paris, 239 p.

Comité interprofessionnel des vins de Touraine, Tours. — 'Le vignoble de Touraine' (Vineyards of the Touraine), 18 p. (19 square Prosper-Mérimée, 37000 Tours, France).

Morlat R., Puissant A., Asselin C., Léon H., Remoue M. (1981). — 'Quelques aspects de l'influence du milieu édaphique sur l'enracinement de la vigne, conséquences sur la qualité du vin' (Some Aspects of the Soil's Influence on Vine Root Growth and the Consequences for Wine Quality), *Bull.Ass.Fr.Et.Sol*, No 2, pp. 125–146.

Puisais J. (1985). — 'Les vins de la Loire' (Wines of the Loire), Nouv. République, Tours.

Previous page: The hill at Sancerre. The vineyard slopes overlie marl and argillo-siliceous formations of Cretaceous and Eocene age. The track in the foreground is virtually parallel with the fault (Photo. Macaire).

Above: A typical small valley in Vouvray. The cellars behind the wine-growers' houses are hollowed out of the tufa rock-face. The vineyard growing chenin blanc is located on the plateau in the background (Photo. Macaire).

Below: Chinon at dusk (Photo. Macaire).

Lorraine

The vineyards of Lorraine are synonymous with those of the Moselle, the river that was once a frontier of the Roman Empire. Ausonius the poet and winegrower was praising its hillsides clad with flourishing vines as long ago as the 4th century AD. This made them without doubt the best known vineyards of the Roman era. The wines were transported northwards along the Moselle, a much less hazardous operation than using the Rhine (which was not used as a waterway until Carolingian times). The Lorraine section of the Moselle valley was an important Roman route linking large centres of civilian population (Toul, Metz, Triers) as well as numerous spa towns on each side of the river (between Plombières and Sierck-les- Bains), and at that time was something of a wine-growing paradise in miniature, rather as the area between Triers and Koblenz is today.

History of the vineyards and their people

Rise, fall and re-emergence

Rooted as it was in Rome and the Episcopacy, Lorraine inevitably became an important centre of monasticism. Convents and basilicas had already been established in the episcopal sees by the 4th century, and their ranks were increased by the many abbeys set up when the monks of Ireland brought Christianity to these eastern outposts. In this region more than any other, the neighbouring abbeys and their extensive vineyards were an important stimulus to establishing and maintaining vineyards in the most favoured sites.

Metz had been the capital of a Celtic tribe, the Mediomatrices, and later became the seat of the Carolingian dynasty. The vineyards around Metz became enormously popular in the 12th and 13th centuries, an era of cathedral building, general prosperity and bustling commerce. The auxerrois grape variety was developed at Laquenexy on the southeastern fringes of Metz.

Saline springs gave rise to a salt production industry, followed by the discovery of iron ore at shallow depths and the introduction of forges. These resources had long constituted a reservoir of non-agricultural activities, but from beginnings in the 13th and 17th centuries they brought a degree of prosperity to the population of the Duchy of Lorraine and its "Three Bishoprics" by providing alternative employment. Conversely, the march of industrialisation put vineyards in retreat, at first around the towns and then in the apparently favoured sites. The working population had long wavered between peasant wine-grower and manual worker. The scientific and industrial revolutions of the 19th century finally tipped the scales in favour of increasingly well-paid industrial work.

At this point lesser vineyards would have given in completely and disappeared. The wine-growing region of Lorraine held out despite some powerful adversaries, such as fast rail deliveries of cheap wine from other regions, a delayed outbreak of phylloxera and an excessively wet climate. Though today only a shadow of the vineyard that once was, it is a model of vitality and seems to imply the beginnings of a re-emergence. These scattered remnants of a paradise lost were granted VDQS status in 1951, and in the nineteen-eighties two appellations were defined, known as "Côte-de-Toul" on the western side of that town, and "Vins de Moselle" in the regions of Sierck-les-Bains, Metz and Vic-sur-Seille. They just happen to be close to old abbeys.

Vines and soils

Landscape, exposure and geology

These hillside vineyards face mainly east or southeast into the sun, due to the deep, winding nature of the Moselle valley which runs from south to north. The tabular structures of Triassic and Jurassic age which back onto the massif of the Vosges and dip towards the Paris Basin alternate between calcareous and argillaceous formations. They have been subjected to erosion and continental extremes of temperature for over 100 million years, and the limestone has formed uplands or plateaux separated by lowlying argillaceous plains. The ensuing concentrically arranged morphology gives rise to a sequence of uplands known as the Côtes de Moselle, the Côtes de Meuse, the Côte de Bars and the Côte de Champagne.

Thus the somewhat dry calcareous upper slopes enjoy a sheltered climate, providing suitable conditions for vines and orchards. The plateaux or lowlands, on the other hand, are more suitable for cereals or grass.

South of Metz, however, the tidy arrangement of formations was disturbed somewhat by tectonic features with a northeasterly orientation. These undulations are due to earlier synclines and anticlines which obliged first the Meurthe and then the Moselle, instead of flowing along the edges of the hills, to incise the hills longitudinally, creating isolated outliers to the east between Nancy and Metz.

The geological formations underlying the vineyards of Lorraine are seen to be progressively younger from north to south. At Sierck the vineyards are on dolomitic Muschelkalk and Keuper, at Metz they overlie Dogger, and at Toul they are on Malm. A tour of all the vineyards will give a complete cross-section from Early Triassic to Late Jurassic.

Climate

Lorraine represents the eastern extremity of the Paris Basin where it encounters the edge of the Vosges Massif. Its climate combines continental and oceanic influences, giving rise to pronounced extremes of temperature. As a result, rainfall occurs throughout the year at an annual average, varying from south to north, of between 720 and 770 mm. Even though the prevailing southwesterly rains are only partially tempered by the high ground of the Côtes de Meuse and the Côtes de Moselle, the vineyards are located in rain shadows.

Mean annual temperature is 9.6°C, mainly because of long, cold winters (January average 1.4°C). Yet although there are likely to be over seventy days of frost, only a few of these will be consecutive. Summer averages are at least 2° lower than in Alsace (July average 18.1°C).

Sunshine hours are drastically reduced by frequent cloud cover. Nineteen cloudless days contrast with seventy-one sunless days. Average hours of sunshine vary between 1 500 and 1 600 per annum, with 1 100 of these occurring between April and September. Relative humidity of 72 per cent in summer and 90 per cent in winter, with over sixty days of mist every year, are further characteristics of the climate in Lorraine, which at first sight seems better suited to grazing land than vineyards.

Vine varieties

The Lorraine wine-growing district uses grape varieties from Alsace or the Rhineland. Although there are still many direct hybrid producers, they are likely to disappear since they are no longer accorded VDQS status. Vins de Moselle and Côtes-de-Toul are derived from pinot blanc and pinot noir, auxerrois blanc, and very occasionally auxerrois gris (locally called auxerrois de Laquenexy, indicating its Lorraine origins) together with a little of the riesling and sylvaner varieties.

Varieties from outside Alsace include the meunier gris, which is also used in Champagne. It gives fresh, pale-red wines with a fairly high alcohol content, though less fine than wines derived from pinot. Gamay is another highly recommended variety. It is a black grape with white or tinted juice, and though highly productive it is early, and therefore sensitive to frost. It grows well in deep, clayey soil giving pleasantly fruity grey or red wines for drinking young. When used with pinot noir, the resulting wines are more supple.

Muller-thurgau is also allowed in VDQS Vins de Moselle. This variety is a riesling-sylvaner cross developed in 1882 by H.Muller (from the Swiss canton of Thurgau). It is vigorous, usually prolific and early, and though its wine is slightly lacking in acidity, in Lorraine it gives a well-balanced and particularly fruity wine.

A brief word about the elbling or burger blanc, which is a near relative of the gouais blanc from the Rhône. This variety was introduced from Germany after 1870, but is banned from use in appellation wines. Volume producers of "vin ordinaire" in Luxembourg plant this variety on their estates in France. Elbling was once sold in Germany by the vintners of Triers for making "champagne", but was also sent to Champagne itself before being prohibited by laws passed in 1908 and 1911.

The speciality wine of Lorraine is "vin gris", a very pale rosé wine made from red varieties and vinified as if it were a white, that is pressed before fermentation (without macerating the must).

Wines of the Moselle

There were as many as 6 200 ha of the Côtes de Moselle district under vine in 1893. Today scarcely 200 ha are dedicated to vineyards, and these are unequally divided between three regions. In fact, a total of 887 ha, shared by 18 village districts, have been designated VDQS, yet of these less than 10 ha claim this appellation today. They base their output on auxerrois, pinot and muller-thurgau varieties, and production is limited in official terms to the "60–90 hl/ha range". There are also many hybrid or excluded vines on the 200 ha in use.

The Sierck-les-Bains region

The vineyards in the loop of the Moselle between Haute-Kontz, Contz-les-Bains and Sierck are bustling with vitality. (Of the 238 ha designated VDQS, some 60 ha are in production). Most of the vineyards are owned by wine-growers from Luxembourg, who are not interested in producing wines of VDQS status. They prefer to grow the elbling, since it produces a prolific amount of ordinary wine, and the grapes are processed at the cooperative wineries in Luxembourg. Small growers from Lorraine may not claim VDQS status for their original elbling varieties, but they are now allowed to use the muller-thurgau variety which is so popular in Germany and well suited to Lorraine's soil and weather.

Itinerary

Near the centre and to the south of Sierck, the Montenach stream is incising the basement of the old Rhineland massif: Taunus Quartzite of Devonian age (quarries), uplands of Hercynian age, residual mountains overlain by sandstone of Late Buntsandstein age. This red micaceous Voltzia-rich sandstone forms the Moselle valley floor.

"La colline du Stromberg" (Mount Stromberg) rises like a mountain peak to the north of the town. On the shelly and marly-dolomitic Lower Muschelkalk sandstone of its southern slopes stand vineyards which owe their longevity as much to the Carthusians of Sierck as to the spa town of Contz. The journey from Contz to Haute-Kontz first crosses a fracture field of Keuper age and then brings us to the Schliewerberg vineyard, which stands on variegated marl with dolomitic banks of Late Keuper age and argillaceous sandstone of Rhaetian age.

Calcareous sandstone facies thus predominate in the vineyards around **Sierck**, engendering a fruity lightness in the white wines produced from pinot, auxerrois and muller-thurgau. The latter variety is one to look out for. Pinot noir also does very well on these soils.

The Metz region

This region is typical of the Côtes de Moselle. It was once the most extensive, and nearly 550 ha have recently been designated VDQS, even though several villages which once produced highly respected wines have given up wine-growing altogether. The region produces light rosé wines called "Clairets de la Moselle", as well as some less popular reds.

The vineyards grow on the left bank of the Moselle. They stand on the upper hill slopes overlooking many villages which have been transformed into small towns by the industrialisation of the valley.

To the east, the argillaceous Liassic plain supporting grass and crops has been incised by the Moselle. Marly Toarcian formations and even Pliensbachian argillaceous sandstone occur in the valley bottom. The uplands to the west consist of Dogger formations. The first few metres date from the Aalenian, then there is marly calcareous limestone with accumulations of iron-rich oolites which were once extracted from the hillsides by drift mining. Nowadays Lorraine iron is worked by mine shafts penetrating the tree-clad Haye plateau, the edge of which forms the calcareous cuesta of Early and Middle Bajocian age (note the many retaining walls). The limestones here are of the spathic, coral, shelly and oolitic varieties, which break down to form scree slopes overlying the Toarcian marls. The resulting soils are almost exclusively the domain of the Metz region vineyards. Vines which face east or southeast benefit from the stoniness of the broken limestone surface as well as from the mineral-rich argillaceous subsoil with its good water retention characteristics.

Itinerary

At **Marange-Silvange**, about ten kilometres north-northwest of Metz, is the last remaining vineyard in the district. The location conforms perfectly to the morphological and geological criteria mentioned above. The road to Malancourt climbs the cuesta. After a kilometre, a quarry of fossil-rich Bajocian limestone can be seen to the right of the road. Limestone workings (Jaumont Oolite) are also common to the east of Roncourt.

Due west of Metz, in the wide blind valley of the Montvaux (N 43), which faces south-east, is a group of wine-growing villages consisting of **Châtel-Saint-Germain, Lessy, Scy-Chazelles, Sainte-Ruffine, Jussy and Vaux**. A further 5 km to the south (D 6) we find Ancy, Dornot and Novéant. At Ancy, which produces a well-known red, the scree is mixed with silt.

Cross the Moselle at Corny into the southeastern sector of the region, where the vineyards stand on the eastern slope of the Côte de Faye. Here the river has dissected the limestone plateau lengthwise (Pont-a- Mousson Anticline). The Côtes de Moselle are east of the river. The wine-growing district is defined as the villages of Fey, Marieulles- Vezon and Lorry-Mardigny. The geological characteristics are the same here, except that we find quarries working the Liassic marls: some 600 metres west of Fey a quarry is working the Pliensbachian argillaceous formations; north of Jouy-aux-Arches, on the eastern side of the N 57, the firm of Jouy-Tuilière is exploiting the same formations as well as Middle Liassic sandstone and Toarcian paper shale.

It is also worth travelling 8 km to the southeast of Metz (D 999) to Laquenexy on the Liassic plain, where the vineyards on the Lotharingian limestone and marl are steeped in antiquity. A viticultural research centre was established here in 1902. It became a centre for research into fruit in general, but is soon to return to its original purpose.

The Vic-sur-Seille region

The presence of brine springs in the vicinity of **Château-Salins** has made this region a scene of human endeavour since the New Stone Age, and particularly so in Gallo-Roman times. The salt drew the abbeys to the area in the Middle Ages (Vergaville), fomenting rivalry between the bishops of Metz and the Dukes of Lorraine. Rock salt was mined in the 19th century, first and foremost around Vic, and this activity certainly generated long-term support for the vineyard's products. The 'vin gris' produced around Vic is popular. Some 3 ha of the present 16 ha of vines are dedicated to VDQS, yet more than 100 ha have been designated VDQS in the area, implying that the vineyard was once an important source of income for the village.

As at **Haute-Kontz**, the vineyard stands on dolomitic marl of Late Keuper age and its overlying Rhaetian argillaceous sandstone. Horizons of red marl (Chanville and Levallois) enclose these formations and can easily be seen on the hill to the north of Vic which is dissected by a stream called Quatre Rupt. Here, on the slopes of the buttes known as Haute- Borne and Noires-Montagnes, are vineyards of pinot, auxerrois and gamay.

A visit to the **Musée du Sel** (Salt Museum) in Marsal shows how, at the dawn of history, salt was made into 'briquettes' using terra cotta vessels.

Côtes de Toul

It was certainly a bishopric, some time around the 4th century at Toul, which established vineyards in the region. Eight villages on the western side of the town have taken up the VDQS appellation which was granted in 1951 and confirmed by decree in 1983. This means that 800 hectares could again be planted with gamay noir, pinot noir and auxerrois blanc, but at the present time only 64 ha are producing around 4 000 hectolitres of grey, red and white wines.

Toul is located in a loop of the Moselle which shows that at this point its course was captured by a tributary of the Meurthe. In fact, when the Moselle had intersected the Bajocian limestone plateau and crossed the Woëvre clay formations, it used to join the Meuse at Pagny via the Malm limestone. This latter section was abandoned during the Quaternary for various topographic and tectonic reasons, and is now a dry valley known as the Val de l'Ane, occupied by the puny Ingressin.

Soil of the Late Jurassic: the vineyards, then, are located at the foot of the Côtes du Toulois, or Côtes de Meuse, on the upper portion of the Woëvre clay formations: Callovian-Oxfordian marls are overlain first by Oxfordian flints, in the form of a hard layer of siliceous limestone and lamellibranch-rich sandy marl; then by oolitic limestone with Argovian and Rauracian coral reefs. These limestones and flints break down into scree which is then immobilised by the underlying marl.

Itinerary

The wine-growing villages are practically on the same line of longitude. Wines from Lagney exist only in memory. Lucey and Bruley account for 4/5ths of the vineyards around Toul, with over 100 designated hectares in each village. These vineyards are perched picturesquely on slopes, each village with its own retaining walls. We recommend a visit to the quarry in the flint formations some 800 metres north of Pagney- derrière-Barine, on the way up towards Pagney woods. Here you will find very hard siliceous limestone interbedded with occasionally shaly marl. The coral-rich and oolitic limestones can be seen in several old quarries 500 metres northeast of Ecrouves.

South of the former Moselle valley, the situation of Domgermain, Charmes-la-Côte, Mont-le-Vignoble, Blénod-lès-Toul and Bulligny is identical to that of the north. Here, Bulligny produces from an area of 16 ha whereas Charmes has some 237 ha of territory.

The vineyards in the Toul region expand a little more each year, and are promoted by the 'Confrérie des Compagnons de la Capucine', which was established at Toul in 1962. Wines of the VDQS Côtes-de-Toul are valued for their fruitiness when young. Only the red wines made from pinot noir will age gracefully.

Wines of Lorraine and gastronomy

The present re-emergence of the wines of Lorraine is therefore taking place mainly in the vineyards at the northern and southern extremes of the wine-growing region (Sierck and Toul respectively). Their quality is continually improving, and they are finding favour as wines to accompany entrées and second courses, with such dishes as Lorraine sausages or Quiche Lorraine.

To round off your meal, Lorraine can offer you its own digestif, a clear spirit called Mirabelle. Nowhere else will you find one as fruity.

FOR FURTHER INFORMATION

Geology

'Guide géologique: Lorraine-Champagne' (Guide to the Geology of Lorraine-Champagne), 1979, by J.Hilly, B.Haguenauer et al., Masson, Paris.

IN SEARCH OF LOST VINEYARDS
THE PARIS REGION

From the Middle Ages until the 18th century, the Paris region was one of the main wine-growing regions of France, but nowadays only a few relics remain, such as the vineyards at Argenteuil, Suresnes (Mont Valérien) and Montmartre. We may include the many small plots of land still under vine, right up to its traditional northern growing limit around Laon (fig.106). Why did these vineyards originally flourish, what caused them to decline, and what part did geology play in any of this?

The natural conditions in the Paris region (a great variety of rocks and soil, undulating landscape, temperate climate) are basically not so very different from those in the Champagne or Orléans regions. In fact, the winding, chalk and limestone meander slopes of the Marne and the Seine, and the undulating slopes of the marl buttes capped with Fontainebleau Sands, as well as the many sites facing in easterly, southeasterly and southerly directions, all add up to a favoured setting for viticulture (fig.107).

Wine-growing expanded rapidly under the Carolingian kings. Even at that time, mention was made of the vineyards at Montmorency, Cormeilles and Mont Valérien, where the predominant varieties were pinot (for red wines) and fromental (for white wines, better appreciated in the Middle Ages than today). These wines were transported on the waterways: on the Seine to Rouen and England, or on the Oise towards Picardy and then to Flandres and the Low Countries.

In Carolingian Paris of the 9th and 10th centuries, vines flourished at Charonne, Belleville and Montmartre, with England acting as an important outlet. But as the population of Paris grew, an ever-increasing share of the wine-harvest found its way to the capital. Or, to be more precise, two shares: one for the middle classes, which would nowadays be called 'owner-bottled', and the other for the people, of a lower quality, which the wine-growers of the 'flat lands' sold to the tavern-keepers.

The latter flow was stemmed by an act of the Paris "Parlement" dated 14th August 1577, forbidding inn-keepers from "going to buy wines in the country". Since wine was at that time as essential as the motor-car is today, it was naturally seen as a source of tax revenue. It was these "entry taxes" which affected the wine trade at the time, and prompted the inn-keepers to emigrate beyond the taxation perimeter set up by Louis XIII and reinforced by the construction of barriers at which the taxes were levied.

Beyond these barriers the "guinguettes", or open-air café bars, prospered and multiplied from 1675-1680 onwards in the districts of Pologne, Les Porcherons and Nouvelle France, as well as the Courtille district further east (fig.108; Dion, 1959). Among the café bars closest to Paris were those of the "Barrière Blanche", at the northern end of the Chaussée d'Antin. This barrier owes its name to the convoys of workers who came down from the gypsum-quarries of Montmartre via the Rue Blanche.

These barriers became symbols of fiscal oppression, incurring the wrath of wine-growers and consumers alike — not to mention the ingenuity of smugglers, who used tunnels (one of which was around 800 metres long), or even launched weighted balloons from scaffolding, in order to get round them.

The authorities started to construct a perimeter wall around the city limits of the era of Louis XIII. Called the "Mur des Fermiers Généraux" (Wall of the Farmers General), it would have brought the "guinguettes" within the area of taxation. This

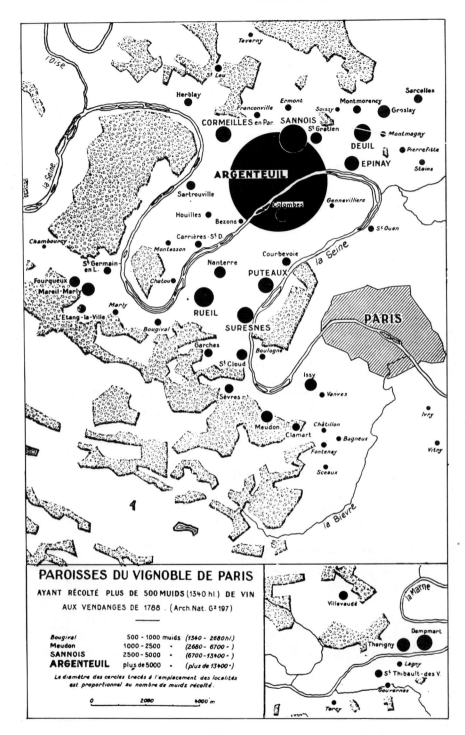

Fig. 106. — The location of vineyards and the size of harvests in the Paris region in 1788 (adapted from Dion. 1959).

PARISHES IN THE PARIS WINE-GROWING AREA PRODUCING OVER 500 HOGSHEADS (1340 hl) OF WINE FROM THE 1788 GRAPE HARVEST (Arch. Nat, G2 197). The diameter of the circle drawn at each location is in proportion to the number of hogsheads produced.

Laon, Vue

Fig. 107. — Laon and its vineyards around 1789 (water-colour by Tavernier de Jonquières: Bibliothèque nationale).

générale.

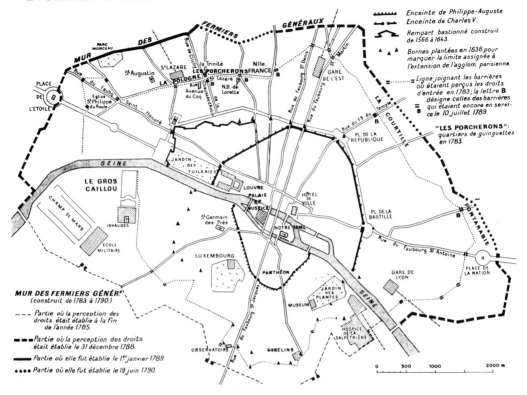

Fig.108. — Plan of Paris in 1789. Some place-names and the shaded areas relate to paris in modern times (adapted from Dion. 1959).

Legend (top right)
City boundary at the time of Philippe-Auguste.
City boundary at the time of Charles V.
Fortified ramparts constructed between 1566 and 1643.
Boundary-posts erected in 1638 to mark the limit assigned to the expansion of Paris.
Line joining the barriers where entry duties were levied in 1783: the letter B indicates those barriers still operating on 10th July 1789.
'LES PORCHERONS': the 'guinguettes' districts in 1783.

Legend (bottom left)
MUR DES FERMIERS GENERAUX (Wall of the Farmers General) (built between 1783 and 1790)
Sector where duties were levied at the end of 1785.
Sector where duties were levied 31st December 1788.
Sector where duties were levied 1st January 1789.
Sector where duties were levied 19th June 1790.

plan infuriated the populace, and on 11th July 1789 the Barrière Blanche was attacked and burned. The following day other such incidents occurred, foreshadowing the Storming of the Bastille (Dion, 1959).

As demand increased, vineyards expanded from the hillslopes onto the plains (flat lands), and the noble grape varieties were replaced with the higher-yielding gamay. This was the start of the debasement of the vineyards during the 18th century (Dion, 1959), which continued into the 19th century, when yields at Argenteuil reached 200 hectolitres per hectare from soils heavily manured with Parisian night soils (Lachiver, 1982). The resulting wines were mediocre. They included the *'Picolo d'Argenteuil'*, the *'Petit Bleu de Suresnes'* and the *'Ginglet des coteaux de Cergy et de l'Hautil'*.

Although the vineyards of Languedoc were attacked by phylloxera as early as 1863, the Paris region was still producing 84 million hectolitres of wine in 1878. Paradoxically, the phylloxera outbreak revitalised the Parisian vineyards, which were protected from the initial outbreak by the vine-free area of La Beauce (the first insects did not reach Arpajon until 1886). But the railway outpaced the phylloxera, and the vineyards of the Ile de France "which had survived every attack by insect and by mildew, and were preparing to overcome the phylloxera outbreak, were defenceless against wine delivered to Paris at 10 Francs per hectolitre" (Lachiver, 1982). Overproduction in the Midi, culminating in the crisis of 1907 and the resulting wine market collapse, was such that "there remain today only the merest traces of the great vineyards which, for fifteen centuries, mirrored every major aspect of the political and social history of the City of Paris" (Dion, 1959).

There are, of course, living reminders like the museum-vineyards at **Montmartre, Suresnes and Argenteuil.** To these can be added a few place-names, such as the Rue de Retrait, in the 20th "arrondissement". The name of the street is a corruption of "Ratrait", who was the proprietor of a famous vineyard in Ménilmontant. The Rue des Morillons in Vaugirard commemorates a variety of grape similar to the pineau. Some administrative districts in the Ile de France also have names recalling the vine: Chanteloup-les-Vignes, 10 km south of Pontoise; Nouvion-le- Vineux, 7 km south of Laon; Vignemont, 10 km northwest of Compiègne; Saint-Thibault-les-Vignes, 2 km from Lagny; and Vigneux-sur-Seine, 15 km south of Paris. These relics survive to perpetuate the glorious memory of a vineyard now gone forever.

> FOR FURTHER
> INFORMATION

Geology

'*Guides géologiques*' (Geological Guides) Paris, Masson: '*Bassin de Paris, Ile-de-France, Pays de Bray*', (1968, 3rd edition 1986), by C.Pomerol and L.Feugueur; '*Paris et environs, les roches, l'eau et les hommes*' (Paris and District, Rocks, Waterways and Population), (1979), by P. Diffre and C. Pomerol.

Oenology

Lachiver M. (1982). — 'Vin et vignerons en région parisienne du XVIIe au XIXe siècle' (Wine and Wine-growers in the Paris Region from the 17th to the 19th Centuries), *Soc.historique et archéologique de Pontoise*, 37, rue de Chantereine, 78250 Hardricourt, France.

LYONNAIS

A journey from north to south down the western edge of the Rhône graben follows an almost unbroken succession of vineyards, some of which are more famous than others: Bourgogne, Mâconnais, Beaujolais, Côtes du Rhône. Yet there is a surprising gap. Between the south of Beaujolais and the north of Côtes du Rhône, the region around Lyon is almost devoid of vines. Why is this? And was it always so?

For as back as records go, the Rhône corridor has been a busy trade route between the Mediterranean and countries in the north. When the two most important Gallo-Roman cities of Lyon and Vienne were developed, vines were introduced by Greek or Roman merchants as an adjunct to the active Mediterranean wine trade. The introduction of the vine occurred between Villefranche-sur-Saône and Condrieu, around precisely the two great cities from which vines have today disappeared.

It is known that these vines originated from the Mediterranean area (they were of the viognier and serine varieties). It was not until the 13th or 14th centuries that the gamay variety, having been excluded from Bourgogne, reached the Lyonnais district.

M.-T.Lorcin (1974) has re-examined the 14th-century founding of the Lyonnais vineyards and followed their subsequent development. He found that in the 15th century (fig.109), vines were established in widely separated areas around the river Azergues and along the valley of the Brévenne (Saint-Jean-des-Vignes, Bessenay) but were more densely implanted on the terraced hillsides along the right bank of the Saône and the Rhône, between the Azergues and Condrieu, with an incursion along the whole of the Gier valley. It can thus be seen that vineyards were planted on any type of soil, the over-riding consideration being that they should face south or east. In this way, vines colonised all types of alluvial formations along the Saône or Rhône, whether old, recent, fluviatile or glacial. They covered the slopes of the Mont d'Or sedimentary formations, limestones, clays and sandstones alike. They adapted to the crystalline soils, especially around the Brévenne, the Gier and the district of Condrieu. The wine-growers needed all their ingenuity and doggedness to overcome the generally poor qualities of the soil, including the direction of ploughing, erection of retaining walls, terracing, and so on. That is why the lie of the land, and therefore the climate, played the major role. Yields would have been fairly high, but the quality mediocre, generally described as "convent wine".

From the 16th century, the Lyonnais vineyards expanded considerably. Eastwards they reached the slopes of the Dombes range. To the west, they covered the Lyonnais plateau, reaching the lower slopes of the Lyonnais uplands and Mont Pilat. It was certainly not quality which contributed to this expansion. The areas of high yield continued to be the slopes south of Lyon (Grigny, Millery), and those of Mont d'Or and Condrieu. Vines did not advance northwards, however, except in the area of Villefranche-sur-Saône. Cereals were the main crops at Fleurie, Morgon and Moulin-à-Vent (as the name, "Windmill", implies).

During the 17th and 18th centuries, the Lyonnais vineyards regressed. They disappeared in the reverse order in which they arose. Soon there was only the Mont d'Or and its surroundings (Champagne, Ecully, for instance), the slopes south of Lyon, some of the Gier, and Condrieu. The corollary, or even the cause, was the development of the Beaujolais vineyards.

The vineyards of Lyonnais were to have another, weaker expansion towards the middle of the 19th century: fluid intake was needed by the mining and other industries around Saint-Etienne and the Gier valley. Thus there were still 16 000 hectares under vine in 1877 when the phylloxera outbreak occurred. The vineyards were then

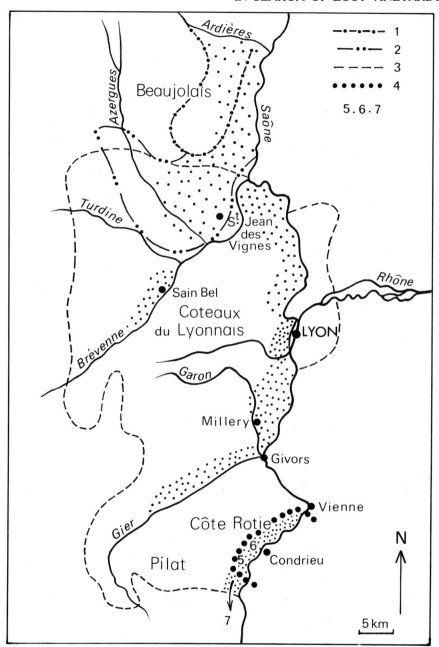

Fig. 109. — The extent of the Lyonnais vineyard (dotted area).

1. Southern boundary of Beaujolais 'grand cru'; 2. Southern boundary of inferior Beaujolais; 3. Boundary of the Lyonnais district; 4. Boundary of the Côte-Rôtie vineyard; 5. Appellation 'Côte-Rôtie'; 6. Appellation 'Château-Grillet'; 7. Côtes du Rhône.

replanted, reaching their maximum extent around 1902, and regressing ever since. Orchards have replaced vines on all the well-exposed sites (peach and pear trees, etc., to the south of Lyon; cherry trees around Brévenne).

As G.Durand (1979) says, it can be seen that the vineyards expanded according to three strategies: around the consumer townships and the estate owners, they were circular (as happened with the oldest ones); later, their expansion was linear, on the

357

well-exposed slopes along valleys and local routes (Azergues, Brévenne, Gier, Condrieu); and lastly, expansion was interstitial, that is using all favourable sites, so long as the main demand came from outside the region.

Nowadays only a few traces of the former Lyonnais vineyards remain: Millery, Saint-Laurent-d'Agny, Sain-Bel and a few neighbouring villages. Since 1984 they have been brought together under the appellation "Coteaux du Lyonnais", but total production is hardly more than 10 000 hectolitres per annum. A little further south, downstream of Vienne, one of the oldest vineyards still clings perilously to the cliffs of Mont Pilat. The appellation "Côte-Rôtie" covers 106 hectares of crystalline shale and produces 4 600 hectolitres of red wine. The "Condrieu" appellation is reserved for a rare and exceptional white wine (16 ha, 400 hl) and another, the "Château-Grillet", is one of the most geographically restricted appellations in France (2.5 ha, 90 hl).

It would no longer be possible to slake the thirst of the inhabitants of Lyon if the third river which flows into the town, the Beaujolais, had not considerably increased its flow in the course of time as it ran parallel to the Saône.

FOR FURTHER INFORMATION

Geology

Guide géologique Lyonnais — Vallée du Rhône (Guide to the Geology of the Lyonnais Region and the Rhône Valley) (1973), by G. Demarcq et al., Masson, Paris.

Oenology

Lorcin M.-T. (1974). — 'Les campagnes de la région lyonnaise aux XIVe et XVe siècles' (The Country around Lyon in the 14th and 15th Centuries), *Bosc.impr., Lyon*, 548 p.

Durand G. (1979). — 'Vin, vigne et vignerons en Lyonnais et Beaujolais' (Wines, Vines and Wine-growers of Lyonnais and Beaujolais), Presses Univ., Lyon, 540 p.

Durand G. and Garrier G. (1980). — 'Vin, vigne et vignerons en Lyonnais et Beaujolais' (Wines, Vines and Wine-growers of Lyonnais and Beaujolais), in: 'Hommes et terroir', *Ass.Amis.Mus.Lyon pub.*, pp. 55–90.

FRENCH WINE QUALITIES: A COMPARATIVE CHART

YEAR	Red Bordeaux	White Bordeaux	Red Burgundy	White Burgundy	Côtes-du-Rhône	Alsace	Pouilly-sur-Loire Sancerre	Anjou Touraine	Beaujolais	Champagne
1928	*	••••	*							
1929	••••	*	*							
1945	*	*	••••		••••					
1947	*	••••	••••		••••			*		
1949	*	••••	*		••••			••••		
1955	••••	••••	••••	•••	••••			••••		
1959	•••	••••	*	•••	•••	*		*		
1961	*	*	*	••••	••••	••••		•••		
1962	••••	••••	•••	•••	•••	••		•••		
1964	•••	•	••••	•••	•••	•••				
1966	••••	•••	••••	•••	••••	••••				
1967	•••	*	•••	•••	••••	••••				
1969	•	••	•••	••••	•••	•••		•••		
1970	*	•••	•••	*	*	•••		•••		
1971	••••	•••	••••	••••	••••	*		•••		
1973	•••	•••	••	••••		••••		••		
1974	•••	•••	•••	•••	••	••		••		
1975	*	••••	•	•••	••••	•••		•••		
1976	••••	••••	••••	••••	••••	*		•••		
1977	••	••	••			••		••		
1978	••••	•••	*	••••	*	••	••••	••••	•••	
1979	••••	•••	•••	*	•••	••••	•••	•••	••	
1980	••	•	••	•••	••••	••	•••	••	•	
1981	••••	•••	••	•••	•••	••••	••	•••	•••	
1982	*	•••	•••	••••	••	•••	••••	•••	••	
1983	Some good quality wines with regional variations									

Champagne column note: The best years were 1975, 1976, 1978 and 1979. Some notable vintages are shown. Wines without a year are generally blended from the wines of several years under the supervision of each winegrower.

Minor year	Average year	Good year	Great year	Exceptional year
•	••	•••	••••	*

The table gives the average quality for a given year only.
There are exceptions to prove every rule.

This chart is published by kind permission of the 'Institut National des Appellations d'Origine des vins et eaux-de-vie' (INAO). The INAO is the French Government Agency responsible for laying down and supervising the production conditions for French AOC wines.

Ma	ERA	PERIOD	EPOCH		AGE	OTHER UNITS
2	Cenozoic	Tertiary	Quaternary			
5	Cenozoic	Tertiary / Neogene	Pliocene		Piazencian = Astian	Lower Villafranchian
					Tabianian = Zanclean	
			Miocene		Messinian	Pontian
					Tortonian	
					Serravallian	Helvetian
					Langhian	
					Burdigalian	
24					Aquitanian	
		Palaeogene	Oligocene		Chattian	
36					Stampian = Rupelian	Stampian ss
						Sannoisian
			Eocene		Priabonian	Ludian
					Bartonian ss	Marinesian Auversian
					Lutetian	
55					Ypresian	Cuisian
						Sparnacian = Ilerdian
			Paleocene		Thanetian	
					Montian	Vitrollian
65					Danian	
	Mesozoic	Cretaceous	Late	Senonian	Maastrichtian	Rognacian Begudian
					Campanian	Fuvelian Valdonnian
					Santonian	
					Coniacian	
100					Turonian	
					Cenomanian	
			Early	Neocomian	Albian	Vraconian
					Aptian	faciès Urgonian
					Barremian	
					Hauterivian	
135					Valanginian	
					Berriasian	
		Jurassic	Late	Malm	Portlandian	Tithonian
					Kimmeridgian	- Sequanian
					Oxfordian	- Rauracian
			Middle	Dogger	Callovian	- Argovian
					Bathonian	
					Bajocian	
					Aalenian	
			Early	Lias	Toarcian	
					Domerian Carixian	Pliensbachian = Charmouthian
					Sinemurian	Lotharingian Sinemurian
195					Hettangian	
		Triassic	Late		Rhaetian	
					Norian	Keuper
					Carnian	
			Middle		Ladinian	Muschelkalk
					Anisian = Virglorian	
230			Early		Scythian Werfenian	Buntsandstein

360

Ma	ERA	PERIOD	EPOCH	AGE		
230	Palaeozoic	Permian	Late	Turingian		
			Early	Saxonian		
280				Autunian		
		Carboniferous	Late	Silesian	Stephanian	
					Westphalian	
					Namurian	
			Early	Dinantian	Visean	
345					Tournaisian	
		Devonian	Late		Famennian	
					Frasnian	
			Middle		Givetian	
					Couvenian	
			Early		Emsian	
					Siegenian	
395					Gedinnian	
		Silurian	Late		Ludlovian	
					Wenlockian	
435			Early		Llandoverian	
		Ordovician	Late		Ashgillian	
					Caradocian	
			Early		Llandeilian	
					Llanvirnian	
					Arenigian	
500					Tremadocian	
		Cambrian	Late		Potsdamian	
			Middle		Acadian	
570			Early		Georgian	
	Precambrian	Protero-zoic			Brioverian	
1 000					Pentevrian	
2 600		Archean			Icartian	
3 800						

SIMPLIFIED GEOLOGICAL TIME-SCALE

This table is partly based on the work of F.W.B. van Eysinga (Elsevier, 1978) and of necessity takes the form of a diagram. It should especially be noted that the = sign does not always signify strict equivalence on the chronostratigraphic scale, nor that facies are always identical. During the Upper Pliocene, for instance, the Piazencian was essentially argillaceous whereas the Astian was mainly arenaceous. Similarly, dates shown in millions of years in the left-hand column are approximate only, and the uncertainty increases with remoteness in the past.

The lines are too straight to convey a true impression of the subtleties of stratigraphy. The Urgonian facies corresponds to the Barremian-Aptian in the Alps, for example, whereas in the Pyrenees it is generally younger (Aptian-Lower Albian). The Quaternary is divided into two very unequal parts: the Pleistocene, which lasted until about 10 000 years ago, and the Holocene, corresponding to the last 10 000 years (post-glacial). Geological units not shown in the above table are defined in the glossary. These units are all discussed in detail in three volumes called 'Stratigraphie', 'Paléogéographie: Précambrien' and 'Paléozoïque, Mésozoïque, Cénozoïque' by C.Pomerol and C.Babin, Doin édit., Paris.

GLOSSARY[1]

Alluvials : Clastic river deposits

Amphibole : Dark green mineral, elongated crystals of a ferro-magnesian silicate

Anticline : Fold convex towards the top

Arkose : Feldspathic sandstone

Basalt : Dark volcanic rock accounting for 95% of the continental and oceanic lavas

Bauxite : Aluminium ore, weathering product rich in hydrated aluminium oxides

Benthonic : Descriptive of bottom-dwelling organisms

Bioclast : Fragment of organic origin incorporated in a sediment

Bioclastic : Descriptive of a rock formed of bioclasts

Biodetritic : Synonym of bioclastic

Boulbène : Not very fertile soil in the Aquitane Basin, sandy-clayey, red, yellow or grey, sometimes cemented at depth. Silty soil of a specific, podzolic development

Calcedony : A siliceous mineral

Calcimorphic : Soil developed in the presence of abundant limestone

Ceratites : Group of Cephalopods (molluscs at present mainly represented by the Nautilus and the cuttlefish) with a convoluted shell which lived during Permian and Triassic times (see Geological Time Table)

Chert : A siliceous rocktype

Chloritoid : Needle- or plate-like mineral, a green ferro-magnesian silicate closely related to mica

Cluse : River valley at right angles to a fold axis

Colluvium : Slope deposits of fragments originating from nearby rocks

Crinoid : Group of Echinoderms attached to the seabed by an articulate stem. The fragments are the main constituent of crinoid limestone

Cryoturbation : Soil movements caused by repeated freezing and thawing

Cuesta : Escarpment at the edge of a slightly inclined plateau

Diaclase : Crack or fissure in the rock without displacement of the separated parts

Diorite : Dark coloured magmatic rock, wholly crystalline, consisting mainly of feldspars and amphiboles

Dolomite : Calcium-magnesium carbonate rock

Echinoid : Descriptive of a carbonate rock containing abundant fossil fragments of sea-urchins and starfish

Fault : Crack in the rock with displacement of the separated parts

Falun : Unconsolidated sedimentary rock with abundant shells

Feldspar : White or rose-coloured mineral abundant in granites, a potassium-aluminium silicate (orthoclase) or a sodium-calcium-aluminium silicate (plagioclase)

Flysch : Sedimentary rock consisting of alternating detrital coarse (sandstone) and finegrained (pelite, marl) beds

Foraminifer : Unicellular marine animal encased in a calcareous or chitinous shell

Gabbro : Very dark magmatic rock, wholly crystalline, consisting mainly of plagioclase and pyroxene

Garnet : A reddish-brown mineral with spheroid crystals. A complex silicate typical of metamorphic rocks

Gelifraction : Frost-shattering of the rock

Geothermal gradient : Increase in temperature with depth (approximately 3° per 100 metres)

Glauconite : A green mineral in sedimentary rocks. An aluminium-iron-potassium silicate

Gleysation : Reduction of iron in badly drained soils resulting in a mottled appearance

Gneiss : Metamorphic, banded rock composed mainly of quartz, feldspar and mica

Graben : Depressed block lying between two fault zones

Granite : Light coloured magmatic rock, whitish or reddish, wholly crystalline, consisting mainly of quartz, orthoclase and mica. Granite is a common surface rock

Greywacke : Sandy sedimentary, dark coloured and finegrained rock with a clayey matrix

Grit : Detrital accumulation, coarser than coarse sand and finer than fine gravel

Gypsum : A white or translucent mineral formed during the evaporation of sea water. A hydrated calcium sulphate

Holocene : Most recent Quaternary Epoch: the last 10 000 years

Horst : Uplifted block lying between two fault zones

Hydromorphic : Descriptive of a water-rich soil

Kyanite : A blue, rod-like mineral. Kyanite is an aluminium silicate typical of metamorphic rocks

Lapiaz : Dissolution furrows on the surface of a limestone plateau

Laterite : Red, superficial residual rock, rich in clay, iron and aluminium, originating from tropical or subtropical weathering or a variety of rocktypes

Latdorfian : Age practically equivalent to Late Ludian (Late Eocene)

Lignite : Carbon-rich rock originating from the transformation of deeply buried vegetation

Lithographic : Descriptive of a fine grained limestone formerly used in the printing industry

GLOSSARY

Lherzolite : A rather uncommon magmatic rocktype, rich in ferro-magnesian minerals and relatively poor in silica

Loam : A mixture of clay, silt and sand

Loess : A finegrained, windblown mixture of clay, silt and sand

Magmatic : Descriptive of rocks formed by the solidification of magma. They include volcanic rocks (basalt, rhyolite) solidified at or near surface, and plutonic rocks (granite, diorite, gabbro) solidified deep in the earth

Marl : Sedimentary rock consisting of a mixture of clay and carbonate

Metamorphism : Transformation of rocks by increase in pressure, temperature and interaction with their surroundings. The metamorphic rocks (micaschist, gneiss) are generally laminated

Micrite : Calcareous mud consolidated to form a calcareous rock

Millstone : Siliceous sedimentary rock, coloured brown by iron oxides, either cavernous or massive

Mica : A platy mineral common to magmatic and metamorphic rocks. A complex silicate of varying composition. Micas are usually colourless or black, rarely green

Molasse : Thick sedimentary formation consisting of alternating sandy and silty beds, deposited near mountain chains

Monoclinal : Descriptive of structures where the bedding is inclined in the same direction over a long distance

Moraine : Glacial deposit consisting of a mixture of big blocks, boulders and finer grained material

Nappe : A complex rock mass, of often enormous dimensions (allochthone) overthrusting a stable terrain (autochthone) along a horizontal or slightly inclined plane

Oolite : Small sphere with a diameter of 0.5 to 2 mm

Orthoclase : Potassium feldspar

Outlier (butte) : An erosional remnant consisting of a mass of younger rock completely surrounded by older formations

Pelite : Detrital, fine grained, consolidated rock consisting mainly of clay minerals with minor quartz or mica

Pericline : Intersection of the nose of an anticline or syncline and the surface of the earth

Phyllite : A fine grained, schistose rock, intermediate between slate and schist

Pillow lava : Lava consolidated into pillow-like masses, typical of submarine extrusion

Pisolite : Small sphere with a diameter in excess of 2 mm

Plagioclase : Sodium-calcium feldspar

Pleistocene : Longest Epoch of the Quaternary, preceding the Holocene

Podzol : Soil consisting of three horizons: a top horizon rich in humus, a middle horizon rich in silica and a bottom, iron and humic acid-rich horizon, often sandy

Pollen diagram : Graphic representation of the pollen content in a sedimentary sequence

Porphyry : Magmatic rock consisting of bigger crystals set in a fine grained or glassy groundmass

Psammite : Sandstone with a clayey cement and micaceous layers

Pseudoporphyritic : Rock with a porphyritic appearance but in which the bigger crystals have grown after solidification

Pyrite : Yellowish metallic mineral composed of iron sulphide

Pyroxene : Black mineral, elongated crystals of ferromagnesian silicate

Quartz : The most common form of silica, whitish or translucent crystals

Quartzite : Sandstone of quartz grains in a siliceous matrix

Rendzine : Soil formed over a calcareous rock, with a top horizon of dark coloured, pebbly, crumbly and humic acid-rich material, and a bottom horizon of more or less fragmented and altered calcareous rock

Rhyolite : Volcanic extrusive rock consisting of small quartz and feldspar crystals in a glassy, light coloured matrix

Riss : The second-last Ice Age (appr. from 100 000 to 200 000 years ago)

Sandstone : Sedimentary rock consisting of cemented sand grains

Schist : Foliated metamorphic rock, usually originating from fine grained sediments

Shale : Indurated, fine grained detrital rock

Silky shale : Carbonaceous shale, displaying a silky lustre

Sink hole : Circular depression on a limestone plateau due to dissolution

Slumping : Sub-aqueous sliding of waterlogged sediments along a slope resulting in complicated contortions of the bedding

Solifluction : Sliding of waterlogged rocks down an incline

Sphene : A honey-brown mineral occurring in globular masses. A fluoro-silicate of calcium and titanium

Staurolite : A brownish mineral of prismatic habit. An aluminium silicate typical of metamorphic rocks

Stylolite : Columnar, interdigitating structure in calcareous rocks, commonly explained as a pressure phenomenon

Syncline : Fold concave towards the top

Tectonics : The structural deformation of the rocks inflicted after their formation

Till : Glacial deposit containing heterogeneous fragments in a finer grained matrix, similar to moraine

GLOSSARY

Tillite : Rocktype consisting of consolidated till

Tufa : Calcite deposited directly from supersaturated waters

Unconformity : Deposition of horizontal sedimentary strata on a folded substratum

Vertisol : Humic acid and clay-rich soil

Würm : Last Ice Age (appr. from 80 000 to 100 000 years ago)

[1] The interested reader should refer to: The Penguin Dictionary of Geology (Penguin Books) for more detailed definitions and descriptions.

INDEX OF THE VINE VARIETIES

INDEX OF THE PRINCIPAL
WINE DISTRICTS

© 1984–1986, Éditions du Bureau de recherches géologiques
et minières
BP 6009, 45060 ORLÉANS Cedex

© 1984–1986, TOTAL-Édition-Presse
25, rue Jasmin, 75016 PARIS

© 1989 English language edition
Robertson McCarta Limited
122 Kings Cross Road
LONDON WC1X 9DS

Publishing director: Claude Cavelier
Chief editors: Jean Ricour, André Combaz
Managing editor: Jacqueline Goyallon
Production: Marie-Claude Guimbaud
assisted by Annick Cinçon and Véronique Sabaton
Illustrations: Odile Férnandez, Jean-Michel Ihigo

This edition
Cover design: Christine Wood
Cover photograph supplied by Images Colour Library
Production: Grahame Griffiths
Typeset by Columns Design and Production Services, Reading

English translation based on 2nd edition, *Terroirs et Vins de France*, revised and corrected, 1989

British Library Cataloguing in Publication Data
The wines and winelands of France.
 1. French wines 2. France. Wine – growing regions –
 Visitors guides
 I. Pomerol, Charles II. Terroirs et vins de France.
 English
 641.2'2'0944

 ISBN 1–85365–108–7

Printed in Italy by Grafedit S.P.A., via Bergamo 23/25,
24052 Azzano S. Paulo (BG)